I0118687

PRAISE FOR
STOP THE ROAD

Ev Paull masterfully documents the untold story of plans for a series of super-highways that changed the face of Baltimore over the last 80 years, taking readers through the many twists and turns, and buttressing his research with interviews from both prominent and all-but-forgotten participants, the opponents and advocates... Paull's book is at once scholarly journal, urban history and personal observation, while highlighting individual accounts of "ordinary people doing extraordinary things..." Drawing on Baltimore's experience, neighborhood by neighborhood, he provides a cautionary tale for future highway and city planning, as well as an instructive guide for the federal government as it now turns its focus to correcting mistakes of the past.

—William F. Zorzi, former journalist, *Baltimore Sun* / writer,
The Wire and *We Own This City*

Evans Paull has written a scary book about how close Baltimore came to losing its chance at future renewal. His villains are 1960s politicians, planners and civic leaders who backed misguided schemes that would have rammed expressways through ... destroying thousands of homes in the process. His heroes are activists of all races and backgrounds who stopped the worst excesses. Paull's surgical dissection of the 40-year battle produces a book that is essential for understanding today's Baltimore--and the many other American cities that experienced similar highway wars.

—Antero Pietila, author of *Not in My Neighborhood:
How Bigotry Shaped a Great American City.*

Stop the Road is an engrossing saga of Baltimore, not just because the events depicted are so significant for our city, but also because the history is enlivened by in-person storytelling. You will marvel how this combination of community protectors, civil rights activists, preservationists, 1960s idealists, and environmental advocates gained the upper hand over the road building establishment.

—M. J. ("Jay") Brodie, former Baltimore Housing Commissioner and President of Baltimore Development Corporation

Paull's marvelously detailed work provides an instructive example of how different groups, race, ethnicity, and education came together for a common goal—to stop something that was destroying the fabric and essence of a community. This [unity] is sorely lacking in many ways today.

—Philip J. Merrill, Co-founder & CEO, Nanny Jack and Company, LLC

It was people, not politicians, who stood up and saved Baltimore from the ravages of the East-West Expressway. With few material resources, diverse citizens united to protect their neighborhoods—to resist, regroup, persist and finally prevail. Ev Paull has found many of those courageous people and made their "highway stories" a compelling human history of the challenges that faced post-war urban Americans.

—Mark Reutter, Senior Editor, *Baltimore Brew*; author, *Making Steel: Sparrows Point and the Rise and Ruin of American Industrial Might*

STOP THE ROAD

Stories from the Trenches of Baltimore's Road Wars

E. EVANS PAULL

Boyle
&
Dalton

Book Design & Production:
Boyle & Dalton
www.BoyleandDalton.com

Copyright © 2022 by E. Evans Paull
LCCN: 2022916551

All rights reserved.
This book, or parts thereof, may not be
reproduced in any form without permission.

Hardback ISBN: 978-1-63337-643-4
Paperback ISBN: 978-1-63337-644-1
E-Book ISBN: 978-1-63337-669-4

Printed in the United States of America
1 3 5 7 9 10 8 6 4 2

CONTENTS

Dedicated to Rosemarie.

I. INTRODUCTION

So, when you're telling the expressway story, I want it to be told…in terms of people, and in terms of the sacrifice that some people made for the majority. And to me, they are the heroes…And just somewhere I want recorded the people who saved their own community.
Then City Councilperson [later Senator] Barbara Mikulski, 1974[1]

Speaking of the Black neighborhoods that would be eliminated by a proposed East-West Expressway in Baltimore, Robert Moses…would not mince words. "The more neighborhoods that are 'wiped out,'" Moses said, "the healthier Baltimore will be in the long run."
Secretary of Transportation Anthony Foxx, referring to Robert Moses, the New York highway mogul whose 1944 Baltimore Arterial Plan served as the forerunner of all subsequent highway plans.[2]

During a visit to her former neighborhood in 1988, Mercedes Stevens succinctly summed up Baltimore's battle over interstate highways: "If the expressway had been built, you'd say, 'Well, who wants to live there anyway?'"[3] Stevens was talking about her family's former home on South Decker Street in Canton, but she could have been talking about Montgomery Street in South Baltimore, William Street in Federal Hill, Ellamont Street in Rosemont, Aliceanna Street in Harbor East, or Lancaster Street in Fell's Point.*

Twenty-seven years prior, in 1961, Baltimore's team of consulting engineers released the highway scheme I have dubbed the "Future Investment

---

* Readers may want to briefly review the "supplements to the book" section of the Stop the Road website, www.stop-the-road.com/the-book/. Appendix 1, the Neighborhood Battlegrounds and the major highway alignments, located at the end of this book, is also recommended as background, especially for non-Baltimore readers.

Prevention Program." It now seems as if it had been designed expressly to prevent Baltimore's old-line waterfront neighborhoods from becoming havens for young people renovating houses and enlivening storefronts. The plan called for an eight-lane East-West Expressway to cross South Baltimore at Montgomery Street, swipe through Federal Hill (taking a large chunk out of Federal Hill Park), cross the Inner Harbor with a fourteen-lane low level bridge, occupy Harbor East with a colossal six-level interchange, rip through the heart of Fell's Point at Broadway and Thames, and then follow the Canton waterfront all the way to the Canton industrial area, thereby cutting off all southeast neighborhoods from the harbor. From our modern-day point of view, it is hard to imagine anything—save, perhaps, a nuclear power plant—that would have had a more deadening effect on future urban vitality.

Thankfully, the plan was halted before the Road Gang[†] started laying asphalt, even though it had the backing of Baltimore's economic and political establishment, all apparently beguiled by the promise of almost limitless federal dollars devoted to bringing cities into the automobile age. That Baltimore is not saddled with expressways barging their way through these historic waterfront communities is testament to a rare victory of powerless outsiders over powerful insiders. This is the story of those outsiders and how they managed, against all odds, to gain the upper hand.

But there is a parallel story that is equally compelling as a civic tragedy. In 2016 Anthony Foxx, Obama's US Transportation Secretary, was looking for a place to hold a staff retreat, a place to illustrate the point that past transportation programs and policies have too often been inequitable for communities of color. Foxx decided that Baltimore's "Highway to Nowhere" was just the backdrop he needed: a highway originally conceived as "Negro removal" and constructed in spite of the known risk that it may never link up to the other 2,115 miles of I-70.

The tragic side of the highway fight takes us also to the African American

---

† The term "Road Gang" may sound like it is meant to denigrate the pro-highway forces, but the term was coined by highway-affiliated businesses and interests in 1942. The organization (also referred to as "Washington's Transportation Fraternity") continues to bear that name today. See: www.theroadgang.org.

communities of Sharp Leadenhall and Rosemont, the former a textbook example of the detrimental impact of the all-too-prevalent practice of using highways for slum clearance; the latter revealing Baltimore's low regard for a stable middle class African American neighborhood. These issues need to be exposed and probed and take their place in this country's much needed reckoning over race.

The stories behind both the triumphs and the tragedies will take us on a journey to meet Baltimore's unsung heroes. Amongst this ragtag band of neighborhood activists, preservationists, environmentalists, and 1960s idealists, there is only one household name: US Senator Barbara Ann Mikulski. While the senator's good name does deserve to be on the marquee, there were so many others—ordinary people doing extraordinary things.

Baltimoreans should know and revere the names of the saviors of Fell's Point: Bob Eney, the beloved Fell's Pointer whose unmatched knowledge of and unbridled enthusiasm for eighteenth and nineteenth century architecture could "turn a slum landlord into a preservationist"[4]; Lu Fisher, who was thrust into leading the battle to save Fell's Point after the ill-advised purchase of a condemned house (bought with 100 percent love and 0 percent due diligence); and Jack Gleason, the guy who miraculously bonded the ethnics with the preservationists, thereby uniting southeast Baltimore in opposition to the road.

Modern-day Baltimoreans also owe an enormous debt of gratitude to Tom Ward, the cantankerous ex-councilman and judge who almost single-handedly carried the anti-expressway banner through the mid-1960s and saved the Mount Royal cultural district from death-by-expressway.

My interviewees ran out of superlatives when they described Joe Wiles and Mary Rosemond, two of Rosemont's stalwart leaders. Wiles' quiet but effective diplomacy forced a rerouting of I-70 around Rosemont,‡ a legacy that was largely unknown until Wiles was prominently featured in author Earl Swift's sweeping history of the interstate highway system, *The Big*

‡ Rosemont, readers may have noticed, appears on both the "triumphs" list and the "tragedy" list. Indeed, it is both.

3

Roads. Out of tens of thousands of anti-highway activists all across the country, Swift chose Wiles to represent "the human obstacle" to building highways through cities.

Another ordinary guy, Harlem Park's John Wells (a bus driver and former resident of public housing) won an astonishing victory for all displaced families when he convinced the city, the state, *and the federal government* to offer up to $5,000 ($25,000 today) over "fair market value" for acquired homes.

Councilman Norman Reeves, a muscular dystrophy victim, brought incredible strength and determination to the cause of saving Leakin Park. Civil rights activist Stu Wechsler played a starring role in creating the first large-scale inter-racial protest movement, the aptly named Movement Against Destruction (MAD). Sharp Leadenhall's Mildred Moon brought her community back from the gallows after two highway plans and one urban renewal plan almost obliterated her proud African American community.

Change agents also came from within the bureaucracy. Referring to themselves as "the fifth column," Robert Embry and M.J. Brodie of the Housing Department quietly supported highway opponents. The unsung heroes also took up residence in Baltimore's highway consulting team— Nathaniel Owings and Stew Bryant quite literally saved Federal Hill and the Inner Harbor, acting in complete contravention to the wishes of their clients.

The Road Warriors left a remarkable legacy, all due to regular folks rising to the occasion and defying conventional wisdom. Refusing to be silenced or dissuaded, they took the mantle of leadership when their elected leaders failed to represent the interests of the community.

Baltimore has managed to gain notoriety at both ends of the expressway controversy spectrum. While famous nationally for saving Fell's Point, Federal Hill, and the waterfront, the city is also *in*famous for building the Highway to Nowhere. This is a story of Baltimore at its best and at its worst all at the same time, a story of the mob retaking Mobtown, a story of monumental struggle for the Monumental City.

II. 1940s

ROBERT MOSES MEETS THE RESISTANCE

Mrs. Rufus Gibbs, the last of the speakers, read a letter from H. L. Mencken in which he said the expressway probably will be adopted because "it has everything in its favor, including that it is a completely idiotic undertaking."
The *Baltimore Sun*, referring to a March 19, 1945,
city council hearing on the Franklin Expressway[5]

In 1944 Robert Moses arrived in Baltimore with highway backers hoping that the strength of his persona would carry the day—that highway obstructionists and doubters would be swept away by the forcefulness of his vision. There had been proposals to build an East-West Expressway in 1942 and 1943, but they had failed to rally public support. Moses' engagement in Baltimore lasted only seventy-five days, but the legacy of his work would last four decades, finally unraveling in 1981.

By all accounts, Moses was an articulate and influential advocate for freeways, with a reputation as "the power broker," the go-to guy to get public works and highways built in the New York metro area. Cities like Baltimore brought Moses in to create that same sense of purpose and resolve. He had cachet; he was the face of the movement to modernize cities by building freeways.

His vision for Baltimore, detailed in the 1944 "Baltimore Arterial Report," was to expand the Route 40 corridor, converting the street to a limited access freeway with service roads on both sides. The "Franklin Expressway," as Moses termed it, approached from the southwest, followed the Franklin-Mulberry to downtown, veered slightly north to traverse Mount Vernon via a depressed section only one block south of the Washington Monument, then followed Orleans Street/Route 40 through East Baltimore. (See Figure 1.) With service roads and enjoining open spaces, the road cut a wide swath, dislocating an estimated 18,000 people.

However, the master builder was also a master-race kind of guy, and one has to wonder if Baltimore's leaders understood this (or cared). Robert A. Caro's Pulitzer-prize-winning book, *The Power Broker*, details how Moses' work encouraged the segregation and exclusion of minorities and poor people. Caro describes how Moses purposely designed the Southern States Parkway, which connected the Big Apple to Jones Beach on Long Island,

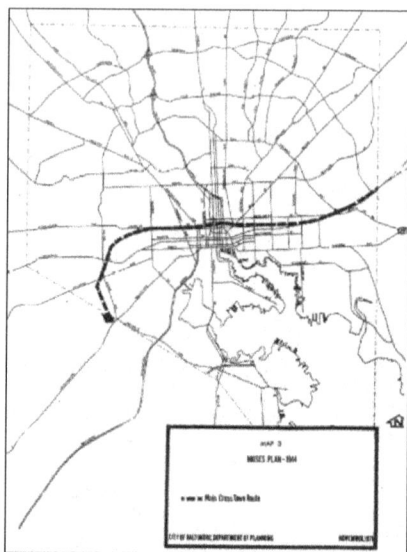

Figure 1. 1944 Franklin Expressway (Robert Moses) plan (Source, Baltimore City Department of Planning, 1972)

with bridges that were too low for buses to "restrict the use of state parks by poor and lower-middle-class families"[6]; and how Moses opposed Black war veterans moving into Stuyvesant Town, a Manhattan residential development complex created to house World War II veterans.

In later chapters, we will meet city planners who abandon all pretense of objectivity and adopt the advocacy planning model to aid dispossessed populations impacted by the highway. Moses abandons objectivity for the opposite purpose—to bulldoze the dispossessed. He blatantly advocated for clearing out dilapidated neighborhoods: "Some of the slum areas through which the Franklin Expressway passes are a disgrace to the community, and the more of them that are wiped out the healthier Baltimore will be in the long run…. The expressway…is a long step toward destroying slum houses."[7]

Moses reassured residents of Baltimore's better neighborhoods, stating, "We do not propose to tear down familiar and cherished landmarks which cannot be replaced. Nothing which we propose to remove will constitute any loss to Baltimore." But a *Baltimore Sun* article released in the wake of Moses' report counted the losses that Moses so easily dismissed: two hundred blocks completely leveled and countless more partially razed; a recently built school that would cost $500,000 to replace; large parts of the recently completed Somerset Homes and Armistead Gardens public housing projects; School No. 176 for Handicapped Colored Children; twelve churches; and scores of businesses.[8]

Further, as Figure 2 shows, the new expressway would be bordered by new high- and mid-rise low-income apartments to keep the undesirable displaced households from invading the "good" neighborhoods: "It is neither necessary nor desirable to disperse this class [lower income Black residents] to other areas," the report bluntly pointed out.

Figure 2. Franklin-Mulberry corridor 1944 plan—existing slums to be replaced by (choose your adjective) "modern" or "Soviet-style" public housing (source: Baltimore Arterial Report, 1944)

In historic Mount Vernon the expressway would be depressed, going under Cathedral and Charles Street bridges, then elevated to go over St. Paul Street. As Figure 3 shows, there were four partial interchanges sandwiched between Eutaw and St. Paul Streets, shoehorned into the heart of Mount Vernon.

MOSES MEETS HIS MATCH
IN JANE JACOBS

Robert Moses' run as the successful highway dealmaker came crashing down in the mid-1960s when he tangled with Jane Jacobs and New York City activists over the ten-lane Lower Manhattan Expressway.

Jacobs, the author of *The Death and Life of Great American Cities*, first faced off with Moses over a 1955 plan to put a four-lane road through Washington Square. Moses demeaned the Committee to Save Washington Square Park as "nothing but a bunch of mothers." But Jacobs and the mothers prevailed, not only stopping the road but also banning all traffic from Washington Square.

Moses envisioned a ten-lane elevated expressway in Lower Manhattan that would carve out sections of the Lower East Side (Broome Street), Chinatown, The Bowery, Little Italy, and what later became SoHo, while displacing more than two thousand families and eight hundred businesses. The area contained "one of the greatest collections of cast-iron architecture in the world." Countless historic buildings including the Haughwout Building, a cast-iron gem and home of the first commercial elevator, would be collateral damage. "When you operate in an overbuilt metropolis," Moses remarked, "you have to hack your way with a meat axe."

Jacobs and a ragtag group of supporters protested the highway by wearing gas masks and staging a New-Orleans-style funeral march, carrying signs that read "Death of a Neighborhood" and "Little Italy—Killed by Progress." The group rallied public support, gaining an influential letter from noted planner and urbanist Lewis Mumford, who, incidentally, had earlier published a scathing critique of Jacobs' book. Mumford lambasted the plan as "the first serious step in turning New York into Los Angeles. Since Los Angeles has already discovered the futility of sacrificing living space to expressways and parking lots, why should New York follow that backward example?"

Following Jacobs' rule of thumb, "you have to kill a highway three times," the highway plan was "de-mapped" from the city plan in 1963, only to be revived after Moses rallied business support. Congressman (and later Mayor) John Lindsay shifted his position on the road at least three times.

In a 1968 hearing (which seemed mere window-dressing for community input, one of the final checkboxes before the plan would be implemented after decades of wrangling and indecision) the crowd grew impatient and started chanting, "We want Jane." Jacobs finally gained the podium and then invited supporters to join her. In the resulting melee, the stenographer's table was upended. The record of the meeting was therefore compromised, and the bureaucrats were not pleased that they would be unable to "check that box."

Jacobs was arrested and charged with second-degree riot and criminal mischief. The case caught the attention of the press and became a cause célèbre in New York as artists, socialites, and dignitaries sponsored highway opposition events and held legal defense fundraisers. The charges were reduced and Jacobs was freed. The expressway plan was now an object of ridicule that no politician could support. Lindsay declared the project dead on July 16, 1969.

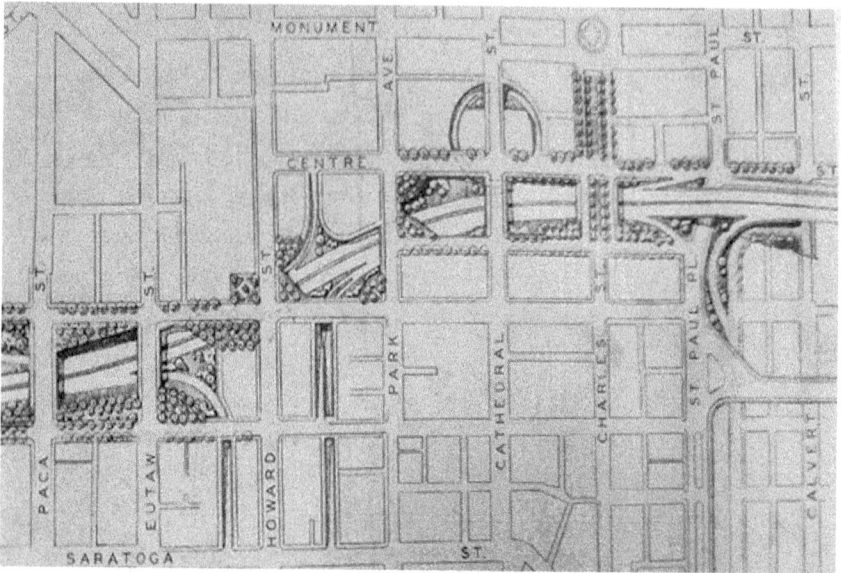

Figure 3. Franklin Expressway (1944) traverses Mount Vernon at Centre Street with a series of full and partial interchanges between Paca Street and Calvert Street (source: Baltimore Arterial Report, 1944)

Undeterred by the facts, Moses assured Baltimoreans that "experience in other cities has shown beyond a shadow of a doubt that the type of development recommended in this report results in a permanent substantial increase in the value of adjacent residential property." This claim is patently false. While expressway interchanges in commercial and industrial areas often attract investment and improve property values, the Franklin Expressway directly targeted Black residential areas, and the highway itself brought noise, air pollution, and division of previously cohesive neighborhoods. Moreover, limited relocation options for displaced minorities, already hemmed in by discriminatory real estate practices, promised overcrowding and blight.

The populace was unconvinced. The dawn of Baltimore's anti-expressway movement occurred at a city council hearing on March 21, 1945. The *Sun* reported that "1,500 people filled the auditorium...cheers, boos, and other interruptions were so frequent that City Council President C. Markland Kelly gave up any attempts to quiet the crowd." An attorney named Herbert Bloom said the highway would create "a mountain of human misery, [because it contained] no specific or adequate provision for the 19,000 to be removed from their homes."[9]

The *Sun* and the *Afro-American* both reported a mixed-race audience and highlighted the testimony of Willard Allen, a Black insurance executive who would be displaced in the plan. Allen warned: "We are twenty percent of the population of Baltimore and live in two percent of the area.... If 13,000 Negroes are dumped on the other population in the city, there will be an insurrection. They are anxious to live to themselves and live in peace. They have always gotten what is left over, and, with this project, there would not be anything left over."

However, Baltimore's African American population remained largely disenfranchised. It would be twenty-five years before the Movement Against Destruction (MAD) formed a multi-racial coalition to fight the expressway. Even though they represented a small percentage of those displaced, it was the White neighborhoods in southwest Baltimore and Mount Vernon that mounted an effective opposition and stalled the Franklin Expressway.

On December 9, 1946, five hundred incensed White residents formed the Southwest Baltimore Civic and Improvement Association, the first anti-highway coalition. A *Sun* article concluded with an ominous and implicitly racist tone: "Most speakers admitted that an expressway was inevitable, but all insisted it could be mapped so as 'not to cut the heart out of *our communities*,' in southwest Baltimore or elsewhere." [Emphasis added.]

The freeway plan was never fully defeated, but it stalled as condemnation bills and funding authorizations were delayed or turned down. At one critical juncture, Moses' own words were used by opponents to sink a state appropriation of $4.5 million. Opponents twice quoted Moses as advocating for sufficient preliminary spending to get to a point of no return: "Mr. Robert Moses made the statement [that agencies should] spend $10,000,000...to acquire property along the route and then the taxpayers will be hooked and have to go through with the project."[10]

The *Sun*'s editorial board was aghast at the parochial political considerations that kept progress at bay. In 1946, when city council turned down a modest request by chief engineer Nathan Smith to establish the expressway's entry point into the city, the *Sun* called the action "deplorable."[11] In 1947, they editorialized,

"Never has a commendable undertaking been subjected to more bitter criticism, more political dealings, more outright misrepresentation, than this one."[12] They reserved their most scornful language for sentimentalists trying to protect Mount Vernon from a superhighway thrusting through historic property:

> The third surviving argument is just about as wrongheaded as it could be. It is that a freeway skirting the northern edge of the downtown district—the route generally follows Centre Street— will wreck an historical section of the city and destroy or impair the beauty of Mount Vernon place. This is wrongheaded because, save for a handful of ancient houses, mostly small and in decay, there is little to be proud of in that part of the town.

Thankfully, most Baltimoreans were in the "wrongheaded" camp.

Aside from Moses' plan, six other plans were advanced from 1942 to 1949, but only one offered up new and notable concepts—the 1949 plan developed under the direction of Planning Director Arthur D. McVoy. (See Figure 4.) Published as a "Tentative* Master Transportation Plan," the document is notable for several "firsts": McVoy's plan was the first to map a route across the southern edge of South Baltimore and cross the harbor at Fort McHenry enroute to the Canton industrial area (later built as I-95); it was also the first to propose a northwestern route

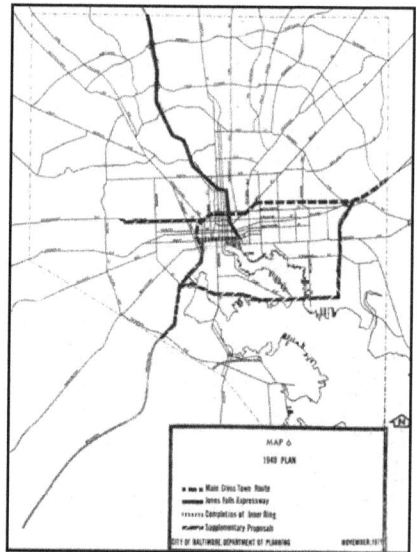

Figure 4. Planning Commission 1949 Transportation Plan (Source: Baltimore City Department of Planning, 1972)

---

* "Tentative" is an interesting choice of words – when you have had six plans rejected in seven years, it is probably best to hedge your bets.

coming down the Jones Falls to the Central Business District (CBD) (later built as I-83). These highway plan concepts get high marks for boosting economic development with minimum residential displacement.

TRANSIT, TROLLEYS, AND THE URBAN FORM IN THE 1940S

There was one astonishing finding in Moses' 1944 report: Baltimore's buses and street cars were carrying two-thirds of all trips, totaling 1.3 million transit trips in a single day. To be fair, the transit mode split was artificially high, boosted by war-time restrictions on driving; still, most Baltimore residents were getting around on public transit, with the trolley system far outpacing buses as the leading transit mode. (See Figure 5.)

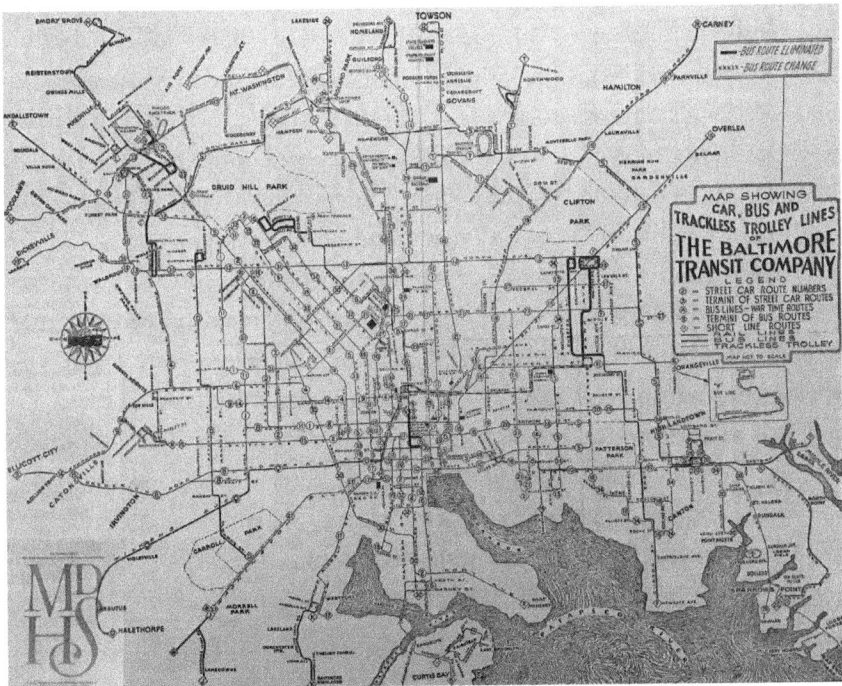

Figure 5. Trolley, trackless trolley, and bus lines, 1945 (source Maryland Center for History and Culture archives)

Those numbers were reminiscent of European cities, but Europe maintained that high transit mode split after the war and to the present day. Europe and the US took radically different paths after WWII. The US invested in highways that facilitated sprawl, then subsidized the dispersal of middle-income households through FHA and VA loans as well as tax-deductible interest on mortgages. In Europe, investment in transit rivaled or outpaced investment in freeways. The growth of cities was controlled with an eye toward strengthening the center; even outward extensions were relatively dense, compact suburbs where it made sense to extend transit lines.[13] Here is the first fork in the road where the US arguably took a wrong turn. Had we followed the European post-war model, cities like Baltimore could have been strengthened rather than weakened in the post-war decades.

Some would argue that the demise of the Baltimore trolley system was another wrong turn. Wartime restrictions were a boon to the Baltimore Transit Company (BTC), the private business that ran the trolley system, but post-war trends (highways, cars, and subsidized sprawl) caused the return of financial strain. In the late '40s BTC fell under the control of National City Lines (NCL), a holding company formed by General Motors, Firestone Tire and Rubber, Standard Oil of California, and Phillips Petroleum.

NCL acquired or controlled forty-six transit systems for, as one author put it, "the express purpose of acquiring and dismantling urban streetcar operations. In so doing, they allegedly created lucrative and long-term markets for their own products."[14] While this contention is not universally accepted, I'm inclined to agree with the conspiratorial point of view based on admittedly circumstantial evidence. Carmakers, tire manufacturers, and oil companies have one thing in common: they each make money on buses. Regardless of NCL's motivation, the Baltimore trolley system was dismantled over the next two decades. On November 3, 1963, the last streetcar, PCC No. 7407, made its final run.[15]

But imagine an alternate universe where highways, cars, and suburban sprawl did not conspire to sink the mainstay of 1940s transit. What if the strongest trolley lines had been maintained until the early '70s, when transit became worthy of public capital investment and public operating subsidies?

Some cities have revived trolleys as a tourist amenity (San Francisco, New Orleans) by modernizing them with new light rail cars (Boston, Newark, Philadelphia, Pittsburgh, and Cleveland), or by rerouting them through tunnels beneath congested areas (Newark, Philadelphia, Boston, and Pittsburgh).

To understand why present-day Baltimore has a second-rate public transit system, one needs to look to the past, starting with the choices made in the post-war years of the 1940s. Baltimore is now paying for the road not taken.

> The value of public transit is not just as a means to get to work, to lower pollution, or as a substitute for destructive highways. It is all of those things, but it is also an intricate part of urban neighborhoods where people and businesses want to locate because they are alive, vibrant, walkable, and just plain more fun than monolithic suburbia.

III. 1950s

IKE'S HIGHWAYS AND CITIES

Perhaps we should forgive his inattention to detail. After all, Dwight D. Eisenhower was accustomed to carrying out weighty missions where the future of the Free World hung in the balance. Still, it is more than a little shocking that President Eisenhower misunderstood several basic aspects of his signature piece of legislation, the Federal-Aid Highway Act of 1956. That legislation (and Ike's misunderstandings of it) heavily impacted cities like Baltimore for the remainder of the twentieth century.

Eisenhower's first foray into the world of interstate travel must have left a lasting impression. In July 1919, seeking a break from the mind-numbing peacetime routines of army life at Camp Meade, Maryland, Ike volunteered to serve on a cross-country brigade of heavy army trucks. At the time, the country was crisscrossed with "roads," only in the loosest sense of the word. The seventy-two-vehicle caravan was sent to test the army's equipment, aid in training the army's Motor Transport Corps, and explore the viability of long-distance truck travel using these roads.[16]

Traveling cross-country on the Lincoln Highway, there were frequent breakdowns, and the heavy trucks "crushed scores of bridges, fourteen in one day, by Eisenhower's count—which trailing soldiers scrambled to rebuild," according to author Earl Swift in his wide-ranging history *The Big Roads*.[17] The caravan made it to the Great Salt Lake, then to Fisher Pass. On August 20, the caravan's descent from Fisher Pass "floundered in hip deep dust…one vehicle after another spun its tires until the frame bottomed out. It took all day and most of the night to jack up the trucks, stuff the holes beneath their tires with sagebrush, and ease them on their way—after which they all too often re-stuck themselves."[18]

Then things went from bad to worse. On a detour through the Salt Flats, virtually every vehicle broke through the thin crust and became mired in the muck. The determined commanders then harnessed up to a hundred men, who towed the trucks across the flats using brute force. Much of the caravan outran their supply trucks (a mistake that Eisenhower presumably did not repeat as commander of the Allied forces in Europe), and food and water were severely limited; that night, guards had to be stationed around the water tanker truck.[19]

Two and a half decades later, while Eisenhower was quite literally off saving the world, Franklin D. Roosevelt engineered a new and little-noticed section of the 1944 Federal Aid to Highways Act envisioning a 40,000-mile interstate highway system.* In the next decade, roads and highways advanced haltingly, with state and federal roles lurching forward and backward. When Eisenhower was elected in 1953, the system envisioned by Roosevelt in 1944 still existed mostly on paper.

Ike later expressed how his experiences with the truck convoy and WWII converged: "the old convoy had started me thinking about good two-lane roads, but Germany [which used the Autobahn to strategic advantage in WWII] made me see the wisdom of broader ribbons across the land."[20] The Federal-Aid Highway Act of 1956 was thus conceived as a "three-fer": part defense highway, part job-creating infrastructure, part facilities to meet community needs. Fortunately, the defense functions have not been tested, but one would have to be somewhat concerned if our nation's security depended on military vehicles fighting their way through rush hour traffic on I-95.

The adopted bill showed little resemblance to Ike's vision, however, and this is where Ike's mastery of detail is found lacking. The president was, according to Swift, "not much of a reader and couldn't sit through long briefings."[21] Embarrassingly, he did not even realize that a national interstate highway program had been on the books since 1944, or that a plan had already been adopted for where those highways were to go.

---

* The term "interstate" had been substituted for the term "inter-regional" because Republicans thought the latter descriptor "had been coined by planners whom they regarded as leftist pains in the neck." (Swift, p. 141)

Ike's knowledge of the subject apparently came primarily from a fourteen-page paper written by Walker G. Buckner, a golfing buddy and securities analyst with interest (but no apparent expertise) in transportation. The paper was appended with a gas station map with hand-drawn routes crisscrossing the states.[22] The Buckner-Eisenhower proposal was for a series of "self-liquidating" toll roads, even though the Bureau of Highways had concluded ten years earlier that toll roads were completely inadequate to the task of building 40,000 miles of interstate highways.

Eisenhower's vision was for a rural program that connected but did not go through cities. Incredibly, through two full years of congressional debate and even after the program had been operating for several years, Ike believed the National System of Interstate and Defense Highways Act reflected this vision. There is one version of Ike's discovery of urban freeways that bears repeating:

[In] the spring of 1959, so the story goes, the president...was in the back of a limousine headed out of Washington for Camp David when the car became bogged down in a highway construction snarl. Ike asked what was going on and learned that the highway in question was an interstate. This was far too close to Washington to comply with the president's notions of a largely rural, intercity system.... Riled, Eisenhower demanded an explanation—and so, according to one school, discovered that "his" highway program wasn't.[23]

Ike expressed grave concern that the original legislative intent had been somehow thwarted, even though there was very clear language in all the bills going back to 1944. This led to the first fork in the road for the interstate program, a road-not-taken of immense importance to cities like Baltimore: In what might now be characterized as an attempt to create "alternate facts," Eisenhower hired General John S. Bragdon, an old friend and tolls advocate, to undertake a broad review of the interstate program with a specific emphasis on the urban issue.

Bragdon carried out an exhaustive critique, with case studies of eighteen cities. Some of his early recommendations would have horrified city leaders, such as his recommendation that highways "ordinarily pass close to, or around, but not through congested areas."[24] Beltways around cities would get the highest priority, while urban routes would only be eligible for conventional (50/50) federal aid, not the 90/10 formula adopted in the 1956 Highway Act.

In an April 1960 meeting attended by the president, Bragdon faced off with Bert Tallamy, the first federal highway administrator and a disciple of Robert Moses.[25] Tallamy bluntly attacked the Bragdon Committee, saying it was Bragdon (and, by implication, the president) who was attempting to undermine legislative intent. He called the president's attention to the "yellow map" of planned federal interstate routes, many going directly through center cities, noting that this map had been on the desk of every congressman who voted in favor of the Highway Act.

Finally understanding the legislation he had championed, Ike appears to have simply given up on the issue of routing highways through cities. A memorandum of record from the 1960 meeting states that he "reiterated his disappointment over the way the program had been developed against his wishes, and that it had reached the point to where his hands were virtually tied."[26] Not long after the meeting he appointed Bragdon to a post on the Civil Aeronautics Board, and the work of the Bragdon Committee was dismissed and forgotten.

This is a critical fork in the road that was simply missed as the road-building bureaucracy went back to business as usual. We are left to wonder what could have been. Bragdon's work could have set a more modest course correction, not eliminating highways through cities but establishing certain principles for the altogether different circumstances presented by heavily urbanized areas. Bragdon recommended that urban expressways be spurs to downtown rather than inner loops and routes swiping *through* central cities,[27] and that they should be implemented in a comprehensive local planning process that included robust citizen participation. Finally, the Bragdon report could have laid the groundwork for a public transit share of the Highway Trust Fund—one finding was that "a rapid transit rail facility can move 40,000 seated passengers an hour whereas it takes 40 lanes of freeway to move an equivalent number by car."[28]

These changes would have been enormously helpful to cities like Baltimore. The spurs-instead-of-through-routes issue drove Baltimore to the edge of community madness. Twenty tumultuous years after Bragdon's work ebbed away unnoticed, Baltimore's highway planners finally acceded to the opposition and accepted one through-highway (I-95, moved away from downtown and neighborhoods to an industrial corridor) and two spurs, I-83 and I-395, truncated highways that improved downtown access but avoided the more destructive aspects of a highway system that looked great on a map but would have ripped the heart out of affected communities.

However, the story has gotten a little ahead of itself. Baltimore's role in the 1956 Federal-Aid Highway Act goes far beyond that of recipient or victim (depending on how you look at it). Baltimore also played a critical role in the genesis of this federal law that changed the face of America.

FALLON'S FORMULA

George H. Fallon seemed like an average guy, a lifelong Baltimore resident who worked at his father's business, the Fallon Sign Company. Although known for his part in launching the interstate program, Fallon personally disliked driving, especially freeway driving, and he commuted to his Washington congressional office via the Pennsylvania Railroad. In a retrospective after his death, the *Baltimore Sun* described him as a "quiet and unpretentious man... who would rather have thrown out the first ball at a sandlot game in Clifton Park than at Memorial Stadium.... Another politician might have used his chairmanship to twist arms. Mr. Fallon was benign. He made sure no congressman was slighted."

"Benign" might not be the right term to describe Fallon's run for Congress in 1944. The election was a face-off that seems like a head-scratcher today: Fallon, the conservative Democrat, accused Republican incumbent Daniel Ellison of being a left-leaning radical who was out-of-touch with the electorate. He called out Ellison's votes "against the committee that was appointed to investigate un-American and subversive activities," and "to keep certain communists in key Federal positions."[29] Fallon slammed his opponent, saying rhetorically, "On what ticket is Ellison running: Republican, Democrat, or Communist?"[30]

The Red-baiting strategy worked, and Fallon was elected by a narrow margin. Thereafter, Fallon was re-elected thirteen straight times. Except for the Highway Bill of 1956, his record was unremarkable; indeed, he often seemed to benefit from his status as a "safe choice." By 1960 Fallon's longevity had become his greatest asset; his campaign slogan was "an investment in seniority." In 1965 Fallon became the Chairman of the House Committee on Public Works, one of the chief committees that dispensed federal pork barrel largesse. In this role Fallon was able to secure funding for the completion of the Baltimore-Washington Parkway[†] and for the construction of the downtown federal building which bears his name.

However, outside Baltimore, Fallon was known only for the 1956 Federal-Aid Highway Act. He is credited with developing the winning combination of a gasoline tax and several highway user taxes, all linked to the inviolable Highway Trust Fund—the additional taxes generated would be dedicated to funding expressways and only expressways. The bill passed Congress on June 25, 1956, and President Eisenhower signed it on June 29.

With a dedicated funding source and an irresistible 90/10 federal/local split, highways suddenly became a focal point for cities wanting to keep pace and take advantage of federal largesse. Suburban car culture seemed to be winning, and cities welcomed the opportunity catch up. What's more, highway funding was seen as an opportunity to clear slums using a funding source that was far more favorable (both in size and in the federal-local split) than the Urban Renewal Program.

But the flipside of that formula was that city leaders were seduced by the dollar signs, and decisions were made opportunistically without full consideration of their impact. Further, a circularity of effects (Figure 6) was set in motion: more roads led to more driving, which led to more Trust Fund revenues, which led to more roads. One commentator crystallized the argument

---

† The Baltimore-Washington Parkway, built between 1947 and 1954, is an example of an expressway spur, Bragdon's preferred form for expressways that traverse cities.

against the Trust Fund: "If it is justifiable to use gasoline taxes exclusively for highway construction, the federal tax on alcohol should be spent to promote and expand the liquor industry."

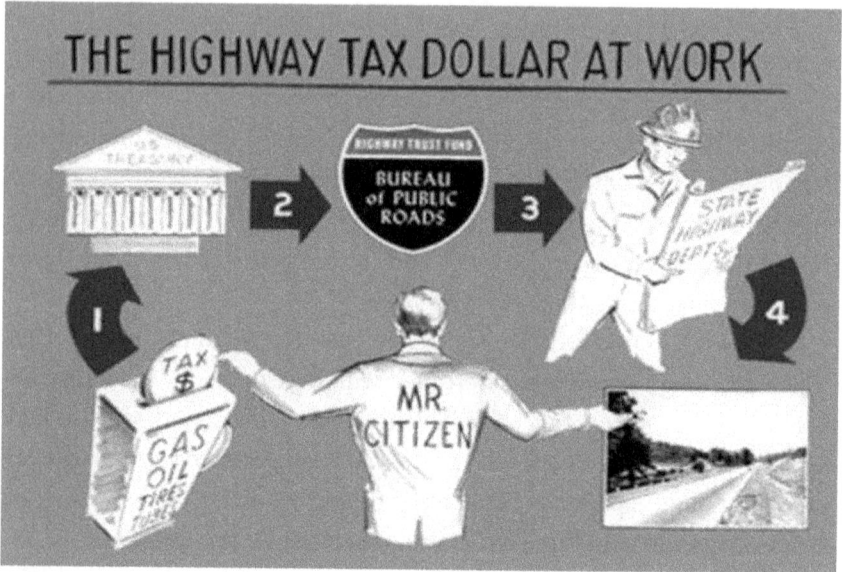

Figure 6. Circularity: An illustration from the Bureau of Public Roads, but highway opponents might have used precisely the same graphic

Recently built highways were becoming congested far faster than projected. Highways were not just meeting demand, they were generating demand. "Induced traffic"‡ came partly from transit riders switching to cars. The resulting drop in transit ridership caused a spate of private transit companies to go out of business; some were replaced by publicly run and subsidized agencies, but the needed subsidies soared as many systems lost middle-class patrons and were left with a lower income clientele who could not afford fare increases.

---

‡ My son Daniel, age three at the time, seemed to have an innate understanding of the concept of "induced traffic." Stuck in a sea of automobiles one day, I muttered, "I wonder why there is so much traffic out today?" Daniel, from his car seat in the back, offered up: "Daddy, I know. It's because all the cars got unparked."

Additionally, highways encouraged outer suburban growth, often featuring car-dependent cul-de-sacs that were miles farther away from the workplace. These growth patterns generated more demand for road capacity while simultaneously exacerbating urban-suburban inequities, segregation, and a host of issues connected to sprawl.

The cost-benefit scales should have been taking neighborhood issues into account: bisecting formerly unified communities, destroying historic properties, disrupting businesses, generating noise and air pollution. In removing blighted properties, lower income and minority residents were disproportionately impacted, bearing the brunt of displacement issues. Replacement housing was limited in the discriminatory housing market, and "fair market value" payments to displaced residents were insufficient to purchase or rent decent accommodations.

If urban highways had had to compete with other claims for the federal purse, their downsides would have been quickly perceived, and resources likely would have been shifted to transit as the more urban-friendly method of transportation. Instead, because of the self-funded Highway Trust and the irresistible 90/10 split, cities continued to force highways through their communities, "damn the costs" to residents and businesses. As architect Nathaniel Owings phrased it, "Part of the tragedy is that the cities themselves have rushed with a strange sense of urgency to cooperate in their own mutilation."[31]

Later efforts to "Bust the Highway Trust" would play out nationally and locally in parallel spheres, with George Fallon at their intersection. Back in Baltimore, highway planners were buoyed by the new abundance of 90/10 dollars and produced a more ambitious highway plan in 1957, but it ran into obstacles that were completely unanticipated.

TINY TYSON STREET, BULWARK AGAINST THE 1957 HIGHWAY PLAN

In 1957, the 900 block of Tyson Street—all four hundred feet of it—oddly became the focus of a national highway symposium. Tyson Street's rejuvenation was a story that struck a chord. That one-block stretch had been cited in national magazines and even the *Encyclopedia Britannica* as an example of private urban revitalization. Formerly dilapidated homes had been fixed up by artists, artisans, and same-sex couples (groups that seem to be always on the vanguard of reinvestment in run-down neighborhoods), and the new folks were mixing congenially with the Black population that preceded them. However, Tyson Street was now threatened by the East-West Expressway.

At the symposium, Federal Housing Administrator Albert M. Cole said of Tyson Street, "On a tiny scale here is an unusual example of private enterprise, of neighbors acting together to achieve something." He showed pictures of the tidy, recently renovated rowhomes, painted in pastel colors and featuring neatly planted window boxes. Then he turned to fellow panelist Bert Tallamy, the Federal Highway Administrator. "Mr. Tallamy has on his hands a gigantic task of urgency and gravity," Cole said. "From his point of view our carefully planned redevelopment of the slum section may be a threat to progress. He may fear his splendid roads may have to be relocated, perhaps at heavy cost. My plea to the Administrator and his coworkers is simply this: keep in mind the little places with the window boxes—the Tyson Streets."[32]

The lure of 90/10 funding had emboldened Baltimore's highway planners to offer up a more ambitious expressway plan. The '57 plan included several firsts: Two expressways approached from the west, including one that raked its way through Leakin Park and Rosemont; the southwest expressway came across South Baltimore at Montgomery Street and Federal Hill, then crossed the Inner Harbor to meet up with I-83; and the mid-town section that had traversed Centre Street was moved up to Tyson and Chase Streets to appease the defenders of historic property near the Washington Monument. The main route followed Chase Street to the rail corridor and through Northeast Baltimore. One supplementary route extended I-83 through southeast Baltimore, roughly following Fleet and Aliceanna Streets through Fell's Point then along the Boston Street waterfront. The other supplementary proposal was the Fort McHenry alignment that much later became I-95. Notably, all of the above were linked together by an inner loop that surrounded downtown.

It looked great on a map (Figure 7), but once again failed to justify the human costs to a skeptical Baltimore populace. A March 1957 public hearing brought out eight hundred opponents, mostly from the southwest neighborhoods of Carroll Park, Mount Vernon, and Tyson Street.[33] If there were activists out there advocating Fell's Point and Sharp Leadenhall (and all the other neighborhood battlegrounds featured in later chapters), they must have been operating stealth-like behind the scenes.

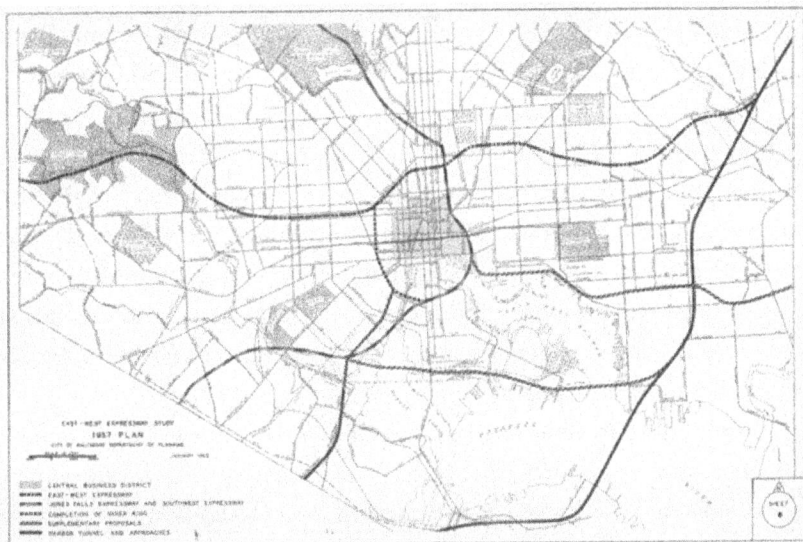

Figure 7. 1957 East-West Expressway Study (Source: Baltimore City Department of Planning, 1972)

The biggest problem in Mount Vernon was the proposed interchange at Chase Street and the Jones Falls Expressway, which was under construction at the time. Opponents characterized the interchange as a "Chinese wall," a description oft-repeated by critics and the media. Highway planners responded with a design scheme for a depressed highway, which one opponent called the Panama Canal plan. In truth, there was not a solution. You cannot hide a full interchange that is cheek by jowl with historic Mount Vernon.

But it was the picturesque one-block section of Tyson Street that garnered the most attention because it represented new urban hope with appealing principles: It was history versus modernism, rehabilitation instead of clearance, and private renewal without a single dollar from the public trough—it was David's well-placed slingshot compared to Goliath's urban renewal bulldozers.

The Maryland General Assembly did not ordinarily mettle in local highway plans, but when the city needed blessings for a $20 million bond bill to finance the local share of the expressway, the Assembly said fine—but not for Tyson Street. (In the forty-year history of the Road Wars, there was only one other time they said no to a city highway plan—for the Fort McHenry harbor crossing, a Chesapeake Bay Bridge-like structure that would loom over the Fort McHenry National Monument.)

The plans were modified to narrowly miss Tyson Street, but then engineers determined that segment would need to be eight lanes instead of six,[§] and the death knell for Tyson Street was struck again.[34] Public Works Director George Carter said he was quite sure that decision-makers would determine that "the expressway is more important than Tyson Street,"[35] and that the city would finance that segment with funds not limited by the General Assembly's amendment to the bond bill.

Tyson Streeters, however, were winning in the court of public opinion. In a move that would later be copied by the Society for the Preservation of Federal Hill and Fell's Point, they organized a Tyson Street house tour, attracting an astonishing 2,700 people and raising over $4,000 (almost $40,000 today) for the Save Tyson Street Fund.[36]

In March 1958, the Maryland House of Delegates passed a broader resolution, not linked to a bond bill, against the Tyson Street segment.[37] Both the condemnation ordinance and the bond bill languished in city council. Fourth District Councilman Solomon Liss urged highway planners "to reexamine their plans and leave Tyson Street as a beacon for the future of Baltimore."[38] In September the Greater Baltimore Committee sided with Tyson Streeters. This led Mayor Thomas D'Alesandro Jr. to authorize a new study to explore minor shifts that would make the current alignment palatable. However, Planning

§ This unquestioned determination that the city needed an eight-lane highway through the Mount Royal Cultural District is symptomatic of the rule of engineering in the 1950s. The engineers said "jump" and the City said, "How high?"

Director Phil Darling took this opportunity to scope out a completely different alignment through central Baltimore: the 1960 plan to destroy the Inner Harbor, which we will shortly describe.

All those later credited with saving Fell's Point, Canton, Rosemont, Leakin Park, and Federal Hill owe an enormous debt of gratitude to the 1957 protesters, especially the determined defenders of tiny Tyson Street. All those communities would have been obliterated long before the opposition got organized, except that the city was, once again, forced to go back to the drawing boards.

IV. 1960–1966

Most of the direct benefits from those highways would accrue to suburban residents; owners of central business district properties and industrialists.
Anthony Downs, Real Estate Research Corporation,
"Economic Overview Analysis" for Design Concept Team, 1968

As the story moves into the 1960s, there is a growing realization that running highways through cities brings out a cornucopia of issues and trade-offs. In Baltimore two proposed plans would have gutted most of the waterfront that later led to Baltimore's revitalization. That Baltimore's civic leaders were more than willing to make this sacrifice is dismaying to say the least. Public sector decision-making had been skewed by the abundance of 90/10 funding and the over-influence of self-interested engineers. However, there was at least one admirable objective: Highways were seen as the means to keep cities competitive with suburbs in an auto-dominated age.

Historically, local efforts to increase Baltimore's accessibility reaped massive rewards—the B&O railroad transformed Baltimore from backwater town to thriving metropolis. Now, local officials, engineers, and planners saw the interstates in the context of just that kind of mission. Dimento and Ellis' book *Changing Lanes, New Visions of Urban Freeways* sums it up:

> [Up until the 1960s] most engineers and many planners viewed freeways as the indispensable framework for a bold new city of high mobility and economic efficiency. The old neighborhoods near the central business district seem chaotic—obstacles to be cleared away and replaced by new super blocks and wide thoroughfares. As businesses and residents fled the city for the suburbs, planners and politicians search for ways to modernize the old cities, contain the spread of blight, and bolster the sagging land values of the central business

28

district. Building a new network of high-speed roads atop the old city grid seemed a critical part of this metamorphosis.[39]

Larry Reich, Baltimore's Planning Director (1965–1980), was later called upon to articulate the case for keeping up with the suburbs, as follows:

Since the early 1960s, when the Beltway began exerting its centrifugal attraction, there has been a strong trend toward the location of stores and manufacturing plants along and adjacent to that route. It is easier today…to travel to Beltway shopping concentrations…than to Baltimore's CBD.… Suburban residents are also increasingly able to find employment in the growing numbers of industrial firms and office complexes in the counties…

However, if the present forces continue there will undoubtedly be a further weakening of the city's economy as people and business firms move and a loosely knit, weakly centered, low-density urban region spread over a wide hinterland develops.… Baltimore needs an expressway system to maintain a competitive position within its metropolitan area and with other urban areas. Nowhere is the problem of access as critical as in the CBD and the Port.… Traffic destined for the CBD must be able to find smooth-flowing, high-speed routes leading to the city's heart, if Baltimore is to remain the region's focal point.[40]

As the city's chief planner for most of the Road Wars, Reich might have proposed a different future for Baltimore's waterfront. In the 1980s he does do exactly that, but in the '60s Reich was still constrained by the mayor's policies. Which leads to the first stop back in 1960, a remarkable example of short-sighted planning authored by Reich's predecessor.

1960—PLANNING'S HARBOR ROUTE: THE SHOCKING PLAN TO DESTROY THE INNER HARBOR, FELL'S POINT, AND CANTON

Automobile driving along regular city streets is usually a rather dreary and dismal experience… Driving on urban expressways is often stimulating and even exciting. Not only is there the pleasure of being able to proceed continuously and at good speeds through highly congested areas, but also expressways sometimes can provide the opportunity for interesting and even spectacular views of the city.... Expressway driving in many cases can be an exhilarating experience.

Baltimore City Department of Planning,
Study for the East-West Expressway, 1960

To the critics of the urban planning profession, Planning Director Phil Darling's 1960 highway plan is a marvelous illustration of the point that planners have no better crystal ball than the average person on the street. The plan moved many pieces on the highway chess board, almost all in a disastrously wrong direction. Darling (the guy whose job it was to think in the long-term) proposed moving the downtown section of the East-West Expressway to the Inner Harbor, occupying the land between Pratt Street and the Inner Harbor basin. But that was only the start of this wrong-headed masterplan. (See Figure 8 and Figure 9.)

Darling's plan deleted one good idea from the 1957 plan—the mostly industrial route with the harbor crossing at Fort McHenry and on to the Canton industrial area. It repeated the ill-conceived idea to put I-70 through Leakin Park/Rosemont and to route the southwest expressway through Montgomery Street and Federal Hill. One more hallmark and a first: It moved the primary East Baltimore segment from the rail corridor to the Fell's Point/Canton waterfront (which had been a "supplementary proposal" in the 1957 plan).

There is no mention of the neighborhoods that would suffer a wide swath of asphalt where houses, stores, and churches had been: Fell's Point, Rosemont, Canton, Sharp Leadenhall, and Federal Hill did not warrant even a mention in the sixty-one-page plan. Nor did it address Tyson Street and its feisty defenders. But the *Sun* reported: "The embattled bohemians of Tyson Street had another fight on their hands. The new east-west plan includes a spur that would strike off to the northeast toward the Jones Falls Expressway. It would come so close to Tyson Street houses that a Tyson Street housewife, emptying a dish pan out the back door would empty it into the expressway right-of-way."

Instead of describing neighborhood impacts, the report offers a blanket Robert-Moses–like explanation: "As a matter of fact, not only would the clearance of many of the buildings along the proposed route not harm the city, one can go further and say that their removal would be advantageous." Then, in defending the proximity of the Harbor Route to the CBD, the report maintained that, "In many cases, the easiest place to locate an expressway is in the belt of slums that surrounds the central business district."[41]

That Darling in 1960 had a completely opaque Inner Harbor crystal ball would be forgivable if it had preceded any viable vision for revitalizing the Harbor. However, it was Darling's predecessor, Arthur D. McVoy, who first conceptualized the Inner Harbor redevelopment in 1956. McVoy's plan featured an entirely new vision of the Inner Harbor basin, with industrial and port-related uses replaced by parks, public recreation facilities, hotels, office buildings, restaurants, and high-rise apartments. McVoy maintained that Baltimore could be "one of the most exciting cities in the world," and he viewed the Inner Harbor as "The [single] most significant area from the standpoint of civic design and a fine architectural setting."[42]

Figure 8. The Department of Planning's concept plan for the downtown section of "the Harbor Route," 1960

ARTHUR D. McVOY

This current work stands alone, as far as I know, in tracing the Inner Harbor vision back to McVoy's 1956 plan.

Sadly, McVoy passed away only a year later, a victim of pneumonia at age forty-seven. His vision for the Inner Harbor was not the only thing that he had gotten right. It was McVoy, as noted previously, who first proposed the industrial corridor expressway with the harbor crossing at Fort McHenry. In 1950 he elevated that plan to second priority, right behind completion of the Jones Falls expressway, and he farsightedly recommended a tunnel instead of a bridge. It took another twenty-five years before Baltimore's leadership came around to that same point of view. Had McVoy lived, Baltimore almost certainly would have taken a few shortcuts to implement a viable highway plan, not to mention that Darling's disastrous "Harbor Route" would never have seen the light of day.

The *Baltimore Sun's* obituary called McVoy "a young man of bold and imaginative vision."

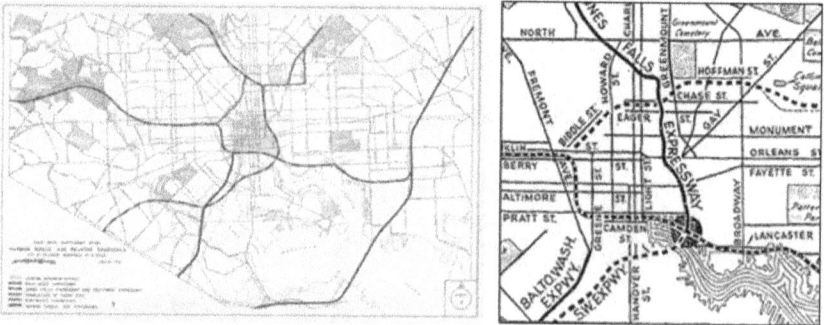

Figure 9. Baltimore City Planning Department's 1960 highway alignment (Source, map at left: Department of Planning, 1972; map at right: Baltimore Sun*)*

Darling contended that his highway plan might co-exist with or even complement McVoy's Inner Harbor vision. Astonishingly, he points out that McVoy's plan was mostly park space between Pratt Street and the water, and "the construction of the expressway might bring the park into being at an earlier date than would otherwise be possible," and that park development might be "facilitated if the Harbor Route served to reduce the present heavy surface traffic around the Inner Harbor."[43]

Darling's plan does not fare well in hindsight. However, it should be pointed out that Darling had plenty of company on the bandwagon that almost prevented the Inner Harbor from taking shape: Darling gained the endorsements of Baltimore's heavy hitters, including the city housing and redevelopment agencies, Committee for Downtown, the Greater Baltimore Committee, the Association of Commerce, the Retail Merchants Association, the Port Administration, and Citizens Planning and Housing Association (CPHA).[44] From this lineup of economic development interests, you can see why Darling's plan was not dead on arrival: The Harbor Route brought the expressway much closer to downtown retail and the Charles Center office core than any other plan. If you buy into the notion that expressways are the key to keeping downtown competitive with the suburbs, then you might be willing to give up on a promising Inner Harbor plan that might turn out to be a pipedream.

The 1960 plan had only a brief stay on the front pages of the highway saga, as the Department of Public Works hired a team of engineers to revisit the highway plan in 1961. But Darling did not go quietly.

1962—10-D PLAN: THE "FUTURE INVESTMENT PREVENTION PROGRAM"

I loved the sketches of that bridge [Federal Hill to Harbor East]; we used to call it an engineer's wet dream.
    Joe McNeely, Director, Southeast Community Organization

If a 1960s-era Baltimore resident wanted to devise a program to discourage young people from returning to the city, fixing up houses, and giving new life to struggling neighborhoods, they might have boldly and brazenly designed a highway that crossed South Baltimore at Montgomery Street, swiped through Federal Hill, crossed the Harbor with a fourteen-lane low level bridge, occupied Harbor East with a six-level flyover interchange, and then followed the Fell's Point/Canton waterfront all the way to the Canton industrial area, permanently cutting off those neighborhoods from the harbor. The 1962 10-D plan, amazingly, did exactly that.

The 10-D plan, as shown in Figure 10 and with more detail in Appendix 1-B, was very likely born of inter-agency rivalry. The Department of Public Works Director Bernard Werner was not keen on the Department of Planning stepping into the lead on highway planning. He hired a team of three engineers and traffic planners, with J. E. Greiner as the lead. The study was initially described as "technical" (to make sure that Darling's plan worked from a technical point of view)—after all, it had been prepared *without* engineering involvement. But under Werner's direction the new study grew into a full-fledged analysis of alternatives to the 1960 plan.

As this little inter-agency drama unfolded, Werner apprised Darling of difficulties in the 1960 plan, and Darling responded with ways to overcome those difficulties. Then, in September 1961, Werner stopped returning Darling's calls and memos. When the report came out, Darling regarded it as a personal affront. The main difference was that the Pratt Street segment was removed and traffic approaching downtown from the west was guided to the more southerly Montgomery Street/Federal Hill corridor. The bridge crossing the harbor at

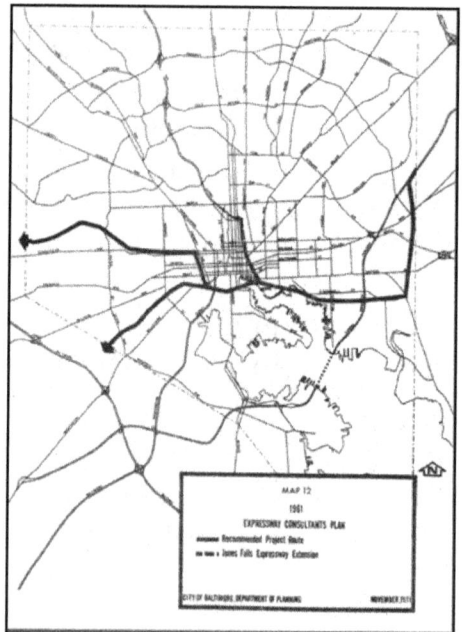

Figure 10. The 1961-62 10-D plan (Source: Baltimore City Department of Planning, 1972)

Federal Hill grew into an unwieldy fourteen lanes due to the absence of any alternative east-west route.

Darling, now in open warfare with Werner,* attempted to rally support for his Pratt Street route. Marty Millspaugh (in charge of the Charles Center redevelopment) sided with Darling because the Pratt Street corridor would provide "a natural barrier" that "would contain the Central Business District and permit the development of different types of land use to the south." He opposed 10-D because it would "promote growth of the Central Business District in a southerly direction," thereby weakening the core.[45] This, coming from the future Director of Charles Center Inner Harbor Management, is more than a little surprising, stunning really. Millspaugh was not alone, as Walter Sondheim, Chairman of the Urban Renewal and Housing Commission, and the city's Renewal Director Richard L. Steiner also supported Darling's plan.[46]

When the Greater Baltimore Committee (GBC) sided with DPW's 10-D plan, however, that tilted the scales. GBC withdrew their support for Darling's plan because the Pratt Street segment would "impose a physical and psychological barrier" between the central business district and the Inner Harbor. In January 1962, the Planning Commission's Master Plan Committee narrowly voted (3-2) for 10-D, then the full commission voted overwhelmingly (7-1) for 10-D.[47] Mayor Grady then endorsed 10-D, which led to one of the more disorderly public hearings in the long history of acrimonious expressway community meetings.

Highway supporters did themselves no favors in this January 1962 hearing. Bernard Werner expressed little sympathy for those impacted, saying, "You can't build an expressway without tearing down some homes... Somebody's going to

---

* Darling and Werner repeatedly butted heads over highway plans from 1961 to 1965, when Larry Reich took over as planning director. A news account on January 8, 1964, captured the two in a juvenile standoff over the lower section of I-83—Werner supporting the eastside Jones Falls route, Darling supporting a westside alignment near Mount Royal. An irked Werner walked out of a Planning Commission meeting where these options were being discussed. When CPHA sided with Planning, favoring the west-side alignment, Werner called it "ridiculous." Four days later, after McKeldin ordered a study of the westside route, a news article recounted: "Before trudging off into a realm of silence, both Bernard Warner and Phillip Darling, the chief antagonists in the argument over expressway plans, claimed victory from the mayor's ruling."

have to be displaced no matter where we build it." J. E. Greiner's Bruce Herman†
dispassionately stated that "many of the neighborhoods affected have already
been earmarked for slum clearance." The crowd responded with "a chorus of
boos…interspersed with shouts of 'Who says?' and 'My home's no slum.'"

With emotions riding high, City Councilman William Bonnett grabbed
the microphone from a highway supporter representing the Jaycees and
shouted that they must "live in the County." The *Sun*'s account of the fracas
continues, "Mr. Werner struggled with Mr. Bonnett for possession of the
microphone, but the determined councilman held on, [stating that] 'About
15,000 people are going to be put out on the street because of this expressway.
They are the people who ought to be heard, not those who live in the county.'
With this, Mr. Werner finally regained the microphone and ordered Mr.
Bonnett to his seat amid jeers and cries of 'Let him talk!' from the crowd."[48]

Mayor Grady just wanted to be done with the issue, and said in July
1962, "At this point, we don't care where the east-west goes, as long as it goes
somewhere."[49] But State Roads Commissioner John Funk wanted to wait for
the results of a regional traffic study, which put everything on hold for about a
year and a half—everything, that is, except the community opposition, which
was gathering steam, especially in Southwest Baltimore. One meeting drew six
hundred protesters, and an early anti-highway coalition was formed called the
No Route Association.[50] In city council a voting block emerged to gain leverage—seven councilmen from three districts said they would vote as a block,
which meant each representative needed to be satisfied with the road plan.

Theodore McKeldin was elected to a second stint as Baltimore's mayor
and took office in the fall of 1963. He promised a prompt and thorough review
of the expressway plan, but he too needed the results of the regional traffic studies. In this waiting period an enormous opportunity was missed, and this speaks
to the "engineers rule" mindset of the day. Why did no one think to re-examine
the highway plans from the point of view of the communities impacted and
the city's broader land use and economic development objectives? Surely that

---

† Herman would later win status as highway villain for forcing the removal of George Nilson,
attorney representing Leakin Park's communities, from the *V.O.L.P.E. v. Volpe* lawsuit. See
Leakin Park chapter.

would have led the city to dust off the 1949 plan for the Fort McHenry harbor crossing, the only route that involved virtually no residential dislocation, no loss to the city's tax base, and enormous economic development upsides.

The anxiously awaited traffic study was carried out by Wilbur Smith Associates (WSA) over a twenty-eight-month period and at a cost of over $800,000 ($7.2 million today). It was released in a preliminary form on October 5, 1963.‡ WSA recommended burying the city in concrete with forty-eight miles of expressways (compared to 10-D's twenty-two miles) connected by an astonishing twenty-seven interchanges. Completely new routes were mapped out, including an east-west belt along Cold Spring Lane, a new northeast connector along Harford Road and Perring Parkway, a new northwest expressway that would link the Cold Spring Freeway to the (later named) I-795, and the Arundel Freeway (Route 10) extension into the city along Hanover Street. (See Figure 11.)

Further, the study maps and accompanying description were so general that they did not address the more fine-grained decisions faced in the city. There was one very wide routing line going through Baltimore's Inner Harbor, and you could not tell if it was Darling's Pratt Street route or 10-D's Federal Hill route. It appears no one wanted to tell John Funk he had needlessly waited for a study that did not even speak to the main decision points. The study was essentially dismissed by those whose opinions were not unduly warped by a misguided desire to impose a Los-Angeles-style freeway system in the City of Baltimore.

Clearly, the underlying assumption of the WSA report was that anyone

---

‡ There is an entertaining *Baltimore Sun* account of the release of the WSA report. Mayor McKeldin wanted to know what WSA recommended as priorities and when SRC would give the "go-ahead sign." WSA said that information would be in the full report, which would be available in six weeks (it actually took nine more months). Not satisfied, McKeldin bored in, leading to the engineers arguing among themselves as to "whether work should proceed on the outskirts and [move] toward downtown or start at the center and move outward." McKeldin, growing impatient, asked when he could have the data. Funk: "Monday or sometime next week." Mayor: "What about this afternoon?" They settled on the following Wednesday. McKeldin boldly claimed that he had just shaved six weeks off the highway decision timeline, which is positively comical in hindsight—it would take another seventeen years before Baltimore implemented a highway plan.

who wanted to get somewhere faster than they can now needs their own expressway. Except that WSA missed one: they failed to propose the sole highway alignment that made sense—the industrial route with the Fort McHenry harbor crossing. The WSA plan has the worst batting average for implementation—only five miles were built from the forty-eight proposed! (And those five miles were essentially "gimmes," such as the downtown section of the Jones Falls Expressway.) They thankfully whiffed on almost 90 percent of what they dreamed up on John Funk's dime.[§]

Funk Unwittingly Aiding Highway Opponents

If Baltimore's anti-expressway advocates ever had a reunion, they should have paid homage to Funk's decision to place everything on hold for eighteen months while his consultants wasted $800,000. Every delay worked to benefit the opposition, and that was a big one. It was especially important because in 1966 federal laws were enacted to protect parks and historic areas from highway incursions. Funk's delay helped his opponents get to the post-1966 era when they gained new tools of obstruction.

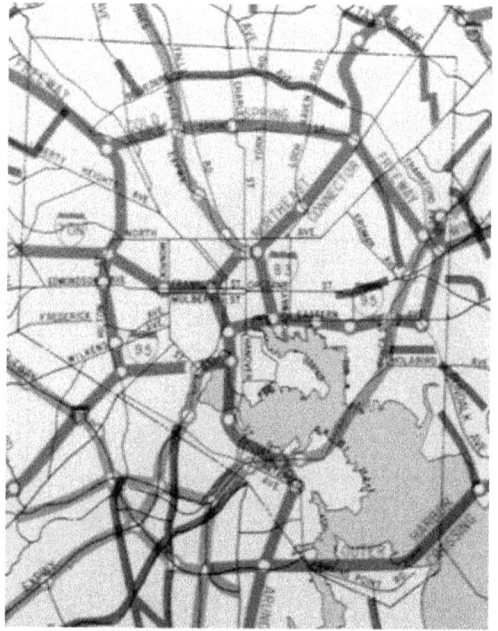

Figure 11. WSA Baltimore Metropolitan Area Transportation Study, 1963 (Note the thin dark lines are major streets, not expressways)

§ In 1974, Charles Pratt, Principal at Wilbur Smith Associates, testified in the MAD lawsuit that, if the full 3-A expressway system was not built, "Baltimore would never make it." "Downtown," he said, "would near breakdown." (*Baltimore Sun*, April 19, 1973.)

The WSA report was interpreted as supporting the 10-D alignment, and the Pratt Street route went into the ever-deepening dustbin of discarded highway plans. Probably influencing this decision, it was also in 1963 that McKeldin began forming committees and authorizing studies for a massive redevelopment of the Inner Harbor. It is reasonable to assume (although research has not unearthed a paper trail) that McKeldin, Millspaugh, and Sondheim began to see the full potential of the Inner Harbor and therefore rejected the Pratt Street route.

Although McKeldin endorsed the 10-D plan, he did not ingratiate himself to the engineers who created it. In 1964 he formed an advisory committee on highway design, saying that engineers, if left to their druthers, would produce "grotesque eyesores bringing ugliness and a sense of revulsion to the citizens." The Public Affairs Committee of the Baltimore Chapter of the Maryland Society of Professional Engineers took offense, saying, "We believe that the opinions the mayor expressed are his own and represent but an infinitesimal portion of the population of the city."[51]

From 1964 to 1966, McKeldin and the city began pushing through condemnation ordinances for 10-D in the areas where they had the councilmanic support they needed. Other segments were re-studied, including the southwest/Carroll Park area, but a satisfactory solution to that segment eluded highway planners until the Urban Design Concept Team (UDCT) arrived on the scene in January 1967.

In 1966 McKeldin's battle for good design centered on the bridge from Federal Hill to (the later termed) Harbor East. He called the preliminary design "hideous" and authorized a $40,000 study of alternatives, saying the bridge "could become Baltimore's trademark in this century and the centuries to come."[¶][52] Author Earl Swift pilloried that idea, saying the bridge "would be a mammoth fourteen lanes wide and the signature feature for which

---

¶ Some of the 10-D critics, including Planning Commission Chair Barton, realized they were not going to stop the 10-D steamroller; so, they became advocates for an unusual design concept for the Inner Harbor bridge. Lev Zetlin, an Israeli-American civil and structural engineer, created a design later described as: "multiple decks carrying 14 lanes of traffic, supported by an innovative 'cat's cradle' system of force and counterforce cables."

Baltimore would become known the world over—as instantly recognizable, its straight-faced backers claimed, as the Golden Gate Bridge."[53]

In 1965, after another disastrous hearing (this time for the condemnation bill), federal and state officials pressured the city into giving up some of its autonomy over the highway planning. The result was a unique multi-level agency with equal responsibility shared by city, state, and federal government. The Interstate Division for Baltimore City (IDBC) managed highway planning with streamlined access to decision-making authority at all three levels of government. It may have been streamlined for transportation decision-making, but the highway fight that was only then starting to brew, was about those operating *outside* the transportation silo who were demanding to be heard.

CITY COUNCIL SKIRMISHES—TOM WARD'S LONELY FIGHT

Baltimore must resort to mass transportation for a solution to its conveyance problems and restore the pedestrian and bus riders to a first-class citizenship. Inner Baltimore must cease being used as a convenience parking lot for county dwellers.

Tom Ward, from a 1962 statement[54]

While other councilmen pressed for adjustments to lessen the impact on their communities, there was one, and only one, who opposed the totality of the expressway plan. That was Tom Ward.

In 1964 Ward attempted to remove $27 million in capital funds designated for the East-West Expressway. While his colleagues did not want to turn away all that 90/10 federal money, Ward contended, "Whether we'll lose the federal money isn't the question. The point is do we need the East-West Expressway?" He further stated, "What we really need is a well-developed mass transit system."[55] Ward was initially willing to consider expressways if they also accommodated mass transit. Later, his position hardened—he was the "green eggs and ham" highway opponent. He did not like them here; he did not like them there.

In 1965, before he settled in as the no-highway-nowhere guy, he put out an alternative highway plan that he dubbed the $50 transportation plan, an obvious dig at the $800,000 Wilbur Smith plan, which Ward accurately portrayed as causing "unparalleled destruction." Ward advocated for eliminating I-70 and building what he called an "on-surface expressway" (really a boulevard) through the Franklin-Mulberry corridor—a landscaped urban parkway wide enough to allow for a future rail line. I-83 would similarly become a boulevard in the downtown area. Ward saw "no critical need" for I-95, but said he could accept an alternative alignment in the spirit of compromise. Ward's plan gained editorial praise but had little impact beyond embarrassing the State Roads Commission for wasting $800,000 on the WSA study.[56]

Ward also contributed to two delays of a condemnation bill during his tenure as vice chair of the Transportation Committee. Ward contended that those delays cost almost two years on the timetable (1965 to 1967), with a result that the highway team then had to contend with new federal rules related to impacts on historic districts and parks. Ward described the delays in a 2015 interview:

I said "Mr. chairman…the vote is illegal. Because…you are going through a city park [Federal Hill] and…you haven't got the permission of the Park Board. And the law of the city requires you to get permission of the Park Board and you didn't do it." Schaefer [then chairman of the committee] starts shouting at D'Alesandro [president of city council]…So, they sent the ordinance back to committee…. They go before the Park Board and they pass it… They come before the city council again… I say "Mr. President, you do not have the correct process…. You have changed the masterplan of the city, and you did not get permission of the Planning Commission."…Back to Committee she goes again.

The interviewer asked Ward, "Did you wait to add that second part to buy yourself more time?" And Ward replied, "Yes, I certainly did."

41

Ward's memory of these events was less than perfect, and we cannot attribute a two-year delay to these actions alone. Sixth District councilmen put up a united front against the condemnation line in the Carroll Park area during this time too. Regardless of the primary cause, this two-year holdup of the condemnation ordinances, combined with Funk's eighteen-month delay for the WSA study, created the bridge to the post-1966 era when new legal tools strengthened their hand.

In 1966 Ward was the only "No" vote against the condemnation line for Franklin-Mulberry. In November 1967, as the lone opponent of the final condemnation bill, Ward promised that he would not go quietly. He threatened to sue and later followed through on that threat, losing one lawsuit and winning another.[57] The final condemnation bill authorizing the full 10-D system passed city council on November 20, 1967. However, there was one piece of the highway map that was interrupted, and it was largely due to Tom Ward's influence that Baltimore was later able to establish the Mount Royal Cultural District.

THE WESTSIDE CONNECTOR

Tom Ward was mostly tilting at windmills trying to stop the 10-D juggernaut, but he did have one extremely significant win—he led the fight to eliminate a six-lane expressway that would have barged its way right through the middle of the Mount Royal Cultural District. This "Westside Connector" would have been a very unfriendly neighbor to Mount Royal Station and the Lyric Opera House, divided Mount Vernon from Bolton Hill, hemmed in both the University of Baltimore and the Maryland Institute, prevented the later development of the Meyerhoff Symphony Hall, and thwarted the later use of the Mount Royal area for events like Artscape.

In September 1965, Ward introduced city council Bill 1102 to eliminate the Westside Connector from the city's masterplan. By November, Ward had amassed an anti-expressway coalition impossible to ignore: The Lyric Opera

House; Maryland Institute College of Art;** Maryland General Hospital; two churches; seven community organizations representing all of Mount Vernon, Bolton Hill, Seton Hill, and Tyson Street; and two political clubs.†† Notable for Ward, he had set aside his differences with the Mount Royal Improvement Association (a rival to Ward's Mount Royal Democratic Club) and enrolled them as active participants.

City council punted the hot-potato issue back to the Planning Commission for further study in December. McKeldin's instructions came right out of the highway opposition handbook: "A decision on any one highway must represent a balanced judgment in which traffic requirements are weighed against the damage which its construction would entail. Important human and cultural values should not be sacrificed to the seemingly insatiable needs of the automobile."[58]

Two and a half years passed before the Planning Commission issued their report, finally voting to remove the Westside Connector from the masterplan in June 1968, presumably with

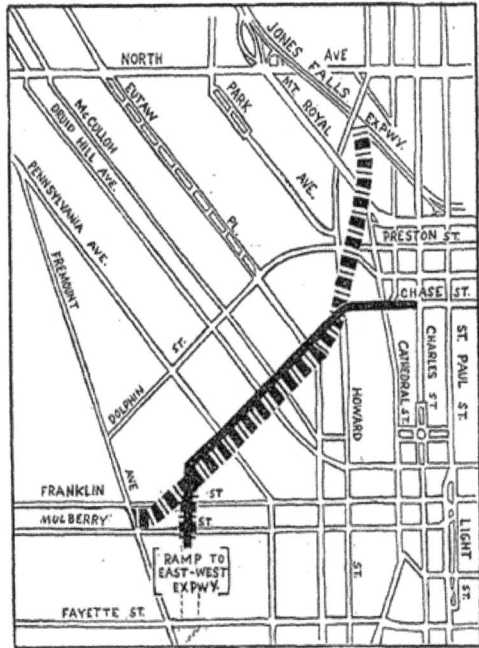

Figure 12. Westside Connector (striped line shows the 1965 expressway version); black line shows the 1968 boulevard version (source, the Baltimore Sun)

** The Maryland Institute College of Art acquired the historic Mount Royal Station in 1964, then carried out an adaptive reuse plan that was hailed as a national model. When they joined the opposition, Darling discounted their opinion, saying they had purchased the B&O station at their own risk and should have planned for the expressway.

†† Oddly, the Philadelphia Symphony Orchestra was on record opposing the Westside Connector, while the Baltimore Symphony remained silent.

the blessings of the new mayor, Thomas D'Alesandro III. As Figure 12 shows, the Commission substituted a boulevard that veered east to avoid the troublesome nexus of Mount Royal Station and the Lyric Opera House.

Much like many of the ever-so-slow gains made by highway opponents over the next decade and a half, the person most responsible for the victory, Tom Ward, was not in a position to enjoy the accolades—he lost the 1967 Democratic primary due to underhanded and racially motivated election tactics.

YOU JUST CAN'T HIDE AN EXPRESSWAY

In 2019, Gene Bober of the Interstate Division Joint Development staff recounted how fellow planner Les Graef attempted to lower the Westside Connector's impacts with a design somewhere between a full-fledged expressway and an at-grade boulevard.

> We worked very studiously…to minimize the effect that this highway would have on the west side…. Les really went to work on all the details of trying to narrow that roadway, for example…integrating the gutter pans into the roadway…. We would have these long, protracted arguments with the engineers… The roadway got narrower, and the signs got smaller, but it still ripped across the urban grid, and there wasn't any mistaking it.
>
> …We made a presentation to the [Housing] Department planners…One of the planners said, "You know, I've got to tell you, you've done a lot of work here—I'll give you… credit for it. But in the end, it's still putting a mink coat on a turkey."

THOMAS WARD, BULLDOG FOR THE HIGHWAY FIGHT IN THE SIXTIES

Trying to gain strength from a bout with a debilitating disease, 80-year-old Tom Ward had renewed his habit of taking daily lengthy walks around the city. On one of these walks he saw a man in a neighbor's yard and suspected a robbery in progress. When Ward confronted him, the man, later described as 40 years old, 6 feet tall and husky, climbed the fence and attempted to flee. Ward (5'8", 170) tackled him and was able to keep him down until police arrived.[59] Had the robber known any of Ward's opponents in the road wars fight (or in any myriad of other public controversies), they might have advised him not to tangle with the combative ex-councilman.

Ward is a Hall-of-Fame Road Warrior with a tragic side—a highly principled but also cantankerous and rigid man. More libertarian than liberal, the word "compromise" was oddly missing from his political vocabulary. He was stubborn, determined, and could be vindictive to people who crossed him. You could make a good argument that Ward's contributions to the Road Wars are unequaled. However, his penchant for picking fights and holding grudges is on equal display, marring an otherwise stellar record. In his later years, Ward tried to remind people of the legacy left by the original founders of the Preservation Society (of which he was one), but he did so with enmity, trying to tear down the legacy of everyone's favorite Road Warrior, Senator Barbara Mikulski.

Ward started out his public life as a primary organizer of the Mount Royal Democratic Club, originally conceived as an alternative to the Jack Pollack-controlled Democratic machine. He won a city council seat in 1963, then lost it four years later, leaving an overwhelmingly positive legacy. Ward was a lead sponsor for the city's first minimum wage law, as well as the bill that established the Baltimore City Commission for Historic and Architectural Preservation. He stood with civil rights activists in supporting fair housing bills‡‡ and led a movement to expand funding for urban tree planting.

---

‡‡ As one small example of Ward's contribution in the category of "race and change," Ward paved the way for two African Americans (Philip K. Merrill and Joy Owens) to serve on the board of the previously all-White Preservation Society. Merrill, incidentally, told me he did not find other board members to be welcoming of this diversity.

Ward chaired the council's Public Transportation Committee and used this post to promote public transit to a mostly tone-deaf audience. He championed the creation of a statewide mass transit agency to take over Baltimore's fading private transit system. The state's Mass Transit Administration was created in 1971, four years after Ward's council stint, but it was really Ward who got the ball rolling.

Moving to his Road Wars legacy, Ward's imprint on the Baltimore's highway system is extensive and all to the good.

In 1967, Ward teamed up with Lu Fisher to form the Society for the Preservation of Federal Hill and Fell's Point. He identified and analyzed the provisions of the Highway Act of 1966, which became the basis for the court challenge that would later sink the highway through Fell's Point. Ward also secured legal assistance for the Preservation Society in 1969, enlisting the help of Norman Ramsey, a highly respected attorney at Semmes, Bowen, and Semmes—this resulted in Geoff Mitchell being assigned to the case.

Ward was instrumental in delaying the 10-D condemnation bill, filed the first lawsuits to challenge the highway through Leakin Park, and engineered the defeat of the Westside Connector, a heated battle that also revealed Ward's combative side. When a number of city council members switched sides in November 1965, Ward wrote six bitterly angry letters. One to William Hodges read: "I am 38 years of age, in good health, and intend to be around for a long time, and I am sure that your actions of yesterday will rise up and haunt you in the future."

Henry G. Parks, the respected African American owner of the Parks Sausage Company, also received a Ward missive: "To say I am disappointed in you would be the massive understatement of the year. I have always stood beside you in some most difficult matters, and it is now apparent to me that I cannot count on you in matters that are of acute interest to me." Parks replied in kind, "This acknowledges your unfortunate letter of November 9. I am extremely sorry that you are proving to be so shallow and that you are severing our good relationship based on a pre-determination of my judgment."[60] When Parks voted against an anti-highway amendment in 1967,

Ward accused him of "making flowery speeches about Negro rights [while] doing almost nothing [for] Baltimore's Negroes."

In 1968, Walter S. Orlinsky and fourteen members of the Mount Royal Democratic Club split off and formed the New Democratic Club. Some objected to Ward's support for the Vietnam War and his opposition to gun control; others argued that Ward treated the club as his own personal fiefdom and the club's newsletter as his mouthpiece. All accounts agree that Ward's vitriol toward Orlinsky and the NDC group never abated, even decades after the split.

Ward lost his council seat in 1967. In that election there were two integrated tickets (including Ward's Mount Royal Democratic Club), an all-White ticket, and six Black independents who were long-shots for the three posts. The all-White ticket put out a "vote Black Power" flier in majority Black neighborhoods a few days before the election—it supported the independents, taking votes away from the integrated tickets and thus defeating Ward. A grand jury convened to examine the issue said the campaign had "employed the most insidious of the techniques of false propaganda and was calculated to inflame and exploit racial tensions to gather additional votes."§§61

There was an upside to Ward's loss: He could now devote more time to the formation and growth of the Preservation Society and to identifying and taking full advantage of the changes in federal law—the harbingers of a new day for highway fighters.¶¶

---

§§ A similar campaign trick in the Third District used a flyer targeted to conservative White voters. Under a banner of "Citizens for Equality," the flier appeared to advocate for three candidates described as "Liberal-minded men" (Embry, Curran, and Smith), while criticizing three others (Pica, Gallagher, and Best) for voting against integrated taverns, more antipoverty funds, open housing, and busing. The flier was actually put out by supporters of Pica, Gallagher, and Best who were catering to racial fears and attitudes among those voters.

¶¶ Ward found it abhorrent when the Preservation Society offered a heavily conditioned endorsement of the Fort McHenry route that was later built as I-95. In March of 1971 Ward resigned from the Preservation Society over this issue. In his resignation letter, he characterized the society's position as "a disgrace… The same old stuff…hurt someone else…as long as we are not affected…. My opposition to the expressway did not come because it went through Fell's Point. I am opposed to it because it is injurious to the city…" He later came back into the fold.

TOM WARD, "TELLING IT LIKE IT IS"

As a judge, Ward was regarded as fair minded and straight shooting, although on one occasion his habit of "telling it like it is" got him in trouble. A jury pool was dismissed because Ward's instructions to the jury were a little too close to the truth.

The defense attorney on the case quoted Ward as saying: "In criminal cases the job of the prosecution is to convict. It is the job of the defense to get his or her client off no matter how. [Both] will try to confuse you and get away from the case."

When the statement came to light, Ward seemed surprised that anyone would regard this as an inappropriate instruction to jurors. As the controversy brewed, a letter to the editor of the *Baltimore Sun* hit the nail on the head: "Judge Ward was always straightforward with people... No one has more honesty, integrity, and fairness than Judge Ward. This is exactly how he got where he is."

NEW AMMUNITION—THE FEDERAL LANDSCAPE CHANGES

[The freeway fighters] were successful only to the extent that they used the tools provided by new legislative mandates to challenge, confront, delay, and litigate against the road builders. In an ironic turn, the same federal government that financed interstate construction had also legitimated the activities of freeway opponents.[62]

Raymond Mohl, author of numerous books and articles about the volatile intersection of cities and highways

The Federal Aid to Highways Act of 1966 and its counterpart, the Historic Preservation Act of 1966, were not well understood at first. Many assumed the new provisions were minor bumps in the road requiring more check-boxes and more paperwork with more expansive justifications. Few thought these new requirements would fundamentally alter business as usual for highway planners.

The 4(f) provision of Federal Aid to Highways Act stipulates that the Secretary of Transportation may not approve the use of federal funds in projects requiring "any land from a public park, recreation area, wildlife and waterfowl refuge, or historic site" unless "no feasible and prudent alternative" exists. Projects that claim "no feasible alternative" justification must provide for "all possible planning to minimize harm."

The Historic Preservation Act of 1966 supplements the Highway Act. Section 106 of that law is nebulous by design—there are no prohibitions, nothing that says you cannot build a highway through a historic district. The provision instead requires federal agencies to take into account the effects of their projects on historic properties and to provide the Advisory Council on Historic Preservation with a reasonable opportunity to comment. Federal agencies must consult with the State Historic Preservation Offices (SHPO) and members of the general public with an economic, social, or cultural interest in the project. If the project is found have an "adverse impact" on historic properties, there is a structured process to determine if and how the adverse impacts can be mitigated.[63]

Back in Baltimore, the highway protest movement matured, coalesced, and became a force to reckon with in 1967 and 1968 thanks to the hope provided by these two federal laws. Although protesters had no better understanding of the new laws than the road-building establishment, it was a turning point; protesters could tell their friends and neighbors that this was not a waste of time. The federal government was now of two minds: the expressway funding side saying "build it," and the regulatory side saying, "not so fast."

In 1969 Congress passed the National Environmental Policy Act (NEPA) requiring environmental impact statements (EIS) for all federal actions with significant environmental effects. Protesters in Baltimore quickly learned what constituted an acceptable EIS—disputes might not result in a substantial change, but a delay of several months was a huge win for anti-highway forces.

Also in 1969, the nature and timing of public hearings were changed to favor more substantial community input. Highway planners were now required to conduct two hearings: a "location hearing" before final decisions were made, and a "design hearing" after the alignment was selected. In Baltimore, this might have been termed the "Bernard Werner override provision." The DPW chief (and the chief advocate for a public-be-damned method of ramming through the highway plan) might have seen this coming—he resigned in December 1968.

Then, in 1971 the Supreme Court handed down the landmark *Citizens to Preserve Overton Park v. Volpe* decision, holding that the lower courts erred in backing the government defendants' argument that "changing the route to avoid the park...was more costly and more disruptive." The High Court held that "the fact that the alternatives are more costly and disruptive does not constitute a reason to dismiss those alternatives as imprudent and infeasible." Suddenly the 4(f) provision had real teeth.

These alterations of the federal landscape were the harbingers of change at the local level. Nowhere was this change more evident than in Baltimore.

IMPORTANT NOTE

This concludes the chronological accounting for the years 1940 to 1966. 1967 to 1975 are the years when everything changed—by the end of 1975 the highway protesters had, shockingly, gained the upper hand. This is the core of the Road Wars. At this point we depart from a chronological account so that we can take a deeper dive into the community battlegrounds (each with their own chronology) and cross-cutting city-wide issues. We will return to the chronological account in 1976.

V. BLOWS AGAINST THE EMPIRE I

1960S ACTIVISTS JOIN THE CAUSE

Never underestimate the power of a small group of committed people to change the world. In fact, it is the only thing that ever has.

Margaret Mead

It was the late 1960s. As Preservation Society volunteer Charlie Duff put it, "If you weren't knocking on doors or marching for some good cause (or bad cause), there was no point being alive." Up until about 1967, anti-highway activists were essentially folks trying to protect their neighborhoods along with a smattering of historic preservation and civil rights advocates. But in the late '60s, young people, both White and Black, began questioning pretty much everything the establishment stood for, from military colonialism to the pursuit of material wealth. Baltimore's establishment quite clearly stood for the Road, so young activists held the highway plans up for scrutiny and found what they suspected: economic interests were controlling the process to the detriment of dispossessed communities.

Anti-highway groups found new foot soldiers for the cause—veterans from the anti-war and civil rights movements brought a new level of energy along with some left-wing slogans that had to be tempered lest pro-road forces paint them all as out-of-control radicals. In nearby Washington the regulars apparently failed to tamp down the lefties, as shown in this sign (Figure 13) linking the 3-Sisters Bridge to US colonialism.

Baltimore was tame by comparison, using mostly conventional

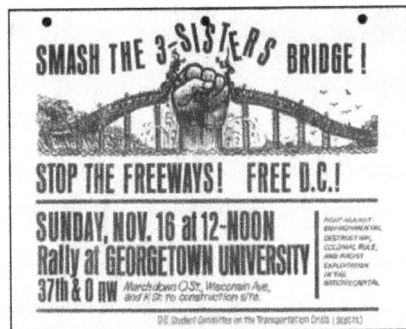

Figure 13. DC Protest Sign

51

tactics. When the Movement Against Destruction (MAD) needed a rab-
ble-rouser at a hearing, they brought in Sammie Abbott from Washington.
Abbott's peace and civil rights activities had earned him "an invitation" to
testify before the House Committee on Un-American Activities. He was one
of the main organizers of the Emergency Committee on the Transportation
Crisis (ECTC), a DC anti-highway coalition. Abbott had a confrontational
style unmatched in Baltimore—he was arrested thirty-four times while carrying out seventy-five street protests. Not unlike Barbara Mikulski in Baltimore,
Abbott had a way of capturing the essence of an issue with a memorable
phrase, for example, "They take seven cents out of every gallon and use it
to bury us in concrete," and the oft-repeated slogan, "White men's roads
through Black men's homes."[64] Abbott, who was White, described himself as
"perpetually mad…I'm living to fight the goddamned thing. I'm too mad to
sleep." He advised against civility, saying, "Once you're committed to a sense
of decorum, you're screwed."

Abbott and Reginald Booker, ECTC co-chairmen, lay claim to perhaps
the greatest winning percentage of any anti-road group in the country: only
10.7 of 36.4 planned miles were actually built. More than $1 billion in high-
way funds were later shifted to building the Metro.[65] When Abbott died in
1990, fellow Road Warrior Angela Rooney was quoted in the *Post* as saying,
"When people fly into Washington, they marvel at how pretty it is. Well, it
wouldn't look that way if not for Sammie Abbott."*

At the invitation of Baltimore's highway opponents, Sammie made several
appearances at highway hearings. Just as advertised, Abbott was unrestrained
by decorum. He referred to highway planners as "smiling idiots," "finks," an
"autonomous bunch of flunkies," and "dehumanized technocrats."[66]

Gene Bober, a former IDBC staffer, recounted a memorable hearing at
Edmondson High in which Sammie confronted hearing officers taking comments from the audience. "He grabbed [his] shillelagh, and he marched right

---

* Abbott later became the first and only socialist mayor of Tacoma Park (AKA "The People's
Republic of Takoma"), but was voted out in 1985, partly because he could not resist using his
office to advance left-wing causes (such as establishing Tacoma Park as a "Nuclear Free Zone")
that had little to do with running local government.

onto the stage, and…he took over the room. He said, and this is a quote that I'll take to my grave, 'More cities have been destroyed by city planners wielding magic markers than all the wars in history.'"

Baltimore's highway dissenters may not have had the same fervor as Abbott, but the spirit of 1960s activism played a major part in the expressway battle. Idealists and activists brought new energy and zeal to the fight, not to protect their own neighborhoods, but because their involvement fit into their sense of purpose and worldview—that working class and minority neighborhoods were being victimized because they were powerless.

Anti-road activism was a two-way street: The movement benefitted enormously from people who brought experience from anti-war

BILL HELLMANN ON THE OTHER SIDE OF THE FENCE

In my interview with Bill Hellmann (IDBC Chief in the late 1970s), he reflected on being on the receiving end of these insults, saying, "Our job was not a pleasant job, when it came to meeting with communities. Let's be honest, who was in favor of it? GBC and the mayor. The communities impacted—why would you expect them to be in favor of a road?" He credited Locust Point as the only community that was always polite and respectful. Other communities, Hellmann said, "abused you personally. They said things that were horrible. You know, we were doing our job."

and civil rights causes, but expressway fighters often went on to other endeavors where they selflessly promoted social change. The Road Wars were both the progeny and the breeding grounds for spirited community activism. Fell's Point activist Jack Gleason, in a 1974 interview, called his fellow road fighters "some of the greatest people [he's] ever known." William Donald Schaefer had a standard retort to highway protesters, which was, "Why can't you be FOR something?" The Road Warriors, operating in other walks of life, were more than just FOR something—they DID something.

In 1955, civil rights icon and anti-highway activist Dr. Helena Hicks refused to leave Read's drug store when she and six other Morgan State students were refused service. The resulting standoff generated bad publicity for Read's, leading them—and many other businesses who followed suit—to integrate all of their stores.[†] Norman Reeves, a litigant in the campaign to save Leakin Park, was a leader of the University of Maryland Black Coalition and endured a frightening encounter with neo-Nazis at a protest supporting open hotel accommodations. Martin Appell Dyer, active in the highway fight in West Baltimore, was the first African American to enroll at St. John's College in Annapolis. Esther Redd, President of the Relocation Action Movement in the late 1960s, was involved in civil rights protests to open up Baltimore's department stores.

If one were preparing a list of "Who's Who" for Baltimore community development activities, you would see tremendous overlap with the Road Fight. Charlie Duff, a young Preservation Society volunteer, has led Jubilee Baltimore to a place of prominence, as perhaps the longest standing and most effective community development organization in the city. Lucille Gorham, part of the Southeast Community Organization (SECO) and Southeast Council Against the Road (SCAR) coalitions, founded and directed Citizens for Fair Housing, a highly successful East Baltimore community development corporation (CDC). Michael Seipp, a community organizer for the campaign to save Leakin Park, later led community development organizations in both East and Southwest Baltimore. Joe McNeely, the first director of SECO, became a national expert on community organizing—he started and ran the Development Training Institute, which national columnist Neal Peirce called "the country's premier trainer of CDC leaders."

[†] Hicks later described the incident with a mix of pride and amusement: "They wouldn't serve us. They kept telling us we had to leave. We didn't belong in there. And we decided we weren't going to leave... We were worthy as anybody else. So, we had no problem sticking to our guns. About 30 minutes into the standoff, police came. The police were baffled. They didn't want to lock us up [because] we weren't doing anything wrong. What they did was keep calling more policemen. So, here we have all these police cars for seven students just trying to get warm until they get a bus to take them to school." She was also amused that this was described as the first civil rights sit-in, because "They hadn't invented that word 'sit-in.'" (Source: David Collins, "Building that held first civil rights sit-in for sale in Baltimore," WBAL-TV, Feb 28, 2020)

The Road Wars were also a notable training ground for women in leadership roles. Like many SECO/SCAR veterans, Betty Deacon started out as a housewife-activist. Her leadership skills first emerged when she chaired the Southeast Truck Task Force, but she later applied those skills to the Southeast Desegregation Coalition as well as the Racial Justice Center, an offshoot of the YMCA, where she taught "White awareness anti-racism training."[67] Betty Hyatt, another former housewife active in SECO/SCAR, later led Citizens for Washington Hill, spearheading a widely acclaimed redevelopment project.

We also find Road Warriors leading anti-poverty efforts. Bea Gaddy was known mostly for organizing massive holiday meals that served thousands of less fortunate Baltimoreans; she also ran the Patterson Park Emergency Food Center. Less well known, she was active in the Road Fight as a SECO/SCAR anti-highway activist.[‡] Leakin Park activist Millie

NECO ORGANIZES AGAINST A FICTITIOUS HIGHWAY

In 1972, Planning Director Larry Reich wrote a curious letter to Joseph Curran, Councilman for the Third District in Northeast Baltimore. Reich was frustrated because the Northeast Community Organization (NECO) kept hounding his office about a fictitious highway following Cold Spring Lane. As you recall, there had been a regional highway plan prepared by Wilbur Smith Associates in 1964 that did, indeed, propose a Cold Spring Lane Expressway. It never advanced beyond the concept stage and never had any status.

Reich, clearly at his wit's end, said it "frankly baffles me. Over the past three years we have met with [NECO representatives] on several occasions and have tried to convince them that the city has no plans for such a major highway project at all. This message is either not getting through to them, or else they… simply want to use the idea to develop a political base of their organization."

Larry's theory was undoubtedly correct. Nothing quite like having an expressway as a whipping boy for community organizing, even if said expressway is little more than a rumor.

---

‡ If you wanted to turn people out for a protest or a hearing you would start with Gaddy because, as Joe McNeely told me, "Bea was a crossing guard—she knew everybody…she was a natural organizing point every morning and every afternoon."

Tyssowski organized the nonprofit Women Entrepreneurs of Baltimore to help low-income and disadvantaged women gain self-sufficiency. Westside highway opponent Betty Merrill started and ran the Baltimore-based Human Development Institute, which provided a path out of welfare dependence via job training and job placement services.

In 1966, as the spirit of activism was taking hold in youth and minority groups all across the country, highway opposition began to take on new forms. Organizations were created for the sole purpose of altering or stopping expressways. First, the Relocation Action Movement (RAM) was organized in November 1966 to represent the Black West Baltimore communities of Harlem Park and Rosemont (see the Harlem Park chapter for more detail). Next, Fell's Pointers and historic preservation advocates pulled together and formed the Society for the Preservation of Federal Hill and Fell's Point (Preservation Society) in February 1967 (see Fell's Point chapter). In January 1968 RAM, the Congress for Racial Equality (CORE), and other westside anti-highway activists joined forces under the banner of the Expressway Coalition of Neighborhood Improvement Associations (ECONIA). Later in 1968 the eastside communities banded together to form Southeast Council Against the Road (SCAR).

So far so good, but skin color and geography represented parallel dividing lines—eastsiders were overwhelmingly White and westsiders were predominantly Black; plus, there was inefficient and uncoordinated intelligence-gathering and strategic thinking. In the summer of 1968, leaders of these disparate groups began meeting to explore the creation of a citywide anti-highway coalition. The main instigators of this group, dubbed the "Expressway Conference Committee," were Stuart Wechsler (RAM, CORE, and ECONIA), Jack Carr (the city planner hired by the Archdiocese and responsible to the Interfaith Urban Committee), Lu Fisher (Preservation Society), and Stew Bryant (working surreptitiously while staffing the Urban Design Concept Team by day—more on that fascinating side story shortly).[68]

The Conference Committee put out a July 1968 position paper and call to action that must have struck a chord—on August 3, thirty-five organizations met and created the Movement Against Destruction (MAD).[§] The *Sun* described the meeting as "an angry parley," keying in on the need for unity because "the Black and the poor are [both] victimized."[69] A later account said that Stu Wechsler was elected as the group's first president after he "made an impassioned speech, with stimulating slogans."[70]

The emergence of MAD was a coming-of-age moment for the anti-highway movement, a highwater mark from any number of points of view. The overwhelming majority of impacted communities were represented among the member organizations. More significantly, MAD was completely integrated, as Lu Fisher said, "the first alliance of Black people and Whites in the history of Baltimore."[71] Art Cohen (MAD's second president) said, "Baltimore was ready for an interracial citywide coalition. After the civil rights experiences that this town had been through in the '50s and '60s…the city was ready to put aside differences and get people from low-income White communities to sit in the same room [with the Black communities]."

In a 1974 interview, Lin Butler (who played an invaluable role as MAD's secretary) described the initial meetings of MAD: "There was a lot of energy, a lot of excitement." But the sessions were also "long, stormy" affairs, which he further describes as, "like going to a great ethnic carnival or fair—I was awestruck by the amazing coalition of Baltimore neighborhoods around the expressway issue."[72]

On August 5, 1968, MAD announced themselves with a simple dichotomy, saying, "The question is whether the City of Baltimore is to live in or to drive through. For twenty years most politicians and highway officials have behaved as if it were to drive through. Now it is time to hear from the people

§ According to Art Cohen, the group met for a period of time without a name. He said the name came from a young Black psychiatrist whose practice was in West Baltimore. The psychiatrist (whose name Art long ago forgot) only came to two meetings. As he left the second meeting he said, "I'm not going to come to any more meetings, but I'm going to leave you with a suggestion for the name of your group: 'Movement Against Destruction' (MAD)."

who believe the city is to live in." Typical of MAD, this statement was only a lead-in to a longer and well-documented fifteen-page position paper.

MAD was a bit of an oddball in the highway protest movement. MAD eschewed the kind of protest rallies that are designed to make the 6:00 news (gatherings with cleverly worded signs, anti-highway chants, and inflammatory speeches). While they certainly helped rally anti-highway forces for public hearings, much of their work was more in the category of "a war of words": they believed that they were in a battle to win over public opinion.

Even on points where they ostensibly lost, MAD's critiques caused highway planners to backtrack, revisiting and defending their assumptions, data, and citizen input processes. As every sports fan knows, it is hard to move the ball forward when you are constantly on the defense. MAD benefited enormously from the involvement of Barbara King. With PhDs in math and science, King demystified technical reports and exposed poor assumptions. When King returned to her native Tennessee, Allan H. Marcus, a Johns Hopkins University mathematics professor, became MAD's technical analyst. His critical analysis of the 1972 Leakin Park Draft Environmental Impact Statement was one of the factors that led to a three-year delay of that segment.

Below, we profile three of MAD's presidents, each representing a different aspect of MAD's modus operandi: Stu Wechsler, whose deep involvement in the civil rights movement helped forge the inter-racial coalition, bringing eastsiders and westsiders together in common cause; Art Cohen, who kept up the spirits of the protest movement through music and a multi-faceted campaign of wry ridicule; and Carolyn Tyson, whose analytical approach enabled anti-highway activists to challenge the government's crew of paid experts.

STU WECHSLER, PROFESSIONAL POT-STIRRER

Stuart Wechsler responded enthusiastically to my interview request, but he also warned me, "Once I get going, you might not be able to shut me up." I had a hard time editing my interviews with Stu; the guy has some war stories. Stu is now soft-spoken and grandfatherly, someone who could effortlessly fill in as a department store Santa Claus. He readily hands out accolades to those he worked with while deftly sidestepping my characterization of him as a key leader of the highway fight. He says he was more like "Forrest Gump, a much better second banana than a lead."

Wechsler's resume puts him in the upper echelon of unsung anti-highway heroes. He served as the local director of the Congress for Racial Equality (CORE) and brought them into the Road Wars. He also helped lead the Relocation Action Movement (RAM) and guided a momentous reform in the compensation system for residential acquisitions. He was instrumental in the creation of MAD, then served as MAD's first and third president in 1968 and 1969. He was a logical choice for leadership both because MAD was in no small part his vision, and because he was a White guy with unequaled credibility in the African American community.

Examining Wechsler's experiences as a civil rights activist, one author ticked off the list, as follows, "By the summer of 1967, [his] resume...included sit-ins, rent strikes, picket lines, several arrests and jail stays, a caning and kidnapping at the hands of Florida bigots, and up-close views of several shotgun barrels, all in the service of the Congress of Racial Equality (CORE)."[73] He was arrested thirty times.

Stuart's evolution at CORE started with helping organize a new CORE chapter in his native New York City. He was then assigned to the "upper-south freedom rides," leading to his first arrest in Elkton, Maryland, where he was protesting public accommodations along Route 40. In 1964, three CORE freedom riders were killed in Mississippi: Michael Schwerner, Andrew Goodman, and James Chaney. Wechsler knew two of them personally and asked to be re-assigned to the South, leading to a stint in Gadsden County, Florida. At this North Florida location there were a number of memorable and frightening incidents: their car was rammed by a pickup truck, their office was sprayed with shotgun pellets, and they received mail addressed to "N----- Lovers, Quincy, Florida." Stu commented, "It was postmarked only the day before arrival. Now that's efficiency!"

But the most harrowing story was his caning experience. Wechsler and two other CORE staff were carrying out voter registration activities on a farm where the owner, Tom Smith, was particularly antagonistic to their mission.

Stu recounts what happened as follows:

We were on the plantation… talking to an [African American] man on the porch… While we were talking to him, a car and a pickup truck pull into the yard, and the man I am talking to says, "Oh, my lord. It's Mr. Tommy [Tom Smith]." Smith motions towards me, and he says, "Get off the farm." And I said, "I came from Northern Florida voter education project, and we have permission to be here."

[Needless to say] that did not work… Tom Smith jumped out of the car with a cane. I thought oh my gosh, he's crippled. [But then] the other five jumped out… They all had canes. I am thinking no way [there are] six crippled crackers coming after me.

I ran into the swamp but… they caught me, and they whacked me around; and then they started a debate as to whether or not they will kill me [or] have me arrested. At that point, the two [CORE] guys I was with, got back in our car and took off. One of the [cracker] guys says, "Oh, he was with somebody else. Should we go get them? And Smith said, "No. You will never catch them." This was fortunate because the guys did not know how to drive with a stick; so, they drove all the way back to Quincy in first gear.

Stu, to this day, does not know if the death threat was real or just an attempt to scare him. If it was real, he was only saved by the fact that the other two CORE workers were potential witnesses, now making their way back to civilization *in first gear*.

"Smith called the police," Stu said. "The sheriff came, and the two deputies patiently wait while Smith and his crew work me over with canes a little bit more, and then I was arrested. I was charged with trespassing."

The legal issue boiled down to: Are voter registration activities protected or are they subject to trespassing laws? Wechsler's case was appealed and might have gone all the way to the Supreme Court, except that the Court of Appeals ruled on a similar case, finding that voter registration activity was not subject to trespassing laws, and the Supreme Court let that decision stand.

In 1966, CORE asked Wechsler to lead a campaign in Baltimore as a trial run for projects in other northern cities. Rosemont anti-highway advocates encouraged his involvement in the highway issue, leading to Wechsler's key roles with CORE, RAM, and MAD. Wechsler now sees many parallels between the anti-highway and civil rights movements, saying that when "People really felt that they were involved, something [important was] at stake, and that they could play a role, that is when they get really committed to it, and it becomes a mass movement."

Although modest and deferential, Stu accepts some credit for "bringing together the disparate elements of the battle against the expressway. I think, if there was anything that I did, it was to serve as a connection between those different groups because I had that perspective.... I think people pretty much took [that] and ran with it."

Wechsler later became an expert on housing and real estate finance, with stints at the Columbia Association, the US Co-op Bank, Freddie Mac, and the Maryland Department of Housing and Community Development. Was he able to continue his role as a change agent within the constraints of workplace hierarchies? Stu, always ready to illustrate a point with a wry twist, tells me that he once taught a course on "Mortgage Banking and Community Organization." So, the short answer to that question is "yes."

REGISTERING MISS PEARL

Wechsler had one other especially memorable experience in Florida. "One of the highlights of my life [was that] we registered a woman who had been enslaved. This is in 1964. She believed she was somewhere between 106 and 113 years old. She remembered the Emancipation Proclamation. She remembered Abraham Lincoln."

Stu later went back to take "Miss Pearl" to the polls on election day. Although Stu was arrested again (this time for having a campaign sticker on a car less than 600 feet from the poll), Miss Pearl did cast her first vote in her 106-plus year life.

As Stu was being cuffed, he told Miss Pearl, "I do not want you to get upset, but I am being arrested." She said, "I ain't upset. They aren't arresting me. They are arresting you." Then he realized: She was over 100 years old and born a slave. What the hell would scare her?

ART COHEN AND MAD HIJINKS

Somewhere in the bowels of the National Archives, there is a recording of Art Cohen singing his self-penned highway protest song, "The Baltimore Road Building Blues," at a 1974 hearing. Baltimore did not have a perpetually pissed off Sammy Abbott–like character, but we did have the merry trouble-maker, Arthur Cohen. Where Sammie used a sledgehammer, Art's weapon of choice was the lampoon. "There is nothing quite like deserved ridicule to generate public support and enthusiasm," Art told me.

Always affable, always ready to spin a yarn, Art still gets a gleam in his eye when he recounts his activities with MAD, even fifty years hence. Like many of the activists in this book, Art had experience with race and equity issues. He came to Baltimore in 1967 as a Legal Aid attorney, got caught up in defending those arrested during the 1968 Baltimore riots, and then had to change jobs to maintain balance. Art initially filled in as legal counsel for MAD, then became its second president in December 1968. He is most remembered for bringing music and some much-needed levity to the high-way battleground, for example the 1972 City Fair stunt, an attention-getter that brought the wrong kind of attention but led to a creative solution.

"I got a bunch of sheets and stitched them together on the cobblestone street," Art said. "It was the width of the expressway as if it had gone across the harbor. It was like two hundred feet long, and it said 'Stop Mayor Schaefer's road.'" Art gathered with some protesters, and they walked into the City Fair and unfurled the sign. "It took them twenty minutes to see what we had done, and then they threw us out. ...The next year what we did was we rented an airplane. We each kicked in twenty-five dollars, and we had it fly over the City Fair. And there was nothing they could do about that."[74]

Art fondly recalls other clever MAD promotions: They made and sold buttons that said *Who's Afraid of Jerome Wolff?* targeting the State Roads com-missioner. It was reported that Wolff ran into a MAD button peddler and bought twenty-five of them.

In another campaign, MAD created a mock alternate highway plan, which was distributed as a satirical flier at the City Fair. It proposed a new

A-1 highway route that required the acquisition of only six houses—those of the principal highway promoters—"all of whom have expressed delighted willingness to make the essential sacrifice," the flier stated. Art remembers that this one was conjured up by Jack Bond, MAD's third president. Bill Boucher (president of the Greater Baltimore Committee and one of the targeted highway proponents) feigned alarm when he was shown that the new plan included his dwelling at Bellefield Farm in Cockeysville. Boucher indicated that he was "terribly upset" that no public hearings had been held on the group's new route; he further denounced MAD's secrecy in developing the plan, saying "I was excluded from those talks." Still, he added respectfully, "The A-1 deserves to be looked into."

But it is Art's song, "The Baltimore Road Building Blues," that is his mostly fondly recalled contribution to highway (in)sanity. Accompanying himself on the squeezebox, Art performed the song at multiple meetings and hearings, including the Board of Estimates and in front of an audience of engineers.[¶] It was also on jukeboxes all over southeast Baltimore. The melody was based on "Tobacco Road." The lyrics, as you can tell from this excerpt, were anything but subtle:

Pave over the city, pave it with concrete
If the road gang has its way, we'll just be one big street.

One billion dollars, that's what it's gonna cost
If they build this highway, this city will be lost.

Bill Boucher makes another appearance in Art's favorite anecdotes. Art was peddling his record at the Inner Harbor when he ran into Bill. Bill's wife said, "Come on, Bill, we can buy one of these." So he did—for one dollar.[**] If

---

¶ Mayor Schaefer suffered through Art's rendition at the Board of Estimates. Art said, "His only comment was, 'Can't you be *for* anything? Why are you always *against* something?' He was irritated." No surprise there!

** Did MAD miss this PR opportunity? Banner headlines: "Bill Boucher secretly donates cash to MAD."

Art and Bill had both signed and dated that 45, it would be quite the Road Wars collector's item.

In the fall of 1969, Art was offered and accepted the job of executive director of CPHA, telling the board that he would resign as president of MAD but remain active in the expressway battle as a concerned citizen. The board agreed. Steve Zecher, a former Urban Design Concept Team staffer who worked for Art at CPHA, was impressed that Cohen produced "a really fine team working together and supporting each other.... I found him to be really a supportive leader at a professional level but also [working really well with] many people and groups that were involved in CPHA."

However, CPHA's board soon saw things differently—Art read the handwriting on the wall and resigned after a one-year stint. Art later heard that (then city council president) Schaefer engineered the show of non-support, apparently unimpressed by Art's resignation from MAD and finding him guilty by association.

Now retired from a long career in public health, Art has gone back to his MAD roots as a public transit activist, assisting in the Red Line light rail planning and the Baltimore Transit Equity Coalition. He even authored his own transit proposal: a five-mile trolley line on North Avenue, end-to-end.

If Art is remembered for adding a bit of levity and song to the highway fight, Carolyn Tyson's later leadership of MAD is marked by the group's increasing ability to counter punch on an analytical and technical level.

CAROLYN TYSON, TEACHER, ADVOCATE, ANALYST

I think they sense the direction that the wind is blowing, change is coming, opposition is rising. It's not just a bunch of little old ladies in tennis shoes anymore.

Carolyn Tyson, 1974 interview[75]

In 1974 the city was in the throes of a fiscal crisis—teachers were on strike and the city was crying poor. One city teacher had a unique vantage point: Carolyn Tyson, who was also president of MAD. Tyson produced an analysis of the city budget that unmasked how the city had been hiding the fiscal impacts of the expressway system. While claiming the expressways were 100 percent funded by Motor Vehicle Revenues (MVR), the city had been making massive shifts of other activities that were formerly funded by MVR dollars (e.g. local street improvements), and moving those activities to local funding sources. Tyson said, "I am convinced that the city is spending so much for highways that it cannot pay teachers and other expenses."[76] Her analysis claimed that highways actually cost at least $0.23 on the city's property tax rate.[77]

The point hit home—Baltimoreans who might have been otherwise neutral on the expressways paid attention to two issues they all cared about: taxes and schools. This was typical of Tyson's stint as president of MAD from 1972 to 1974, challenging the data and assumptions that constituted the basis for the highway plan. Tyson performed these fiscal analyses every year from 1973 to 1976; her last critique in 1976 argued that the expressways were costing $1.34 on the property tax rate.

While Tyson steered MAD toward a more "policy-wonk" approach, she also had passion and fervor. David Hollander, active in VOLPE and the fight against I-70, said Carolyn "infused the organization with backbone and energy."[78] Art Cohen characterized her as a "strong, powerful woman. Very determined." Mary Logan, a MAD activist, said, "She was terrific. She was a dynamo...strident about the issues she cared a lot about." Mary found it amusing listening to Carolyn espouse "her progressive views" with a distinctive southern drawl.

Carolyn was born and raised in Little Rock, Arkansas. She was the class valedictorian, then earned her teaching degree from Texas State College for Women in Denton. In Little Rock she organized the area's first integrated preschool program, bucking prevailing attitudes. When her husband, George, took a job in Baltimore, Carolyn moved to teaching in Baltimore City Schools. George remembers, "She was a bit of a ham.... She loved to go up in front of a classroom and expound, but she had those big old boys reading poetry."

She and George bought a house near Leakin Park, only to discover that their new neighbor was going to be an eight-lane expressway. They started attending Leakin Park neighborhood meetings in 1970, then joined up with MAD in 1971; Carolyn was elected president later that same year.

In a 1974 interview, Tyson explained how she steered MAD toward a more analytical role, organizing a cadre of experts to speak at design hearings. "We had a man who could read the air pollution statement; we had another person who could speak on the impact on the community and how they had been promised a lot in the joint development process. We had design experts. So that, in the record…they would see that we were making these specific [constructive] criticisms." It is especially notable that some of MAD's critiques and position points were reiterated by federal agencies leading to delayed approvals and stalled segments.

MAD's actions and successes are chronicled in the neighborhood battle-grounds described in the following chapters. But you could sum that up as follows. Rather than any specific action, MAD's legacy was the constant drumbeat steadily undermining the rationale for the expressway plan on every conceivable point—community impact, replacement housing, air quality, fiscal impact, and economic benefit—while also critiquing procedures, the sufficiency of hearings, and community input. From 1968 to 1975 the tone of public debate changed dramatically. You could say that, in the war to win the hearts and minds of Baltimoreans, MAD won.

Our attention now shifts to those neighborhood battles. This is where the resistance took hold. However, Federal Hill is an oddity: Here it was less community activists and more a determined group of architects and planners employed by the State Roads Commission who pulled off a stunning coup d'état.

VI. FED' HILL AND THE INNER HARBOR

CONQUISTADORS OF CONCRETE V.
PLATITUDINOUS PLANNERS

Dave Nutter was a man caught in the middle of the fight for the soul of Baltimore. Nutter was a fresh-out-of-grad-school city planner assigned to be a liaison to Baltimore's federally funded road planning experiment, the Urban Design Concept Team (UDCT)—a multidisciplinary team of planners, architects, engineers, economists, and sociologists meant to replace the narrow rule of engineers, and, it was hoped, alter highway plans to serve rather than destroy inner city neighborhoods. In 1966 Baltimore was chosen as the first of a handful of cities to implement this brave new concept.

Nutter framed the Road Wars as a microcosm of our "national cataclysms" over war, race, and young people expressing "an inherent deep desire to make the world a better place," calling 1967 to 1970 an adventurous and extraordinary time. As part of the UDCT experiment, Dave felt like he was on the cutting edge of "creative transportation planning" to fit highways "into the fabric of the city." He recalled, "The soup was being stirred and heated, and it could reasonably be said to be creative chaos."

But our interview took a dark turn. To Dave, the term "Road Wars" is not just hyperbole. This was a war with real casualties. UDCT was "trapped in the middle of this war and they paid a price. When they left Baltimore... [there was] no farewell party. Those men were under tremendous stress..." Dave cited three deaths of road war combatants (John Weese, Joe Axelrod, and Norm Klein), each passing away within a few years after they were embroiled in the knock-down-drag-out UDCT battles. Dave explained: "Well, it was tough stuff. It did not do hearts any good."[79]

The *Sun*'s James Dilts, in a January 1971 look-back assessing the impact of UDCT, stated that several staffers quit partly because of moral qualms over the highway plan and partly because of overwhelming stress. Dilts added, "Others still tried to work for both the communities and the highway engineers and developed cases of professional schizophrenia because of it."[80] We do not ordinarily think of city planning as a profession linked to psychoses or life-threatening levels of stress. But then again, most planning assignments are not at the juncture of our cultural tectonic plates.

Most Baltimoreans think of the Road Wars as a battle that was staged between community activists and the powerful alliance of politicians and engineering interests. However, this part of the Road Wars is less about communities standing up to the power structure, and more about UDCT's band of insurgent architects and planners implausibly overturning the decisions made by the city-state team who paid the tab for their consulting services.

Summing it up after four acrimonious years, UDCT team leader Nathaniel Owings (founding partner, Skidmore, Owings & Merrill [SOM]) spoke at a Greater Baltimore Committee luncheon. He summoned his considerable skills as an orator (and, some would say, his considerable tendency toward pomposity): "To a city and state famous for ingenuity in clipper ships, the B&O canal, and Tom Thumbs, I entrust the concept team's unfinished symphony...we leave you with the paper-thin plans of a vestigial presence." Dilts' account of the meeting referenced the team's number one failure, saying, "The Fell's Point people are singularly unenthusiastic about the new amenities in store for them with the highway." But he also extolled Nat Owings' momentous triumph "to move the main route...to the south where it will traverse mainly industrial land and cross the harbor near Fort McHenry rather than at Federal Hill."[81]

There was no battle more important for the future of the city than this. The 10-D plan, please recall, would have hugged the waterfront through Federal Hill, Harbor East, Fell's Point, and Canton. The later revival of all those waterfront communities would have been jeopardized or prevented by the 10-D alignment. The proposed bridge at Federal Hill was a gargantuan fourteen lanes wide and hovered only forty feet over the water, preventing larger sailing vessels from entering the Inner Harbor. Former Housing Commissioner Jay Brodie said the result would have been "the Inner Harbor puddle."

Dave Nutter characterized it this way: "The Fort McHenry solution was the bravest decision I have ever been [a part of]."

FEDERAL HILL, A SELECTIVE HISTORY

Leakin Park and Federal Hill,* two of the parks that were impacted by the 1962 10-D plan, are oddly linked by an event that may have changed the history of the nation. As the Civil War was breaking out, Baltimore was under scrutiny. Many thought Maryland might join the Confederacy, an eventuality that would have been disastrous for the North—Washington, DC, would then be an island surrounded by Confederate-controlled states, surely an untenable position. General Benjamin Butler stepped into the fray, apparently acting without orders, and took steps to ensure that Maryland would stay loyal to the Union whether they wanted to or not.

He sent a train to Frederick to arrest leaders of the pro-Confederate contingent, but that was a diversionary tactic to disguise his real intention, which was to put Maryland under martial law, enforcing its allegiance to the Union. After leaving the city, Butler uncoupled the westbound train and returned to Baltimore under cover of darkness. The next morning, May 13, 1861, Baltimoreans awoke to find that Butler had occupied Federal Hill and was enforcing Baltimore's and Maryland's loyalty to the Union by pointing dozens of cannons at downtown Baltimore. Absent these unauthorized and daring actions, Maryland's allegiance—and the ultimate outcome of the Civil War—would have been very much in doubt.

The link between Leakin Park and Federal Hill? It was none other than Ross Winans who was arrested by General Butler's troops in Frederick that day. Winans was regarded as the leader of southern sympathizers in Maryland; his estate was later purchased by the city and became Leakin Park. Orianda House, the Winans villa, is still standing, one of many historic landmarks threatened by road plans.

While General Butler's conquest of Federal Hill did not involve much

---

* I once had a quite memorable experience while visiting Federal Hill. My daughter, Mackenzie (four at the time), and I were admiring the statue of Sam Smith. I thought, *Why not give Mackenzie a little history lesson while enjoying the view?* So I started reading the inscription to her, but Mackenzie was on a whole different plane. She interrupted the history lesson and said, "Daddy, how do people become statues?"

of a fight, the second battle for Federal Hill was quite a struggle. It pitted not soldiers against soldiers or even communities against politicians; rather it was an all-out battle between professions.

PAVEMENT PLUTOCRATS AND
CONQUISTADORS OF CONCRETE

Widening roads to solve traffic congestion is like loosening your belt to cure obesity.

Walter Kulash, a traffic engineer from Orlando, Florida

Stu Wechsler (RAM, CORE, and MAD) expressed disappointment that the catchphrases he invented to characterize Baltimore's engineers never caught on. We now give Stu his due so that his "conquistadors of concrete" and "pavement plutocrats" can stand along with Barbara Mikulski's more famous epithets. In the spirit of what Art Cohen termed "deserved ridicule," we offer up several examples of the engineering mentality run amok.

In 1948 the Army Corps of Engineers announced a campaign to drain the Everglades in a highly entertaining documentary entitled *Waters of Destiny*. The narrator, summoning his best movie trailer voice, describes the water of the Everglades as "hideous, unrelenting, shrieking its rage. The vicious scourge of mankind."[82] Of course, taming the Everglades proved to be both impossible and unwise, as were many engineering measures undertaken in the '40s and '50s. The parallels with urban highways are both obvious and irresistible.

More deserved ridicule: John B. Funk, Chairman and Director of the State Roads Commission, addressed an organization of highway builders in December 1964, saying, "These ribbons of concrete are not merely the expression of basic necessity, to be tolerated with shame. They are masterpieces. They are the Mona Lisa, and we are their da Vinci." The *Evening Sun*'s local section skewered "John (Leonardo) B. Funk" with a pictorial essay: a picture of Jones Falls Expressway signs was titled "Behold: A Sign." Funk's "latter abstract period" was represented by an aerial view of a highway cloverleaf titled "Lines and Circles, Signifying Nothing."

70

In the early days of interstate planning, engineers had carte blanche; they created many engineering marvels, for example, the astonishingly beautiful I-70 route through Glenwood Canyon in Colorado. Highways historically were funded by narrowly focused transportation agencies and designed by even more narrowly focused engineers. Most had been built through rural areas where the main obstacles were topography, soil conditions, rivers, and the occasional influential property owner—all problems that engineering firms were expert at solving. Objectives were similarly well-defined: move traffic from point A to point B at maximum speed, satisfy travel demands, solve bottlenecks, minimize cost per mile, and project and meet future demands. It was all very cut-and-dried, but not especially suitable to urban areas.

WHY NOT NUKE THOSE MOUNTAINS?

In *The Big Roads*, Earl Swift cites another entertaining example of the unconstrained engineering mentality. In 1963 engineers proposed to get I-40 through California's Bristol Mountains by "detonating twenty-four nuclear bombs…at least sixty times beefier than that deployed at Hiroshima and Nagasaki, combined." Swift's account of Project Carryall continues, "The engineers promised that…radioactivity, fallout, and air blast…would [pose] no hazard…or cause significant structural damage or endanger local inhabitants."

By the late 1960s, the scales had fallen from our collective eyes, and highway engineers were under attack. Of the 41,000 miles of interstate, it was those last 200 miles that went through cities that revealed the emperor had no clothes. Impacted communities shined a light on a decision-making process that left them out in the cold. The attitude was typified by a Baltimore Relocation Action Movement flier that railed against highway engineers who viewed people "as just another obstacle, like a hill to be leveled or a valley to be bridged."

Baltimore's 10-D plan was a case study of urban engineering myopia, representing the triumph of traffic movement objectives over all other considerations. DPW's Bernard Werner, J. E. Greiner Co., and the State Roads

Commission (SRC) were all in the 10-D camp, all wanting to ram it through with a bare minimum of community-determined alterations. These were the pavement plutocrats who first opposed and then tried to tie the hands of the Urban Design Concept Team.

PLATITUDINOUS PLANNERS†

Since the engineer regards his own work as more important than the other human functions it serves, he does not hesitate to lay waste to woods, streams, parks, and human neighborhoods in order to carry his roads straight to their supposed destination. As a consequence, the "cloverleaf" has become our national flower and "wall-to-wall" concrete the ridiculous symbol of national affluence and technological status.

Lewis Mumford

Lewis Mumford was perhaps the most influential figure in urban planning from the late 1950s through the early '70s. He relentlessly railed against engineers, highways, and the sprawl they generated, describing expressways as "funnels that help to blow the urban dust farther from the center, once the topsoil of a common life has been removed."[83]

You might think the broader discipline of city planning better suited to situate urban highways with greater sensitivity to community factors. But planners had their own set of blinders and tended to guide highways to areas where they saw large numbers of substandard and overcrowded housing units. Joseph Dimento and Cliff Ellis observed: "These data, along with a superficial scan of building facades, could reveal a 'slum' where there was actually a reasonably stable low-income community. Thus, the scientific 'objectivity' of planning studies was compromised by biases built in the methods of analysis."[84]

Landscape architects had similar blinders: Wanting to design a work of beauty, the architect might propose a tree-lined parkway with a wide

---

† "Platitudinous Planners" is my own little contribution to the competition for the Road Wars best epithets.

landscaped median. This might enhance the driving experience, but it also doubles the amount of right-of-way required and knocks out even more homes and businesses.

Further, the involvement of all these disciplines was paid for and accountable to the engineering-influenced political and bureaucratic leadership, which did not question the necessity of expressways; the real agenda was to make just enough changes to mollify the community and get the damned road under construction. That was the usual case. However, Baltimore's engineering-political alliance was completely unprepared for the challenge posed by their own consultants: enter Nathaniel Owings, the Urban Design Concept Team, and a tale of revolution from within.

NATHANIEL OWINGS AND THE INSURGENT PLANNERS

We've been prompted by the best in the business. These young [planners] come around at night to describe the bad points of the expressway and then we go to their bosses the next day.

Tom Fiorello, a Fell's Point community organizer

In 1966 there was a lucky confluence of local and national interests, both motivated to try new models for urban highway planning after meeting with stiff opposition from anti-expressway activists. The US Department of Transportation had belatedly realized that giving engineers carte blanche over urban highway planning was a formula for just the kind of resistance they were getting.‡ The old blueprint had been largely successful, but building highways through heavily urbanized areas, officials belatedly realized,

---

‡ A 1968 report entitled "The Freeway and the City," prepared by "The Urban Advisors to the Federal Highway Administrator," sensibly recommended a broad application of the multidisciplinary approach that was tried in Baltimore. However, the number one recommendation was to "expand the application of the techniques of systems analysis and operations research as the most rational approach to the problems of planning, locating, and designing urban freeways." In other words, the Urban Advisors wanted to put their faith in continuation of a technocratic method of highway planning, somehow improved by plugging in more variables, running it through a more complex decision matrix, and hoping a magic bullet solution popped out at the other end.

KERMIT PARSONS

Kermit Parsons was a Cornell University professor who wrote a 378-page manuscript titled *The Baltimore Wars*, originally intended as part of a biography of Nathaniel Owings. *The Baltimore Wars* took on a life of its own, centering on the Urban Design Concept Team and the momentous change from the 10-D/Federal Hill crossing to the 3-A/Fort McHenry harbor crossing. Parsons passed away before he could complete and publish the document.

This chapter relies heavily on Parsons' draft. His son, Steve, granted permission for its use. To my knowledge, this book is the first published use of Parsons' material. Parsons' archived work resides at the Cornell University library.

required an entirely different approach. However, the old order would not gently step aside. David Nutter reiterated that "there are people wanting the expressways to be built...to an engineering process that is totally linear, has huge amounts of money and government power behind them, and an entire construction industry ready to move and construct the things once they are ready to be built. I mean, you can never forget that."

That Baltimore's UDCT succeeded in changing the single most important piece, the central Baltimore harbor crossing, is testament to their tenacity and willingness to work outside the constraints of normal client-consultant communication and decision-making. Had Nat Owings and his UDCT staff followed the dictates of their client oversight group, Baltimore would now be saddled with a ruinous expressway through the heart of the Inner Harbor.

As author Kermit Parsons recounts, the story behind this momentous change began in 1966 with Fell's Point defender Lu Fisher, who was on a quest for allies in her fledgling effort to stop the highway from ruining Fell's Point. In the fall of 1966, Fisher set up a meeting with George Kostritsky, an architect at RTKL, who brought RTKL partner Archibald Rogers into the discussion. Fisher must have been persuasive, as Rogers became concerned that Baltimore was heading down the wrong path and it would soon be irreversible. This is the first of many, many twists and turns where the ruination of Federal Hill and the Inner Harbor hung in the balance. Keeping tabs on the unlikely course of events in the Federal Hill saga, we'll call Archibald Rogers' involvement "game changer 1."[85]

Rogers was a highly respected former president of the Greater Baltimore Committee—his opinion mattered. He first conceptualized the multi-disciplinary UDCT, then floated the idea with John Funk, Chairman of the State Roads Commission. DPW's Bernard Werner and Interstate Division Director Hugh Downs were both opposed, but Rogers found allies in Planning Commission Chairman David Barton, Richard Ackroyd of the federal Bureau of Public Roads, and William Donald Schaefer, Baltimore's influential highway-friendly councilman. Those four individuals convinced a skeptical Funk—game changer 2—and Baltimore was headed in a new direction fraught with uncertainty.

It was fortunate that the condemnation ordinance for the 10-D plan was still stuck in city council at the time; it's exceedingly doubtful that Funk would have brought in new players if the condemnation ordinance had already been adopted. As it stood, Funk was likely hoping that a few incremental improvements (a depressed highway here, a pocket park there) would blunt the opposition enough to pass the ordinance and start pouring concrete.

The federal Bureau of Public Roads was also beginning to realize the unfamiliar and formidable obstacles they faced at that time. When Funk and Rogers proposed federal funding for Baltimore's UDCT, Lowell Bridwell, Director of the Federal Highway Administration (FHWA), was receptive. He funded a trial run for several cities, including Baltimore—game changer 3.

On September 23, 1967, Transportation Secretary Alan S. Boyd announced a $4.8 million grant to Baltimore with considerable fanfare, saying, "For the first time in any major city, all of the environmental skills available will be brought to bear on the design of a highway from the very beginning. With early planning consideration of the highway's social, economic, historic, and functional impact, this will become not just a road through a city, but an integral part of the city."[86] Baltimore was launching a brave new world in the field of urban highway planning, one that would be carefully watched both for its potential to establish a new model and for the considerable risk of a complete train wreck. Only one thing was certain: It would be different.

Funk asked Rogers to chair the selection committee. In September 1967 Rogers called Nathaniel Owings (Skidmore, Owings, and Merrill [SOM]), a colleague with a national reputation for leadership on design issues (game changer 4). However, Rogers was also thinking politically. UDCT staffer Peter Hopkinson noted that Rogers was quietly but staunchly opposed to the 10-D plan, and "justifiably concerned about the State Road Commission's (SRC's) immense political power to do whatever they wanted with the Greiner Company and Agnew, etc., etc., in charge." Fearing no Baltimorean could stand up to this power structure, Rogers staked his hopes on Owings, a "foreigner" who would be more "credible as a harsh critic of the 10-D."[87]

Of particular interest to Rogers, Owings also had experience, both as a professional and as a private citizen, in defeating or altering at least four highway projects in New Mexico, California, and Washington, DC. His successful effort to protect Big Sur from highway encroachment had been celebrated in California. Parsons adds that Rogers "had noticed [Owings'] excellent design judgment and his ability to achieve the 'impossible' in highly charged political environments. Owings' political clout was impressive."[88]

The decision to hire Owings could almost be termed a "Trojan Horse-type" event. It appears that Funk and Downs hired Owings based on Rogers' recommendation, almost no-questions-asked. There was no competitive bidding because Downs was overly concerned about the delay. Further, I have to suspect that Funk failed to do his own due diligence; would he have hired Owings if he knew Owings' history opposing "the highwaymen," the derisive term that Owings coined in California? Funk and Downs, almost assuredly, later rued the day they hired Owings—they and their successors spent much of the next four years doing battle with a consulting team that, although on their payroll, seemed to be working against their wishes and directives. The manner in which Owings was hired is another turning point (game changer 5).

For his part, Owings was intrigued by the challenge, which Parsons described as:

A major characteristic of Baltimore's history of freeway building has been "intelligent nonperformance"—the ability to not build freeways that were destructive of the social and historic fabric of the city. Owings' sense of this historic ability of Baltimoreans to resist the "inevitable" interested him. It was a quality he thought that should be put to work in the interest of saving those qualities he too believed in.

When Nat Owings arrived in Baltimore in January 1967 the stakes could not have been higher. In an article published in *Traffic News*, Owings announced the new endeavor in the most grandiose terms. "Good news! An enormous stride has been taken toward creating heaven on earth." He described the task: "to lace tubes of traffic through vital parts without unduly disturbing the living organism of the city" and to "produce a unity of knowledge and wisdom much greater than the mere sum of these separate parts."[89] *Sun* columnist James Dilts later commented, "'Blending' a six- or eight-lane highway into the fabric of Baltimore is about as promising an assignment as 'blending' a buzz saw into a Persian rug."[90]

Owings' UDCT team included city planners, economists, acoustical and lighting experts, an "urban psychologist," and an engineering firm (J. E. Greiner, the authors of 10-D, were purposely omitted). With the $4.8 million grant, which would later grow to $7 million, they had the resources for a comprehensive reevaluation of the expressway plan.

Their first task was to examine the alignment of Southwest Freeway (later I-95) and the impact on the neighborhoods near Carroll Park, i.e. the areas where the council reps were standing in the way of the condemnation bill. Frustrated by the ongoing stalemate, Councilman Schaefer had questioned the need for the Southwest Freeway, since traffic could be re-routed to the Harbor Tunnel and I-70 through the planned Leakin Park/West Baltimore segment.[91] UDCT took on the task in October 1966, eight months before their overall contract was inked.

In January UDCT concluded that the southwest freeway was in fact needed, even with the I-70 segment through Leakin Park. They recommended an alternative route through a more commercial/industrial corridor southwest of Carroll Park, eliminating almost all residential impacts. That route had been previously mapped out by Greiner but had run into a federal thumbs-down because of issues with merge lanes and on- and off-ramps. UDCT fine-tuned the plan and found a solution, which became known as "10-D modified." (See Appendix 1-C). Everyone—the community, council reps, mayor, feds, even Werner and the previously engaged highway engineers—was happy.[92] Finally, the city had consensus for the 10-D condemnation corridor, and UDCT's planners were toasted as conquering heroes. That was the last time UDCT met with anything close to universal acclaim. Their revised plan helped the condemnation ordinance sail through city council, but ironically it shackled their ability to evaluate options that involved going outside of those lines.

On April 20, 1967, Nathaniel Owings spoke at the Committee for Downtown and launched the opening salvo in the four-year struggle. UDCT, he boldly stated, would not be relegated to a "window-dressing" role, he claimed, while characterizing the city's current plan as a "giant highway system patently out of scale with man and the fragile fabric of his city and his bay."[93]

He continued, "Now unless the Madison Avenue boys have completely brainwashed us, then we know that running a conventional freeway through a city, using conventional methods of interposing it, is comparable to running a pair of shears through the warp and woof of a priceless tapestry" (note the parallel analogies with Dilts' Persian rug). He compared the developers of Charles Center to Saint George defending Baltimore's central business district against the "freeway dragon"; Owings portrayed UDCT as "the sturdy shafted lance."[94]

It did not take long for the defenders of the freeway dragon to respond. Jerome Wolff said Owings "will accept our dicta, or we don't think he can properly be part of the Expressway program." Werner said, "The Concept Team cannot tell us how we're going to operate," and claimed Owings was trying to "relegate the engineers to...draftsmen." Wolff and Werner held the trump card—at this point they were under no obligation to hire Owings.[95]

Owings may have made a strategic error in baring his fangs before the contract was signed. Werner and Wolff dug in their heels, and Owings had to accept their two non-negotiable provisions: J. E. Greiner engineering was installed as a co-lead on the team, and the consultants' activities were confined to the current condemnation lines. The latter provision became known as "the givens"; UDCT now had to operate within an exceptionally narrow geography—consideration of any and all alternatives to 10-D would violate "the givens."

The agreement was announced on May 27, 1967. Impacted neighborhoods were completely deflated when they read about these provisions. It looked like UDCT would be exactly what Owings had refused to be: window dressing.

10-D condemnation bill

The final condemnation ordinance and UDCT contract negotiations were winding their way through city council almost simultaneously. The 10-D alignment was about to be set in stone, with Owings operating within "the givens." Incredibly, there were only two voices advocating to hold the condemnation bill and give UDCT free reign to consider alternative alignments. Councilman Tom Ward was one; the other was David Barton, Chairman of the Planning Commission. Barton warned, "Once the condemnation ordinance is passed, all leverage the city may have [over the alignment] is gone."

As Figure 14 shows, 10-D spells death to Montgomery Street, Federal Hill, and (the later named) Harbor East, thus justifying my derisive nickname the highway plan, the "future investment prevention" alignment.

The recently organized Preservation Society had no clout; their first position on the Federal Hill route in February of 1967 was not opposition, rather it was to adopt the Lee-Hill Street Route proposed by the Planning Department in 1962.[96] This route was likely a product of the ongoing feud between Planning Director Darling and DPW Director Werner; Darling offered up this option as a compromise between his Pratt Street route and Werner's 10-D Federal Hill alignment. When the Preservation Society resurrected the plan in 1967, Larry Reich had replaced Darling as planning director. Mr. Reich, a visionary when it comes to urban waterfronts, was

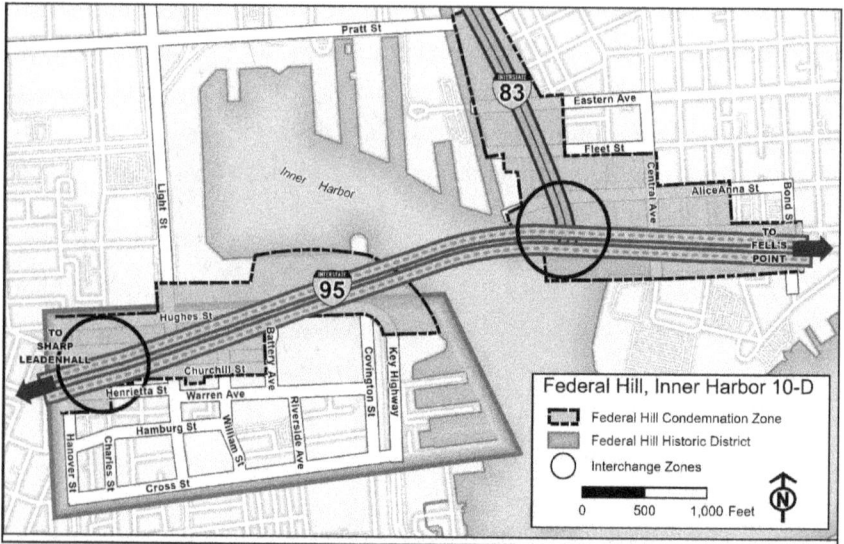

Figure 14. 10-D's wide swath through Federal Hill, the Historic District, and Harbor East. 10-D Modified used the same corridor. (Scott Jeffrey, MS, GISP). (For the full alignment map, see Appendix 1-B—10-D plan.)

likely flabbergasted that his predecessor had proposed a plan that could be a caricature of the narrow-minded rule of engineering.

The plan (see Figure 15) did save Montgomery Street and Federal Hill from direct hits by moving the highway corridor several blocks north over the water. But those viewing the Inner Harbor from Federal Hill would have found themselves overlooking little more than a Los Angeles-style spaghetti of ramps for not one, but two full interchanges—one at Light Street and one at the Harbor East waterfront. That overlook would also feature a lot less of Baltimore's greatest asset: the water itself. One-third of the Inner Harbor basin would have been filled in to accommodate the roadways.[97] Thankfully, the Lee-Hill Street plan received little consideration either when first proposed or later when the Preservation Society resurrected it.

Baltimore City Parks Board was thankful that the UDCT Southwest Expressway plan took Carroll Park off the highway hit list, but 10-D still appropriated 150 acres of Leakin Park and stripped away the northern section of Federal Hill facing the Inner Harbor. Mayor McKeldin had discussed what was called "the Federal Hill Extension," which entailed "building a new hill [on the harbor side] of the expressway and connecting it to the existing Federal Hill by means of a platform bridging the road.[98] The result would have been a highway oddity, an elevated tunnel traversing the park. Apparently feeling railroaded on all the larger park impact issues, the Parks Board oddly decided to take a stand on this issue, wanting a signed commitment, not the nebulous, highly conditioned best effort that Bernard Werner had given them.[99]

Planning Commission Chair David Barton, who later attempted to put much of 10-D on indefinite hold, found almost no one else in the critics' corner. On May 26, 1967, (one day before the UDCT contract was signed) Barton's Planning Commission approved the condemnation ordinance. City council had already voted down Tom Ward's anti-highway amendments seventeen to one. Had the vote been closer, Barton may have attempted a last-ditch fight, but he was up against overwhelming political consensus. After the commission's vote, Barton admitted, "It is a capitulation." He acknowledged, "We are an appointed body; the city council is elected. If elected officials feel otherwise, I feel we should go along."[100] He then added a philosophical note:

Figure 15. Planning Department's 1962 Lee-Hill Street Plan (source: Baltimore City Department of Planning, Report on the Lee-Hill street plan, 1963)

"Unfortunately, in this country, the democratic form of government is geared to mediocrity. It's very difficult to do something very good, but it's also very difficult to do something bad."

Just three days later, the council gave final approval for the East-West Expressway condemnation bill. The Southwest Expressway bill took several more months, passing on November 20. This decision to push forward with 10-D condemnation bills while simultaneously engaging UDCT consultants was a short-sighted and unfathomable mistake. Only thirteen months later the city adopted the 3A alignment, which rendered thousands of 10-D acquisitions useless. In hindsight, the city fathers appear to have operated without the benefit of rational thought. The decision can only be understood in a political context. The East-West Expressway had been stymied by a lack of consensus for twenty-five years. When consensus was finally reached, no one wanted to step back and open the Pandora's box of different alignment considerations.

As the city turned its attention to acquiring properties, UDCT began carrying out their duties: Segment by segment they examined ways to lessen the expressway's impact, meeting with stakeholders and community organizations and flushing out joint development options. These activities seemed to have modest objectives, really nothing more than making the 10-D plan slightly more palatable. However, behind the scenes, UDCT already had a plan.

Genesis of 3-A

Whatever its destiny, Baltimore will one day be regarded as pivotal in the current urban struggle over how and where and whether to build expressways. A kind of Gettysburg in concrete.

David Allison, *Innovation Magazine*,
"The Battle Lines of Baltimore," No. 3, Spring, 1969

It was, if you will allow some literary license, the highway planning version of Che Guevara at Santa Clara: Nat Owings and his guerrilla planners were outgunned and outmanned but prevailed by guile and fortitude. Most Baltimoreans who remember the Road Wars regard 3-A as a failure because the I-83/Canton/Fell's Point segment remained an elevated highway, essentially unchanged from 10-D. However, for the central section of Baltimore, 3-A was revolutionary, and UDCT staffers were the rebel combatants that overthrew the established order.

During their (pre-contractual) analysis of the Southwest Expressway in late 1966 to early 1967, UDCT established communications with city agencies that were not part of the stick-to-10-D alliance. Skidmore's Norm Klein met with major players, including David Barton (Chair, Planning Commission), Larry Reich (Director of Planning), and Reich's staff, who all had severe misgivings about the 10-D alignment. Klein reported that he and the planners were "singing the same songs."[101] In a later meeting with Martin Millspaugh (Charles Center Inner Harbor Management) and David Wallace (Inner Harbor renewal project consultant), Klein heard more concerns about the potential harm to Inner Harbor plan. Result: two more influential allies for the later alternatives to 10-D.[102]

The southwest study also pointed to the single most important problem with 10-D: too much through-traffic was being funneled too close to downtown, causing bottlenecks and driving up capacity demands for that fourteen-lane bridge between Federal Hill and Harbor East. (UDCT later said it needed to be sixteen lanes!) The report found that the Southwest Expressway's route through Federal Hill would "bend many trips out of the desire line pattern toward the central business district," and the findings reference the possibility of an "intermediate circumferential ring,"[103] which would later be termed the Fort McHenry Bypass.

The underlying flaws of the 10-D alignment became more apparent with each UDCT study. But Owings was wary of challenging the design too early. Parsons comments: "From a strategic position, [Owings] believed it was more important for [UDCT] to establish its credibility, to develop more information about the problems of the 10-D design and to further develop arguments for alternative proposals," telling UDCT staff to "Wait for the right time."[104]

By the fall of 1967, Skidmore had drawn up their "ideal freeway scheme, which had been designed in San Francisco. It made use of a 'southern bypass' through Locust Point and Fort McHenry to take most of the non-CBD destined traffic."[105] This solution initially had two harbor crossings, the Fort McHenry route and a narrowed crossing at Federal Hill. The plan was kept under wraps for the time being.

David Wagner[§] was stuck with the thankless job of overseeing UDCT's work on behalf of the IDBC, reporting whenever they strayed outside "the givens," stretched their scope of work, or appeared overly sympathetic to the plight of affected neighborhoods. UDCT kept Wagner quite busy on all three counts. In late 1967 Wagner handed out a harsh slap on the wrist when UDCT staff attempted to respond to Larry Reich's concerns about the Westside Connector and the I-83 route through the Lower Jones Falls.[106] Community meetings were a constant source of irritation; in July 1968 a frustrated Wagner reported that "no matter who is talking, representing UDCT, there is always a tendency to lead the residents...to believe that there are some hopes for changing the system or lowering the standards of the system or for dropping certain segments from the system completely."[107]

Owings and Project Director Weese began to worry, even obsess, that they may never be given the opportunity to introduce their ideas for an alternate alignment. Still, they bided their time. The team won the first exception to "the givens" rule in January 1968 with an airtight case for analyzing alternate routes in Rosemont (see detail in Rosemont section). Wolff warned that this would be "the first and last time" that such permissions would be granted.[108]

In April that Rosemont analysis was presented to the Policy Advisory Board,[¶] but Mayor D'Alesandro decided to stick to the current alignment, a virtual death knell for the neighborhood. The UDCT staff, most particularly

---

§ Wagner, it is interesting to note, moved to the Maryland Transit Administration in 1972. When he was interviewed about the Road Fight in 1974, the interviewer characterized Wagner as having a change of heart about the expressways: "he eventually felt he must leave his position to avoid a conflict... between his job and his personal views." (Source: Maryland Center for History and Culture, Library, East-West Expressway collection.)

¶ The Policy Board included three representatives of the State Roads Commission (the chairman, the chief engineer, and the chief attorney) and three representatives from the city (the mayor, Director of Public Works, and Director of Traffic).

Stew Bryant, was as incensed as the community. Parsons described the growing anger and frustration:

> The irrationality and injustice of the proposed disruption was [unconscionable]. They could see many relatively lower cost alternative solutions which would cause much less and, in some cases, no such disruption. The initial struggle to save Rosemont was lost in mid-April 1968, but the controversy had "heated up" other neighborhoods and other community organizations. In these areas Stew Bryant and other staff members had cultivated contacts and perhaps in legal, but certainly not ethical violation of their agreement with their client, they had provided information about freeway plans. On their own time, as Bryant pointed out, they assisted in the organization of neighborhood opposition to the SRC proposals.

Stewart Bryant and UDCT's bottom-up planners

In the late '60s, young city planners coming out of graduate school were no longer satisfied with serving the status quo—following the teachings of Paul Davidoff, many wanted to be agents for change. "Top down" planning was rejected because it left out the poor and minority populations that were often victims rather than beneficiaries of urban renewal. Planners were schooled in "bottom up" and "advocacy planning," and many saw their jobs as helping to represent the interests of the dispossessed.

Add to this that the most noted city planner and urbanist of the times, Lewis Mumford, was an anti-highway zealot. Also consider that the most influential planning book of that era was undoubtedly Jane Jacobs' 1961 *The Death and Life of Great American Cities*, which laid out the case for lively, mixed-use, human-scale neighborhoods to create stable, safe, and vibrant cities. Mumford and Jacobs did not agree on many fronts, but they were united in their opinion that interstate highways were the antithesis of what cities need to be attractive places to live and work.

It was in this context of professional upheaval that many of UDCT's young planners were operating. It was UDCT staffer Stewart Bryant who was the personification of UDCT planners who felt more allegiance to highway-impacted communities than to the interests of their clients.

Bryant, according to fellow UDCT staffer Steve Zecher (interviewed in 2018), was a veteran of the Free Speech Movement at UC Berkley. Zecher indicated that Bryant had gotten his degree in Environmental Design at Berkeley, where "he would get on the back of trucks and drive around Berkeley, talking to people about the [Free Speech] Movement... Because of that activity he [may have been] blacklisted from getting jobs, planning jobs in the state, in cities and with companies... in... California."

With this liberal/left background, it follows that Bryant adopted advocacy planning with a bottom-up approach to practicing the profession. Fast forward to 1967 and 1968, when UDCT solicited community input on highway plans. It sounds innocuous enough. But multiple sources claim that Bryant and other UDCT staff helped school highway opponents, sharing insider information about policy decisions, outlining how to use federal regulations to slow the Road, and advising opponents about weak points in official documents such as environmental impact statements.

In April 1968 two things happened that further radicalized Bryant and the UDCT staff: Martin Luther King's assassination and the subsequent riots crystallized issues of Black victimization under expressway plans. Then, only three weeks after the riots, the mayor turned a blind eye to the plight of Rosemont. This is when Bryant went several steps beyond "giving information to the enemy." From May to July, Bryant surreptitiously helped to create the Movement Against Destruction (MAD). Parsons says that Bryant "began assisting [Stu] Wechsler in drafting and editing a statement that [MAD] would make public.... Bryant's working outside the formal decision-making structure seems a difficult one, but Bryant had no ethical difficulty with his...'secret life' as an 'opposition planner'...because he felt that the objective, of defeating those who would thrust a freeway through the Rosemont community, justified such means."

Bryant always emphasized that he carried out these activities on his own time. However, Parsons describes Bryant's subterfuge as also including press leaks of SRC's "more quotable angry statements" to embarrass the city or engineers on the team.** He justified this tactic by saying that "it increased the long-term credibility of [UDCT's] community relations function." Needless to say, these actions made SRC furious. (Alert readers have probably put two and two together and concluded that Bryant was, in all likelihood, [*Sun* columnist] James Dilts' own "Deep Throat." Dilts always seemed to have inside information on the inner workings of the Concept Team and their overseers—now we know why.)

Stuart Wechsler said that Bryant "talked about how Greiner was bugging offices and really gangster stuff." Wechsler puts the onus on Greiner, saying, "But those guys were dirty.... evil, evil people. They were the big pushers for [the 10-D]." Parsons also refers to likely spying on the UDCT staff.[109] Joe McNeely (Southeast Community Organization's [SECO's] first director) said the city "sent Greiner in to lock up the jail and get the inmates back into their cells... Of course, they were trying to put the genie back into the bottle." No matter how you look at it, it is fairly astonishing that the road builders were paying guys who were out in the community sowing the seeds of discontent.

While UDCT staff seemed to be working hard to undermine the highway plan, their day jobs were still geared to making community-friendly modifications that would lessen the negative impact of the expressways. They produced volumes and volumes of joint development plans. However, most communities saw this effort as nothing more than a sales job designed to

---

** It is little wonder that Bryant became (IDBC chief) Joe Axelrod's worst nightmare. Gene Bober (former IDBC Director of Joint Development) recounted a humorous anecdote:

[There] were four or five of us standing around a drafting table at the Interstate Division.... Our office was between [Axelrod's] office and the men's room, so, we saw a lot of Joe on his way to the men's room. And one day [Joe] hears us talking about Stu Bryant.... He started [complaining] about Bryant, but [then he goes right into] talking about growing up in South Philadelphia, and that when he was 15 years old, he met this girl Mary Beth. This is a 5-minute story in which this girl initiates him into the mysteries of sex... And he excuses himself, and he goes to the men's room. And we're going, "What the hell was that about?" We're completely flummoxed. He comes out of the men's room, he starts walking back to his office. He turns around and looks at us and said, "You know, from Mary Beth, I learned about sex. But from Stewart Bryant, I learned about getting screwed."

blunt community opposition, and they said so in no uncertain terms. UDCT staffers were getting raked over the coals by the engineers, the city, and the communities, too.

"The givens" give way

When UDCT lost their bid for Rosemont, they also changed their above-board tactics. Obviously, as Parsons points out, they could not prevail on "social, economic, and aesthetic grounds. From then on, [UDCT] attacked the highway plans on the one basis the [road] gang could understand: traffic service."[110] In January and February 1968, the team focused on traffic data that would be the Achilles heel of the 10-D plan: 43 percent of traffic projected to use the Federal Hill crossing was through traffic, meaning there would either be an enormous bottleneck or an unwieldy number of lanes in that area.

The Fort McHenry route, still under wraps in March 1968, might not have advanced any further except for Nat Owings' personal connection to Federal Highway Administration Director Lowell Bridwell[††] (they both served on Lady Bird Johnson's Committee on Beautification). Bridwell was invested in UDCT innovation as a policy matter, and Owings had been keeping him up to speed. Never one for going through proper channels, Owings assuredly pitched the Fort McHenry alignment using this informal method of communication.

In April 1968, Bridwell had a meeting with state and local stakeholders. The agenda included the Rosemont Bypass but not the harbor crossing issue. Bridwell brought that topic in by asking about solutions to the bottleneck that seemed to be "concentrated in the downtown interchange area... Why didn't they consider getting the through traffic completely out of the center city area,

---

[††] Parsons commented: "Lowell Bridwell...had not been a member of the 'highway establishment.' His work as a journalist critic of urban development and as a junior administrator in the Kennedy and Johnson [Bureau of Public Roads] BPR had provided him with experiences that suggested substantial changes were needed in the urban freeway design process. He initiated programs that within less than a year led to substantial changes in policy."

perhaps on another route?" According to Parsons, UDCT's project manager John Weese responded that they felt "strongly about a system of this nature but it was not within their 'givens.' Bridwell then asked to see a presentation of Weese's system so that he could determine if it was a valid alternative."

Weese, seemingly operating on the fly but more likely according to Owings and Bridwell's blueprint, unveiled the plan that would later be known as 3-A, sketching it onto an overlay of the 10-D plan ("one assumes rather dramatically" as Parsons mused). I-95 was moved south to Fort McHenry, with a spur to downtown via Sharp Leadenhall, and several previous expressway links became boulevards instead of expressways.[‡‡] The Harbor crossing at Federal Hill was eliminated. UDCT's long-incubated plan was hatched.[§§] (The full 3-A map is in Appendix 1-D.)

According to Parsons, "Bridwell was impressed. He said if the new plan gave a 'better solution to the problem, it should be investigated.'" Outflanked and outranked, Wolff agreed, and "the givens" were finally breached. This (game changer 6) was a crucial turning point, but also an exceedingly unlikely event, except that Owings was operating outside the conventional channels of client-consultant communication.

In the spring and summer of 1968, a months-long struggle ensued over which alternatives would be flushed out and to what degree each would be analyzed. IDBC Chief Downs (with the backing of Werner and the blessings of Wolff) used every decision-point to curb the pursuit of all options that were not 10-D or its slightly revised hybrids. But UDCT kept right on going because they had Bridwell's endorsement and (probably) the backing of high-ranking city officials, including Housing Commissioner Bob Embry, Larry Reich, and David Barton, who each shared a concern that 10-D would stifle the Inner Harbor.

One new and critically important economic study was completed in May

---

[‡‡] If Parsons' description of Weese's plan is correct, UDCT was recommending eliminating I-83 through Fell's Point and Canton, replacing it with a boulevard. Some versions of 3-A also turned I-170 into a boulevard.

[§§] The plan was likely incubated on a piece of "bumwad" that should have been preserved and enshrined, a monumentally significant artifact in the history of Baltimore.

1968. Tony Downs, a highly respected economist working with UDCT, outlined the overwhelming economic advantages of the Fort McHenry option over the Federal Hill harbor crossing. "There were significant positive benefits for the Port, as well as other industries in Locust Point and in the Canton and Dundalk industrial sections of Baltimore: improved truck access and increased potential for industrial development of adjacent properties."[111] Downs further outlined the benefits of removing through traffic downtown and concluded that the Fort McHenry route would displace far fewer residents and businesses and expand the city's tax base.

In July 1968 Joe Axelrod replaced Downs as Interstate Division chief.⁑ Axelrod, having served under Werner in DPW, was in the 10-D camp, but the team was so far into the weeds of various alternatives that it took some time for him to get up to speed. That complexity worked in their favor— Owings plowed ahead. Then, in August there was an external event: Wolff's political mentor, Spiro Agnew, was nominated for vice president, and Wolff "was distracted by [Agnew's] imminent rise...to higher political office."[112]

Bridwell called another meeting, which happened at the end of July. The traffic studies that formed the basis for the Fort McHenry Bypass were not complete, so that was not the main topic. However, Bridwell bored in on the Inner Harbor bridge part of 10-D. Informed that the bridge might need to be sixteen lanes, he said he would "never approve a crossing of [that] magnitude."[113]

All of these factors were favorable, but it was still unclear whether any of this was going to see the light of day. The exploration of alternatives to 10-D was happening without public knowledge, except that actually it wasn't...

When MAD was formed on August 4, 1968, MAD President Stu Wechsler demanded a moratorium on highway implementation to enable real community input. He also said MAD would withhold judgment until a new report

⁑ Parsons speculates that Axelrod may have been installed at IDBC because Downs had not been able to reign in Owings and his renegade staff.

was completed that included "new routes [that were already] drawn up." Parsons commented that "the MAD decision seems to have been based on their privileged knowledge of the contents of an unpublished UDCT report for a radically new freeway system design. Who told them? It seems very likely that Bryant did."[114] The secret plan for the Fort McHenry Bypass was not a secret after all.

MAD, probably with the help of Stew Bryant, orchestrated a series of letters and communications designed to make their movement appear to represent a significant shift in public opinion, while also supporting this new alternate route. I imagine Wolff got more than a little hot under the collar as his inbox filled with letters urging consideration of a highway alternative that was supposed to be confidential.

Then MAD requested a meeting with the mayor, and specifically asked that SRC and DPW *not* be included. Activists presented the case for a moratorium on all further highway planning "until the citizens affected by such construction have a chance to approve the plans." All sides described the meeting as a positive exchange of ideas.[***]

The "piling on" and the meeting with the mayor coincided beautifully with the emergence of the not-so-secret 10-D alternatives, making it appear that the 10-D plan—which had passed city council by a 17 to 1 vote only a year before—was suddenly under assault from all sides.

At the Policy Advisory Board meeting in August it all came to a head. UDCT staff presented the results of their analysis of seven alternatives for the harbor crossing, four of which included options outside "the givens." The 10-D/Federal Hill route ranked below all the alternates that included the Fort McHenry crossing.

There were still 10-D adherents. "In my opinion," Werner said, "any major deviation from the given alignment…would be fatal to the entire expressway system in Baltimore City. [I will] take a firm stand against any changes, alterations, deletions, or major additions to the existing condemnation ordinances

---

*** In August 1968 a MAD flier compared the expressway system to the dinosaurs, with the caveat that "the dinosaurs had the good sense to die at the end of their era."

at this time."[115] David Wagner wrote a memo to Axelrod castigating the team for unauthorized work.[116] This was technically true—Owings had not bothered with contract amendments. Oral agreements, he had found, could be interpreted to grant wider latitude.

This put Wolff in a difficult position—he had been in the 10-D camp, but policy had been determined at the federal level, and anti-highway activists already knew about the new alternatives. He recommended that the Policy Advisory Board officially sanction consideration of these new alignments. The board reluctantly agreed, and the shackles of "the givens" were officially removed. The discussion turned to the merits of the other alignments, and by the end of the meeting, 3-A and 3-C were the two surviving alternatives to 10-D,††† but 3-C had garnered the most attention.

3-C was a compromise between 10-D and 3-A, with Harbor crossings at both Federal Hill (narrowed to four-to-six lanes) and Fort McHenry. For easier remembrance we are renaming 3-C, calling it "3-C(2)," shorthand for two harbor crossings. (See Figure 16.) Now, if you take a colossally bad idea (the Federal Hill harbor crossing) and cut it in half, it's still a bad idea. But for 10-D proponents there were two advantages of the 3-C(2) plan: Engineers had seven more miles of interstate to design, and politicians and policymakers faced less embarrassment because 3-C(2) made use of the 10-D right-of-way. No one wanted to admit that the 10-D condemnations had been an unfathomable mistake.

One more matter was addressed in this watershed meeting: the role of UDCT's insurgent planners. Axelrod "railed against the team for releasing information which should not have been released… Several of the schemes which were presented in the transportation analysis, he said had 'flown into the hands of the anti-expressway groups.'"[117] Axelrod insisted that UDCT clear all information with IDBC before sharing it outside the organization. Owings had no choice—he agreed.

Consideration of the new 3-A and 3-C(2) options were announced by

---

††† 10-D was renamed "1-A" and included some modest changes. I keep the name 10-D throughout to avoid confusion.

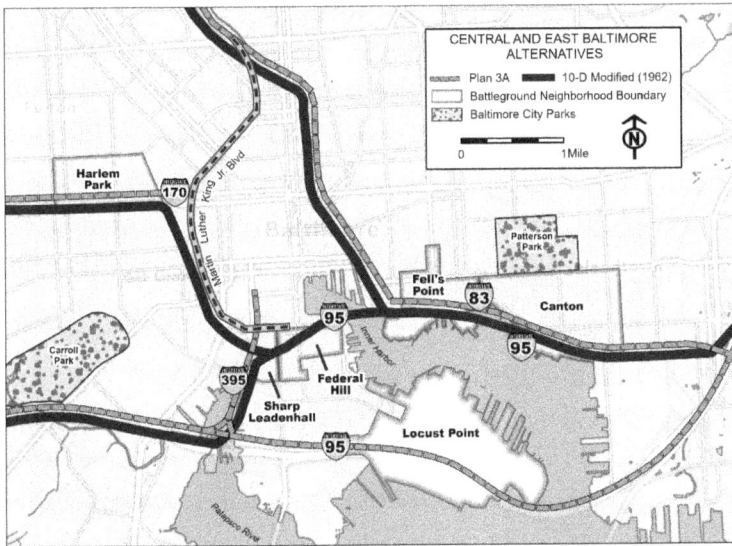

Figure 16. The black line represents 10-D (one harbor crossing at Federal Hill). The grey dotted line represents 3-A (one harbor crossing at Ft McHenry). 3-C(2) combines the two, with two harbor crossings, at both Federal Hill and Fort McHenry. (Scott Jeffrey, MS, GISP)

Mayor D'Alesandro and Jerome Wolff on August 22. The *Sun's* follow-up editorial was overwhelmingly positive:

> Now . . . at last some fresh thinking shows promise of dealing with the traffic realities. The Concept Team has proposed, and city and state officials have approved, investigation of a more promising arrangement... Free to operate outside the straight jacket of present condemnation lines, the Design Concept Team can now do the job for which, in principle, it has received national acclaim: laying out of an expressway system that enhances rather than runs rough shod on the urban environment.[118]

That 10-D was now on the ropes was testimony to the bold and risky strategy engineered partly by Owings skirting all usual constraints of contract and channels of communication, and partly by UDCT staff working clandestinely with activists while on the payroll of the Road Gang overlords. These elements constitute game changer 7. But there is one more stroke of…it is hard to say. *Genius, madness,* and *courage* are all appropriate descriptors.

Owings coup d'état at CPHA

The next Policy Advisory Board meeting was set for September 26, 1968—the decision-making meeting where the city and state would debate the three options and determine the future of Baltimore's highway plan (and, the author adds parenthetically, the future of Federal Hill, South Baltimore, the Inner Harbor, and Harbor East). All the "heavies" were weighing in, honing their arguments, and lobbying for their favored plan. 3-A got two influential endorsements from David Barton and Bob Embry. But the city's Transit and Traffic Department still backed 10-D; so did Walter Addison, SRC's Deputy Chief Engineer. Wolff's comments at the August meeting seemed to indicate that he favored 3-C(2). The mayor had made favorable comments about the Fort McHenry route largely because it would boost the port and industrial development, but that could be read as supporting either 3-A or 3-C(2).[119] Owings read the tea leaves and projected that 3-C(2) would likely prevail. That prospect did not sit well with him.

This is the point where the Owings penchant for bypassing his clients in the interest of promoting the most sensible plan converged with Stew Bryant's uncanny ability to consort with the enemy without getting fired. Bryant had been a member of Citizens Housing and Planning Association (CPHA) for two years, trying to engage them in the highway debate to no avail. Bryant wanted Owings to present UDCT work "in a dramatic forum to this much respected citizens organization."[120] He got the team's endorsement, then pitched it at CPHA, and a dinner meeting was planned for September 24—two days *before* the Policy Advisory Board meeting.

Bryant ensured that Owings reached the broadest and most receptive audience. Going through official channels (unfamiliar territory for Bryant), he lined up Mayor D'Alesandro to introduce Owings and made sure the invitation list included all of the communities involved. Parsons comments that "Bryant personally invited many of them, and, when he discovered that a number were not coming because of the cost of the dinner, he paid for some dinners himself. Later, he recalled, he may have charged this as an expense to Skidmore."[121] In other words, Bryant packed the house with anti-highway activists whose presence was paid for by his pro-highway clients.

The CPHA dinner attracted five hundred attendees, including the mayor, Council President Schaefer, Hugh Downs, Joe Axelrod, Dave Barton, Bernard Werner, neighborhood and coalition leaders, and city council members. Parsons comments, "In other words, everyone conceivably interested in the subject of expressway decisions."[122]

I have excerpted highlights from Owings' speech here from the Parsons account: [123]

Our short national history is but a faltering step towards the day when the idea of a decent environment will reach the status of a first-class citizen... Man's immortality is gauged by how well, as a builder, he makes peace with his environment. [This] requires that we admit to the fallacies in our policies where they exist and correct them.

Owings then appeals to the audience as collective decision makers in the "fifth dimension of planning," which Owings defined as robust citizen involvement. One can imagine Wolff, Axelrod, Werner, Downs, and company shifting uneasily in their seats. Owings then moves to dangerous territory as he launches a broadside against 10-D, which is still in play, and which still has the backing of some of the members of the Policy Advisory Board:[124]

The Urban Design Concept Team has unanimously agreed that the original proposed interstate system fails as an efficient transportation system. [And] that the system from the day it opens to the public would produce an impossible traffic situation; and that the impact of the proposed east-west harbor crossing would be wholly disruptive upon the human values of the inner-city...

Forcing...twelve or more traffic lanes with massive interchange structures through this area with its highly developed urban, fragile topographical, and historic qualities would be physically destructive and operationally disastrous. The ramps involved could never adequately serve the CBD...By nature, an eight-lane facility wrapping itself around the CBD would tend to choke rather than facilitate the expansion potential.[‡‡‡] The route essentially disregards the growing need for service to the major industrial areas to the southeast and disregards entirely the potential industrial growth in South Baltimore with its Locust Point port facility for which the mayor has great hopes.

Owings then compares Baltimore's highway planning to Vietnam, an analogy that was repeated in the press (and every water cooler conversation) for the next several weeks:

Over a long period of time, something like the Vietnam situation has crept over the scene. Relentlessly, the east-west corridor dilemma has developed, and no one knew how to extract themselves from it. In other words, everyone sensed that it was wrong, but did not know what to do about it...[UDCT proposes] to separate the through traffic that does not want to go downtown from the traffic that does...by developing a harbor crossing through Fort McHenry and adding an interstate route along Gwynns Falls...

Owings has now strayed far off the permissible path, but he is not done. The 3-A bombshell followed:

There are still big decisions to be made between the proposed pared down facility along the given route [3-C(2)] and—hold your breath—no crossing at the Inner Harbor at all [3-A]... If you believe in miracles,

---

[‡‡‡] In rereading this (and all the other accounts) of why 10-D and 3-C(2) would be disastrous, I find that it is positively stunning that the main objection was portrayed, not as an economic development or even a community impact issue, but rather 10-D was attacked mostly on the basis of traffic analysis. Once again, it was a time when engineering ruled, and all other considerations were sidelined.

as I do, then you can hope [for] a more ideal system...the relatively fragile central city would be served by a system of boulevards with access to the main highway system at convenient intervals, and there would be no need for an [Inner] Harbor crossing...

Owings concludes by placing UDCT's work in the context of the larger problems facing Baltimore:

I consider that our job as a concept team is to provide Baltimore with information and unprejudiced solutions to her problems. Transportation must remain subordinate, serving the city, its people, and economy... The ills of the city must be cared for on a priority basis. Highways are way down the list... Neighborhoods in existence in the core city now are the guts of the problem. Repair and additions to these are priority number one... Balanced transportation, mass transit plus normal access to inner-city by car must come, but never at the expense of matters of higher priority.

There are broad areas of the unknown facing us. Your concept team is exploring these areas with your help. Properly nurtured, operating under a favorable climate, we can steer this program through to success. Led by the mayor, supported by the city council, aided by the local architectural profession, who started the whole thing, and downtown interests, supported by neighborhood groups, we can proceed...

A news account said his speech was met with heavy applause and a standing ovation from neighborhood and preservation groups. The article concluded: "The revised alignment proposed last month offered Baltimore the chance to have both its highways and a viable city."[125]

Parsons comments, "Owings, in a very dramatic speech, had taken an enormous chance that the Policy Advisory Board (especially Mayor D'Alesandro and his cabinet) could be convinced of the merits of the 3-A system... In one great stroke in the right place he had shifted the chances of winning for the [Fort McHenry] bypass plan."[126] This was game changer 8, the denouement.

NATHANIEL OWINGS
MISSED OUT ON THE MODESTY GENE

Charlie Duff (Road Warrior for the Preservation Society) read the chapter titled "Small Miracles" in Owings' autobiography, *The Spaces in Between*. His comment was that, "Owings seems to think he himself was a large miracle." Others made similar comments, calling Owings pompous and egotistical. A *Publishers Weekly* review succinctly caught the major objections to the book: "Essentially it is a salesman's story, replete with promotional style descriptions…heavy with namedropping."

In his book, Owings refers to the Baltimore UDCT as "a crusade beyond all tangible things. It was a song of action." He then adopts a sanctimonious tone: "[Officials] were unwilling to drop one strand of the strings of job-giving patronage or share any of the influence that might accrue in the decision-making at high federal levels. My interference was resented, and I was forbidden in writing to even visit the federal-related authorities. I ignored this and proceeded to carry on as before. The risks? Contract termination, perhaps, but the goals were worth the risk."

My take: Only an arrogant SOB could have mustered the strength to overthrow the Road Gang's plan to ruin Baltimore's Inner Harbor. Archibald Rogers knew it was going to be a tough job; he brilliantly chose Owings—the right man, in the right place, at the right time.

If his clients had been unhappy about Owings going over their heads with Bridwell, who at least was within the fraternity of highway planners, you can imagine how they felt about him going over their heads to the general public. Axelrod, in Parsons' account, lambasted Owings' "appeal to lay people for the pushing of public opinion pressure buttons…any rejection of Concept Team proposals [would now be] low minded, culturally deficient, arbitrary and capricious."[127]

Axelrod shut down UDCT's community outreach activities in early October, calling UCDT staff "professionals who forgot their professional assignments and got emotionally involved with the people…. We're not looking for feedback where residents don't want an expressway because they're going to get an expressway."[128]

A *Sun* editorial responded with sarcasm, "It is shocking to believe, although Mr. Axelrod leaves little doubt, that men have infiltrated Baltimore's expressway planning who are soft on people. Mr. Axelrod moved fast to suppress weakening influences, as he must if the State Roads Commission is to preserve the principle that traffic movement takes precedence over all other considerations."[129]

Greiner's staff disputed Owings' characterization of the Team's recommendation as unanimous. One engineer said, "Owings' sponsorship of 3-A was unilateral."[130] Wolff castigated Owings and UDCT in a scathing letter with a long list of grievances: Owings had "approached Bridwell in violation of [his contract]"; "caused intense embarrassment" to SRC at the CPHA meeting, promoting the 3-A route "without consultation and approval of the members of [his] team"; "retained consultants at such high individual costs that [Wolff] had refused to approve them"; and provoked hostility against SRC.[131] Further, Owings had held meetings before data was complete, jeopardized a pending bond offering, and generally produced sloppy, unprofessional work. Wolff concluded by threatening to stop contract payments until Owings satisfactorily answered "all of the points raised herein."[132]

Skidmore had to endure a financial crisis resulting from Wolff's cutoff—unreimbursed salaries totaled a whopping $640,000 ($5.1 million today), and the firm had to take out short-term loans.[133]

While Owings' overseers vented their anger, 3-A became a rallying point for community groups, elected officials, and the editorial boards of Channel 13 and the *Sun*. The newspaper's October 1 editorial echoed Owings' Vietnam analogy, and marveled that Owings had managed to transform Council

President Schaefer from "expressway hawk" to "expressway dove… his faith shaken, [Schaefer] left the meeting no longer convinced that the expressway was needed."[134]

In October there were several meetings where Wolff, Axelrod, and Greiner's engineers attempted to put the 3-A genie back in the bottle. Owings was outnumbered; then he knuckled under to the pressure, and on October 18 the Policy Advisory Board adopted the team's "unanimous recommendation" in favor of 3-C(2).[135] The result was not released to the press, but it was an open secret in Baltimore. Controversy swirled: the secrecy was presumed to mean that the report was being altered so the technical analysis matched this position. There was also a widespread belief that Owings and perhaps the whole Skidmore team had been threatened with being fired; so, no one believed that Owings had really changed his mind.

Owings later defended his change in position saying, "he was not too concerned…because he knew that Bridwell, Mayor D'Alesandro, and several of his staff members, especially Embry and Reich, were leaning toward the 3-A scheme, all for different reasons."[136]

There ensued a two-month policy cliffhanger, with all eyes on the mayor. It did not start out as a cliffhanger, though. On October 31, D'Alesandro set the odds as, "it is 99 chances of 100 that we adopt 3-C(2)."[137]

City development officials orchestrated a campaign to persuade D'Alesandro that he should endorse 3-A. David Barton, Bob Embry, Marty Millspaugh, and Bill Boucher all weighed in with concerns about 3-C(2)'s impact on the Inner Harbor, as well as the economic development advantages of 3-A.

Owings had hoped the passage of time would soften Wolff, but he was finally required to respond to Wolff's scorching letter. His response was equal parts apology and "pursuit of the greater good." A very uneasy peace broke out.

Two external events weakened 3-C(2) adherents. The Nixon-Agnew ticket won the election on November 5, shifting Wolff's attention as he prepared to go to Washington (so he could continue collecting bribes for the VP, as we learned two years later). Then Bernard Werner retired as Director of Public Works. Pierce Linaweaver, his replacement, was an expressway advocate, but he was less dogmatic and closed-minded than Werner; more importantly, he concentrated on internal DPW reforms and was simply less engaged with the expressway battle.

The October 30 *Sun* editorial said, "Now is the time for others who have objections to the [3-C(2)] plan to bring their points to the fore… Critics should make themselves heard."[138] More interested parties moved into the 3-A camp, including CPHA and William Donald Schaefer.

In a 2020 interview, Pierce Linaweaver remembered how the mayor struggled with the decision to endorse 3-A or 3-C(2), saying, "It was one of the toughest decisions that I can think of… and I am now eighty-six years old…He was being pulled in totally different directions at every move… Well, he slept overnight and came back and said 3-A." That decision was game changer 9. The mayor called the 3-A plan "the most compatible with the environmental, commercial and social development of the city."[139] Later he added, "I don't want to be responsible for what may be regarded as idiocy or worse in years to come."[140]

Wolff resisted any temptation to go against the mayor. He endorsed 3-A on behalf of the State Roads Commission, but he and Werner both registered their misgivings. Werner, more than a little obsessed with the matter, publicly urged D'Alesandro to reconsider on January 2, 1969, a week after the mayor's decision and two weeks after he had resigned from his post at DPW.[141]

On his last day in office, January 17, 1969, Bridwell approved the 3-A plan recommended by Mayor D'Alesandro and SRC, saying, "a long-standing log jam in Baltimore has been broken."[142] (The full 3-A map is in Appendix 1-D.)

Owings later came to regard Baltimore's 3-A decision as the greatest achievement of his long and distinguished career. In a 2018 interview, Bill Hellmann (former IDBC chief and later Secretary of Transportation) called the 3-C(2) "this crazy bridge across the Inner Harbor, which would have been a horrible decision, nobody in their right mind can argue that."

Against all odds, the platitudinous planners had prevailed over the conquistadors of concrete.

UDCT and 3-A: Controversies continue to the end

UDCT was only halfway through their contract when 3-A was adopted; you might think the warring parties would make peace and get down to the more modest issues of improving the agreed-upon alignment. However, the remainder of UDCT's time in Baltimore was just as contentious as the battle over 3-A.

In March 1969 an *Architectural Digest* article entitled "How SOM took on the Baltimore Road Gang" painted Owings and Skidmore as valiant truth-tellers doing battle with myopic engineers and closed-minded bureaucrats. Stew Bryant was quoted as saying, "We reacted out of a sense of integrity. This is a part of professional ethics." The clear implication was that the Road Gang was lacking in both integrity and ethics. The author phrased this as a white-hat–black-hat dichotomy, saying that Skidmore had triumphed over "the all-powerful Baltimore Road gang, which for years had been *terrorizing the citizens* with plans for turning the historic heart of the city into one big interstate highway interchange… The new scheme eliminates most of the predecessor's *worst features*" [emphasis added].

Again saddled as the villains in the Road Wars saga, IDBC and SRC were livid. A month later, Bryant and Norm Klein, the only UDCT members who were interviewed for the article, were re-assigned within Skidmore.[143] The news media connected the dots, and another scandal ensued. Bryant and Klein were subsequently brought back to the Baltimore project because of a combination of bad publicity and complaints by neighborhood groups.

In July 1969, a consequential disagreement developed over which segments would get funding and scheduling priority. News coverage pointed to internal division within UDCT, with Greiner pushing forward the surviving elements of their 10-D plan and Skidmore advocating for the new 3-A segments.[144] §§§ The city and state finally settled priorities in September, backing the Greiner plan to go first with I-83 (Fell's Point), then I-170 (Leakin Park/West Baltimore). The newer elements of 3-A (the Fort McHenry Bypass and connecting boulevards) were somewhere between low priority and no priority.[145] The Planning Commission, over objections lodged by Robert Embry and David Barton, adopted this same priority scheme. With only so much

---

§§§ Owings again went public, saying, "At no time will I allow any infraction of the spirit or the physical fact of the 3-A scheme." He added, "We're either going to have a contract and get going or we're going to get out." But Owings was, once again, more bluster than bite. If you are counting, this is the third time Owings backed down after staking out a confrontational position.

local match to go around and a federal deadline looming, only segments listed in the city's six-year capital plan would advance. I-83 and I-170 were in the plan; the Fort McHenry Bypass was not.[146] Its low-priority status had the potential to indefinitely postpone the centerpiece of UDCT's hard-won expressway plan.

In June 1970, GBC's Transportation Sub-Committee put out a position paper attacking those priorities. It pointed out that both the I-83 and I-170 segments would have to overcome serious legal issues, and that building those segments without the bypass would exacerbate traffic congestion downtown and in the Inner Harbor, stifling new investment and limiting the Inner Harbor's turnaround potential.[147] GBC suspected that the state's decision was tainted with self-interest because they were having trouble selling bonds for the Outer Harbor Tunnel,¶¶¶ speculating that "[SRC], with the unofficial backing of the Federal Bureau of Public Roads, is using every influence that it can to delay progress on any 3A segments which would [divert] traffic and therefore revenue from the existing harbor tunnel and the proposed Outer Harbor Tunnel."

The plot thickens. Were city officials who harbored antagonism to 3-A duped into being complicit with the state, while not knowing what the real agenda was? In October, GBC and the Baltimore Regional Chamber of Commerce wrote a joint letter to Governor Mandell and Mayor D'Alesandro strongly urging a shift in priorities. The position paper attached to the letter centered on the economic development benefit of the Fort McHenry Bypass, while reiterating the need to channel through traffic away from downtown and the Inner Harbor, "just now on the threshold of a major redevelopment opportunity."[148]

The voices of two of the most influential business groups in Maryland carried the day, and the Fort McHenry Bypass jumped to the top of the priority list in 1971 (game changer 10). While the GBC was a strong advocate for the entire 3-A system, including segments we now view as mistakes, we credit them with this exceptionally wise and far-sighted choice.

But there is a lingering question: Why did it take this overwhelming force of the state's two top business advocacy groups to get the city and the

---

¶¶¶ At the time, the plan for the I-695 Outer Harbor crossing was a tunnel, not a bridge.

state to prioritize the one highway segment that had no legal complications, would stimulate jobs and economic development, preserve residential neighborhoods, add to the city's tax base, and divert through traffic away from the congested downtown/Inner Harbor area? The suspicion is that pride of authorship had a lot to do with it, but there was one additional concern that turned out to be legitimate: It would prove to be exceptionally difficult to establish a new condemnation line.

In December 1970, UDCT was closing up shop. They had won two great victories with the adoption of 3-A: rerouting I-170 around Rosemont and saving Federal Hill and the Inner Harbor by adopting the I-95 Fort McHenry Bypass. But no one in Baltimore seemed inclined to offer up any words of gratitude. To the road-building establishment, they were subversives and amateurs; to communities, they had failed to produce any gains on the segments they most cared about: Leakin Park, Fell's Point, Sharp Leadenhall, and Canton. Worse, they had tried to sell the highways with joint development plans meant to (but failing) appease the opposition.****

Mayor D'Alesandro reflected on their accomplishments in an understated way, "In my own personal critique, it has been a plus. They got me thinking away from the original route. It would have been the ideal situation if the concept team had come here without routes already being laid out. They came in with a cloud, with encumbrances... Hopefully, within the decade we'll see the completion of the jugular vein†††† of the transportation system of Baltimore."[149]

**** UDCT staffer Steve Zecher resigned in August 1969, but on his way out, he gave voice to his overwhelming frustration that the Team had been kept from making an honest and objective assessment, and further that, "in a sense, [UDCT] is hustling for the highway lobby. If there are prostitutes in the expressway program, you might say the consulting team is their pimp."

†††† The mayor's choice of terms, "jugular vein," unintentionally captures the dichotomy of the highway plans. To some these highways were primary life-supporting arteries. But highway opponents were looking for the other meaning: the vulnerable point where The Road plans could be slain if one aimed the blow with exacting precision.

The *Sun's* James Dilts noted that, because of UCDT, "Baltimore's anti-expressway groups developed sophisticated knowledge of the highway plans and the ways to combat them."[150] Joe McNeely described how UDCT's young planners aided anti-highway forces: "Without them leaking us information, we would never have stopped the highway... They not only gave us information, they taught us—they were our tutors." To state the obvious, IDBC did not count this aid in the plus column.

But the last word on UDCT comes back to 3-A and the Fort McHenry Bypass. As Dave Nutter phrased it, "3-A became a compromise between the two warring armies." Like many compromises, no one was all that happy with the result. We started this section saying that Baltimore's UDCT experiment would be watched closely because of both "its potential to establish a new model and for the considerable risk of a complete train wreck." Really, it was both.

LOCUST POINT FIGHTS BACK

GBC President William Boucher was more than a little frustrated. He had successfully fought to prioritize the Fort McHenry Bypass, but when road planners organized a community meeting in Locust Point, he was one of only three supporters—the city administration had performed a disappearing act. He was heckled and jeered, unable to finish his speech until meeting organizers intervened to quiet the crowd. At a hearing two weeks earlier on a different segment, he had been the only proponent. In a letter to Mayor D'Alesandro that conveniently found its way to a news reporter, Boucher chided, "We have become increasingly distressed at the failure of the City Administration and its appropriate departments to appear in justification or even explanation of the 3-A system."[151]

The Fort McHenry harbor crossing had one enormous problem: the proposed 180-foot-high bridge was seen as a desecration of the Fort McHenry monument.[152] Intense community opposition supplemented by well-organized veteran's organizations achieved a quick result rivaled only by Tyson Street. In April 1971 the Maryland General Assembly passed a resolution draped in patriotism: "a call to...all veterans groups and all other patriotic Marylanders and

Americans to aid and support the protection of our national heritage in Fort McHenry." It specifically requested that the State Roads Commission "fix an alternate route for an extension of I-95 so that Fort McHenry will not be jeopardized."[153] All three Sixth District (South Baltimore) council representatives were also opposed, even though the highway involved no residential displacement.

The issue of the harbor crossing had to be re-opened—the defenders of 10-D (gleefully, one presumes) dusted off the plans for the Federal Hill crossing. With the words of now-retired DPW Director Werner ringing in his ear ("any major deviation from the given alignment, in any way whatsoever, would be fatal to the entire expressway system in Baltimore City"), D'Alesandro asked for new studies of two possible tunnels, one at Federal Hill and one at Fort McHenry.[154]

The Planning Commission authorized the new study over the objections of Commission Chair Barton.‡‡‡‡

Baltimore's return to the drawing boards brought an incisive and satirical essay from *Sun* columnist Edgar L. Jones:

> Baltimore's 30-year history of expressway indecision could only be understood if one started with the assumption that what officials had been trying to do all along was NOT build an expressway system. Viewed this way, each unpalatable change in route alignment and recourse to fresh consultants can be seen as a clever conspiracy to avoid construction without risking direct confrontation with the federal authorities and the highway lobby.[155]

The new consultants produced an interim report in only two months, presenting it in August 1971. Some suspected that the state may have influenced the findings, again along the old fault lines of 10-D vs. 3-A. While the report

---

‡‡‡‡ David Barton, again on the losing side of the Planning Commission's actions, had a few choice words for the "highway people," saying, "the only kind of action [they] understand is do they get the money. After that you can forget about planning. And without it you get this thing stuffed down your throat." Barton, we are coming to understand, was not a go-along-to-get-along guy.

found that both tunnels were feasible, it recommended a "3-A modified" plan: an eight-lane tunnel at Federal Hill. Again, for easier remembrance, we are renaming "3-A modified," calling it "10-D(T)," because it was the old 10-D alignment through Federal Hill with a tunnel (T) instead of a bridge.

The tunnel at Federal Hill was 7,600 feet, beginning at Charles Street on the west side and emerging just past Wolfe Street on the east side. The land parts of the tunnel were cut-and-cover,§§§§ so many historic buildings would be lost in Federal Hill and Fell's Point. The consultants maintained that this alignment would save $268 million (44 percent) relative to the Fort McHenry tunnel, but they also found that the Federal Hill crossing would have insufficient capacity in the long run—that a second harbor crossing would be needed later.

The same interests that had spurned 10-D and 3-C(2) came together to oppose 10-D(T).

David Barton, Larry Reich, Bob Embry, GBC, and certain downtown business interests all dusted off their former position papers, perhaps using white-out to substitute "10-D(T)" for their previous disparaging references to other Federal Hill crossing plans. Barton said that combining local and through traffic in the CBD was "tantamount to pushing a grand piano through a transom."¶¶¶¶

The chorus of naysayers neutralized the issue for the 1971 election cycle. William Donald Schaefer was elected mayor in November, then launched a comprehensive review of the expressway plan. Everything came to a halt for a couple months, which provides a convenient opportunity to pay homage to Locust Pointers Shirley and Victor Doda. The Dodas are generally credited as the Locust Point masterminds who forced the road establishment to build a tunnel instead of a bridge at Fort McHenry. It was seen as a compromise at the time, but please imagine a Chesapeake Bay Bridge-like structure looming over Fort McHenry. This was no small victory.

---

§§§§ A "cut-and-cover tunnel" involves digging down from the surface, in contrast to a "bored tunnel" that involves no surface disruption.

¶¶¶¶ As Chair of the Planning Commission, Barton never adopted the language of "planner-ese." The "piano through the transom" characterization is rather more "Mikulski-esque."

Shirley and Victor Doda:
Locust Point activists sink the Fort McHenry bridge

Shirley and Victor Doda were admired by both friend and foe. Senator Mikulski had a little extra charge in her voice when she brought up the Dodas; she called them "a force of nature in their own right." Bill Hellmann (IDBC) was a very close friend to the Dodas despite being on the opposite side of the fence. Bill said they had a friendly bet: "We had a deal. That if the tunnel got stopped, or if the project got stopped, they would invite us to the party. And if we got the approval, and we built the tunnel, then we would invite them to the party at the groundbreaking and the ribbon cutting, and we did."

It was much the same with Mayor Schaefer—when he ran for re-election in 1975, the Dodas hosted a neighborhood "Thank Mayor Schaefer" party even though he had threatened to cut off municipal services if they did not support the highway plan. Shirley explained: "We called him every name we could think of, but that doesn't mean we don't think he's a pretty good mayor." Councilman Mimi DiPietro commented, "I don't know how the SOB gets away with this shit."

Shirley Doda self-described their husband-wife team as the "most colorful of the Road Warriors,"[156] (although there was some pretty stiff competition from Art Cohen). Sometimes called the First Lady of Locust Point, Shirley had a knack for attention-getting antics. One protest outside City Hall featured a woman dressed up as a gorilla who handed out bananas inscribed with a warning: "Don't Monkey with Locust Point." Other protests featured neighborhood folks dressed in Revolutionary War uniforms.[157] Shirley led a procession of neighborhood folks (each with a red-white-and-blue hat) to Monday night council meetings, where she would sit directly behind Schaefer. Councilman George Della said, "I was scared to death of the lady until I got to know her, because she had a very strong personality. Schaefer was scared of her, too."

When Victor died after a long illness in 1983, Schaefer gave the eulogy, calling Victor "a man who never gave up." Dick Trainor, another city official who contended with the Dodas' determined opposition, marked Victor's passing in a letter to the *Sun* editor: "meetings were heated and emotional, but Mr. Doda controlled the situation so that it never became personal... At the height of the controversy, we became friends. There is no question that his efforts changed the proposed deal for the benefit of all."

When Shirley passed away in 2007, city official Floraine Applefeld characterized her this way: "She was dynamic—that's the only word I can use to describe her—and a good-hearted woman who, when she decided to do something, it was best to just get out of her way."

STRANGE BEDFELLOWS:
SCHAEFER/GBC AND MIKULSKI/MAD AGREE

Newly elected William Donald Schaefer held expressway hearings in January 1972,***** only weeks after he took office. Critics called it a charade—Schaefer's position was a matter of public record going back at least twelve years. Still, he won editorial accolades for a more inclusive and transparent process. The supporting materials for the hearing described the city's current plan as 10-D(T), with the harbor crossing in a tunnel at Federal Hill. Four months later, after the Schaefer Administration consulted with a host of stakeholders, federal authorities, and experts, Schaefer announced that he supported the earlier version of 3-A, with a tunnel harbor crossing only at Fort McHenry. Getting to that point required some complex maneuvering and a back-room deal, but there is another important element of that equation...

***** Charlie Duff imparted a memory of these hearings: "There was a ginormous city council hearing... They allowed 90 speakers...against [the highway]. It was Baltimore in August, and City Hall wasn't air-conditioned. It ran till about two in the morning, and even I got to speak at that thing. I spoke on the behalf of people in my generation and told the city council, in case they didn't realize it, they are going to try to want to get people from my generation to live in the city. In Fell's Point, in Federal Hill [there are] the kinds of buildings [and] neighborhoods that we wanted. If you wanted to get us, you should provide, preserve our natural habitat." Then Duff remembers the feedback he got from this thoughtful and visionary statement: "In private, Councilman Mimi DiPietro told me to 'shut up, you Irish prick,' and that was about all that came of that."

Federal Hill—National Register

Up to this point there has been little mention of the Preservation Society in regard to the Federal Hill crossing. They and the South Baltimore and Federal Hill neighborhood organizations were persistent opponents of all the Federal Hill alignments. MAD activist and former South Baltimore resident Mary Logan remembers, "fighting the road was the main item on our agendas...between 1970 and 1973."[158] Larger forces (city development agencies and GBC) were at work, pressing for the Fort McHenry crossing and against the Federal Hill crossing. The community and the Preservation Society were relatively minor players in this battle, except for one critical matter: placing Federal Hill on the National Register of Historic Places.

Fell's Point activists Bob Eney and Jack Gleason (two of the original members of the Preservation Society covered in greater detail in the Fell's Point chapter) repeated their Fell's Point spade work for Federal Hill and succeeded in gaining National Register status in April 1970. This was a critical step that evened the regulatory scales with Fort McHenry; otherwise, it is easy to see how the Department of the Interior, pressured by powerful veterans' groups, would have stood their ground and said no to the Fort McHenry crossing even if it was in a tunnel.

The Federal Hill Historic District was also incorporated into the Fell's Point lawsuit in August 1973. By that time Schaefer was already pushing for the Fort McHenry crossing, but the threat of adjudication undoubtedly helped convince others that the Federal Hill crossing faced too many obstacles. The Preservation Society's success in gaining National Register status can be ranked as yet another turning point: game changer 11.

The Mikulski deal to final OK

Mayor Schaefer's January 1972 hearings were meant to clear the air, make decision-making more transparent, and get interested parties on

110

BARTON RESIGNS WITH
A FURIOUS VERBAL ASSAULT

Those 1972 hearings claimed one victim on the anti-highway side of the fence: David Barton, the one official who had argued in favor of precisely the expressway plan that the city later settled for when I-70 and I-83 were dropped.

Larry Reich, Director of Planning, had been called upon to present the big picture for why the city needed these highways. Barton was incensed that Reich was espousing a position that did not represent the Planning Commission's views. When the city council president asked a question, Barton was not permitted to respond, presumably because it would have looked like the city was not speaking with one voice.

Barton resigned after the humiliation of being muzzled, but he did not go quietly. He called the hearing "one more charade in the history of the highway saga." He maintained that Reich's presentation was made "without knowledge or authorization from the Commission." After the hearing, Barton met with the mayor and concluded that their views were not reconcilable. In Barton's account, Schaefer said "he wants a team," but Barton responded, "What you mean is a benign Planning Commission, and that's not in the City Charter." He added, "The former two mayors ignored the Planning Commission. The present one wants to *be the Planning Commission.*"

(Source: James Dilts, "Barton quits Planning Commission," *Baltimore Sun,* Feb 18, 1972)

the same page. However, the most notable result was a host of side conversations outside official proceedings that led to an off-the-record meeting, ostensibly brokered by newly elected Councilperson Barbara Mikulski. The minutes of the GBC Transportation Subcommittee in March 1972 state:

Councilwoman Barbara Mikulski, a well-known opponent of the expressway, asked for an off the record meeting to include the community people, the industrial people directly connected to the Canton area, the attorney for the lawsuit, members of the opposing organization MAD, and the GBC.[†††††] At this meeting Councilwoman Mikulski proposed accommodation of the 3-A system if certain provisos were met. As spokeswoman, she asked for commitments to:

1. The Expressway in a tunnel at Fell's Point and relocation of the road southward to go farther out into the harbor.
2. A reduction of lanes from four lanes to three lanes.
3. A reduction in industrial zoning where it encroaches on the neighborhoods.
4. Inclusion in the capital improvement program of a new school and playgrounds.

In exchange for these commitments Councilwoman Mikulski said she would support passage of the two remaining condemnation ordinances [needed for I-95/Fort McHenry] and the community would drop its lawsuit.[159] [‡‡‡‡‡]

It appears that at least some of the elements of this deal were, in fact, followed. No lawsuits were dropped, and Mikulski's expressway-stopping ordinances stayed in the hopper. However, MAD and Councilpersons Mikulski and Fitzpatrick all dropped their previous opposition and endorsed the I-95/Fort McHenry crossing.[160] And in the fall of 1972, the city began evaluating

[†††††] Oddly, the listed parties do not include anyone from the city. It appears to be simply assumed that the city would happily jump on board to any deal that would get GBC, Mikulski, and MAD on the same page. Probably a good assumption.

[‡‡‡‡‡] I strongly suspect that the phrasing of the GBC minutes ("Mikulski proposed an accommodation of the 3-A system") made the deal sound bigger than it was. That phrase was assuredly meant to refer only to 3-A's Fort McHenry crossing, not the rest of 3-A. Mikulski, Fitzpatrick, and MAD would not have agreed to drop opposition to the highway through Leakin Park as a tradeoff to getting a tunnel around Fell's Point.

tunnel options for Fell's Point, including, for the first time, putting the tunnel off-shore, south of Fell's Point.

The former no-highway-nowhere opponents took significant heat for the change in position. A news account said that MAD's Carolyn Tyson "was harassed and called names by flag waving citizens of Locust Point as she was going to city hall last week." Victor Doda indicated that "his group was about to embark on a 'national campaign' to save the Fort. 'We are tired of fooling with local politicians,' he said."[161]

No matter the reason (but likely due to the Mikulski deal), when the anti-expressway crowd backed the 3-A Fort McHenry Bypass, that was the final nail in the coffin for 10-D(T). Schaefer now had solid justification and almost universal backing for doing what he had wanted to do anyway: change the harbor crossing from Federal Hill to Fort McHenry, albeit for a tunnel instead of a bridge. This was game changer 12.

Technical studies were completed in April 1974. There were three options for bypassing the Fort, but the mayor favored the most complete (and expensive) solution, which moved the tunnel to the east and south, adding another 330 feet. The visual impact of the highway was virtually eliminated.

These options finally went before the Locust Point community in December 1974. Victor Doda said the community was still concerned about the impact of construction vibration and air pollution, but the condemnation ordinance passed in a 12-5 vote on January 23, 1975.[162]

Mikulski voted no. Her announced reason was that she wanted to be consistent with her original promises as a candidate to oppose the whole expressway system. I suspect the real reason was that her 1972 deal was predicated on Schaefer adopting the underwater tunnel route south of Fell's Point. In the ensuing three years the mayor waffled back and forth but was still considering a destructive landside cut-and-cover tunnel. So, the deal was off.

AFTERMATH

I-95 with the Fort McHenry tunnel opened on November 3, 1985. The tunnel cost $750 million—even with 90 percent federal funding, the non-federal share was almost $80 million. The city and the state worked out an agreement with FHWA so the tolls collected would pay the non-federal share.[163]

It had taken thirty years to find an east-west passage through Baltimore, but it was hard to argue with the result: there was no residential displacement,[164] very little business relocation or lost tax revenue, and Baltimore's port and industrial areas got a real boost from the superb access that I-95 provided to the entire eastern seaboard.

In the 1970s and '80s, Baltimore Economic Development Corporation developed three city-owned industrial and business parks in the I-95 corridor: Holabird Industrial Park, Crossroads Industrial Park, and Caton 95 Office Park. These investments are still paying off, generating thousands of good-paying industrial jobs. The Canton-Seagirt Marine Terminal, built with the dredge spoil from the Fort McHenry tunnel, is now classified as "one of the highest productivity container operations on the US East Coast," generating over thirteen thousand jobs.[165] The breakbulk and RoRo terminals at North and South Locust Point advertise, "When it's time to hit the road, no marine terminal gets you rolling quicker… Locust Point has Interstate 95— the 'Main Street' of the East Coast—literally running past its front door."[166]

While restructuring and foreign competition caused major employers like General Motors and Westinghouse to close, new uses were waiting in the wings. Today Amazon's warehouse occupies most of the former GM facility, employing three thousand workers. Across the harbor at Port Covington, the city is heavily invested in the Under Armour headquarters; the Sagamore (now Weller) redevelopment plans, now well underway, promise to bring $4.4 billion in new investment, thousands of jobs, and 2.5 miles of restored waterfront. The Port Covington website boldly advertises "three direct access points to I-95, visibility and accessibility to 42 million cars annually."

Back up at Federal Hill and Harbor East, there is really no need to cite statistics or state the transformative change that 10-D, 3-C(2), or 10-D(T) would have prevented. These neighborhoods have become anchors and center points for reinvestment, for young people giving new life to districts that might have been written off by previous generations.

Baltimore today would almost certainly be living with a catastrophic eight-lane superhighway through the heart of Federal Hill and the Inner Harbor but for an incredible chain of events: 1) Lu Fisher's meet-up with George Kostritsky, who brought in Archibald Rogers; 2) Arch Rogers conceptualizing and then selling the UDCT concept to the state; 3) Federal Highway Administrator Bridwell's receptivity and his creation of the UDCT demonstration program; 4) Rogers' choice of Nathaniel Owings; 5) Downs unintentionally facilitating that choice by eliminating the competitive bid process; 6) Owings going over the heads of his clients to Bridwell; 7) MAD, armed with information surreptitiously supplied by Stew Bryant, creating a groundswell of opposition to 10-D and 3-C(2); 8) Owings' shocking and courageous coup d'état at CPHA; 9) D'Alesandro's decision to back 3-A over 3-C(2); 10) the Preservation Society successfully getting Federal Hill placed on the National Register; 11) GBC and the chamber joining forces to take Fort McHenry off the back burner and thrust it to top priority; and 12) strange bedfellows Schaefer, GBC, Mikulski, and MAD coming together to back 3-A over 10-D(T), thereby overcoming the last barrier, the formidable challenge from Locust Point.

Was Baltimore just lucky, or was this a case of good ideas rising to the top? Probably both.

If you are looking for a black-hat–white-hat dichotomy in the road wars saga, Don Schaefer, Bill Boucher, the GBC, Interstate Division, and Nathaniel Owings all get mixed reviews for the broad brush of their involvement in the highway fight. But in this chapter, they can proudly lay claim to the white hats—perhaps wide-brimmed ones with golden spangles. With a supporting cast that included David Barton, Bob Embry, Barbara Mikulski, Bob Eney, Marty Millspaugh, Stew Bryant, Norm Klein, and Larry Reich, their collective role in guiding I-95 out of the Inner Harbor to the Fort McHenry alignment was a stunning achievement of such significance that it is hard to exaggerate.

If only they had stopped there, as David Barton had suggested, and said "We don't need the rest."

VII. RACE, HARLEM PARK,
AND THE HIGHWAY TO NOWHERE

*[This is a] White man's road going through the Black man's neighborhood.
The city has ruined Black neighborhoods of elderly homeowners and has
forced many onto welfare. The expressway will be of no benefit to surrounding low-income Black communities. It will just help White people who left
Baltimore to work in the city and then take money out of the city.*

Esther Redd, representing Rosemont and Movement Against
Destruction (MAD) at a community meeting at the Freedom House on
September 17, 1971[167]

West Baltimore resident and arts activist Denise Johnson refuses to drive on
the Highway to Nowhere, the regrettable 1.3-mile segment of I-170 that
cleaved its way through West Baltimore but remains unconnected to the rest
of the 2,115-mile-long interstate highway. Denise's personal protest is based
on the same line of reasoning that led Anthony Foxx, Obama's Transportation
Secretary, to bring his staff to Baltimore to see firsthand how transportation
decisions can have a devastating impact on minority communities.

In 2016 Foxx was preparing to launch the Ladders of Opportunity
Program, a national initiative designed to bring equity considerations into
Department of Transportation policies and programs. Foxx brought his senior
staff to Baltimore where they heard directly from Denise Johnson and other
longtime West Baltimore residents. We can only imagine them shaking their
heads in disbelief—how had their predecessors let this happen? Who was
complicit in this fiasco of decision-making? When I interviewed Secretary
Foxx in 2020, I found him forceful and persuasive, but not overbearing, with
a unique ability to simplify complex issues (much like his former boss). He
framed the issue this way:

What happened—remember that this is pre-Voting Rights Act—there were a lot of places where African Americans were disenfranchised. A lot of these decisions were being made by elected bodies. You layer on top of that who is making the decisions at the state level. It becomes a case of [Jim Crow defenders like] Bull Connor saying "Mind Over Matter. I don't mind and you don't matter," because if you can't vote people out, what's the consequence of bulldozing your neighborhood?

Secretary Foxx (also a former mayor of Charlotte, North Carolina) brings a wealth of experience to issues that revolve around race and transportation, including personal experience: His grandparents' house in Charlotte was cut off from the larger neighborhood by two expressways. In a speech at the Rotary Club in Charlotte, Foxx said, "It became clear to me only later on that those freeways were there to carry people through my neighborhood, but never to my neighborhood. Businesses didn't invest there. Grocery stores and pharmacies didn't take the risk. I could not even get a pizza delivered to my house." Fox later said of the meeting, "It's probably not the speech they were expecting to hear."[168]

Foxx explained why he chose the Highway to Nowhere as a backdrop for the Ladders of Opportunity Program: "I didn't want the issues to be abstract to my team. A lot of times, when you talk about rectifying wrongs of the past, they get reduced to platitudes and opaque concepts. Going to Baltimore for us was a 'feel it' kind of moment, where we wanted our team to talk to people who lived through it, which we did." Foxx also put Baltimore in a national context as one of many cities that used highways as a vehicle for slum clearance, including New Orleans (the Claiborne Expressway), Los Angeles (I-10), Seattle (I-5), and Syracuse (I-81). "History doesn't repeat," Foxx said, "but it rhymes."

Baltimore's part of that rhyming history is deeply embedded in a sordid past—our city went the extra mile, first attempting to enforce segregation, then using urban renewal as "Negro removal."

HISTORICAL PERSPECTIVE—RACE AND THE ROAD

On December 25, 1910, the *New York Times* devoted more than a full page to a story under the banner headline "Baltimore tries drastic plan of race segregation."[169] The *Times* introduced the article with words both historical and hysterical, "On last Monday December 19th the City Council of Baltimore passed and the mayor signed what was probably the most remarkable ordinance ever entered upon the records of town or city of this country... It may be said to mark a new era in social legislation... Nothing like it can be found in any statute book or ordinance record of the country."

The law established that it was illegal for a Black citizen to take up residence in a block that was more than one-half White, and it was equally illegal for a White person to take up residence in a block that was more than half Black. Mayor J. Barry Mahool defended the action, saying, "It is clear that one of the first desires of a Negro after he acquires money and property is to leave his less fortunate brethren and nose into the neighborhood of White people... These Negroes of the better class commenced some ten years ago to attempt to worm their way into White residential districts."

Edgar Allan Poe (distant cousin of the legendary author and Baltimore city attorney at the time) added the philosophical underpinnings of the new law: "It cannot be denied that the greatest problem that confronts the South today is the Negro problem. This problem exists not because of mere race prejudice but because experience and time have conclusively proved that the co-mingling of the White and colored races is an absolute impossibility, and that any attempt to bring about such a result invariably leads to grave public disaster."

When the courts twice struck down the ordinance, the determined Baltimore City Council twice refashioned and reinstituted the mandated segregation law. In 1917 this class of ordinances was finally struck down by the Supreme Court, causing Baltimore to turn to more widespread use of deed restrictions to accomplish the same purpose. Author Antero Pietila describes the neighborhoods of Guilford and Roland Park as "some of the earliest communities in the nation to bar Black residents through property deeds."[170] Once again, Baltimore had distinguished itself in the cause of racial segregation.

Pietila's groundbreaking book, *Not in My Neighborhood*, catalogs Baltimore's contemptible history of discrimination and segregation in real estate. One of the most revealing findings is how differently Black and White people viewed blockbusting. To White people, blockbusters were money grubbers, gaining unseemly profits by preying on people's fears. In Baltimore, among the many unscrupulous practices, one was the use of reverse psychology: blockbusters would pay a White guy to walk up and down the block carrying a sign that read "Resist: I'm not selling." Easily panicked White residents got the message that racial change was imminent.

However, to Black residents hemmed in by deed restrictions and the "unwelcome wagon," blockbusters were liberators and freedom fighters. How else, Black leaders said, was the supply of decent housing available to Black people going to expand? The alternative to blockbusting was severe overcrowding as the growing Black population was limited to the districts they already occupied. In a 1957 article, the *Baltimore Afro-American* newspaper called the Manning-Shaw real estate firm (one of the leading blockbusters) "Baltimore's most progressive real estate brokers."[171]

In addition to groundbreaking legal maneuvers to further the cause of segregation, Baltimore was also a pioneer in the use of eminent domain for "Negro removal." In 1911, Pietila explains, "America's local governments had not yet widely discovered condemnation as a land acquisition tool, and none had used it to pursue racial goals. [Mayor James H.] Preston was a pioneer on both counts." What is now known as Preston Gardens (the linear park that parallels St. Paul Street near Mercy Hospital) resulted from Mayor Preston's novel use of eminent domain, likely to serve two purposes: downtown beautification and the elimination of a Black neighborhood. Pietila theorizes that Preston was concerned that African Americans "might spill over into Mount Vernon."[172]

Another abuse of urban renewal took place in the 1950s when the city leveled twelve hundred houses near Johns Hopkins Hospital. The promised low-income replacement housing never materialized; instead, Johns Hopkins took possession and built housing for their interns. Thereafter, the area was derisively known as "the Compound." Former MAD President Stuart

Wechsler explained: "The urban renewal regulations said…replacement housing is going to be built for people with the same income as the folks who were being removed. Well, interns…weren't making anything at the time. So, Hopkins…built the housing, built a fence around it, had its police department patrolling the area; and then they built a Sheraton Hotel and supermarket there." Wechsler concluded, with considerable understatement, "That bred resentment."

In the 1960s, Tom Ward (former councilman and founder of the Preservation Society) and Julian Lapides (former state senator and influential Preservation Society member), got their start in politics opposing the Linden Avenue Urban Renewal Plan. Five blocks of Linden Avenue (plus several adjoining blocks) in Bolton Hill were cleared, removing two thousand mostly Black and lower income people. Middle to high income housing replaced the lower income tenements. The Mount Royal Improvement Association backed the plan, saying the project would remove "this pestilence that divides us," and establish Bolton Hill as a "gracious place for downtown living."[173]

Ward and Lapides formed the "Homeowners Opposed to Housing Authoritarianism," opposing the project partly because many houses were architecturally and historically significant and partly because the removal of the Black population was, according to Ward, simply "immoral."[174] Ward thought the historic character of the houses would attract renovators and hoped the area would evolve into an integrated section that would complement upscale Bolton Hill.

Ward and Lapides lost, but there is one more thought-provoking intersection of policy and people for the Linden Avenue Renewal Plan. When Larry Reich was hired as the city's new planning director in 1965, he moved his family into one of the new houses in the 300 block of West Lafayette Avenue, a product of the Renewal Plan. Larry was lured away from Chicago by David Barton, Chairman of the Planning Commission. Reich no doubt felt the sting of criticism from Baltimore's increasingly vocal Black community. We do not know if he ever connected the dots—that his Bolton Hill home was, in fact, part of the city's legacy of unfairness to its Black population.

WHITE RELOCATION FEARS

Most White residents did not bat an eye at highway plans that impacted predominantly Black populations. But on further reflection there was a huge problem: displaced residents had to go somewhere.

In 1959 the Baltimore City Council voted down a $10 million expressway bond issue. A *Sun* article covering this action said, "It has been pointed out that several thousand Negroes live in these slum properties and that the razing of the houses and relocation of the Negroes would speed up their moving into predominantly White areas."

In 1968, alarms went off in Northwood when rumors circulated that the neighborhood might be nominated for a highway-related housing relocation plan that included low-income housing. Top mayoral aides were dispatched to a jammed community meeting where angry residents vented their fears.

The rumor was quelled, but the issue of relocation was now front and center. Baltimore's high rise public housing was a response to these concerns—the least disruptive and only politically feasible way to house residents displaced by the highway and urban renewal plans. Many of those high-rise projects were torn down or switched to elderly housing in the 1990s.

These are the stories behind the statistics. As one analysis found, "Between 1951 and 1964, 89% of the city's displaced families were Black... These families were effectively barred from large segments of the housing inventory, not only by discrimination, but also by the fact that the cost of decent dwellings was beyond their means."[175]

With this historical perspective, the channeling of the East-West

Expressway to Franklin-Mulberry and Harlem Park should be viewed not as an isolated event, but part of a pattern where underlying policies reflected segregationist attitudes and low regard for functioning but poor African American neighborhoods. While the highway builders' primary purpose was to improve transportation, Harlem Park was viewed as acceptable collateral damage. That damage assessment, one assumes, did not consider Harlem Park's notable history.

Harlem Park, a selective history

In 2004 a large section of inner West Baltimore, including Harlem Park, was placed on the National Register of Historic Places under the name "Old West Baltimore." If this had been accomplished back in 1967, Harlem Park could have been afforded the same protections that were the key to saving Fell's Point and Federal Hill. Nancy Schamu, a noted Baltimore historian, commented, "It breaks your heart that the Highway to Nowhere was built at a time before anybody, including the Maryland Historic Trust, paid any attention to what Section 106 [of the Historic Preservation Act of 1966] meant. The highway goes nowhere and destroyed a mile of the city."

Baltimore Heritage summarizes Harlem Park's history this way:

> In the early twentieth century, the area transformed into a spiritual and cultural center for West Baltimore's Black community. Across the decades, builders, residents, and religious leaders left a legacy of unique landmarks including Lafayette Square, the former Harlem Theater, a wealth of magnificent churches and grand brick rowhouses. These buildings still stand as monuments to the generations of people who built Harlem Park, and they remain important assets as community leaders continue to build a stronger future for the neighborhood.

The name Harlem comes from the original late 1700s settler, Dutch merchant Adrian Valeck, whose palatial estate and farm, "Haarlem," was extensively planted with flower gardens and fruit trees. His estate was purchased by Dr. Thomas Edmondson, an avid art collector, and Edmondson's heirs donated the land for Harlem Square to the city in 1867. The main Harlem Park artery bears the doctor's name.

During the Civil War, Lafayette Square served as a recovery center for wounded Union soldiers and sheltered runaway slaves. After the war, developers built stately rowhomes around Lafayette Square and Harlem Square. Baltimore Heritage describes "stylized cornices with jigsaw-cut patterns of sunflowers, butterflies and Japanese fans. New amenities like gas lighting, hot water, and doorbells attracted buyers, including many German-speaking factory owners and shopkeepers from Baltimore's growing middle class." With both density and wealth, the area attracted numerous churches. Many of these still stand. For a period of time Lafayette Square was known as Church Square.

Like a dam breaking at a single weak point, neighborhoods sometimes changed over in a very short period of time. The city's growing Black population was hemmed in by discriminatory practices, deed restrictions, and Baltimore City ordinances that enforced segregation. The Harlem Park dam broke in the late 1920s, and by the early 1930s the area was predominantly Black. In the 1940s the area was characterized as "Black doctors and lawyers in grand houses [living] alongside working-class tenants in boarding houses and smaller alley houses."[176]

A gradual (and unfortunately typical) pattern of neighborhood decline followed. Higher income residents moved west and northwest when those greener neighborhoods opened up to African Americans and more widespread car ownership made up for accessibility disadvantages. Many of the larger houses were cut up into apartments and drew more transient and lower income renters. Absentee landlords contributed to the decline. The 1957 highway plan made the Franklin-Mulberry corridor the official route of the East-West Expressway, further discouraging investment.

Homeownership also declined, but exact numbers are difficult to ascertain because of the prevalence of land-installment contracts (a rent-to-buy scheme often employed because of redlining). One source pegged the homeownership rate at 30 percent in 1957, but another claims it was still close to 50 percent in the mid-1960s.[177]

The city's first urban renewal project aimed to reduce building density in Harlem Park through clearance and demolition of interior block structures. These were the smaller alley houses which were often in disrepair and sometimes lacked indoor plumbing. The plan was to replace them with a series of inner block parks. Some of the parks succeeded, becoming community gardens and basketball courts, but they were plagued with issues that ranged from poor maintenance to crime, safety, and drugs. One analysis concluded that, over time "these pocket parks became weedy, overgrown and filled with trash. They metamorphized from clean community spaces into spaces of neglect occupied by the unfortunate, the homeless, and those looking for out-of-the-way places to carry out criminal activity."[178] This may be a classic case of Baltimore's White city planners misunderstanding Black culture, which is geared more to a collective responsibility for watching kids on the *front* street.

A 1962 assessment of the socio-economic impacts of the 10-D alignment found Harlem Park's residences to be "of generally lower quality," but the majority were in sound condition: "Of the approximately 975 dwelling units affected, 510 are sound, but 375 are deteriorating, and 90 are dilapidated.[179]" Though called a "socio-economic assessment," the report goes no deeper than this simple housing count in predicting the effects of dislocation; it does not even inventory the 62 businesses and 120 jobs lost or the two displaced elementary schools.[180] However, it does take a distinctly upbeat tack by turning to the visual benefits of the highway: "the Franklin-Mulberry corridor would provide a pleasant approach into the city and would have little adverse visual effects on surrounding areas."[181]

This shallow and insensitive assessment of the neighborhood contrasts sharply with residents' view of the neighborhood as poor but fully functioning, a positive place where neighbors helped neighbors and everyone watched out for the children. The neighborhood was so impactful that a group of former residents organized several reunions for friends who had lost touch after I-170 scattered their families.

The *Baltimore Sun* covered the group's 2003 reunion. There were stories of makeshift baseball fields using concrete blocks for bases (resulting in a broken leg, still vividly remembered). There were memories of scrubbing white marble steps every Saturday morning. The friends recalled locals like "Booker Black, a convenience store owner who was 'like a grandfather' to them"; "Hattie Campbell, a hairdresser who worked out of her basement"; and "Ernestine Hunter, who sold snowballs from her home in the 1900 block of West Franklin Street."[182]

Alton West had a unique vantage point: He and his family had been residents and relocatees; later he worked for the City Department of Housing as an inspector covering the western district. He was also one of the organizers of the Harlem Park reunions. Interviewed in 2009, he remembered the shared values that held the neighborhood together:

> Kids were steered to a…higher education than their parents… I don't want to use the word "coerce," but you were pretty strongly guided into a standard of a little higher education. [The community] had values… You were pretty much bound to go to church on Sunday… You were bound to go to school five days a week, you were bound to do chores. But it basically was a place where you didn't have a lot of confusion, conflict, you know, so we pretty much were able to police one another. You know, be another person's conscience… It just really was a haven of sorts… [Leaving it] was like going to the funeral of a loved one. You just don't want to go.

Denise Johnson said of the neighborhood, "When I was growing up… the election wasn't over until the West Baltimore vote came in. It had that kind of power, it had that kind of swag, it had that kind of strength, it had that kind of togetherness." But that was before the late 1960s when two forces of destruction—the MLK riots and the Road—left Harlem Park shattered.

Riots, the Road, and Harlem Park

In an astonishingly forthright moment, Mayor D'Alesandro connected road building and racial unrest at a February 1968 meeting of the American Road

Builders Association, only three months before the King assassination riots ripped Baltimore apart. Sounding more like the president of MAD than the mayor, D'Alesandro said the expressway "will displace thousands of families, will dismember neighborhoods and communities, will disrupt industry and commerce, and will destroy parks and historical landmarks… The problem of the dislocation of people is particularly critical… Over 25,000 people will have to find a new place to live." He foretold coming events, calling the dislocations "a major cause of unrest," and calling on public officials to "demonstrate to the public that the balance of good versus bad roadbuilding is more nearly even."[183]

D'Alesandro thought Baltimore was in a better position to address these issues than other cities because of the Urban Design Concept Team, but the mayor was deep in the woods of self-deception if he thought UDCT's brand of band-aids was any match for the anger that led to the Baltimore riots.

Baltimore erupted on April 6, 1968, three days after the King assassination, when someone lobbed a brick through a store window on Gay Street. The next day the trouble spread west. On April 8, the *Sun* reported that "to drive through West Baltimore…was to enter an ugly no-man's land in which throngs of Negro youths roamed unchecked by airborne troops, National Guard soldiers or city police."[184] According to Art Cohen, the riots devastated Edmondson Avenue. "Edmondson was pretty well developed in terms of small West Baltimore shops.… I think a lot of people just closed up shop and left."

Only two weeks after the riots (as detailed in the Rosemont section), the mayor decided to stick with the 10-D Rosemont destruction route instead of the bypass recommended by UDCT. Perhaps the mayor should have reread his own speech.

BUILDING THE INFAMOUS HIGHWAY

When the interstates were being planned in the 1960s, Robert Moses had long since departed the Baltimore highway scene, but the underpinnings of the Franklin-Mulberry plan followed Moses' philosophy of using expressways for slum clearance. To Clarence Landrum, a co-chair of the Relocation Action Movement (RAM), it was particularly galling that "the expressway is mostly for the people in the county, and those are the same people…[who] voted down open housing."[185]

The evidence paints a damning picture. Baltimore decided to proceed with a highway plan that would (in D'Alesandro's words) "dismember" West Baltimore even though the benefits were almost nil unless the highway was connected up to I-70 through Leakin Park. It turned out to be a very bad bet, and not just in hindsight. The Leakin Park segment faced overwhelming legal obstacles, as well as community opposition, and these hurdles were well-known at the time.

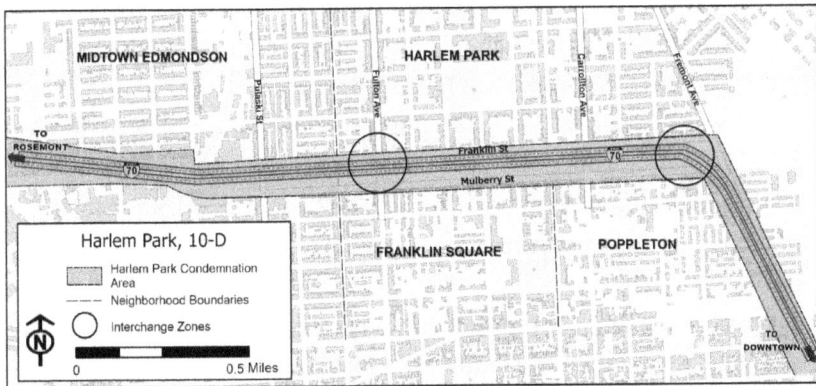

Figure 17. The highways' path through Harlem Park, Mid-town Edmondson, Franklin Square, and Poppleton. All three major highway alignments (10-D, 10-D Modified, and 3-A) followed this Franklin-Mulberry corridor). (Scott Jeffrey, MS, GISP)

The first East-West Expressway plan to cleave through West Baltimore along the Franklin-Mulberry corridor was hatched in 1942. Of the fifteen plans considered post-1942, all but two included that same route.

In 1967 Mayor McKeldin was ushering through the final condemnation ordinance for the 10-D plan, including the Franklin-Mulberry section of Harlem Park. The Relocation Action Movement (RAM) knew they were going to lose on the condemnation bill, so they concentrated on compensation, which led to a meeting that Stu Wechsler still remembers, but not for the compensation issue. Wechsler wishes he'd had a tape recorder during RAM activist Spencer Bradford's speech, but Wechsler's retelling frames the deep injustice at the core of the Highway to Nowhere:

Spencer Bradford was a bear of a guy.... We had planned the agenda, and he kind of jumped in and started talking about the flowers at Druid Hill Park. I'm thinking, "Oh man, this is not going to go well." He starts making a speech... "All these different flowers...blues and greens and reds and yellows and each growing in according to their nature, but together a garden, a masterpiece of beauty." And then he says, "You've got to open up the doors of opportunity and stop this oppression and let us thrive, so that we can, just as a garden, grow together, thrive as a garden.... Because, if the doors of opportunity aren't open, we'll have no choice but to rip them off the hinges and walk through them ourselves."

I was sitting next to Gene Feinblatt, who was one of McKeldin's advisors, and he turned and he had tears in his eye... Of course, me, as a hardened community organizer, I couldn't admit that I was choking up, too.... It was a moment.

It was timely and appropriate that Bradford addressed these comments to Mayor McKeldin in 1967. In his first stint as mayor (1943-47), McKeldin supported Robert Moses' Franklin Expressway, which was quite explicit about the "Negro removal" objective. In his second term (1963-67), McKeldin pushed through an anti-discrimination measure establishing equal opportunity in employment, education, accommodations, housing, and welfare.[186] Yet these progressive views did not cause him to reconsider the 10-D plan and its ruinous collateral damage to the African American neighborhoods of Rosemont, Harlem Park, and Sharp Leadenhall. The same could be said about Mayors D'Alesandro and Schaefer—both progressives on race, both oblivious to the injustice endemic to the highway plan.

Figure 17 and Figure 18 portray the highway's path through the southern section of Harlem Park, while also affecting the predominantly African American neighborhoods of Mid-Town Edmondson, Franklin Square, and Poppleton. The city demolished 971 homes, 62 businesses, and a school, mostly in Harlem Park. Twenty blocks were cleared, and two thousand lower-income Black residents were relocated from 1966 to 1973.[187] The Highway went under construction in June 1973, exactly one year *after* I-70 through Leakin Park was stopped by a court-ordered injunction. I have found no record that the city ever paused to reevaluate the Franklin-Mulberry segment in light of that injunction.

Figure 18. Schematic representation of the future Highway to Nowhere. Schematics, of course, are intended to make the subject matter look good. But it's hard to see anything but harm. (Source: Urban Design Concept Associates, Corridor Development, Segment 10)

RAM and John Wells: Be careful what you wish for

Transportation planning seems to proceed backwards. When you built the Bay Bridge, you didn't start it and then say, well, let's find some way to get it across the bay.

Stuart N. Wechsler addressing Jerome Wolff
at a RAM/State Roads Commission meeting[188]

The Relocation Action Movement (RAM) was the voice of those displaced by the highway, advocating for expanded relocation benefits and just compensation for residents. It was an uphill climb, but RAM and its president,

John Wells, succeeded, really an astonishing win for all those in the path of the highway. However, that success blew back on Wells in ways he surely did not anticipate.

Organized in November 1966, RAM was an oddity in the highway battle. Some observers categorized them as more militant than other groups. Their affiliation with the Congress for Racial Equality (CORE) suggested a sympathy with radical Black power. Their positions often cited the discriminatory effects of the highway plan, couching their arguments in terms of racial injustice. One of RAM's papers threatened, "We will make our stand in the streets and the doorways of our homes. Unless Black people's demands are satisfied, the expressway WILL NOT be built."[189]

If you dissect that last sentence, RAM's stance was conditioned opposition, a more moderate stance than later groups that were in total opposition. RAM primarily worked toward "replacement value" over "fair market value" for acquired houses, expanded relocation assistance, and eligibility for rental assistance. "Fair market value," RAM supporters maintained, was depressed precisely because of the highway plan. Rather than fight what was likely a losing battle against the expressway condemnations (such that they may end up with no concessions), they chose to work on issues where they thought that fair-minded people would be on their side.

In July 1967, RAM notched its first victory when city council adopted an ordinance asking for a moratorium on property acquisitions until there was an investigation into "fair replacement value" versus "fair market value." The resulting analysis did reinforce RAM's complaint. "The average replacement cost was found to be approximately $3,000 ($25,000 today) over and above the amount received from the city for the old property. Significantly, however, the average additional cost was different in the two areas. In the I-70 (Black) area, the difference was $3,900; whereas, in the I-95 (White) area, it was $2,500."[190]

Now with data to back their contention, in October 1967 RAM and CORE met with Governor Agnew. Agnew called it "one of the most fruitful meetings he had ever held." He requested that the state's attorney general and the Legislative Council study the issue of just compensation.[191]

The following spring, with the support of the city and the governor's office, RAM succeeded in the Maryland General Assembly: Senate Bill 365 revised the definition of "fair market value." The bill allowed as much as $5,000 ($41,000 today) compensation over fair market value, but it was dependent on federal participation. The bill passed on April 11 and was signed into law on June 1, 1968.

This led to a high-level meeting in Washington. RAM had secured the participation of Mayor McKeldin and other senior officials to make sure the feds knew that this policy had backing at the top. As the meeting progressed, Stu Wechsler recalls, "We were getting a very bureaucratic response, but then this guy Alan Boyd, Commissioner of Roads, walked into the meeting. He wasn't the most senior person in that room. Boyd comes in and…says, 'We'll provide the additional compensation to bring it to replacement value not market value.' It was a dramatic moment."

For John Wells and RAM it was "mission accomplished," a huge gain for all those displaced by the expressway. However, Wells' personal experience was not a story of triumph. James Dilts interviewed Wells and his wife, Ada, for the *Baltimore Sun* in October 1968, almost four and a half months after the new policy was supposed to go into effect. Wells, a bus driver, had purchased his house in 1949 for $6,949; with improvements and interest his investment was about $13,000 ($113,000 today). Ada said, "It was a beautiful block. It had two beautiful trees. We lived in the projects before, so this is the first house we've had of our own. It was one of the best-looking neighborhoods in the city. Now, it's a haunted village."[192]

When the highway plans became more imminent, landlords stopped making repairs, the city stopped issuing permits, and decline accelerated, which, of course, reduced fair market value. The city relocation office offered $5,200. Wells held out until the new "replacement value" standard came into effect. But others took what the city offered. That is when a bad situation became intolerable.

Mrs. Wells recounted how, with most of the properties vacant, the area was subject to dumping and attracted rats; fires in the boarded-up buildings were a regular occurrence; further, they could not make repairs. Conditions were "just not fit for people," she said. "Staying in a house like this is fearful…

I get upset and depressed… I'm scared to death." Mrs. Wells had taken to walking the floors at night because, "If I'm asleep the house can burn down with the kids."

Dilts asked John Wells if all the effort he put into replacement value was worth it. He said, "I've asked myself that a million times. It may have been that we should have taken the $5,200 and left. My wife is in a nervous condition… She's been to the hospital twice and has been seen by a private doctor. They couldn't pin anything physical down—it's just nerves."

A RAM meeting with the State Roads Commission brought angry complaints from those waiting for the extra $5,000 before moving out. One woman said, "It would be OK to sit and wait as long as you got a decent place. But I'm one of only two people on the block; all the windows are broken, and I can hear the glass fall out at night. I'm afraid."

Wells, in great frustration, said, "We need something right now, not tomorrow, not next week. My roof is leaking; my plaster is falling down. Pay us and let us get out now. I waited two years for this bill, and I can't wait three more months."

What happened to the expanded replacement value? The article indicated that the federal department of transportation could not make up its mind, that officials seemed to be waiting for a new federal law to go into effect. The city said it was waiting for federal funds. Finally, in early October 1968, Wells received word that his payment was on the way. The Wells family had had enough of urban living—they moved to the Liberty Road area in the county.[193]

"The Platform" and joint development

UDCT joint development plans for the Franklin-Mulberry corridor called for a new school, parks, playgrounds, and new low-income/low-rise housing.[194] The centerpiece of the plan was intended to help knit the divided community back together: a three-block platform over the depressed highway with schools, a multi-service center, housing, recreation facilities, a shopping center, and/or a community health center.[195] (See Figure 19.)

The platform was never built, and few of the other improvements were implemented, but the key question is: Was this ever a serious proposal, or was it just put out there to quell community opposition in full knowledge that it would never happen?

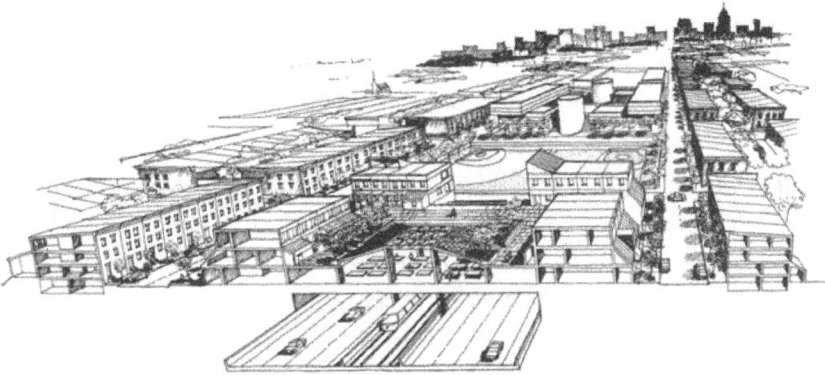

Figure 19. The platform: One of several schemes showing the highway underneath (and dwarfed by) unspecified (but cool-looking) uses, as well as parking. (Source, Urban Design Concept Team, Corridor Development, Segment 9)

Gene Bober, former Chief of Joint Development for IDBC (in a 2017 interview), indicated that the platform itself would have been awfully expensive. "Putting a lid on the highway would have come with a hell of a premium." On this point, news articles indicated that the feds had agreed to 90/10 funding, which Planning Director Reich called a "first ever" for federal highway funds.[196] One article estimated the extra cost of the platform as $4 or $5 million over building the same facilities on the ground. Still there was a great deal of support for the concept in the Bureau of Public Roads.[197] But those federal 90/10 dollars were for infrastructure (the platform itself) and replacing one school, not for other facilities. There was no special funding for improvements other than infrastructure and beautification, and even those items had to be sold to the feds case by case.

In 1968 UDCT made Franklin-Mulberry and the platform their top-priority joint development project. Impressively, they secured endorsements from the

Baltimore School Board, City Planning Department, the mayor's office, Housing and Community Development, the State Roads Commission, the US Bureau of Public Roads, and the US Department of Health, Education, and Welfare.[198] The design was presented at a national conference and written up in a publication of the Highway Research Board, a division of the National Research Council.[199] The platform had the potential to be a model for lowering the impact of highways in dense urban areas, so the plan was garnering national attention.

Then it all started to fall apart. The Maryland Department of Health and Mental Hygiene raised concerns about air quality in schools and living space over the highway.[200] The community and the school board chose an alternative site for the school. Five years went by before I-170 construction started, and increasing vacancy in the neighborhood (mostly attributable to blight spreading out from the highway corridor) made the platform proposal almost an anachronism—why pay for a platform when there is an abundance of vacant land that could house the same facilities? And as time passed, commitments made by previous officials were not always honored by current ones.

Moreover, common sense may have replaced the hope stirred by the misleading visions of architects. Did people really want to live or take their children to parks and playgrounds that were right next to (or on top of) a smog- and noise-generating expressway? Was this an environmental justice issue in the disguise of prettied up plans? The community never pressed the city to fulfill the joint development promises—either their enthusiasm waned or so many were forced to move that the constituency dissipated.

Back to the fundamental question: Was this plan a serious proposal or a malevolent way to gain begrudging community support? Was RAM activist Esther Redd right when she said of joint development, "They're still trying to dupe us"? Gene Bober said, "I think Skidmore [the lead consultant for UDCT] really believed that it would be a good idea from just a land formation point of view. But these guys were not real estate economists. They had some interesting drawings with some interesting visions and maybe a few bullet points of how implementation could happen." But Bober added, "The only way you're going to build that sort of thing is if it's in a high-dollar neighborhood. And, of course, if it's a high-dollar neighborhood, you're not putting a highway in there."

In June 1972, Dick Trainor (Interstate Division) described the platform as "in limbo." When the highway went under construction in 1973, the platform and most other joint development concepts had been put on the shelf. All those renderings that made the highway seem, if not attractive, at least palatable, were in the dustbin. On March 22, 1974, Trainor reviewed the status of all 3-A joint development projects in a memo to the mayor. The platform did not appear on the list.[201]

In retrospect, it is likely that the Skidmore team was well-meaning, but the process was deeply flawed, and residents were likely taken in by unrealistic plans. The city fathers did not actively conspire with planners to deceive the community, but the result was the same as if they had. No one in charge asked the key question: Is it fair to show the community these grandiose plans when the chances of it actually happening are dim? Esther Redd was correct—the community was duped.

Although Redd is no longer around to ask this question, several of my interviewees turned the tables and asked me the following question:

What were they thinking?

It was a cliffhanger. Gene Bober described the manner in which Franklin-Mulberry went under construction in June of 1973. There was a hard-and-fast federal deadline for going under construction by July 1, 1973, but construction could not start before the MAD lawsuit was settled. Bober described it as follows:

> [Bill] Hellmann and [David] Wagner [IDBC staffers] were really very hardworking guys. The judge hadn't yet decided [the MAD lawsuit]. So, the contract had been awarded but not yet started. Trainor and Hellmann had the courthouse staked out waiting for the judge's decision. And as soon as the judge said, "Okay, the highway can go," Hellmann got on the phone to the contractor, who already had the bulldozers on the site waiting to go, so that they could say to the Federal Highway Administration, "Okay, we've met the deadline."

Construction started just before the deadline, with Hellmann and Wagner undoubtedly receiving accolades from the mayor for going above and beyond the call.

About thirty-eight years later, Bob Leonard, one of the West Baltimore arts activists whom we shall meet shortly, characterized the Highway to Nowhere as "West Baltimore's Katrina," but with longer-lasting impacts: "An inner-city catastrophe that comes along with [the highway], for instance, looks like the effects of a hurricane that stays. Decades long in its motion, and the turmoil is continuous."

It is a stunning juxtaposition—the city was so anxious to start construction on a highway later characterized as a permanent natural disaster.

From Secretary Foxx to West Baltimore community leaders of both yesteryear and today, the Highway to Nowhere certainly has the appearance of a racial justice issue. It adds insult to injury that Franklin-Mulberry was authorized to proceed even though the plans to connect it up were in doubt. Can we now, fifty years hence, reconstruct and dissect the decision to proceed?

Most people, myself included, assumed this was Mayor Schaefer trying to demonstrate his determination to implement the highway plan and show that opposition was futile. As Bill Hellmann phrased it, the mayor wanted to "build everything you can as fast as you can." The road plans were blocked in other areas, so Schaefer was making progress in the only place he could. A number of additional factors may have been at work.

First, there was a possibility that the city would have to repay the federal government for cost of acquisition, relocation, and preliminary engineering studies already incurred. News accounts at the time parroted the city's contention that estimated these costs at $5 million ($34 million today). The prospect of having to return federal funds looms large in Schaefer's 1974 correspondence with the New Democratic Club.[202]

Highway opponents believed this was a trumped-up justification, and I am inclined to side with the opponents. A 1972 legal analysis by Preservation Society attorney Geoff Mitchell found no precedent for these kinds of repayments. MAD's Carolyn Tyson also researched cases in other localities where highways were dropped and concluded that "reimbursement has never been sought and received from any state or city, not even for the completed but unused section of the Embarcadero in San Francisco, finished more than seven years ago."[203] Former IDBC staffer David Chapin recalled some discussion of repayments in connection with other segments, but my own research uncovered no evidence that repayments entered into the consideration of any of the other dropped highway segments. Secretary Foxx commented, "I'd just be surprised if Baltimore or Maryland as a state got to a place where they knew the project was never going to be fully completed and just decided to do it anyway because they thought they would be asked to pay back all the money they had used in the plans."

Other factors add perspective if not a solid justification. Bill Hellmann pointed out that the Leakin Park segment was not the only option to link up Franklin-Mulberry. The other proposed connection (later named I-595) would have extended I-170 west and south to I-95 (traversing a section of Gwynns Falls Park), so the mayor was not 100 percent banking on getting Leakin Park approved. This is technically correct but does not provide a convincing rationale. The I-595 link was dropped in 1983 because it was judged to be of minimal transportation benefit relative to its cost. In a January 1983 editorial, the *Baltimore Sun* maintained that the I-595 plan "would not connect one freeway system to another, only to itself. The result would be a five-mile loop in southwest Baltimore for people not going anywhere... About the only purpose of a connector to I-170 is to give some semblance of purpose to that [Highway to Nowhere] folly."[204]

There is one other mitigating circumstance: timing. Gene Bober commented that "the Leakin Park segment was going to be iffy. But the mayor was saying, 'We gotta do something or we'll lose the whole thing.'... There was always the danger of federal highway money being reallocated elsewhere out of Baltimore City or even out of the State of Maryland." The looming federal deadline, linked to a loss of federal funds, forced the decision to be made before there was a resolution of the injunction.* This argument still leaves the

---

* The city, in an apparent attempt to meet the requirements of the court injunction, held hearings and redrafted the EIS for Leakin Park in December of 1972. However, the EIS was not approved, which meant that the city would not have been able to go back to the courts prior to the June 30, 1973, deadline to start construction.

matter in the category of a very bad bet. In the Leakin Park chapter we will document the city's half-hearted attempts to address the court's requirements for lifting the injunction. In other words, the city did darn little to change those betting odds and connect up Franklin-Mulberry.

The role of the Federal Highway Administration is another question: How and why did they allow this segment to proceed? At least one federal highway official, John E. Hirten, argued that the city "should not be allowed to begin work in the corridor until the suit over the parks was resolved." Hirten was overruled by superiors after the state highway administrator, David H. Fisher, argued on behalf of the city, saying, "the City of Baltimore feels that Franklin-Mulberry is a needed facility and should proceed regardless of the parks controversy."[205] †

There is one final and critical question: Did racial bias affect the decision? In a later chapter Schaefer is shown to have a degree of racial bias, but he largely overcame these inclinations and worked easily and productively with the Black community. The decision to proceed with Franklin-Mulberry absolutely reflected bias, but it was mostly the mayor's pro-highway bias that skewed the matter. My opinion: You could classify the decision as "implicit racism," an unconscious bias that affected decision-making.

Here, it must be pointed out that the blame does not land solely in William Donald Schaefer's lap—by the time it got to Schaefer in 1972, he was faced with only bad outcomes. The corridor was acquired under McKeldin and cleared under D'Alesandro—all before Schaefer took office. If Schaefer had not built the highway, he would have faced an enormous task in redeveloping Franklin-Mulberry.

All these city leaders stuck to a plan hatched by Robert Moses and others with dubious motivations. All three mayors would bristle if they were accused of using the highway as an excuse for "Negro removal," but they each carried out a plan that initially had exactly that as an explicit objective. They each failed to reevaluate.

---

† Hellmann additionally pointed out that federal rules should have prohibited the Highway to Nowhere scenario. He said, "property acquisition and relocation assistance should not occur till a complete section of highway received Federal approval, e.g., Franklin/Mulberry Corridor."

Bill Hellmann said it succinctly in a 2017 interview, "I think, in retrospect, proceeding with the Franklin-Mulberry Corridor was a terrible decision." He paused and then repeated for emphasis: "Let's just say it was a bad decision."

POST-MORTEM

In a 2009 interview, former Harlem Park resident and housing inspector Alton West was asked if he thought the highway was responsible for the decline of Harlem Park. "Oh, without a doubt! Without a doubt," West said. "There's not one scintilla of doubt as far as what caused all this to happen... I gotta say that [the highway] probably impacted on the integrity and character of the neighborhood. It really did."

West described how the blight spread out from the highway corridor first to the adjacent blocks, but then beyond: "Just call it the domino effect or whatever you want... [I]t just fell and kept going... [By the] late seventies it was like the spread of cancer, I guess. It was just inoperable. And then the methods which you try to bring out for rehabilitation and that sort of thing, [the city government] didn't have a clue."

As early as 1968 (only one year after acquisitions had started), the Harlem Park Council expressed deep concern and frustration about the spreading blight: "The vacant land and houses in the Franklin-Mulberry-Fremont corridor have greatly increased the rat population in the Harlem Park area. This destruction has caused filth and debris to litter Harlem Park." The council asked the city to "gas the Harlem Park area to reduce rat infestation."[206]

The population declined from an overcrowded 22,000 in 1960 to an undercrowded 4,000 in 2000. The 2000 census also found that 41 percent of housing units were vacant, almost 80 percent of occupied homes were rentals, and 67 percent of residents earned less than $25,000 per year. A 2017 City Health Department report cited more grim statistics, for example, the adult and youth homicide rates were both more than twice the citywide average. The neighborhood ranked first (out of 52 city neighborhoods) for drug- and alcohol-induced deaths.[207]

Alton West's comments come from a deeply personal point of view and need to be tempered—the decline of Harlem Park should not be solely attributed to the highway. A more dispassionate analysis would additionally take account of the impact of the riots, the loss of good-paying manufacturing jobs, and the destructive impact of crack cocaine as equally or more responsible for the decline of Harlem Park.

There have been sporadic efforts to revive Harlem Park and the Highway to Nowhere corridor. In 1997, Mayor Kurt L. Schmoke sent up a trial balloon that suggested removing the highway and rebuilding the area, mostly with new affordable housing.[208] The plan never gained traction, probably because the neighborhood had gone so far downhill that a plan focused on the Franklin-Mulberry corridor would not work unless the entire neighborhood was revitalized, the cost of which was difficult to ponder.

Artists and the highway

Denise Johnson ran a unique program, trying to make lemonade with Baltimore's most embarrassing lemon: using the arts to uplift the expressway-impacted community, now besieged by a host of urban ills. City planners can rattle off many examples of distressed neighborhoods where artists are pioneers, leading to later general reinvestment and revival. But Denise's program was different, using the highway that had divided the community as a focal point for an arts and culture program that would knit that community back together.

Denise was one of the West Baltimore residents that Secretary Foxx invited to his staff retreat to tell the story of the highway's impact, but she also has a long resume as a culture and arts organizer and leader in the African American community. Her connection to the Highway to Nowhere goes back to her childhood. Her parents were separated, but her father lived on Franklin Street and had to move in advance of the highway.

While working at the Bon Secours Foundation, now called Community Works, she met Ashley Milburn, a Maryland Institute student artist who was bringing people together to talk about the Highway to Nowhere, what it represented, and the potential for arts and culture to aid this distressed community. Denise felt a strong connection to the concept, because "This was part of my story, too." She adds:

> In doing that work, I think it was the first public conversation in the community about the Highway to Nowhere, the loss. We were for-tunate enough to be able to gather some members in the community who were elderly... These...folks, people up in the eighties, close to nineties, when they shared the story about the loss, they were still very emotional, and that tugged at my heart... I was a little girl when that happened, and I had no idea of that loss, that impact that it had on those people. It makes it even more real... If you think about people in their eighties still upset. Having that remembrance and shedding tears about that; it's pretty heavy.

The abandoned highway was such a strong symbol of defeat and decline—if the community could come together and make the Highway to Nowhere part of a hopeful and life-affirming endeavor, it could be a game changer for the people of Harlem Park. The resulting program, CultureWorks, received a grant from the Open Society Institute. Denise became the director, charged with turning the Highway to Nowhere into a positive focal point for grassroots community action.

The theme for CultureWorks was "remembrance, healing, and celebra-tion." Note the absence of terms usually associated with attempts to revive downtrodden neighborhoods. This was not about "physical renewal" or devel-oping "a revitalization plan" to tear out the highway and build something else. This was renewal of the spirit—in Denise's words, "about raising the cul-tural value of West Baltimore in the minds of the people in West Baltimore."

CultureWorks organized numerous events in an eight-year run from 2007 to 2015, all using the arts as a vehicle for community organizing and community awareness. The centerpiece was the 2011 ROOTSfest, located right on the infamous Highway to Nowhere. CultureWorks produced the fes-tival with Alternate Roots, a national group with a similar focus on using the arts as a means of empowerment. The City of Baltimore did not support the event. "We had folks [in] power who felt that we didn't know what we were doing, felt that, if we had the festival in West Baltimore, all kinds of terrible things are going to happen," Denise said.

Brian Francoise, another CultureWorks activist, put it this way: "Sometimes this work happens in more comfortable places, and so Ashley [Milburn] was challenging them [Alternate Roots] to have their 35th anniversary festival...someplace [where people might]...start to see the neighborhood differently, where the pain and the scars are now a potential asset, a healing place."

The festival attracted eleven to sixteen thousand participants from Baltimore and points beyond, successfully (and peacefully) engaging a diverse audience. It started with a three-day "National Learning Exchange" consisting of workshops, story circles, panel discussions, and readings, all geared to the intersection of art and social justice. ROOTSfest then culminated in two days of live performances, punctuated with nationally known artists, authors, and musicians, held right on the Highway to Nowhere. "It was magical," Francoise said. "I mean people were so appreciative. People came who would normally never come to West Baltimore." He said that even West Baltimoreans were shocked that their neighborhood and the misbegotten highway were the focus of an artistic celebration.

Denise now directs the Arch Social Community Network, continuing to work at the intersection of art and activism. Arch Social Club, founded in 1905, has been a mainstay of African American culture and music for more than a century. Its location on Pennsylvania Avenue in Upton makes it a centerpiece for efforts to revive Pennsylvania Avenue as a center of African American culture.

A play is one of the lasting achievements of this unlikely marriage of arts and the highway. Stories collected by Ashley Milburn and CultureWorks became the inspiration for the play *Last House Standing: A Play About the Highway to Nowhere*, scripted by playwright Sheila Gaskins. It has been staged five times in Baltimore: at ROOTSFest 2011, at the national Imagine America Conference in 2015, and a three-night run at the Arena Playhouse in 2016.

The play revolves around EV, a teenage girl whose family is faced with a tough choice: stay and fight or recognize reality and move. Gaskins' script involved not just EV's family, but also the house itself in the protest—the marble steps sing several soulful numbers as the "Marblettes." When EV finally gives in to inevitability, her mother advises that "sometimes it is as important to keep your head high and move on in defeat, as it is to fight in the first place."

A reviewer for the Johns Hopkins Newsletter commented, "It was…a reminder of what theatre can and should be: a representation of people and situations which matter, and which ought to be remembered and exhibited."[209]

Of the Highway to Nowhere, Gaskins said, "I think there's an opportunity for hearing more stories… I think there's still more meat about this… It's an ever-growing conversation." Secretary Foxx phrased his hope for the future of our country using some of the same words: "It's really important for our society to have this conversation." Denise Johnson joined Foxx on a US Department of Transportation video that opens with a simple message: "Transportation should not create division; transportation should be the solution to past division." Foxx saw his agency's support for the Red Line in precisely that context.

Red Line

The best hope for the Highway to Nowhere and Harlem Park was the Red Line light rail plan. In 2015 Governor Hogan canceled the project, which had been ten years in planning. He called it a "boondoggle" and said it was "not the best way to bring jobs and opportunity to the city."[210] Revenues from a 3.5-cent increase in Maryland's gas tax, passed in 2012 and intended to fund the Red Line, were redistributed primarily to suburban growth areas.

A vital transit connection between the inner city and suburban job centers is largely missing in the Baltimore area. Glenn Smith of the Transit Equity Coalition stated, "It is estimated that access to job centers from West Baltimore takes roughly 95-plus minutes if transit is running with no obstacles. Data shows that less than 35 percent of residents of West Baltimore have access to an automobile."[211]

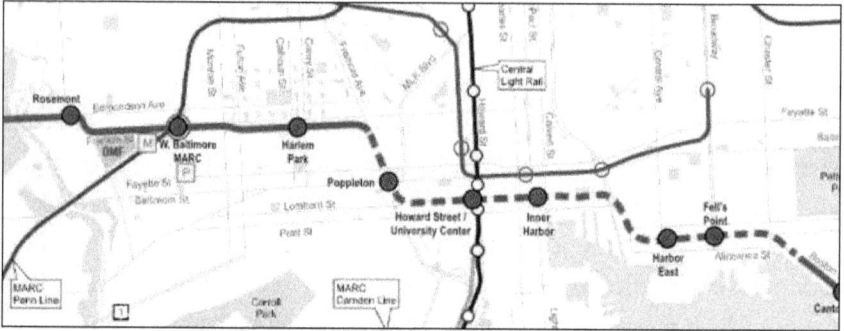

Figure 20. Red Line plan (Source WBAL, July 11, 2014)

Secretary Foxx said they had planned to commit $1 billion to the Red Line before it was cancelled by the state.[212]

Some community activists involved in planning the Red Line still had vivid and bitter memories of the Highway to Nowhere. Zelda Robinson, a leader of the West Baltimore Coalition and longtime resident, said the Highway to Nowhere "divided the communities and it hasn't been the same since."[213]

Joyce Smith, a Franklin Square resident whose family was displaced from the 400 block of Gilmor Street, said, "I remember people were just so upset... We didn't have a voice... It separated our churches, it separated our services, it separated our families. The whole sense of community was shattered. It had a devastating effect."[214]

The Franklin-Mulberry/I-170 segment was completed in 1979 at a cost of $101 million.[215] There is no record of a ceremony to commemorate the completion. What positive words could be said about this milestone? That Baltimore ruined a decent and functioning African American neighborhood to save commuters less than two minutes in their journey downtown?

In 1983, after the last possible option for connecting Franklin-Mulberry to the interstate system (I-595, coming up from I-95) was abandoned, the city unceremoniously changed the signage: I-170 was no more. It was back to Route 40. As Mayor D'Alesandro aptly described it back in 1967, Harlem Park had been "dismembered" so that I-170 would have a brief four-year run as an unconnected part of the 40,000-mile interstate highway system.

The dysfunctional highway has remained essentially unchanged for almost forty years. Hope has been rekindled by the Biden Administration's infrastructure program—the good news is that there is a carve-out for "Reconnecting Communities"; the bad news is the original $20 billion proposal was cut to $1.0 billion. Baltimore will be in a heavy competition with other cities, all trying to rectify the mistakes made when highways and engineering were king, but decision-makers would be hard-pressed to find a better poster child than Baltimore's Highway to Nowhere.

VIII. THE BATTLE TO SAVE FELL'S POINT

What an astounding thing that one person's knowledge, interest, and energy could have such an impact on all of us who today call Fell's Point home... One passionate soul really can make a difference!

Kathleen Haller, Fell's Point resident,
commenting on Bob Eney's passing in 2016[216]

Perhaps there was some greater-than-life force at work. Indeed, the cosmos seemed aligned in favor of Fell's Point fledgling Road Warriors when unrelated events brought Bob Eney and Jack Gleason from New York City to Fell's Point in February 1967. Only one week after their arrival, Eney and Gleason attended the founding meeting of the Society for the Preservation of Federal Hill and Fell's Point (the Preservation Society); Gleason went on to become its third president. More importantly, in 1971 he was elected first president of the Southeast Community Organization (SECO), thereby achieving what had seemed an impossibility four years before: the White ethnics and the preservationists now marched in lockstep under the banner of highway resistance. But, as important as Gleason's role was, it is Eney's arrival in Baltimore just in the nick of time that feels especially preordained.

To say that Eney found his calling in the Road Fight does not do justice to the pivotal role he played. Eney was a one-of-a-kind marvel—dyslexic to the point that he could not write a sentence but possessed with an unbridled passion for architecture and history, he was the guy who made people look beyond the rundown Formstone-covered houses to see the remarkable-but-hidden potential. He was the guy to fill in the backstory behind those dilapidated facades. Bob's friend (and caretaker when Bob was afflicted with Alzheimer's) Tony Norris said, "Bob was so enthusiastic and persuasive, he could turn a slum landlord into a preservationist." His knowledge, passion, and persuasiveness were a difference-maker for the fate of Fell's Point.

Most Baltimoreans identify the Road Wars with the successful effort to save Fell's Point. However, readers may be surprised to learn that this effort did not start in earnest until 1967, twenty-three years after it first appeared as a targeted corridor and seven years after a 1960 Planning Department plan put a bullseye on Lancaster and Broadway, making Fell's Point/Canton the preferred route through East Baltimore. Fell's Pointers were Johnny-come-latelies to the Road Wars; they owe a huge debt of gratitude to neighborhoods on the frontlines in earlier years. If Tyson Street, Mount Vernon, Southwest Baltimore, and the Mount Royal-area groups had not succeeded in getting various segments blocked, delayed, or changed, Fell's Point would almost certainly be home to an eight-lane superhighway. The Road would have gone under construction before there was any organized opposition or federal protections of historic areas.

Readers may also be surprised to learn that Fell's Point was a very divided community. The Preservation Society in no way represented the whole community—it was dominated by outsiders and a smattering of new folks the long-term residents called "gentrifiers," a decidedly derisive term that connoted a status barely above vermin.

It is Fell's Point's status as a historic community that ultimately saved the neighborhood, so the Fell's Point Road Fight starts with a trip through the archives.

A SELECTIVE HISTORY

A local history blogger captured the essence of Fell's Point history when he called it a "sea-faring frontier." He explained that Fell's Point, much like the free-wheeling western frontier, was a place where "the essence of the American character was forged. [Fell's Point was] created by land speculators, built by risk taking developers, and populated by men and women who were not afraid to push beyond the predominant boundaries of class and the law in their search for wealth and personal freedom."[217]

Here we use Bob Eney's 2003 *Fell's Point Out of Time* living history interview[218] to punctuate a brief history. In 1731, William Fell, a Quaker, was granted the land that later became Fell's Point. William and his wife, Sarah, had several children. One of their sons, Edward, inherited the land when William died in 1741. Eney: "I guess there still weren't too many people because when he [Edward] came to get married, he married his mother's niece, Ann Bond." Ann played the key role in selling Fell's Point after Edward died. Eney: "So, she [Ann] was like a big-time promoter. And she went out, and she sold Fell's Point. Now, Baltimore Town, further up the harbor, ... was still selling off lots. And Ann just went right ahead of them..."

One of Ann's children married a Johnson, who owned most of Greenspring Valley. William Fell Johnson, a descendant of the Fell-Johnson union, was still alive and living in the family mansion when the Road Fight was underway. Eney:

> Old Mr. William Fell Johnson was living there alone in this big house. And we went to him and asked him if he could give us any information or help or anything about the road. And he said he wasn't interested in Fell's Point. He said, "The only thing I have of Fell's Point is a big headache of ground rents," [Johnson continued], "It doesn't bring me enough money to worry about it." He said, "so forget it... Let them buy it [for] the highway." That's what he told us. And so ... he died, *fortunately* [emphasis added].[219]

Bob Eney had a marvelous ability to recall historical detail, all imparted with an inimitable storytelling style.* Storytelling was essential in the defense

---

* Charlie Duff (Jubilee Baltimore) was fifteen when he met Bob Eney. Duff was interested in those mostly abandoned houses near the Fell's Point waterfront. He met with Bob and his housemate Jack Gleason. Expecting a twenty-minute overview, Charlie (later joined by his parents) got a four-hour architecture and history lesson. In a 2018 interview, Charlie said,

of Fell's Point—to the untrained eye, the buildings were mostly common-place, but the stories behind those buildings were rich with lore.

The Fell's Point's raison d'etre was shipping. With a natural harbor deep enough for all manner of vessels, the waterfront was occupied by wharves, piers, warehouses, and shipbuilding operations. Shipbuilding thrived from the mid-1700s to the late-1800s—at its height, there were twenty-two ship-building operations in Fell's Point. The principal goods were flour (milled in the Jones Falls Valley), coffee, sugar, and slaves. Residences were occupied by sea captains, crew, and skilled workers such as blacksmiths, ropemakers, riggers, and sailmakers.

The signature ship coming out of Fell's Point shipyards was the Baltimore Clipper, known for its starring role as privateer[†] in the War of 1812. Clipper ships were fast and maneuverable because of design changes geared to the Chesapeake Bay. To catch the relatively light winds in the bay, there was a lot of sail relative to the size of the vessel. To navigate shallower tributaries, Clippers featured shallow drafts. And Clippers were made with a tapered, sleek hull designed for speed. These features may have made Clippers unsta-ble in the hands of ordinary seamen, but Baltimore crews took full advantage of the ships' speed and agility, especially when those qualities were required in order for privateers to evade British warships. Clippers were the nautical

---

"[Jack and Bob] were fascinating, and they had yards and yards of stories… They were just neat people…. That was the beginning of a beautiful and lifelong friendship… It wound up with my dad head of the Preservation Society in the mid '70s. My mother was Sergeant at Arms…[and] I was doing low-level scout work for the Preservation Society. Knocking on doors, passing petitions, pouring beer at the [Fell's Point Fun] festival."

† Privateering, for the uninitiated, was basically legalized piracy in times of war. Privateers were authorized by the federal government (under "letters of marque") to wreak havoc on the opposition's commercial shipping, disrupting their economy and military supply chain. Captured goods were sold and revenues were distributed to the ship's owner, the captain, the crew, and the government according to a pre-determined formula. It was a high risk/ high reward business—successful privateers made a boatload of money (forgive the pun), unsuccessful privateers were literally and figuratively sunk.

CAPTAIN BOYLE
AND THE CHASSEUR

The Fell's Point privateers were an enormous thorn in the side of the British. The "thorniest" of the privateers was Captain Thomas Boyle and the legendary Chasseur. In a remarkable tale of bravado and guile, Boyle crossed the Atlantic and announced his one-ship embargo of the entire coastline of England and Ireland, surely one of the most audacious claims ever made by a sea captain at war.

His reputation had preceded him, and British commercial shipping was thrown into disarray. Britain re-deployed six fast warships to track him down, but he continued plundering British shipping, much to the embarrassment of the Royal Navy.

The loot included fourteen merchant vessels and cargo worth over $100,000. A year later, after another successful privateering run, Boyle and the Chasseur returned to Baltimore and were greeted by thousands lining both sides of the Patapsco River.

version of Muhammad Ali's boxing strategy: "float like a butterfly, sting like a bee."

In both the Revolutionary War and the War of 1812, the US had almost no navy; the coastline was vulnerable to embargo and sea-based attack. In the War of 1812, privateers outnumbered naval vessels more than twenty to one (517-23). While the Fell's Point privateers contributed mightily to the revolutionary cause, it was in the War of 1812 that the homegrown Baltimore Clippers played an arguably determinant role, as 126 privateers captured more than five hundred merchant vessels.[220]

The success of Fell's Point privateering in general and Captain Boyle in particular (see account in sidebar) provided much of the motivation for the British attack on Baltimore on September 13 and 14 in 1814. As the Preservation Society's website described it, "High up on Britain's list, they wanted to put Fell's Point to the torch. They vowed to set fire to this port that had so vexed them in this war, and burn it to the very cinders: wharves, homes, businesses, boats, shipyards, every last bit."[221]

The Brit's two-pronged attack, by land (through North Point and Hampstead Hill) and by sea (entering the Inner Harbor basin by subduing American forces at Fort McHenry), failed on both counts. On September 16, 1814, there was a "wild celebration"; Fell's Point had survived its first brush with mortality.

In 2012 Fell's Point was chosen as the inaugural site for the Middle Passage Ceremonies and Port Markers Project (MPCPMP),‡ a non-profit organization "established... to honor the two million captive Africans who perished during the transatlantic crossing known as the Middle Passage and the ten million who survived to build the Americas."

The slave trade is barely mentioned in historical accounts of Fell's Point, so it may have surprised many Baltimoreans when MPCPMP chose Fell's Point to launch their national campaign. Why was Fell's Point a major center for slavery commerce? Of course, there is the obvious: Baltimore and Maryland were southern-leaning in numerous matters from slavery to commerce; however, Baltimore's heroic Clipper ships were also, as Wikipedia's authors indelicately phrased it, "especially suited to moving low-density, high value *perishable* cargoes such as slaves" [emphasis added].

In 1808 the US banned the transatlantic slave trade, but the illegal slave trade continued. The fast and maneuverable Clippers were preferred by slave traders because they were superior vessels for evading the authorities. Further, Baltimore's sailors were adept at taking full advantage of the Clippers' swift but somewhat unstable handling. It was another high risk/high reward business, much like privateering—the residents of this "seafaring frontier" understood and perhaps reveled in that exact equation.

Slaves were often held in downtown slave jails and then transported to Fell's Point. As one author phrased it:

---

‡ Clearly the folks at MPCPMP need to take lessons from Baltimore's highway activists in how to create a catchy acronym.

A routine spectacle was the dreary procession of Black men, women, and children in chains along Pratt Street to Fell's Point, where ships waited to carry them south to New Orleans for auction. Weeping family members would follow their loved ones along the route; they knew their parting might be forever, as there would be no way to know where slaves shipped south would end up.[222]

Here we jump forward to the 1960s and '70s, when highway plans had six or eight lanes of elevated expressway ripping through the heart of Fell's Point (see Figure 21). A selection of historic buildings in that right-of-way help us complete Fell's Point's history.

First, the current Thames Point Apartments used to be the old National Can Building on Thames Street. When shipbuilding went into decline in the late 1800s, the waterfront was still bustling with shipping-related commerce—canning businesses, for example, moved into several former shipyards. One account listed six canning and packing plants in the vicinity of Aliceanna and Wolfe Streets.[223]

Next, the London Coffee House on South Bond Street goes back to the pre-Revolutionary War era and is thought to be the oldest coffee grinding and distribution house in America.§ [224] From 1840 to 1900 warehouses and wharves, such as Belt's at the foot of Fell Street and Brown's Wharf at the foot of Broadway, primarily handled coffee from South America bound for inland cities and towns.

Third is the Port Mission still standing today at 813-815 South Broadway. By the late 1800s most of the larger residences in Fell's Point, once

---

§ Romaine Sommerville, who headed the City's Commission for Historic and Architectural Preservation in the late '60s and early '70s, recounted how Fell's Point's bar scene was key in saving the London Coffee House. "When Willard Hackerman gave us some money to purchase the London Coffee House, he said that one of the reasons he was interested in Fell's Point is that the promotional literature from Loyola [College] says that it's near Fell's Point. It's a big attraction to college kids, and he thought, if it was that important to Loyola College in attracting students, there must be something down here."

owned by shipyard owners and fashionable families, had been converted to boarding houses for sailors. As one article characterized it, "Crime, drunkenness, and immorality ruled the streets."[225] Port Mission was established in 1881, one of several efforts to uplift morally afflicted seamen. In 1885 they published a map to heighten awareness of the considerable challenge involved in attempting to bring virtue to Fell's Point—it documented 323 saloons and 113 houses of ill-repute lining the streets. Writer Hamilton Owens speculated that the term "hooker" may have originated in Fell's Point due to the area's hooked shape and the extent of prostitution, saying Fell's Point "may or may not be responsible for this appellation, but it is certain that…there is a good reason for it."[226]

With their services much in demand, Port Mission established the Anchorage boarding house in the Recreation Pier building, later relocating to the site now occupied by the Admiral Fell Inn (another parcel in the 10-D alignment). Sailors flocked to both, perhaps less to be morally cleansed than to avoid being robbed and shanghaied, a not-infrequent occurrence at low-rent boarding houses.

Finally, the Horse You Came In On at 1626 Thames was one of many drinking establishments that would have been obliterated by highway plans. The bar claims a lineage going all the way back to 1775, which makes it the oldest continuously operating tavern in the country.¶

After World War II, waterfront industries that had been the lifeblood of Fell's Point for two centuries went into decline. The culprits included shipping industry changes and the emergence of interstates, which made trucking cheaper than rail or ships. When Fell's Point was targeted for expressway clearance in the early 1960s, that designation was both cause and effect of decline and disinvestment.

Still, its buildings had character and its people were characters.

¶ While the bar's name might conjure up visions of patrons arriving by horse, the real story dates to 1978 when Howard Gerber eyed the building as the location of his dream bar. Gerber made the down payment after a lucky day with the horses at Pimlico. The bar also claims to be the favored drinking establishment of Edgar Allan Poe and the location of Poe's last encounter with the living before his untimely demise, likely by alcohol poisoning.

THE EARLY HIGHWAY PLANS

Chief Engineer Nathaniel Smith's 1945 highway plan was the first to target the Fell's Point/Canton waterfront as a potential expressway corridor, although it was termed a "supplementary proposal." The 1960 Planning Department proposal was the first to advocate for the Harbor Route as the main east-west artery, hugging Pratt Street through downtown then following the Fell's Point/Canton waterfront and meeting up with the Harbor Tunnel Thruway at Boston Street. The plan was silent on the highway's impact on Fell's Point—in sixty-one pages of text (and thirty-six more pages of maps), the authors felt no need to defend the choice to rip through Baltimore's oldest seaport community.

The 1962 10-D plan also channeled the expressway through the heart of Fell's Point, crossing Broadway just above Thames and below Lancaster Street, as shown in Figure 21 below. Again, there was no mention of negative impacts on Fell's Point in the engineer's report or the separately commissioned Blair and Stein Associates report, "The Impacts of the East-West... Expressway."[227]

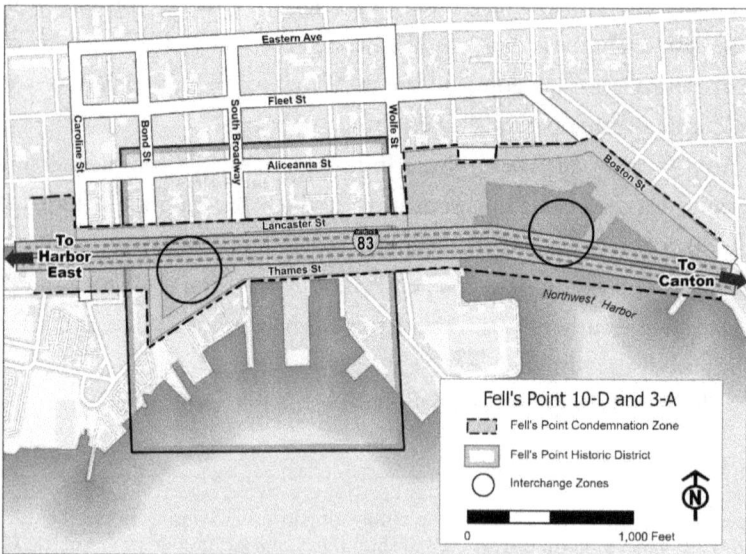

Figure 21. Highway corridor through Fell's Point: 10-D plan (I-95 with an interchange just west of Broadway); later under 3-A (I-83, with a half interchange east of Wolfe Street) (Scott Jeffrey, MS, GISP)

In the early and mid-1960s the expressway was seen as a fait accompli in southeast Baltimore—it was coming, and opposition was futile. Many residents saw the area as a slum and were anxious to use the condemnation money as a ticket to Dundalk or Essex. This point of view predominated among long-time residents; when the Preservation Society was formed, they represented a distinctly minority point of view.

In city council hearings for the condemnation ordinance (passed in a 17-1 vote) there was one memorable interchange. Councilman Tom Ward, the lone opponent, asked a State Roads Commission official if he found "anything of value" in his survey of Fell's Point. The official answered that "he walked around there one day and looked at the buildings, and he did not see anything worthwhile."[228] Acquisition proceeded in May 1967.

PRESERVATION SOCIETY

Tom Ward: *I remember (First District City Councilman) Duffy turned around to me, he says, "Tom, why are you trying to save that rat-infested, rotten neighborhood, Fell's Point? I was born and raised in that neighborhood. It's a horrible place… It's a slum. I want it torn down." He went on and on and on… What he told me was true.*

Interviewer: *If what he said was true, how did you square that with your efforts to save it?*

Tom: *Because it was historic.*[229]

The seeds were sown for the formation of the Preservation Society when Tom Ward and Lu Fisher joined forces in January 1967. The two frustrated Road Warriors met for lunch at Mount Vernon's Belvedere Hotel and conceptualized the group that would devote all its energies to saving Fell's Point and Federal Hill.

It did not seem like a winning combination: Ward (profiled in the "1960-1967" chapter) was a Bolton Hill resident and cantankerous city councilman who failed to line up even one more vote against the 10-D condemnation bills; Lu Fisher was a resident of Ruxton, an aspiring urban real estate investor who failed to perform the most obvious due diligence in purchasing a Fell's Point house. Neither had any connection to Fell's Point residents. It was an inauspicious beginning, and highway proponents can be excused for regarding this new player as a minor irritant, hardly a force to be reckoned with.

Nevertheless, this initial Ward-Fisher meeting constitutes another what-if scenario where the demise of Fell's Point was hanging in the balance—if Ward and Fisher had not joined forces, it is hard to envision other ways that the Preservation Society would have been formed. There would have been no lawsuit and no organized voices to counter those clamoring to get their relocation dollars and get out of town.

Ward and Fisher organized the first meeting of the Preservation Society on February 23, 1967. [230] Twenty-three individuals attended, including Jack Gleason and Bob Eney, newly arrived from New York City. Fisher, Ward, Eney, and Gleason became the core group of the Preservation Society,** but not one of them had experience in community advocacy or connections with Baltimore's movers and shakers. Nevertheless, their combined strengths proved to be exceptionally effective. Sports fans might recognize this as a "team that clicks," where the total is somehow greater than the sum of its parts.

As the Preservation Society's first president, Lu Fisher was a tenacious and inspiring leader, the most quoted spokesperson for many years. In 1966 Lu got connected to the architecture and preservation communities and helped bring them along to the cause. She also used her blueblood connections to raise money and generate buzz among Baltimore's opinion makers.

** This core group, according to my interviewees, deserved the greatest accolades for saving Fell's Point. However, other names also appear prominently in the record. Roland Read was the original proponent of the Fun Festival; he also purchased and renovated the Port Mission building on South Broadway and served as president of the Preservation Society for two years in the early 1970s. Margaret Dougherty also served as president in the mid-1970s. Jean Hepner bought and renovated the Captain Steel House in 1968 and later recalled "carrying her knitting, and a tape recorder hidden within, to tense Road Fight meetings with officials." Julian "Jack" Lapides was active over many years and, as a state senator, lent legitimacy and gave sage political advice.

Tom Ward was a household name after four rancorous years in city council, and, although he burned a few bridges, he could still get his telephone calls returned. As a lawyer he functioned as the Society's legal arm up until the lawsuit. Of critical importance, he reviewed the Federal-Aid to Highways Act of 1966 and found the basis for legal action that would eventually tie up highway plans and force the city to adopt an alternative it could not afford.

Bob Eney was the storyteller, the history and architecture expert who made the case to skeptics by turning mundane details into something remarkable and memorable. Eney volunteered to collect and organize all the documentation needed to apply for National Historic Register status. To anyone else that work would have been drudgery, but to him it was a neighborhood tapestry, a thing of beauty that he gradually unfolded.

Jack Gleason was the organizer, the strategist, and the best bridge-builder in the group. He served as the organization's third president, successfully guiding the legal strategy and partnering with Bob Eney to package the documentation for the National Historic Register.

On February 27 (four days after their first organizing meeting) the *Sun* reported that Preservation Society representatives attended a hearing for the Federal Hill and Fell's Point segments. Their first reported position was not complete opposition but rather to move the Fell's Point segment a block or two north, lessening the impact on historic houses in the Lancaster/Shakespeare Street corridor. [231]

Lu Fisher characterized this time and these positions as heavily compromised because "we didn't have anyone important on our side." Still, Lu forged important alliances that seeded the movement to save Fell's Point.

Lu Fisher, the "Ruxton radical"

Visitors to Fell's Point are immediately aware that Lucretia ("Lu") Fisher is regarded as a heroic figure—the Fell's Point Visitor Center bears her name along with a plaque signed by Senator Barbara Mikulski. Lu was the most visible and articulate spokesperson for saving Fell's Point.

Lu descended from an old and aristocratic family in Pittsburgh. Her father was a physician, and her mother had lineage to the Mayflower. Lu married her second cousin, Dr. Murray Fisher, who hailed from a Maryland horse-breeding family and attended Gilman and then Princeton before entering into practice as an internist at Johns Hopkins. Their 1933 engagement was announced in the *Sun* as an event "of interest to Baltimore and Pittsburgh Society."

The Fishers resided in tony Ruxton, the community that had maintained its isolation from Baltimore's urban grit by fighting and defeating a North Central light rail stop.[††] Some of Lu's light-rail-opponent neighbors must have been aghast that Lu actually attended meetings in West Baltimore in an attempt to put up a united front against the highway. Fellow Road Warriors referred to Lu and her friends as the "Ruxton Radicals."

In 1976 an interviewer described Fisher as "a handsome woman with pink cheeks, blue eyes, white hair, and a marvelous laugh." [232] Bob Eney called Lu "a live wire, a dynamo." Art Cohen referred to her as a "strong, strong personality...who would just not take 'no' for an answer... Well, she was determined, she was fearless." Others called her the visionary that held Fell's Point's anti-road movement together.[233] Geoff Mitchell, a young attorney assigned to help the Preservation Society, said Lu would "walk into meetings with Axelrod. She popped on a tape recorder, and he would say, 'You can't do that.' She'd say, 'Yes, I can.' She says, 'I'm going to record everything you say to me.'"

Aside from her passion for preservation and highway opposition, Fisher wrote two children's books and frequently expressed progressive views in letters to the editor of the *Sun*. In 1963, after a racial incident in Druid Hill Park brought calls for "law and order," Lu wrote to the *Sun*, "How do you teach respect for law and order in an environment that is continually frustrating and utterly lacking in the kinds of satisfactions every human ego needs? ... This is the 'social dynamite' that we ourselves have been guilty of building up in our cities... Let's get at the cause of the disease instead of only being concerned about the symptoms."[234]

---

†† The North Central light rail line, planned and built in the 1980s, connects Timonium to downtown, but there is a five-mile gap between the Falls Road and Timonium Road stations because of community opposition in Ruxton and Riderwood.

The Battle to Save Fell's Point

In 1976[235] and 2003[236] interviews, Fisher describes her introduction to Fell's Point real estate, a history-changing event for the Road Wars that would not have happened had Lu done her homework. In her words:

> I had heard that some architects had been very, very interested in old houses down here. So, my brother, who lived in New York, wanted to come down and see some old houses, and I said, "Well we'd better go to Fell's Point," …I didn't even know where it was.
>
> …It looked almost deserted; very, very few cars there, very few people. And, so, we saw this gorgeous eighteenth century house…. And the [owner of a] little bar next door said, "Just go in, it's vacant." She handed us a flashlight and said if we didn't come back in a half hour, she'd come looking for us. And so we did and we found that it was in… original condition, which really surprised us… We finally found the real estate office, a little office off Broadway…

The realtor (and probably most average Joes on the street) must have known the house was in the condemnation line. But Lu's naivete and impulsiveness were fortunate for the history of Fell's Point. She continues:

> It turned out it was for sale at such a low price, so we were sort of astounded! Right away we put some money down.
>
> That night…we were walking along the waterfront, and [ran into] this man who sort of looked as if he lived here… I said, "We just bought that house over there." I couldn't contain myself. And he said, "Oh yes, that is where they are going to put the expressway. I think they're going to take out three blocks." And my brother said, "Well, you know, we can't fight city hall… This was all too good to be true." …So, he went back to New York.
>
> And then the next day, I came back, and I went up in the house and spent some time. The second floor has got a wonderful room which just must have the best proportions, something that really gets you… So, I thought, well, I'll be damned if I'll let them put an expressway through this fantastic romantic site.

You could say that Lu Fisher bumbled her way into the Road Wars cause, another moment where the future of Fell's Point could have gone the other way—a more considered house-buying decision would have led Lu to retreat to her safe haven in Ruxton, thanking her lucky stars that she had dodged a bullet. Instead, she did buy that house in 1965, Lu's own "damn the torpedoes" moment.

A 1966 letter to the editor of the *Sun* revealed her deeply held desire to save the whole community, not just move the highway a block or two. She said, "Baltimore, born on the harbor, should make the most of its colorful past. Perhaps no other town on the eastern seaboard boasts eighteenth century houses facing the water such as we have here in Fell's Point…. Compared to Europe, America has a small historical heritage to preserve, and the old countries are preserving theirs, but we seem determined to destroy what little we have."[237]

An architect friend got Lu connected to the city's Commission on Architectural Preservation (CHAP). Connections at CHAP led to connections at Baltimore Heritage—she joined the board and helped form an expressway committee. In an effort to leave no stone unturned, in 1967 Lu arranged for an archaeological dig on two of her properties. The effort turned up a skeleton, a mummified cat, and "two long-stemmed clay pipes of the kind used in colonial days."[238] Highway planners did not seem particularly impressed, but they would have been wise to consider the level of effort put forth rather than the easily dismissed archaeological finds.

While there was much to admire about Lu and her key in role forming and leading the Preservation Society, there were more than a few critics. When long-term residents criticized the Preservation Society as the "silk stockings," the gentrifiers, and (what we now call) flippers, Exhibit 1 was Lu Fisher, who had a profitable business in flipping Fell's Point houses. To some people, her involvement in the Preservation Society was tainted by self-interest.‡‡

---

‡‡ Tony Norris, proprietor of Bertha's restaurant in Fell's Point, recounted an instance where Lu and Bob Eney had a falling out over a Fell Street house. "[Bob] loved the house, and so he talked constantly to guy, 'If you ever decide you're going to sell the house let me know.'" One day Bob went to look at the house, and Lu asked if she could come along. "[Bob] is being sort

Lu's defense was undoubtedly accurate. She said, "No big-time investor would ever touch the area with the condemnation ordinance hanging over it. I understood some big investors are waiting, holding back until the ordinance is lifted, but hopefully, by then, all the houses would be in the hands of private owners, people who love them."[239] Bob Eney defended Lu, saying she "liked old houses…and she wanted them saved." She only sold to "people if they said that they would restore them. And she didn't gouge them." Another interviewee commented, "She had the vision to buy property that nobody else wanted."[240] In a *Baltimore Sun* article, Lu said she believed putting her money where her mouth was added to her credibility: "We felt that, if we backed our feelings with cash, we might get our point across."[241]

There was one more downside with Lu: she was not particularly good at bridge building with people outside her socio-economic level. Joe McNeely said that Gleason and Eney were "bridge people," but "Lu always had trouble feeling comfortable in those settings and vice versa." Still, to her credit, the record finds Lu at several Rosemont meetings in 1968 and 1969. The Rosemont folks undoubtedly regarded her as a fish out of water, but they were more than happy to have her in the same pond.

THE COURT OF PUBLIC OPINION—THE '60S

When Lu Fisher rose to speak in opposition to the highway through Fell's Point, she was jeered and heckled by highway supporters, those who wanted the city to buy them out so they could move to East Baltimore County. This was February 15, 1967, one week before the first meeting of the Preservation Society. The *Sun* article said, "The hecklers were most particularly contemptuous of the fact that so many defenders of Fell's Point and Federal Hill lived either in some other part of the city or outside the city." In a later article, Mrs. Charles Jones of 1611 Shakespeare Street echoed this same sentiment, "This

---

of delicate, [avoiding the subject of] money, so walking down the steps, [Lu] says to him, 'How much do you want for this house?' And he says, '$15,000.' She says, 'I'll take it.' So, [Bob] was mad at her for a long time but then they made amends…"

neighborhood is rundown. The people from the suburbs come down here but they don't have to live here. The ships come in here and throw off all that soot… Well, anytime they give me my money I'm ready to move."[242]

That February meeting was a mere warm-up for the raucous May 23 hearing held at the Recreation Pier Building on Thames Street. This time the young Preservation Society was organized but they were outnumbered and blindsided—the hearing was attended by an estimated five hundred people, the majority of whom were adamantly in favor of the current highway plan. They shouted down highway opponents, chanting, "Where were you when Broadway needed you?" They loudly cheered one city councilman who said the members of the Preservation Society "are not interested in you people; they never were interested in you people."[§§]

The *Sun's* account reported that, "After about 20 minutes of shouts and accusations, [the highway supporters] stormed out of the meeting when a man known as Rocky yelled, 'Let's everybody walk out. Let the silk stockings hold their own meeting.'" A shocked Lu Fisher commented, "That was a very interesting meeting, perhaps a little more exciting than we had planned."[243]

Jack Gleason, interviewed seven years later in 1974, was still stewing about what had happened, because the resulting schism had been almost impossible to repair. Apparently an alternate highway plan, essentially a back-of-the-envelope draft by one member of the Preservation Society, appeared to impact St. Stanislaus Church. Although the plan never had any status, the First District Council delegation (all highway supporters), showed it to the pastor, who urged the congregation to oppose the plan at the May 23 meeting. "So, we ran head-on into that opposition," Gleason said, "and that began a separation, a cleavage between the preservationists and the local citizenry that was very difficult to overcome and perhaps to this day has not been totally recovered."

Following these disastrous hearings, the city council passed the condemnation ordinance on May 29, 1967, with Tom Ward providing the only

---

§§ This councilman was not named but was probably Dominik "Mimi" DiPietro, in which case the reader may want to pronounce this phrase the way Mimi undoubtedly said it: "never interested in youzz people."

"nay." 1967 was not shaping up to be a great year for the Fell's Point highway opponents—it would be a long road to win in the court of public opinion.

However, there was a trickle of good news. Articles began appearing in the *Sun* about new investment in Fell's Point. These articles were likely the result of the Preservation Society's "counter-propaganda campaign" designed to offset highway builders' characterization of Fell's Point as a derelict slum that Baltimore should be glad to be rid of. A May 1967 article cited fifteen buildings purchased for redevelopment purposes, including several within the condemnation lines. John Herndon, the owner of one new antique store in the 800 block of South Broadway, described his property as the "second lane of the expressway going east." Herndon had an excellent crystal ball; he was quoted as saying, "There will be a hue and cry in the storm. I don't think they will ever build it here." Eney was reported to be buying a property "smack in the middle" of the expressway alignment. Lu Fisher already owned eight properties.

A bigger step toward winning hearts and minds occurred a few months later, in October. The Preservation Society had been characterized as stuffed shirts interested only in the esoteric principles of historic preservation. As if to give evidence to the contrary, the group decided to put Fell's Point on the map[¶¶] using the Point's reputation as a place for uninhibited fun (not to mention drunkenness and debauchery) to bring attention to their cause. The first Fell's Point Fun Festival was held on October 8, 1967, only eight months after the Preservation Society was formed.[***] Multiple sources credit Roland Read as the mastermind. Tom Ward described it this way:

Roland [said]… "We're going to have Jumpin' Judy Shows, and plays, and poetry readings, and beer stands. We're going to have a train that…

¶¶ Jack Gleason later explained how the name "Fell's Point" had fallen into disuse; residents instead called it the "foot of Broadway." So, the Preservation Society really was responsible for literally putting Fell's Point back on the map.

*** One of the Fun Festival attendees in 1967 was UCDT staffer Stew Bryant. He wrote a memo to Norm Klein and other Skidmore staffers with the subject *The Fell's Point Happening*. He said the festival and parallel interest in houses on the waterfront should be reason enough to consider new options for the highway through Fell's Point. (Parsons, p. 202).

winds around the historic neighborhood." In other words an electric train and...cars that people could sit in. We all thought he was nuts, but he did it....The first Fun Festival had one beer truck that I worked on, and we had the train and we had a fantastic number of people, people came from everywhere. I'd say twenty to forty thousand people showed up. It was so successful. So the next year we had about ten beer trucks and we had a couple trains.

Both Fisher and Eney later admitted that they were initially opposed. Eney said, "I didn't want it, but Roland did. He was determined."[244] Fisher was reluctant because she believed they needed to prioritize the historic survey that would be the basis for their lawsuit. She went along and later admitted it was a brilliant idea.

The *Baltimore Sun* review declared, "They came from all over—from Roland Park, Bolton Hill, East Baltimore—to view the work of 100 artists, witness costume dances by 7 ethnic groups, attend the fife and drum performance of a Revolutionary War drill team, value the wares of auction dealers, and enjoy oysters on the half shell."[245]

More turn-around news: By January 1968, the *Sun* was reporting thirty properties purchased and at least twelve under active renovation. Four of those were storefronts being repurposed for commercial uses.[246] By 1969, there were multiple signs that public sentiment was shifting toward saving Fell's Point and away from the road builders.

In February 1969, James Dilts featured Fell's Point in his highly regarded *Baltimore Sun* column, "The Changing City." His piece "Fell's Point—Goodbye To All That?" articulated what was at stake: "Fell's Point reminds John Dos Passos of the squares of Venice, a place of inherent drama and excitement where the stage seems always set for a play. What makes this waterfront setting especially appealing is that it is completely natural; there's nothing tricked up or Williamsburgian about Fell's Point."[247]

In March the Preservation Society held another promotion/fundraiser, this time directly highlighting Fell's Point's architecture and history. The first Fell's Point Historic Home Tour attracted 355 people touring twelve houses.[248] That was 355 people telling neighbors and friends that the seeds of revival were being sown but that highway plans threatened to scuttle a burgeoning back-to-the-city movement.

Influential organizations were starting to line up with the Preservation Society. On May 26, 1969, the Baltimore Chapter of American Institute of Architects weighed in. Their resolution includes particularly memorable phrasing: "Whereas, the impact on the senses of sight, sound, and smell together with the physical barrier and hazard introduced by the proposed major vehicular thoroughfare bisecting Fell's Point materially deteriorates the character and atmosphere of the area."[†††][249] The resolution included one signatory, M. J. "Jay" Brodie, whose public job as deputy commissioner in the Housing Department was in conflict with his private opinion. Brodie's boss, Robert Embry, was also in quiet opposition to much of the expressway system and likely granted latitude to employees that worked not-too-surreptitiously against the highways.

In the files of the Preservation Society there are letters from organizations one would not expect to be involved in the highway controversy. In a December 1969 letter, the Baltimore Museum of Art registered both support for the historic area and disdain for the highway, saying, "Baltimore appears to be hellbent for self-destruction" by not respecting "the importance of preserving the Fell's Point and Federal Hill areas of our city."[250] Lu Fisher, the maverick blueblood, is presumed responsible for this kind of support from the arts community.

In October 1969 the *Sun* editorial board shifted their stance. Previously, the *Sun*'s attitude had been essentially, "Let's work through these problems and get on with it." Their October 28 editorial concluded, "Unless it can be shown that Fell's Point is the one and only place for the road, it is reasonable to say that one current alternative for Fell's Point is no expressway at all." There may have been a few "silk stockings" mixing with the locals at Fell's Point bars that night.

But all of this would have added up to not much if ethnic southeast Baltimore still wanted the highway to come through and buy them

††† Luckily these carefully chosen words were not read at one of those divisive 1967 meetings. You can almost hear the howls of laughter and derision from the local critics of the Preservation Society.

out. Interstate Division's Joe Axelrod gave an October 1969 speech to the Engineering Society, still portraying Fell's Point's defenders as out of touch with long-time residents. An incognito MAD representative reported, "He described Fell's Point as an area whose historical significance 'was only recently discovered by Johnny-come-latelies.'"[251]

The newly organized Southeast Council Against the Road (SCAR) provided the rejoinder to Axelrod, as well as to those disastrous 1967 meetings. In May 1969 they organized a meeting with ten constituent neighborhood organizations representing most of ethnic southeast Baltimore—the one hundred attendees browbeat their three city council representatives over their support for the highway. The *Sun* reported that, "Councilman Dominic Mimi DiPietro, his face still red from 2 hours of heckling, catcalls, and boos, finally agreed to introduce a bill in the city council that would require the expressway to bypass Canton, Fell's Point, and Highlandtown."[252] DiPietro's bill did not advance, and the councilman soon returned to the fold of highway backers. Mimi was all about patronage jobs, and he knew the city administration would not reward highway opponents.

SCAR also put a charge into the October 1969 Fell's Point Fun Festival. A pint-sized firecracker named Barbara Mikulski was on the megaphone sending out an SOS for "Radio Free Fell's Point." Mikulski launched three of her famous soundbites. She derided UDCT as the "Urban Design Concrete Team"; an anti-road petition was promoted with the phrase, "We are being politically courted but legally extorted"; and the future senator's most famous catchphrase made its first appearance: "The British couldn't take Fell's Point, the termites couldn't take Fell's Point, and God damned, the State Roads Commission can't take Fell's Point either." Fun Festival attendance again moved up the chart, reaching sixty thousand.[253]

The year 1969 closed with a minor coup at a December meeting of the influential Citizen's Planning and Housing Association (CPHA). Tasked with reviewing UDCT's four alternative highway configurations through Fell's Point, the CPHA Transportation Sub-Committee instead recommended a "no build" option. The record of the meeting attributes the change to Barbara Mikulski's strident arguments against the Fell's Point segment.[254]

FELL'S POINT CERTIFIED AS HISTORIC

"Colorful" is not one of the qualifying criteria for the National Register of Historic Places. If it had been, the Fell's Point application might have been quite a fun read, not to mention a cinch for approval. Given this glaring omission, the Preservation Society had to sell Fell's Point's history and architecture as worth saving even though, to the uneducated eye, it was an unremarkable collection of run-down homes and businesses, essentially an old port whose time had come and gone.

In early 1967 Tom Ward reviewed the Highway Act of 1966 and its counterpart, Section 106 of the National Historic Preservation Act of 1966, and saw a potential ally in the US Government, correctly perceiving that National Historic Register status could be the basis of a successful legal challenge to the highway. This new information was undoubtedly the driving force behind the formation and growth of the Preservation Society. Ward and Lu Fisher were able to persuade doubters and skeptics that the Preservation Society had a chance of altering the course of events heretofore regarded as inevitable.

By July 1967 Bob Eney and Jack Gleason were out taking pictures and digging through records to build their case. It was painstaking work, but, at least for Bob, it was a labor of love, really his calling. In a 2016 interview Tom Ward remembers:

> Bob, on behalf of the Preservation Society, examined every building in Fell's Point. And recorded every detail on plats as to the historic items on all the buildings that still exist. Recorded all the buildings. And he did the same thing in Federal Hill…and Montgomery Street. And he turned them all in, these precise drawings, to the National Register of Historic Places… He said I can do this, and he did it… Eney won the battle, and I'm going to say Eney because I'm telling you… I can't speak highly enough of him. He did the work that won the battle.

I examined the application in the Preservation Society archives. It included six three-inch binders of documentation—every property in the proposed historic district was described in terms of its original construction, the architectural elements that made it typical (or atypical) of historical architectural styles, and the known and notable persons that occupied the property. There were usually six pages of information about *each* property. It was an enormous undertaking made a little easier by Eney and Gleason's remarkable knowledge of architecture; Eney would pinpoint the original construction date just by observing architectural details.[255]

The Fell's Point application was the first in the country to be nominated by the state historic preservation officer (SHPO). Maryland's SHPO, Orlando Rideout IV, followed a state-sanctioned process, which gave Fell's Point a leg up.

Bob Eney, in a 2004 interview, offered an additional (and highly entertaining) interpretation of the approval process:

> And we did manage to get on the National Register ████,[‡‡‡] who had worked for Agnew, she took the forms that we had filled out, she took it to Agnew and he sent them over to Dr. Garvey at the Department of the Interior. *And in 3 days*, we were on the National Register [emphasis added]. And the City of Baltimore went crazy.
>
> … But the contractors were furious with Agnew. Because he was so dumb. He had no idea what he had done. He didn't know that he had put us on the National Register for a community that's blocking his highway, that he wanted to build.
>
> Interviewer: He was just doing payback to ████ for all of her work?

---

‡‡‡ Eney's 2004 interview names this person; however, I am withholding the name because I have been unable to obtain any further corroboration of the person's role vis-à-vis Agnew. Nancy Schamu (long time employee of the Maryland Historic Trust) disputed this version of events, saying "I can't imagine where Bob Eney came up with that story." I repeat the story here as essentially just that, "a story."

Eney's version contains another interesting sidebar. He states that, "When the mayor [D'Alesandro] saw that [the listing on the National Register], he fired Romaine Somerville who was head of CHAP [Baltimore City Commission of Historic Architectural Preservation]. He fired Romaine because he was positive she did it. And so, we all called, everybody called the mayor and said, 'Romaine had absolutely nothing to do with this.' And then Maryland Historic Trust, Lenny Ridout, did call the mayor and told the mayor, he said, 'They came to us for help and we helped them. That's what our agency is for.' So, he reinstated Romaine back there, because she was good."

Eney: Yeah. Right. Because she had *bagged for him for so long...* She had gone out and *collected all that graft money* from the different businessmen. *And she was still doing it, even when he was in the White House* [emphasis added]. Unbelievable, isn't it?[256]

Here lies the penultimate Road Wars irony—if Eney's story is true (and I have been unable to corroborate it), Fell's Point obtained the means to fight the highway by virtue of the strategic use of relationships involved in Maryland's entrenched system of engineering and contractor bribery. The nod-nod-wink-wink system that had bloated the bank accounts of both contractors and politicians (providing an underhanded motivation to build highways of questionable value), was employed by preservation advocates in the ultimately successful effort to defeat the highway through Fell's Point, canceling all those lucrative contracts.

Fifty years later it is difficult to discern fact from fiction; however, there is supporting evidence of the political intervention aspect of Eney's version. Fell's Point's initial application, dated November 26, 1968, was turned down; their follow-up application, dated March 24, 1969, was approved on March 27, 1969—this ultra-fast three-day turn-around matches Eney's narrative.[257] Both the speed of the approval and the 180-degree about-face are certainly consistent with someone "greasing the skids." Since the Preservation Society did not have many friends in high places, the involvement of Agnew does appear to fit as a piece of the puzzle.

Bob Eney's work is prominent in the application. This sketch of the Robert Long House (Figure 22), taken directly from the application, is Eney's work.

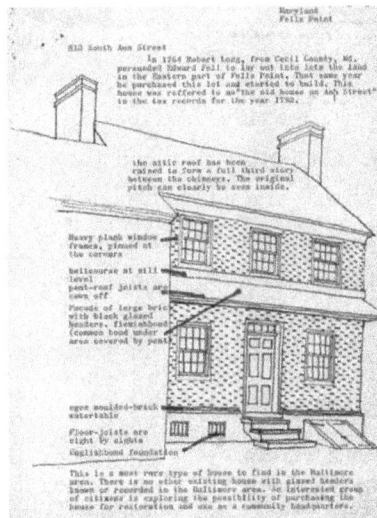

Figure 22. Bob Eney's sketch of the Robert Long House, from the application for National Register status

Bob Eney, Mr. History

Destroy [Fell's Point] and you destroy a major portion of Baltimore's most precious possession, not just tourism potential, but the history, beauty and heritage that belongs to all who live here.

Robert L. Eney, in a letter to the editor of the *Baltimore Sun*[258]

Whenever Fell's Pointers had a question about the history of a house or a park or a shipyard or a bar, they tracked down "Mr. History," Bob Eney.[259] Eney, always glad to commiserate on Fell's Point history and architecture, would spin a yarn that supplied the questioner with ample material for cocktail parties for years to come.§§§

That Eney was there to take on the National Register application in 1967-1968 seems beyond coincidental, one of those inexplicable it-was-meant-to-be intersections of people and history and place. The job combined Bob's three passions: architecture, history, and Fell's Point; it utilized Bob's incredible grasp and memory of architectural and historical detail; and it capitalized on his unique ability to bring history alive through storytelling. Perhaps the cosmos was also in the anti-expressway camp.

Bob was born in Baltimore and spent his formative years in Dundalk, where his father was a business owner. He graduated from Dundalk High School, but, as his friend Tony Norris (proprietor of Bertha's and a long-time Fell's Point resident) explained, "College didn't work for him."[260] Norris said, "Bob was severely dyslexic, and, when he was a young man, they told him that he was stupid, but he wasn't... He was interested in old houses when he was ten years old. [He would] come down here [to Fell's Point] on a streetcar to look at all the houses." His eye for design resulted in his first professional

---

§§§ One of Bob's many entertaining stories: "In my era, the famous thing on Caroline Street was the counterfeiter.... This man had assembled, on the second floor of a building down there, a huge printing press. And he printed money like crazy. They finally tracked it down.... And when they raided this building, they couldn't get the press out of the building because it was too big. And they couldn't figure out how he got it in there. So, they tore off the roof of the building and with a crane lifted the press up and brought it out." (Source: *Fell's Point Out of Time* interview with Bob Eney)

job as a visual display artist for the Lord & Taylor department store on Fifth Avenue in New York City.

While in New York he met Jack, who shared Bob's passion for urban and historical architecture. The move back to Baltimore came as a result of Bob's job offer at Hochschild Kohn department store. Tony said Bob and Jack were "like the odd couple." Bob was impulsive, extroverted, even a little clownish; Jack was the introvert, thoughtful, deliberate, and fastidious. Because the two seemed joined at the hip, many assumed they were a gay couple; however, Tony said Jack was "most definitely straight," and if Bob was gay, he apparently stayed in the closet.

Eney, in a 2004 interview, explains the dawning of this fascination with Fell's Point and its historic houses:

When I was a kid living in Baltimore, I went to art appreciation classes at the Baltimore Museum every Saturday morning. And then, one day they brought us down to Fell's Point and they showed us... [architectural details like] Flemish bond brick... They opened up a door to a house and showed us this black and white marble floor, old, dirty... But, they were telling us that these had been sea captains' houses, and she was showing us different balusters and things. I was very impressed by it and it stuck in my mind.

So later, when I was working in New York, and I got an opportunity to come back to Baltimore to work... I said, "I'm going to go back to Fell's Point and find one of those old sea captain's houses and fix it up." And I got down there and I saw Lu Fisher was already in, looking for houses down there.

Bob's involvement with the Preservation Society was risky relative to his job. Tom Ward remembered that Bob's boss "was in favor of this highway, and he threatened Bob with being fired." However, Bob's display windows were drawing customers. At Christmas time, Baltimoreans "came down by the thousands and looked at these windows." Tom added, "[Bob] was a genius at all that kind of stuff."

Norris remembers, "I never counted them, but we used to say [Bob] had

five thousand architecture books." The astounding thing was that he committed the content of all those books to memory. "I mean, he could tell you if
a house was built between 1790 and 1795 or what it looked like four years
earlier," Norris recalled.

Steve Bunker, a long-time Fell's Point resident, shop owner, and one-
time president of the Fell's Point Community Organization, said, "Other
people could buy the property and…create some political front to fend off
the highway. But for the community to be appreciated in its historical context, it really took somebody like Bob Eney…. Whatever has been done to
save Fell's Point, has been done on the foundation that Bob Eney laid. We
all should be very grateful to him for that." He added, "He's a real nice guy,
too…the salt of the earth. I love Bob."[261]

Toward the end of Bob's life, he was afflicted with Alzheimer's, and Tony
and Laura Norris became his caretakers. There was a poignant moment when
Tony showed Bob a video of his younger self discussing Fell's Point architecture. Bob no longer recognized himself; still, Tony added, "Bob looked at it,
and he says, 'That guy knows what he's talking about.'"

The story will return to Bob Eney's pivotal role in saving Fell's Point, but
for now we close with bittersweet memories recorded when Bob passed away
in October 2016. Senator Barbara Mikulski said:

> Bob was truly one of a kind. Smart, energetic, talented; he had it all
> and was just such a great guy. …The history of Fell's Point was his pas-
> sion, and the people of Fell's Point were his pals… He was one of my
> favorite dance partners, along with Jack Gleason, at the Preservation
> Balls. His idea of fun was having ouzo shooters at Mike Glyphis' bar
> or seeing John Waters at Edith's Shopping Bag… He loved being down
> by the waterfront. We can see his mark on so many things, from the
> Admiral Fell Inn to helping Bertha find her mussels. He helped me
> find my own home on Ann Street, a home that meant so much to me,
> and helped me furnish it with unique items, like chairs from the ladies'
> shoe department at Hutzler's.

Andrew Mazurek, who purchased his family's home from the city after it had been taken by condemnation, said: "Bob loved these houses. If you had a question about a piece of molding, he would draw something on a napkin as he sat in a bar. He was an amazing person." Andrew's wife, Joanne, added: "A half a dozen people have stopped me on the streets and said, 'I wouldn't be here if it weren't for him…'" You could generalize from that—Fell's Point might not be there if it weren't for him, too.

"THE HIPPIE VILLAGE"

Fell's Point was jeopardized not only by the highway but by the long period of vacancy due to highway acquisitions (see Figure 23). This is yet another fork in the road where Fell's Point was almost lost: The opposition had delayed the expressway, and, in the meantime, properties were going downhill almost to the point that there would be no salvaging them. Ninety-nine houses stood vacant, and blight spread as neighboring houses became abandoned too. Joe McNeely recounted how squatters saved Fell's Point in collusion with Bob Embry, City Housing Commissioner:

Figure 23. Vacant houses in Fell's Point in 1980 (source: Society for the Preservation of Federal Hill and Fell's Point)

We occupied a whole bunch of houses in Fell's Point. We broke into them and started to live in them. I think there were seventy; we did it over the weekend and the next week we went to Embry and said, we're in these houses; we want to stay in them; otherwise, they're going to keep deteriorating; that's a problem for the neighborhood. Embry made us a deal. I had one of the houses on Bond Street. I had to pay $70 a month or turn in receipts of $70 that I had invested in the house. And Bob let us do that. He didn't ask Schaefer; we knew he wasn't going to ask Schaefer...

We were kind of a cool collection of people. Like Roy was a cabinet maker and I didn't know anything about carpentry. I knew a little about plumbing...each person was a specialist in something. People would go out in the street and yell, "Does anybody have a big ladder?" Somebody... would come along. The house that I had had electricity but no water. The house next to me had water but no electricity. So, I had a big orange cord going out the back of my house to theirs and they had a hose that came into my house, and that's how we started.

Bob Eney called this free-spirited and completely unplanned movement a "hippie village." McNeely continued with an anecdote that has become part of Road Wars lore:

One day Schaefer was driving down Shakespeare Street and...he sees this guy, Roy Sprengelmeyer, who was about six-foot-three, cabinet maker, going into one of the houses...that Schaefer knows is one of the city's houses. Stops the car, gets out, says to him, "What are you doing here?" Sprengelmeyer looks at him and says, "I live here. Who the hell are you?" Schaefer: "What do you mean you live here?" Sprengelmeyer: "I pay rent to the city and this is my house, I'm going to own it one day. What are you doing here?" Well, you can imagine how that went down.

This story has been repeated (and perhaps embellished) by other Road Warriors. Stu Wechsler's account adds the following: "Schaefer said, 'You know, young man, you're going to lose all this investment when the expressway comes through,' and Sprengelmeyer says, 'Bob Embry says it's never coming through.' Schaefer says, 'Embry get over here!' And he made Embry send out hand-written notes to everybody leasing housing in the expressway right-of-way, saying that the expressway was coming through and they were going to lose their money."

Bob Embry and Jay Brodie's "Fifth Column"

Several of my interviewees gave Bob Embry a lot of credit for saving Fell's Point, partly because of the rental program that prevented irreversible decline. An account later in this chapter reveals that he had a hand in the regulatory review process that was another saving grace for Fell's Point. Embry also influenced D'Alesandro's decisions to spare Federal Hill and bypass Rosemont. Later he is credited with saving 150 homes in Federal Hill by moving the I-395/Light Street connector five blocks north to Conway Street.

In the city archives a March 1974 internal memo said Embry authored a document that advocated for dropping I-83 through southeast Baltimore. Moreover, Stu Wechsler (MAD's first president) said that that Embry and then Deputy Housing Commissioner Jay Brodie surreptitiously helped highway opponents. "Couple of times [MAD and RAM] went up to this office on Sundays and they fed us information. Embry and Brodie were opposed to it."

Brodie confirmed Wechsler's statement. "Yes, we did meet with opponents periodically…including Barbara Mikulski… We saw ourselves as 'the Fifth Column.'" It is reminiscent of UDCT staff actively working with the highway opposition while on the Road establishment payroll.

When I interviewed Embry in 2019, I asked if there was a conflict between his public role and private views. He said no, simply because he did not have "to publicly advocate… that [the highway] be built. So, I don't think there was any tension between my view that it should not be built and any public statement that I made or was required to make."

The mayor put a stop to the rental program. The community raised a ruckus and pestered the mayor to reinstitute it. However, Preservation Society attorney Geoff Mitchell reported, "Bob Embry has told Lu Fisher and myself that the best way to get the rental program reinstituted under his control is for everybody involved to lay off the mayor and stop calling this to his attention. Embry, as you know, was the instigator of the rental program at the outset. In light of this, I think we should do nothing."[262]

McNeely pointed out, "They couldn't evict us again. Schaefer was smart enough to know that wasn't going to look good." So, the rental program continued. "As a result of that," McNeely added, "Bob [Embry] became appointed the Chair of the City Coordinating Committee to get the road done. That was Schaefer's punishment to him…"¶¶¶

DESIGN CONCEPT TEAM FAILS FELL'S POINT

Baltimore's "platitudinous planners," the Urban Design Concept Team (UDCT), had won two bloody and costly wars to save Rosemont and Federal Hill. They had been accused of aiding and abetting the enemy, employees had been fired for sharing too much information, and Nathaniel Owings had not gained any friends when he repeatedly went over the heads of the city over-sight group in the cause of saving the Inner Harbor and Federal Hill. Owings and UDCT had no more arrows in their quiver for the Fell's Point fight.

To some extent this was a matter of unfortunate timing. UDCT eval-uated the Fell's Point segment in early 1968—their four alternatives were reviewed with the community in October of that year. All held to the 10-D alignment, going right through the heart of Fell's Point. It was another year before Fell's Point gained historic status and enjoyed more popular support. But by then, the important decisions had been made and UDCT was starting to wrap up—the end could not come too soon for exasperated city officials. Had Nat Owings gone back to his oversight group and said that Fell's Point's

¶¶¶ Embry confirmed that his appointment as Mayor's Transportation Coordinator came as a result of his opposition to the highway. Source: interview recorded for the "Fell's Point 1975" documentary video, Jacqueline Greff, Tonal Vision, courtesy Montgomery College.

National Register status required them to consider new alternatives, he would have risked life and limb.

The Preservation Society was dead set against all four UDCT options. There was no option to bypass Fell's Point—it was not until 1972 that the city considered a less destructive cut-and-cover tunnel, as well as a tunnel under the harbor south of the community. The Preservation Society's position paper from November 15, 1968, said there were "no meaningful changes in previous route alignments." They had a few choice words for UDCT: they "have proven to be nothing more than a four and a half million dollar sugar pill fed to the people of this city by the State Roads Commission, the mayor, and City Council of Baltimore."[263] A later (February 1969) letter from Lu Fisher reviews a more comprehensive UDCT report and acknowledges the team's success in guiding the highway away from Federal Hill: "The team is to be congratulated for this accomplishment but the results of departure from 'the givens' has not gone nearly far enough."[264]

UDCT's final recommendation for Fell's Point was an elevated highway using the existing condemnation corridor. This was essentially no change from 10-D, except that the Fell's Point segment was now the I-83 connector to I-95 rather than part of the main route. At the time (1970), Preservation Society advocates viewed the 3-A route (which moved I-95 from the Inner Harbor to the Fort McHenry crossing) as a victory for Federal Hill but no gain at all for Fell's Point. In retrospect, however, if UDCT had failed on this alignment issue, Fell's Point and Federal Hill would have been on the main artery for I-95, and it is very doubtful that anything or anyone could have stopped the main highway connecting the entire eastern seaboard.

When asked to explain their recommendation for an elevated highway, an unnamed UDCT staffer (likely Stew Bryant) said, "The Interstate Division said it should go there; they told Greiner Company, and Greiner told us. Why? Because it's cheap." A cut-and-cover tunnel had been considered but rejected because it cost four times the amount of the elevated highway.[265]

UDCT had one other answer to the charge of ignoring Fell's Point: that joint development adjacent to and under the highway would counter negative impacts, making the highway an asset to the community. In their final report, UDCT quoted a subcontractor who said the "construction of an interstate highway presents unique opportunities for revitalizing the area so as to accomplish two major objectives: enhancing the physical, social, and economic conditions of area residents; and improving Fell's Point's position as a distinctive and viable part of the City of Baltimore."[266] If there were a hall of fame for consultants' lies in the interests of their clients, this would rank right up there with whoever pronounced the *Titanic* to be "unsinkable." This folly is revealed in UDCT's renderings of the Fell's Point segment depicting exciting urban life happily coexisting cheek by jowl with the expressway. (See Figure 24.)

In Figure 25, UDCT's architects have taken great liberties in the interest of selling the highway. One might speculate that this plan was never presented at a community meeting because the architects would have been laughed off the stage. The obvious deceptions start with the incredible disappearing highway—only the supporting pillars are rendered. There is complete disregard for the dark, unwelcoming, noisy, exhaust-filled space below. "Tourists shopping" under the highway? Then the ultimate fantasy—the space under the expressway at Broadway is dubbed the "Town Center." No, that is not a joke.

501.51 lancaster street landscaping

Figure 24. The peaceful ambience of the highway at Lancaster Street. (Urban Design Concept Associates, Corridor Development, Segments 4 and 5, 1970)

The absence of alignment alternatives for Fell's Point is a glaring omission from UDCT's otherwise admirable efforts to develop a less destructive highway plan. Nathaniel Owings was defensive about UDCT's treatment of Fell's Point, saying, "it's a questionable historic area… It isn't all that good. You can get sentimental. We can do a better job with reconstruction."[267]

I asked Joe McNeely about UDCT's failure to address Fell's Point. He said, "I think they thought the southeast portion was in the bag. They had the politicians…." He also stressed the unfortunate timing, saying, "It was easier to dismiss Lu Fisher [in 1968] than Barbara Mikulski [in 1972]."

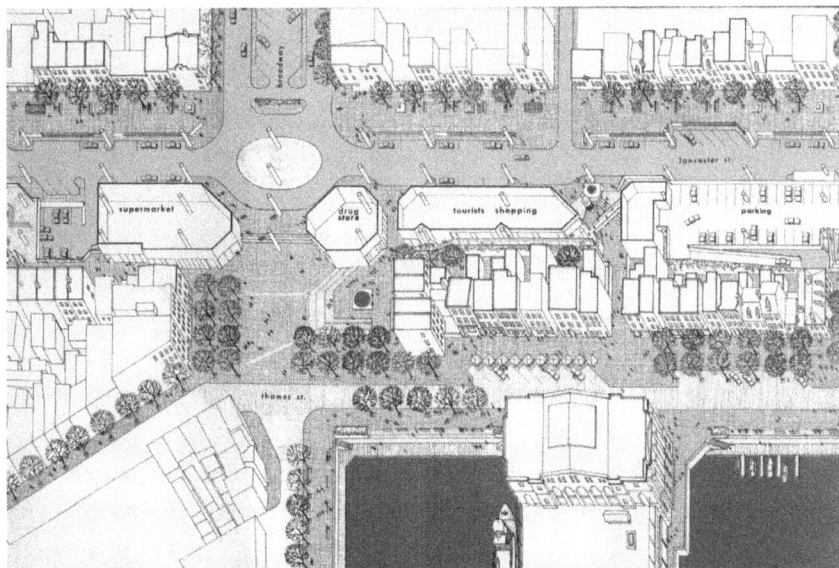

Figure 25. UDCT's joint development plan for the foot of Broadway–look closely because the only evidence of a highway is the support columns. (Urban Design Concept Associates, Corridor Development, Segments 4 and 5, 1970)

THE COURT OF PUBLIC OPINION—THE '70S

In the 1970s the Preservation Society perfected the art of selling fun with the dual purpose of calling attention to their cause and raising badly needed funds, especially for mounting legal costs. In June 1970, the Society organized the inaugural Harbor Ball, held in the ballroom at the Recreation Pier. This became an immensely popular and lucrative annual event. More importantly (and much like fundraisers for Jane Jacobs' legal defense in New York City), the ball attracted Baltimore's movers and shakers. One would have to suspect that Lu Fisher's blueblood connections were a big part of these gains. The first ball netted $900 ($6,800 today), but that number swelled to $2,000 the very next year.[268]

By 1972 the Preservation Society was working with the Maryland Historic Trust on a proposal to feature Fell's Point in the 1976 bicentennial celebration. The Preservation Society's June 1973 minutes indicate that "[City Council President] Orlinsky and Schaefer have been putting pressure on the State Commission to eliminate any Fell's Point funds [for the bicentennial]."[269] The State Commission apparently ignored the city's leaders, perhaps illustrating at least one benefit of the city's diminished power in the state political realm.

By 1973 it was apparent that the Road Wars would not be won in a sprint to the finish line; this was a marathon. Among anti-highway groups, the Preservation Society was uniquely capable of sustaining this effort. The group's April 1973 minutes referenced upcoming legal costs totaling $14,000 ($93,000 today). In the very next paragraph, this enormous hill to climb got a lot smaller. "House Tour: Ms. Fisher reported…a net return of $4162." About a thousand attended—Fell's Point's ambassadors and defenders were again multiplying.[270] The 1973 Fun Festival netted $4,500 ($30,000 today) profit.[271] By 1976 festival profit had almost doubled to $8,000.[272] In 1979 the Preservation Society took over the lucrative beer concession, and revenues more than doubled.****

In 1974 the Preservation Society also staged a coup in the Maryland General Assembly. Astonishingly, they were able to get a bill through, granting $127,000 to fund acquisitions of three historic properties *inside* condemnation lines (a strategy recommended by Society attorney Geoff Mitchell).

**** It is a happy thought that everyone who bought a beer (or two, or ten) at the Fell's Point Fun Festival was helping to save Fell's Point. It is disappointing, however, that Art Cohen and MAD missed this opportunity to create a clever t-shirt. How about *St-hop the Road?*

One of these houses was the Robert Long House built in 1765, reputed to be the oldest surviving urban house in Baltimore. This legislative action was largely engineered by Julian "Jack" Lapides,[††††] a Preservation Society board member. As Mitchell explained in a 2018 interview, "Jack Lapides was a state senator, and Jack's vote was needed by a lot of people on a lot of things. So, we got the Maryland Historic Trust to sponsor a bill and it was enacted."

By 1975, the other anti-highway organizations (MAD, SCAR, and RAM) were running on fumes. They had each left their mark, and some of their constituent communities remained vigilant, but it was primarily the Preservation Society that kept up the fight to make sure Fell's Point would not be scarred by an ill-conceived compromise. In 1977 the Society's membership was seven hundred strong and the annual renewal letter aimed to reach one thousand people.[273]

There was still hostility toward the Preservation Society among long-time Fell's Point residents, the ethnics who derided the preservationists as gentrifiers, a word meant to convey everything they found loathsome and reprehensible about the changes in their community. It was true that the Preservation Society was not representative of long-time Fell's Point residents; their membership was skewed to other areas of the city, the suburbs, and out-of-state populations.[274] And, upscale renovations meant higher taxes, fern bars, and historic preservation standards that most long-term residents could not afford; even if they had the means, most did not care. One old line Fell's Pointer commented, "We don't want to live in a museum. We prefer to live in a community of Poles, Greeks, longshoremen, hippies, hillbillies, winos, seamen, Black people, Catholics, Jews, artists, writers, barmaids, and stray cats."[275]

Community divisions erupted again in the mid-1970s over neighborhood planning issues. Jack Trautwein, Fell's Point's informal historian, remembered the rancor in a 2004 interview:

[††††] In 1974 Senator Lapides also led a legislative effort to have the expressway plan put on the ballot. This effort failed, but it was another potential expressway disaster that Schaefer and highway backers had to expend time and political chits to extinguish.

I never have really experienced such dissension and discord as those meetings...it was almost fisticuffs at every meeting. I mean shouting at each other, spitting at each other... I can remember one of the big meetings we had... The American Legion post had a girls' twirling group and they had won all these trophies. And so, they brought these trophies over and set 'em on the table to show the community. They were proud of this. So, this guy got so angry he...upset the table, broke the trophies, and we had to call the police to get him calmed down, to get him out of there.[276]

After the condemnation lines were finally dropped, the city created a committee to develop disposition and design standards for the ninety-nine houses the city had acquired. Laura Norris, co-owner of Bertha's and long-time friend of Bob Eney, served on that committee. She explained, "It was tough times back then for those of us on the committee. I had people who would spit at me or they would cross to the other side of the street [to shun me]." Bob Eney recalled that "one of the priests at the church stopped [Norris] on the street and told her that he thought that she was one of Hitler's people working in this neighborhood against these poor Poles."

While all that divisiveness engulfed much of Fell's Point civic life through the 1970s, thankfully those divisions were no longer prominent in the Road Fight. That change did not come easily, however—it was the result of probably the most ambitious community organizing effort in the history of Baltimore.

When Southeast Council Against the Road (SCAR) was organized in the fall of 1968, that was the first step toward uniting the ethnic neighborhoods of southeast Baltimore against the Road. However, SCAR was a stepping-stone to a larger vision—an umbrella community organization that would create a unified movement for community reinvestment and capital improvements. When Southeast Community Organization (SECO) was formed in 1971, infighting was put aside and southeast Baltimore was finally united in purpose, with highway opposition as one cornerstone of the plan.

The creation of SECO was a massive effort involving thousands of people, virtually all of whom bought into SCAR's vehement opposition to the highways. But there was an underlying issue that also worked to the benefit of the Road Fight: those thousands of people were part of a vision of hope for the future of the community. The common view that many of these neighborhoods were in decline gave way to this new positive vision. The "take the money and run to Essex" folks were now swamped by neighbors and friends that were going to stay put and fight to make their communities better. "Before SECO," James Dilts wrote, "the question of the effect of the road on the citizens in southeast Baltimore was handled by the First District Councilmen with an indifference that bordered on the spectacular."[277] Joe McNeely added, "They [SECO] were presenting an argument that wasn't so easy to dismiss as upper-class gentrification."[278]

Jack Gleason had contributed his time and expertise to the formation of SECO; when Gleason was elected as SECO's first president in 1971, that sealed the deal. The ethnic communities of southeast Baltimore stood shoulder to shoulder with the Preservation Society in opposition to the expressway. When city council was considering Mikulski's bills to repeal the condemnation ordinance in 1972, it was Gleason, representing SECO (not the Preservation Society), who testified in favor. Other meetings and hearings find Gleason and SECO providing a needed voice advocating for Canton, which did not enjoy the benefits of an historic designation.

Jack Gleason, the unifier

Although hardly outspoken, Jack Gleason was the guy people turned to for level-headed leadership on tough issues, one of the best bridge-builders and strategists for anti-road forces. Gleason, at different points in time, served as president of the Preservation Society, Southeast Development, Inc., SECO, and as chairman of the Fell's Point Planning Council.

My interviewees all characterized Jack as exceptionally thoughtful, deliberate, and wise, a steadying influence in turbulent times. Tony Norris described Jack as "a very serious guy.... Jack thought about every word he had to say, so that he said it right and he didn't offend anybody. He did the right thing in every moment." Tony and his wife Laura filled in the backstory on Jack. (It was an especially fun, anecdote-filled interview, partly because they complete each other's sentences). Jack was born in Ohio and served in the Navy in World War II. He commanded a tank unit in North Africa and earned a Silver Star and three Purple Hearts.[279]

Tony said, "He had a funny nose because—"

"—A bullet just whizzed across his face," Laura added.

"It almost took his nose off," Tony finished.

Joe McNeely remembered that Gleason spent time in New Orleans, where his interest in historic preservation was nurtured. He later moved to New York and had two children, but then got divorced. Gleason was a non-profit administrator for the American Tuberculosis Association in New York. After moving to Baltimore, he specialized in health care administration at the University of Maryland Hospital and the Waxter Center for Senior Citizens.

Gleason met Bob Eney at Trinity Church in Manhattan—their shared love of colonial and early federal architecture was the bond of a lifelong friendship. McNeely recalls, "At one point they collaborated to create both full size and mini colonial rooms for the Brooklyn Museum of Art." Their weekends and vacations were spent exploring, studying, and photographing old houses; their knowledge spanned the East Coast from Maine to Georgia. They planned to publish a book, but it fell by the wayside when they were conscripted into the Road Wars.

Gleason moved to Baltimore with Bob Eney in 1967 when Eney got his job at Hochschild's department store. Gleason's son was a student at Johns Hopkins, so Baltimore was not a hard sell. They bought two houses on Thames Street and renovated them as a single unit. In several iterations of the expressway's path, their houses were either in or directly adjacent to the highway—they had made a risky bet, really a wing and a prayer that the fledgling Preservation Society would somehow prevail.

When SECO was organizing in 1970 to '71, Gleason was out of work for a while, but he used his time to aid in the formation of the group while passing along his knowledge and expertise. Joe McNeely said, "He came to the office every day and coached me through what nonprofit organizations were all about, because I didn't know anything. He really was a stabilizing force."

Lung cancer claimed Jack's life in 1992. Tony Norris added a note of great irony and sadness: When Gleason worked with the American Tuberculosis Association back in New York City, "Jack was the guy who came up with the first warning on a pack of cigarettes… And they did it all in a smoke-filled boardroom. Jack ended up dying from cigarettes, as [smoking had] just totally ruined his lungs and his heart. He just could not quit smoking… and his biggest thing before he died was to make sure his kids stopped smoking."

We close this section with Jack's own words (from a 1974 interview) explaining the evolution of his thinking about the highway, preservation, and the neighborhood.

> My original interest was in bricks and mortar, the old buildings. But when I moved down there, I got to know the people. I got to know the character of the neighborhood. My son married one of the Greek girls from the neighborhood…. While I still have a strong interest in the preservation of historical buildings, my interest today is the preservation of a neighborhood, meaning its total character including the people, their ethnic characteristics, their traditions and heritage.[280]

He succeeded.

LEGAL BATTLE

When you shoot the king, you better get him with the first shot.
Norman Ramsey

Ramsey, senior partner at Semmes, Bowen & Semmes, gave this cleverly worded bit of advice to Preservation Society attorney Geoff Mitchell in 1969. But Geoff's winning strategy was not a knockout punch but glancing blows, a strong defense, and deftly running out the clock. The legal battle for Fell's

Point took place on three fronts: the courts, city council, and the administrative process prescribed by the Historic Preservation Act of 1966. The Preservation Society needed to win only one of these battlegrounds; highway proponents needed to win all three. So, even though governments could draw on endless resources, you could say it was a fair fight. The city council measures were not successful until much later, so this story focuses on the other two.

As you recall, the 4(f) provision of the 1966 Federal-Aid Highway Act stipulated that federal funds may not be approved for projects that impact parks or historic sites unless "no feasible and prudent alternative" existed. Section 106 of the Historic Preservation Act of 1966 is similarly triggered if the project impacts an historic site. If the President's Advisory Council on Historic Preservation (ACHP) finds an "adverse impact," an additional review determines if and how the impact can be mitigated.

The Preservation Society fired the first legal shot across the bow, just two weeks after Fell's Point won its status as a National Register historic area. Their lawsuit on April 7, 1969, alleged that a "4(f) violation" occurred when federal funds were approved for the 3-A plan that routed the highway through Fell's Point.

The Preservation Society had wisely established communications with ACHP before gaining National Register status, and ACHP staff paid a visit and toured Fell's Point with Bob Eney as their guide. Once again, Eney was the salesman for historic designation and the subsequent use of Section 106 as the regulatory hammer. This early on communication reaped enormous benefits down the road.

On April 25, ACHP Executive Secretary Robert R. Garvey wrote to the secretary of transportation requesting that the agency acknowledge the applicability of Section 106 and the involvement the ACHP. Oscar Gray, Acting Chief of Environmental Programs for the Department of Transportation, wrote back on August 11, 1969,‡‡‡‡ agreeing with Garvey's request.

You might assume that highway proponents facing a 4(f) lawsuit, the

---

‡‡‡‡ Every delay works to the benefit of highway opponents. Here, the Department of Transportation took three and a half months to simply acknowledge that the Section 106 process was required.

regulatory involvement of ACHP, and mounting public opposition would initiate a study to avoid or at least lower the impact on Fell's Point. But you would be wrong—that did not occur until late 1972. In the interim, they unwisely dug in their heels and pursued two strategies that would yield no gain.

First, the city attempted to discredit the National Register determination. Geoff Mitchell said, "Interstate Division had retained experts to prove that Fell's Point and Federal Hill were not historic." The Preservation Society's suspicions were aroused because one of those experts was Robert Kerr of the Urban Design Group, reported to be a friend of Dick Trainor (IDBC staff). Gleason and Eney found his qualifications suspect, and they were reserved about sharing information with Kerr. However, Kerr's 1970 report did not find what the city was hoping for. Kerr found that, of 354 structures, 76 percent were of "primary," "exceptional," or "major" consequence for preservation. Kerr finely articulated the case for preservation of Fell's Point as a representation of working class life, saying, "Who is to say that there is less dramatic and human value in the record of the manner in which the average citizen or artisan or mechanic lived out his life than in the artifacts, objects, and setting associated with the great events and moments of human history?"[281]

Undeterred, in 1971 the city continued its campaign to undermine the National Register listing. In their required 4(f) report, the city argued that Fell's Point Historic District was "of questionable significance" and echoed Nat Owings' unfortunate and completely fictional stance that joint development would make Fell's Point "a stronger neighborhood both residentially and architecturally."[282] The environmental impact statement linked to the report made no mention of Section 106, an omission that miffed ACHC's Robert Garvey.§§§§

The Preservation Society left no stone unturned in refuting the city's statement. Jack Gleason wrote a compelling twenty-four-page position paper,

---

§§§§ Garvey's June 22, 1972, letter to the Department of Transportation is harshly worded, saying, "We have taken note of the fact that there is no mention of Section 106, or the consideration of the effect of this undertaking on National Register properties… I would appreciate any advice you can give me regarding the schedule the Department of Transportation will follow in requesting comments."

the clearest statement on record as to why Fell's Point deserved the protections afforded by the 4(f) provision. Then they hired Milton Grigg, a well-regarded preservation expert, using a $5,000 grant from the National Historic Trust and $1,000 from the Maryland Historic Trust. According to Geoff Mitchell, Grigg "came to the conclusion that Fell's Point and Federal Hill were both extremely historic, [and] if these historic districts can be preserved, it would be an economic driver for the city." The Preservation Society distributed both the Gleason paper and the Grigg report far and wide—there is no subsequent record of the city disputing the legitimacy of the historic district.

This brings the story back to highway proponents' courtroom strategy, which also resulted in no gain (unless you look from the Preservation Society's point of view).

Geoff Mitchell was, in his words, "a brand-new associate" at Semmes, Bowen, & Semmes when he was brought in to help the Preservation Society. In December 1968, Tom Ward and Lu Fisher requested legal assistance from Norman Ramsey, who asked Mitchell to take on their case. The Preservation Society paid a $50,000 retainer, likely from a combination of direct contributions and revenues from the Fell's Point Fun Festival and other fundraisers. Mitchell said the assignment later became "a labor of love," evolving into pro bono work. Ramsey was a close friend and supporter of Mayor Schaefer, so I asked Geoff if the mayor ever leaned on Norman to undercut Geoff's role with the Preservation Society. Geoff bristled at the thought, saying, "Nobody ever used Norman Ramsey for any purpose like that. Nobody."

In preparing the complaint, Geoff walked the historic district with Eney and Gleason and got an education on the finer points of Fell's Point eighteenth and nineteenth century architecture. Next, they lined up the plaintiffs, but this was a touchy issue. Given the divisions in Fell's Point, the group wanted some long-time residents in the list of plaintiffs. Polish descent would not hurt, either. Frank Lukowski, a Polish tugboat worker active in the Road Fight, filled the bill, but he passed away before the trial. His wife, Eleanor, signed on; thus, her name is forever enshrined as the lead plaintiff in *Lukowski v. Volpe*.

The complaint claims, "The Secretary, in approving the plans for the alignment of segment 4, failed to conduct a meaningful inquiry and failed to make a determination that there was no feasible and prudent alternative to the use of such land [as required by the 4(f) provisions]." There were several additional points—that certain requirements related to regional planning and public hearings had not been met; however, those points were later merged with a MAD lawsuit that government defendants won. This meant that the Lukowski case, at least from the plaintiff's point of view, hinged only on the 4(f) provisions.

The defendants (city, state, and federal government) primarily claimed that the case was brought prematurely because no final decisions had been made. They also raised two additional issues: The State of Maryland asked that the case against the state be dismissed based on the doctrine of sovereign immunity, and defendants claimed that the proper place for the plaintiff's argument was in the city's eminent domain proceedings, not the courts. As Geoff Mitchell succinctly put it in a 2020 interview, "Well, they didn't get very far with those arguments, did they?" These sideline issues did little but use up time—again, every delay worked to benefit the community.

The case was therefore winnowed down to the 4(f) issue and the defendants' claim that the lawsuit was premature—that no federal funds had been obligated and no final decision had been made. From a layman's point of view, it was obvious that decisions had been made—the city had acquired at least ninety-nine properties in the historic area with the clear understanding that they would be reimbursed by the federal government. Mitchell additionally argued that the federally funded UDCT had been restricted to considering only options that held to the 1962 10-D alignment, so there had been no consideration of alternative alignments since at least 1962. Mitchell's closing argument was that the defendants were "asking the court to divert its attention from the vacant and boarded houses lining Shakespeare, Bond, and Lancaster Streets. It asks the Court not to observe the fact that practically one-third of the historic district has been purchased by the City of Baltimore. Such a characterization invites the Court to overlook harsh reality at the foot of Broadway in Baltimore City. Instead, this court is asked to look to the gleaming bureaucratic machinery of the Department of Transportation— and wait."

Judge Tomsen initially ruled in favor of the government defendants based on their arguments that the Secretary's endorsement of 3-A had been conceptual, that acquisitions had been placed on hold after Fell's Point was declared historic, and that no federal funds had been spent to date. Tomsen said the case should not proceed until the legal triggers related to the federal commitment were clear.

This is when Geoff Mitchell, Bob Eney, and Jack Gleason went back out into the community, knocking on doors, retrieving acquisition letters from the city, and documenting that the city was not only continuing to acquire properties in the historic area, they were also using scare tactics to expedite these acquisitions. Mitchell said, "The patter went like this: 'If you sell us your property today for $5,000, then we will grant you [an additional] $5,000 relocation allowance. But if you don't accept that offer, then we don't know what you'll get.'" Mitchell collected signed affidavits from residents who had been approached in this manner.

Further (and this might have been the clincher), the acquisition letters from the city explicitly referred to federal funding, even providing a funding number. On October 12, 1972, Mitchell presented these new affidavits and written documentation to the court. Mitchell, recounting these events almost fifty years later, departed from his usual just-the-facts demeanor, basking in this "we got 'em" moment:

So Judge Tomsen, a pretty smart and cagey gentleman, looked over at the federal attorneys and the state attorneys. He said, "Is this happening? Is what Mitchell is alleging here—is it true?" They said, "Yes, Your Honor, it is true." He said, "So, of course then, you will agree to stop this until we hear the case." The three attorneys for the state, the Interstate Division, and the feds huddled right at the counsel table. Then they said, "Yes, Your Honor, we will agree that we will stop acquiring property." He said, "Good. So I will enter an order in this case saying… you've stipulated that you will acquire no more property, and at the appropriate time this case can go forward."

One writer quoted the judge as admonishing government attorneys for wanting to "knock down houses and dig holes" before a specific route had been approved by the federal government.[283] In one sense the ruling was a stalemate, postponing the consideration of the 4(f) violation, but it also put the defendants on notice that further acquisitions in the historic area were grounds for adjudication. The government could not build the highway as planned without further acquisitions, not to mention a host of approvals that were now in legal limbo. It was a major setback.

The *Lukowski v. Volpe* case never reached a judicial decision on the core issue, almost certainly because the government defendants thought they would lose. The 1972 order stopping acquisitions in the historic area was a watershed moment, another point in time when the ruination of Fell's Point hung in the balance. Yet again, it was Bob Eney and Jack Gleason, along with Geoff Mitchell, who rescued the neighborhood.

There is one interesting postscript to *Lukowski v. Volpe*. In 1977, Judge Tomsen wrote to attorneys on both sides of the case. He said the "Fell's Point case is much the oldest case on my docket," and asked if the case could be "dismissed without prejudice." Indeed, the saving of Fell's Point was a long, drawn-out affair, and it is hard to pinpoint precisely when and how the community won. However, that does become clearer as the story comes back to the President's Advisory Council on Historic Preservation and the consideration of various highway alternatives for traversing Fell's Point.

PRESIDENT'S ADVISORY COUNCIL— NEW OPTIONS FOR FELL'S POINT

In 1972, in addition to Judge Tomsen's ruling, there was a convergence of local politics and federal regulations that pushed the city to finally begin evaluating alternatives to the elevated highway through Fell's Point. Highway opposition forces were gaining in city council—the 1971 election brought on four to six highway critics (depending on who was counting and how the question was worded). The most vocal was, of course, Barbara Mikulski.

Newly elected Mayor Schaefer held hearings in January 1972 as part of a top-to-bottom review of highway plan alternatives. This led to the off-the-record meeting mentioned on page 111, where Mikulski reportedly brokered a deal that included a tunnel to avoid Fell's Point in return for highway opponents supporting the Fort McHenry Bypass. The written record is not definitive on this point, but it is quite clear that the President's Advisory Council on Historic Preservation (ACHP) began forcing the consideration of alternatives in the summer and fall of 1972.

It started with a meeting between ACHP and highway planners on August 8, 1972. Ben Levy (staff to ACHP) reportedly upbraided highway officials, saying, the highway planners "had not begun to follow any of the procedures set forth in the law [section 106]."[284] The Preservation Society minutes link the genesis of the meeting to the Society's complaint to the ACHP that the city had acquired and razed several warehouses located just *outside* of the designated historic district.

Three years after Fell's Point gained National Register status, the city and its state and federal partners finally had to face facts that their current strategy, somewhere between avoidance and resistance, was not going to get a highway built. They had lost the battle to dispute the historic designation; they had lost the preliminary rulings in the Lukowski court case; and now the ACHP was taking them to task for destruction of properties *outside* the designated historic district. Moreover, they were clearly losing in the court of public opinion. Late in 1972 they finally agreed to undertake consideration of alternatives that would avoid or at least lower the impacts on the Historic District.

This led to a report by Per Hall Zollman Associates, circulated in 1973 and finalized in 1974. They examined nine alternative alignments—all involved tunneling under or around Fell's Point, including bored tunnels, cut-and-cover tunnels, double-stacked tunnels, and a one-way pair of tunnels. Two options placed tunnels under the harbor just south of the historic district.

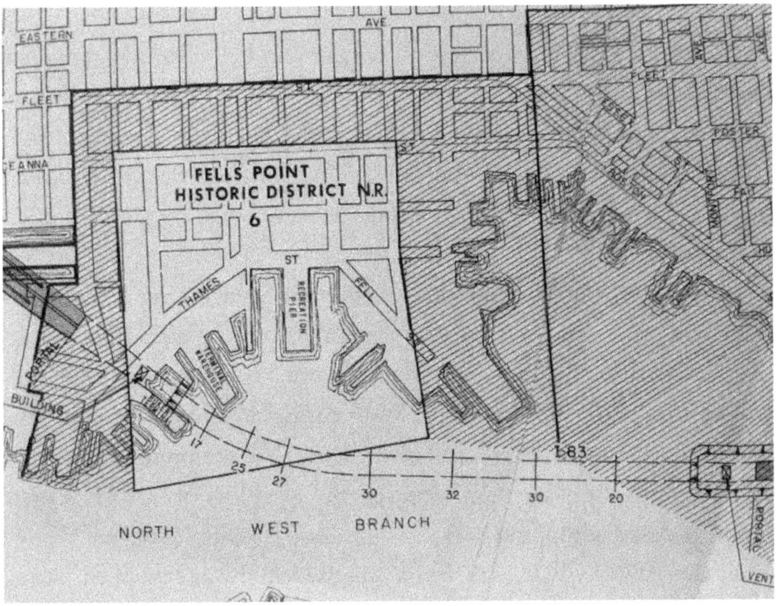

Figure 26. Tunneling around Fell's Point (source: "Case Report, Section 106 for I-83, Gay Street to I-95, January 1977)

The land-side cut-and-cover tunnel options involved razing at least fifty historic structures, but there was discussion of possibly dismantling and reconstructing these buildings after the tunnel was completed. That option brought derision. MAD's Carolyn Tyson said, "People in Fell's Point just laughed at this; they made fun of it. It is beyond the bounds of rationality. So, I think even the Interstate Division knew this was absurdity, but of course they couldn't say so."[285]

In May 1974 Mayor Schaefer announced that he favored a tunnel south of Fell's Point under the harbor.[286] The Preservation Society was reserved in their judgment—this addressed the destruction of structures in the historic district, but they were still worried about the highway's path through the Lower Jones Falls to the west of Fell's Point and through Canton to the east. Plus, they (correctly) surmised that the city would not stick to the tunnel option after the extra costs were taken into account.

At a January 1975 hearing concerns about the waterside tunnel came to the forefront. Disruption of maritime commerce was the main issue in Fell's Point. Fell's Point resident Elleanor Dashiell echoed the views of many when she said, "Take our working waterfront and Fell's Point is gone." Many of those in opposition were now less concerned about Fell's Point but more concerned about Canton and the Lower Jones Falls area. Representing the Canton Improvement Association, Richard Miller said, "the properties under and adjacent to elevated highways would become breeding grounds of crime and vandalism."[287]

The cost side of the equation must have been raising blood pressure among those responsible for the city's fiscal health. The nine alignments had been updated for cost: Land-side tunnel options varied between $124 million and $142 million. A close-in underwater tunnel brushing the south end of Recreation Pier was budgeted at $126 million. One option moved the tunnel further out into the water and achieved the least loss of historic structures and jobs. It cost a whopping $160 million ($871 million today).[288] For comparison, the 1970 UDCT plan for an elevated highway had been estimated at $69 million. The Preservation Society, now with a strengthened hand, opposed all nine alternatives.[289]

The city administration, likely concerned about costs and undoubtedly miffed that none of the build alternatives had won community support, backed off the underwater tunnels in October 1975. Instead, they resurrected landside cut-and-cover tunnels in Fleet and/or Aliceanna Streets.[290] The Baltimore City Council went into an uproar. City Council President Orlinsky, a former highway foe who had turned into Schaefer's floor manager for highway matters, said the whole reason he switched allegiance was that the administration promised to put I-83 in an underwater tunnel.[291] The Preservation Society went back into attack mode, citing the destruction of historic houses, both direct and indirect—they said many structures, already damaged by years of neglect, could not survive the three years of underground digging and vibration from tunnel construction.

In 1976 Interstate Division brought the underwater tunnel back into the mix, but they persisted in scoping out yet another land-side option: a double-stacked tunnel within the Aliceanna Street right-of-way. IDBC cited innovative slurry wall construction being used in the New York City subway system that created less impact at the surface, potentially retaining buildings on both sides of the street. They took a group of Fell's Pointers to New York to see firsthand how it worked.

Former IDBC staffer David Chapin recounted a memorable story of that trip in a 2017 interview. Workers had just declared a strike, and it was a huge mess. "Everyone walked off the job; everyone was complaining; all the business people complaining; so it was not the most successful trip," Chapin said. "We [IDBC] were just about to open I-95 down to O'Donnell Street; so, when we were coming back into the city, [Dick] Trainor told the bus driver, just drive down this highway."

The bus driver said, "It's not open, look at all those barricades."

Trainor said, "Don't worry about it, just drive down there."

Chapin continues, "We drove down there but there was a police car. The guy was taking a nap underneath the Eastern Avenue Bridge... So he put his siren on and stops the bus." When Chapin got to this point in the story he turned on an unmistakable Mimi accent: "[Mimi] DiPietro¶¶¶¶ says, 'I'll take care of this... It's our highway. This is our highway; we're just taking a tour!'"

The Preservation Society was not impressed. Lu Fisher authored their January 1977 position paper in advance of the ACHP meeting in Baltimore. She said the trip to New York "made it abundantly clear that the crippling and destructive effects on the economic, social, and environmental structure of the community were so great that the community would never recover."[292] She softened, just a little, on the underwater tunnel, calling it the "least disruptive plan to date," but she still raised the fundamental objections: the need for the highway had never been demonstrated and air quality impacts would still be harmful.

This double-stacked tunnel in Aliceanna Street was kept in the running until completion of the Section 106 process and ACHP involvement in 1977.

¶¶¶¶ Mimi had no filter between the somewhat convoluted thoughts in his head and what came out of his mouth. Bob Hewitt (the planner for Mimi's First Councilmanic District) was sitting in Mimi's office when Mimi got a call from the Police Commissioner. Bob could only imagine how the conversation got to this conclusion, but it ended with Mimi first looking down at his crotch, then grabbing himself while saying, "What that thing? Oh, that thing hasn't worked in years."

While most of the credit for saving Fell's Point goes to the Preservation Society and SCAR/SECO, here we also acknowledge the contribution of a number of principled public officials who did the right thing, even though their bosses were undoubtedly leaning on them to go the other way.

John Pearce, the Maryland State historic preservation officer, was required to comment on the impact of the proposed highway on historic structures and districts. His input carried significant weight when the issue was put in front of ACHP for the Section 106 review.

Nancy Schamu, noted historian and long-time employee of the Maryland Historic Trust, recounted a meeting that Pearce arranged with Bob Embry, Commissioner of Housing. "John Pearce is a wonderful man, and really knew how to present historic preservation and the decisions he had to make," Schamu said. She recalled that Pearce always warned governments when he was going to make a decision that adversely affected them, and he had scheduled a meeting with Embry to say that I-83 would have "unmitigable adverse effects."

According to Schamu, "So, we went to see Bob Embry, we sat down in his office," but Embry short-cut the discussion, saying, "We shouldn't build I-83 through Baltimore, but we're going to; so, what else do you want to talk about?" Here were two individuals who had the power to equivocate, and in so doing would have earned kudos from their bosses, but they did the right thing instead of the expedient thing.

Schamu continued, "There was a lot of pressure on [Pearce]... It wasn't just I-83. It was every federal activity [that he ranked for historic impacts].... Pearce said, 'If it's significant, it's significant. If it's an adverse effect, it's an adverse effect.' He's probably one of the most courageous men I've ever known in my life." Schamu ranks Pearce right up there with Bob Eney and Lu Fisher as one of the key people responsible for saving Fell's Point.

When Pearce wrote his January 1977 recommendation to the Advisory Council there were still two options: the cut-and-cover double-stacked tunnel in Aliceanna Street and the underwater tunnel just south of Fell's Point. Pearce's recommendations include the following: "I believe that the effects of I-83 from Gay Street to I-95 are so adverse that the Advisory Council can only recommend that this road not be built as currently proposed.... I can see no means by which the adverse effects...can be mitigated."[293] He advised the secretary of transportation "To not approve funding for I-83 unless he finds that no prudent or feasible alternative exists to solve the transportation problems, and he requires...that mitigation be carried out both for future and past adverse effects which have scarred and which would scar the irreplaceable historic fabric of the City of Baltimore."

The Advisory Council came to Baltimore for hearings in February 1977, then held their official review meeting on May 3 and 4. The city, faced with unrelenting community opposition, as well as Pearce's report, withdrew the Aliceanna Street tunnel, leaving only the underwater tunnel option. Since that tunnel completely avoided the Fell's Point Historic District, ACHP's report shifted attention to the approach *to* that tunnel through the Lower Jones Falls. The area was dotted with many historic buildings including four on the National Register: St. Vincent de Paul Church, Shot Tower, the Carroll Mansion, and the Flag House. Numerous other structures had been determined to be National Register eligible.

While this might seem anti-climactic for Fell's Point, the council's judgment on Jones Falls was another nail in the coffin for the whole southeast segment. ACHP recommended: 1) that the highway "should not be constructed as an elevated viaduct through the Lower Jones Falls"; 2) "the selection of an at-grade boulevard...coupled with the harbor tunnel alignment in and beneath the Fell's Point historic district"; and 3) if "for any reason" an at-grade boulevard was not constructed, "selection of a cut-and-cover tunnel for the Lower Jones Falls."[294]

This left the city with two awfully expensive options for the Lower Jones Falls. The boulevard was not eligible for 90/10 money, plus it would interrupt the continuity of the interstate.[*****] Tunneling would add another mile of very

***

costly roadway. The record does not indicate whether there was any effort to have the Federal Highway Administration overrule the Advisory Council, but it appears that highway proponents accepted the recommendation.

The city opted for the tunnel.[†††††] Six months later the cost of tunneling under the Lower Jones Falls and around Fell's Point had skyrocketed to $392 million ($1.9 billion today), a more than five-fold increase over UDCT's 1970 elevated highway plan.[295] The Fell's Point segment would later prove to be beyond the city's ability to hold up its share of highway financing.

BALTIMORE CITY COUNCIL DEALS THE FINAL BLOWS

Up until 1977 highway opponents in Baltimore City Council were largely tilting at windmills. Councilwoman Mikulski, the acknowledged leader of the anti-road faction, had made no real progress. In 1976 she was elected to Congress and was no longer involved.

After adopting the extended I-83 tunnel plan, Schaefer was under intense pressure from Fell's Point groups and city council, especially Wally Orlinsky, to rescind the old condemnation line and release the city-owned houses in Fell's Point. On May 26, 1977, Schaefer announced that his administration would introduce companion bills to authorize the tunnel and repeal the Fell's Point condemnation line.[296] Several council members tried to move forward on the repeal without authorizing the new tunnel alignment, but the mayor prevailed, and the two bills were enacted later in the summer of 1977.

Schaefer had worked overtime, again using the power of his office to bring recalcitrant councilmembers back in line for an expressway that virtually every-one except the mayor saw as too expensive for this cash-strapped city.

At this point, the summer of 1977, Fell's Point's Road Warriors could

---

at both ends, may have required five lanes in each direction, which, ironically, would have been the most destructive of all the alternatives considered for the Lower Jones Falls.

††††† After restudying the Lower Jones Falls segment, the preferred plan that emerged was part depressed roadway and part cut-and-cover tunnel.

take a victory lap—the Historic District had been saved. But it seemed a hollow victory as long as the neighboring areas of Canton and Harbor East remained under the cloud of an anachronism masquerading as an expressway.

IX. ROSEMONT

"THE HUMAN OBSTACLE"

You know what tickles me? Arguing with Jerome Wolff and him telling me that
the route would not be changed. And we said, "It damn well will be changed."

Joseph Wiles

Joseph Wiles, President of the Rosemont Community Association and one
of the most active members of the Movement Against Destruction (MAD),
passed away in 1998, but his obituary does not mention his prominent role in
saving Rosemont from being bisected and destroyed by an eight-lane expressway. Those involved in the Road Fight might regard this as an odd or even
negligent omission.

Author Earl Swift, however, gives Wiles his due. Swift's sweeping
history of the interstate highway program, *The Big Roads*, chronicles the
groundbreaking events and portrays the iconic figures who planned and
built the 40,000-mile interstate highway system. One chapter, "The Human
Obstacle," is a masterful treatise on the largely unanticipated obstacles
encountered in building highways through urban areas, especially minority
residential neighborhoods. Out of thousands of anti-highway activists all
across the country, the person Swift refers to as "the human obstacle" is
Rosemont's leader Joseph Wiles.

It is astonishing that the city once contemplated putting I-70 right
through the heart of this solidly middle-class African American neighborhood, but that was the plan from 1957 to 1970, when the Rosemont Bypass
was finally adopted. That it took thirteen years to figure out an alternate route
is also telling: "Negro Removal" may not have been an explicit or even an
implicit objective in this case, but Baltimore decision-makers were essentially
oblivious to the value of this stable, well-kept, and middle income African
American neighborhood.

Rosemont was first integrated in 1950. Beatrice Simmons became the first Black resident when she purchased a home in the 2300 Block of Lorretta Avenue. One account cited an "instance of vandalism that greeted her arrival."[297] In 1951 the family of Reginald F. Lewis (Rosemont's most famous former resident) moved to Mosher Street, where Reginald spent his formative years. He later graduated from Harvard Law School and had an extraordinarily successful career as a business turn-around specialist. He used his wealth to create the Reginald F. Lewis Foundation which made its largest donation to establish the Reginald F. Lewis Maryland Museum of African American History and Culture, now located at Pratt and President Street.

In 1950 the US Census counted only 89 Black residents in Rosemont; by 1960 it counted only 123 White residents. Baltimore's White leadership undoubtedly viewed racially changed neighborhoods like Rosemont in a negative light, perhaps even "lost causes" in the minds of those trying to maintain a majority White city. This mindset, one has to assume, provided the underpinnings of decisions about where the highway would go.

To Glenn Smith,* Rosemont was the opposite of a "lost cause." Smith currently wears multiple hats as vice president of the Baltimore Transit Equity Coalition, and board member of multiple community development corporations. Smith's family moved to Rosemont on the 2400 Block of Lorretta Avenue when he was four, and they were forced to move in 1968 when he was nineteen. In Smith's words, his upbringing was "like a Norman Rockwell painting. I mean the community was really a tight knit community." He adds:

> My mother passed away when I was about six years old. And I gained about twenty more mothers up and down the block because they kind of took our family under their wings knowing my mother was not

---

* Glenn Smith came to my attention from Denise Johnson—Denise and Glenn got to know each other through the CultureWorks project (see Harlem Park chapter).

there. It was a thing where the neighborhood stayed clean. We had an AFRO clean block campaign; we have marble steps that were washed at least twice a week that were nice and clean. There was no trash in the gutter; you didn't throw trash in the street back then…. We had good elementary schools and high schools. A lot of your professionals lived in West Baltimore, your doctors, your lawyers, your teachers. It was just a thriving community where the children were nurtured, mostly two-parent families… It was just a joy to grow up in that environment. And there was no crime problem.

Smith attributes much of the stability to the fact that "Most people had incomes from… Bethlehem Steel, General Motors, Lever Brothers where you could earn a great living, even if you did not have [higher] education. So… the neighborhood was thriving… I mean the houses were clean, there were no vacant houses. And people took pride in home ownership. It was just very nurturing and a great place to grow up in."

The ties that were built in his formative years have proven to be lasting friendships, even fifty years later. Glenn is part of a reunion group from the old neighborhood—they get together about once a month and share old war stories. "When you know people intimately for fifteen years, those bonds are not easily broken," Glenn said. "Even though they may go to all the different parts of the city, there was still a connection."

A STRAIGHT LINE THROUGH ROSEMONT

Rosemont was first targeted in the 1957 Interstate System Concept Plan. It was clear that I-70 was going to approach Baltimore from the west, and highway planners looked at spacious Leakin Park and Gwynns Falls Park as the path of least resistance. Since previous plans had already established Franklin-Mulberry as the westside corridor to downtown, Rosemont became the connector, the means by which an expressway could cut through Leakin Park and then continue downtown via Franklin-Mulberry. Figure 27 shows the path of destruction, right through the middle of the Rosemont community. Once again, the engineers were holding sway: no deviations from the most efficient alignment.

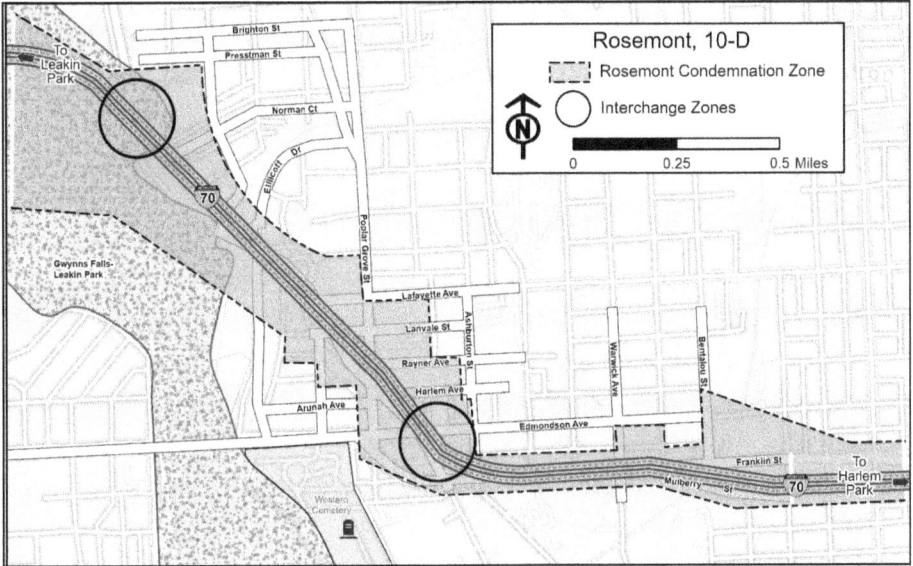

Figure 27. Rosemont bisected by the 10-D (1961-62) plan and 10-D Modified (1967) highway plans. Condemnation line is approximate. (Scott Jeffrey, MS, GISP)

In 1962 the State Roads Commission published a 10-D impact assessment. Of 590 acquisitions in Rosemont, the report said dryly, "530 are of sound condition, 55 are deteriorating and only 5 are dilapidated"—in other words, very well kept, one of the better neighborhoods in Baltimore. The concern that the highway bisected the neighborhood was dismissed, because the current and previous studies "indicate that there is no feasible alternative."[298]

When UDCT studied Rosemont in 1967, the home ownership rate was 72 percent, high compared to 55 percent for the city as a whole, with most owners in their present homes between ten and twenty years.[299] UDCT studies were telling. Mort Hoffman, a consultant, said, "The people have great pride and respect for their property and the appearance of their homes."[300] UDCT's Steve Zecher recalled that a UDCT-funded sociological assessment came to a blunt conclusion: "Regardless of what we spent on [joint] development, none of it was going to repair damage that was caused by the highway over years." Zecher remembered that some of those consultant reports may have been "turned down by the engineers."

Senator Barbara Mikulski (city councilperson at the time) said, "Many of the people who moved to Rosemont were World War II vets who bought their homes in the '40s and the '50s. …They wanted to pay off their houses and… create opportunities for their children. Well, bingo bango, the expressway came through Rosemont and just totally wiped them out."[301]

City council passed the condemnation ordinance in May 1967; 483 homes and 68 businesses were acquired at a cost of $5.3 million.[302] The acquisitions would eliminate or relocate 490 jobs and reduce city tax revenues by $230,000 ($2 million today) annually.[303] In the same month, the city finalized the contract with UDCT, which, only six months after the condemnation ordinance passed, began looking at alternatives for Rosemont. Once again, the city's horrendous decision-making (proceeding with acquisitions while hiring and then shackling UDCT) proved to be disastrous to the Rosemont neighborhood.

With neighborhood pressure mounting, UDCT advised the Policy Advisory Board on December 26, 1967, "that only a different road location could provide a reasonable solution."[304] The following month, making their first exception to "the givens," the board authorized UDCT to analyze alternatives to the 10-D Rosemont alignment.[305] DPW and the engineering side of the Concept Team opposed the exception, concerned about the precedent set in letting the "camel's nose under the tent." On this point they would later prove to be omniscient (see Federal Hill chapter).

As noted in the Harlem Park chapter, Mayor D'Alesandro's February 1968 speech at the American Road Building Association conference was stridently anti-displacement, even predicting that "community dismemberments" will "become…a major cause of unrest." He stressed that Baltimore was in better shape to handle this problem than other cities because of UDCT. Only three months later Baltimore exploded after the King assassination. Two weeks after the riots, D'Alesandro had a chance to save one African American neighborhood, to follow the advice of the UDCT experts he had claimed to value; but he inexplicably, irrationally, and unforgivably failed.

The mayor was an hour late for the April 1968 meeting to consider UDCT's Rosemont alternatives; rather than hearing UDCT's presentation, he got a slanted summary from Jerome Wolff.[306] D'Alesandro's words at that road building conference seemed to have been written in disappearing ink— he decided to stick with the current alignment, really a death sentence for Rosemont. Wolff explained the decision to Joe Wiles, saying, "I think we create more uproar by considering other routes. We were reluctant to consider it in the first place. The route there is the final one."[307]

However, for Joe Wiles and the Rosemont Community Association, this decision was a betrayal. D'Alesandro had promised a different approach. His remarks at the conference were not out of character. For example, as a mayoral candidate, D'Alessandro had promised, "I am not going to run freeways through people."[308] He had "talked the talk," but he was not "walking the walk."

The decision also did not sit well with young UDCT planners like Stewart Bryant, who geared up their assistance to communities and highway opposition groups. They showed Rosemont and MAD activists the rejected alternatives, fanning the flames of discontent. The city later prohibited UDCT staff from going to community meetings, but, at least for Rosemont, the cat was out of the bag.

On May 15, 1968, Mayor D'Alesandro invited Wiles to a meeting with Secretary of Transportation Alan Boyd. Wiles had gained the mayor's respect, even though the mayor's decision had gone against the Rosemont Bypass. It was most likely at this meeting that Wiles impressed federal officials who later leaned on the city and state to avoid Rosemont.

In the summer of 1968 UDCT's camel went all the way under the tent, and a mostly new alignment for I-95 was evaluated (the Fort McHenry Bypass). Although the new charge did not include Rosemont, the general upheaval opened the door for Wiles and Rosemont to press their case with the mayor and others.

JOSEPH WILES AND MARY ROSEMOND, ROSEMONT'S STALWART LEADERS

MAD and RAM activist Stu Wechsler, interviewed in 2019, recalled the west side's three most prominent leaders, Joseph Wiles, John Wells, and Mary Rosemond. "They were just remarkable.... [It was unfortunate that] Barbara Mikulski...cast such a bright light that a lot of these other people, who were great in their own right, [did not get] the coverage." Stu and fellow MAD activist Art Cohen wanted to make sure this book highlighted the critical contributions of Joe Wiles and Mary Rosemond.[309]

Cohen, interviewed in 2019, was effusive about Wiles.

> Wiles was a powerful presence... He just carried himself with great dignity and sincerity. He wasn't loud or boisterous or nasty; he was just always gentlemanly. But he was also passionate, in terms of wanting to preserve that community, what they had built up over the years. They had been in that neighborhood for a long time only to find that it was a target of destruction for this interstate. And they just weren't going to sit still for this. I'm sure he prevailed on local politicians however he could, but Joe Wiles was just an impressive man. And he came to all of the MAD meetings—he always was there. And he was very encouraging to the rest of us in whatever we tried to do. And, if you had Joe Wiles behind you, you knew you were solid. So, he was the kind of guy who just really made MAD a strong coalition.

Earl Swift (author of *The Big Roads*) said that Wiles "rarely made it into the city's newspapers... [but] he was the quintessential background operator, a man whose community activism took quiet but persistent form, who put faith in persuasion and persistence over making a lot of noise." Swift devotes a lengthy section of "The Human Obstacle" chapter to Wiles' background and personal life—it is a story of African American upward mobility that likely shares elements with many of Wiles' neighbors in middle class Rosemont.[310]

Wiles grew up in Brooklyn, the son of immigrants from Barbados. Neither his father (a printer) nor his mother (a homemaker) had a high school education. Still, Swift says, "they had infused Wiles and his four younger brothers with a hunger for learning and service, and with an understanding that 'community' meant more than lines on a map."[311] Wiles won a basketball scholarship to Atlanta University where he studied biology and medicine, graduating in 1941.

Marriage, two children, and multiple stints in the armed services left Wiles longing for a stable and healthy place for him to raise a family. His job in the research lab at Edgewood Arsenal provided a stable income, but the Wileses were locked out of all the neighborhoods close to Edgewood. This led them to a townhome on Ellamont Avenue in Rosemont. The neighborhood provided just the social milieu they were looking for, as Swift says, "The girls instantly made a passel of friends and spent afternoons playing jacks, jumping rope, and riding bikes in the alley. Rosemont became home."[312]

Wiles and his neighbors began working on larger community issues, which led to the formation of the Rosemont Community Association. Swift explains, "At its first meeting, despite his soft-spoken, almost shy manner, Wiles was elected president." The Association directed block cleanups, turned vacant lots into well-groomed green spaces, and organized assistance to older residents that were having trouble keeping up with maintenance problems. Swift continues, "The culture of involvement fed on itself; Rosemont came to seem a village in the city."[313]

Meanwhile Wiles rose through the ranks at Aberdeen Proving Ground, which had absorbed the Edgewood Arsenal; he authored several dozen research papers that were published in pharmacology journals, and he received a patent for the vaccination gun, a.k.a. the "injection pistol."

By the time Wiles took on the expressway in the mid to late '60s, he had honed his leadership skills with quiet diplomacy and the art of persuasion—he simply won people over. It helped that his cause was just.

Mary Rosemond was victimized by highways twice in different cities. Growing up in Jacksonville, Florida, she witnessed her mother's fight against a

MARY ROSEMOND'S MAD
COLORING BOOK

As a teacher, Rosemond had a knack for communicating with children, as seen in one of MAD's many efforts to reach the broadest possible audience, the MAD Coloring Book. Her lovely, simple, and direct message is on each page, for example:

"C is for city, your city, our city, color it silent in the morning. Color the sky clear, color birds singing. Color it contented. Color it peaceful. Color it friendly, the city comes alive with people."

"P is for pollution. Color it hazy. Color it thick. Color it dull. Color it impure. Color the trees dying and dead. Color the people gasping for clean air. This cannot be your city! This cannot be our city!"

highway. "They just broke up the neighborhood," she said. "But my mama wouldn't sell."[314] Then, after acquiring her Rosemont home in the mid-1950s, Mary was shocked to see that the 1957 East-West Expressway would put her through the same trauma. Readers from a White middle-class background probably regard this as a wild, one-of-a-kind coincidence. But for urban African American families, multiple experiences with highway (and urban renewal) relocations were all too commonplace.

Art Cohen was an admirer. He said Rosemond had "a gentle demeanor but underneath it was a steely determination...and a fierce dedication to the people of that community.... She was at the center of community efforts to promote, develop, and preserve...what they had built there."

Rosemond was also a stickler for details and documentation—she retained the association's records, neatly filed away in her basement. After sifting through the records, researcher Brandi Nieland remarked, "What her neighborhood has done for itself is inspiring. Her collection is like Baltimore City's personal diary."

Rosemond's role in stopping the highway is commemorated on a community plaque located, quite appropriately, on Pulaski Street just before the entrance to the Highway to Nowhere.

THE ROSEMONT (IN)DECISION

They would rather run the expressway through Black folks' bedrooms than White folks' cemetery.

A biting slogan adopted by RAM and repeated by MAD

Shortly after D'Alesandro's April 1968 decision to keep the 10-D route through the middle of Rosemont, the tide began turning as Joe Wiles, Mary Rosemond, MAD, RAM, and CORE all pressed their case at every opportunity. Fifth District Councilman Alexander Stark became an important advocate, calling attention to UDCT's alternate routes.[315] Bob Embry weighed in, asking the mayor in an August 1968 memo to consider alternative alignments for Rosemont as part of Fort McHenry alternatives.[316]

Wiles also appealed to the feds, which at first resulted in little policy gain but produced a scathing column in the *Baltimore Sun*. Wiles sent a letter to Alan Boyd, whom he had met at a RAM meeting back in 1967. Frank Turner, one of the original architects of the Interstate System, replied in typical bureaucratese:

Alternate alignment considerations were studied, as you noted, and determination then made . . . that the team should concentrate their efforts in the original corridor toward development of a design solution which would contribute to the environment of the area, and which would bring to bear the skill and the thinking of all planning disciplines so that the final design solution would reflect full public and private interest.

The *Sun's* James Dilts subjected this reply to a journalistic skewering.

What does one make of such official gobbledygook? How, by any stretch of the imagination, can a highway that the Design Concept Team has shown will destroy Rosemont possibly 'contribute to the environment of the area'? Which area? What environment?

[The expressway is] our domestic Vietnam—the same line of reasoning…that we must destroy you to save you… How long, one wonders, will the city engage in urbanicide? When will the federal government recognize the foolhardiness of desperately spending money to build communities such as Rosemont with a Model Cities Program, while busily knocking down the ones they already have with a highway program. Mr. Wiles and the residents of Rosemont hope it will be soon. "The city," Wiles said, "has some devious ways of doing things." Mr. Wiles is the master of understatement.[317][†]

In October 1968 UDCT staff presented new options for the I-95 corridor to Lowell Bridwell, Federal Highway Administrator, including the Fort McHenry Bypass. When discussion turned to Rosemont, Bridwell said he was "not likely to look with any favor on any route that slashed through the Negro neighborhood of Rosemont."[318] We do not know what influenced Bridwell's defense of Rosemont, but I suspect it was two things: Wiles' work behind the scenes and embarrassment over Dilts' scorching column.

In December 1968 D'Alesandro decided in favor of the 3-A/Fort McHenry alignment over 10-D and several other options. While 3-A still went through Leakin Park and the Franklin-Mulberry corridor, the mayor said he wanted to bypass Rosemont as the connector. If you're counting, this is the third time the mayor changed his mind on Rosemont.

The devil was still in the details. There were several complexities, mostly revolving around taking land and moving graves in Western Cemetery just west

---

† This seems like an appropriate place for James Dilts, in his own words, to add a little background to his "journalistic skewering" of the highway plans. Interviewed by Baltimore Heritage in December 2017, he framed his work with highway opponents this way:

There were a lot of interesting groups involved in this fight, the expressway fight. I used to call them the Urban Mafia. We would meet in church basements and stuff like that. There were guys… from CORE, the archdiocese, from a lot of different groups, and they would [each] know different things, and we would all trade secrets… and then I would write about it. I tell you, when I was writing these articles … until like 2:00, 3:00 in the morning, writing this stuff. I was on fire. I was on fire. There was nothing like it.

(Source: Baltimore Heritage, "A tribute to Jim Dilts in his own words," May 2018)

of Rosemont. There were questions about whether condemnation authority could be used for cemeteries. There were tunneling options, but those added significant costs. Jay Brodie (Deputy Housing Commissioner) said he had advocated for the tunnel option but was overruled. UDCT staff produced four alternatives in April 1969. There was no perfect solution—they all involved tradeoffs.

In advance of August public hearings, there was City Hall briefing on July 29. Nathaniel Owings made a surprise appearance and was given the floor as a courtesy. Owings abandoned all pretenses of objectivity, saying, "I'd put my body across the tracks and say the road should not go through [Rosemont].... We don't know if the road should go anywhere, but we know where it should *not* go." Joseph Axelrod (IDBC) quickly clarified that Mr. Owings had expressed "a personal opinion."[319]

The August 1969 Rosemont hearing was a watershed event. Exactly one year before, MAD had been organized as a city-wide multi-racial anti-highway coalition. The Rosemont hearings were MAD's first real chance to pull together its diverse constituency and show its mettle. News articles reflected the success of this unified effort. The *Sun*'s headline read, "An expressway bridges the gulf between people: Rosemont hearings draw opponents from suburbs, inner city into unified front."[320] The article continues:

Several witnesses described the hearings as the greatest boon to race relations here in years. "You did one good thing," an angry woman told highway officials, "you brought White and Black together and this is a beautiful thing." Another witness noted that some officials had felt the expressway issue would pit Negroes against Whites. Instead, he said, "the threat of the roads is acting like a zipper. It's pulling the people together."

White residents from Canton, Highlandtown, and Fell's Point, where homes are also in the path of the East-West Expressway, traveled to West Baltimore during the hearings to express warm sympathy and support for the Negroes of Rosemont.

Biracial mutual support had its own incongruous moments. Whites, at one point, found themselves applauding a Negro militant's threat of a Black powered war if the road went through.

The same news article also highlighted "a growing sophistication about the highway issues on the part of ordinary citizens. Along with the furious shouts and threats that predominated the hearings, there was a good deal of needling that displayed the expertise the public had acquired during its long fight to stop the road."

The hearing was complicated by the presence of a contingent of mostly White suburbanites opposed to the disturbance of their relatives' graves in Western Cemetery. One spokesman said, "Edgar Allan Poe would have loved to have this thing to write about. It's macabre, it's grisly. We used to call them grave robbers."[321]

This odd mix of attendees produced a moment that many participants remember fifty years later. The proceedings started with most African Americans on one side of the aisle and most White people on the other side. One of the White attendees, whose main mission was protecting the graves, switched gears in mid-speech and turned to address the African American side of the room. He said, you don't want the expressway going through your homes; we don't want the expressway going through the cemetery; but we should not be fighting each other, because the answer is that the expressway should not be built, period. In a spontaneous and symbolic movement, the White and African American protesters got out of their seats, crossed over the aisle, and suddenly the multi-racial coalition that MAD worked so hard to create was taking physical shape in this auditorium, before the very eyes of the highway planners.

Although the purpose of the hearing was to air and weigh out the four alternate alignments, only one of fifty testifiers offered up any comment about the alternatives. This was a conscious strategy on the part of MAD and the Rosemont Community Association—by this time highway opponents were starting to see that the "no-build alternative" was not just an exercise in futility, so testimony had been orchestrated to attack the basis of the expressway rather than the particulars. It was an impressive showing for MAD—they had unified the opposition and brought together White eastsiders to aid African American westsiders; they had gained expertise and were now critiquing every assumption and key data point used to justify the highways; and they were not in the mood to compromise.

After the hearing, UDCT's role in assisting the opposition moved front and center. IDBC's Joe Axelrod was examining material submitted in the testimony and concluded that opponents had access to inside information sources. Evidence was piling up: anti-highway fliers appeared in UDCT offices and may have been prepared and copied using UDCT resources; private/internal communications had appeared in MAD testimony; Axelrod even found himself examining the typeface used in opposition materials and noting that it was the same architectural typeface used by Skidmore, UDCT's architectural lead. Axelrod was quoted in the news: "How much of our resources are being used to support the enemy?"[322]

In an October 1969 speech at the Engineer's Club, an incognito MAD representative reported Axelrod's speech this way: Axelrod "felt that the highway people had been put on the defensive by clever spokesmen who claimed the problem was now narrowed down to the choice of a road that would destroy the graves of dead Whites or the homes of live Black people."[323] In other words, MAD and RAM were controlling the public dialogue (a check in the win column for the opposition).

Late in 1969, someone convinced D'Alesandro that he should backpedal and stick to the original alignment through Rosemont. The mayor, apparently prone to making impulsive decisions based on the last person he talked to, announced there would be no change to the Rosemont segment (the fourth time he changed course on Rosemont), citing difficulties in acquiring cemetery land.[324] MAD, Wiles, the Rosemont Community Association, and other allies again ramped up their advocacy of the Rosemont alternatives.

The city's Transportation Coordinating Committee, now very much in the weeds relative to Rosemont (and seemingly ignoring the mayor's latest policy shift), asked UDCT to produce yet more alternatives, this time attempting to avoid both households and graves. Seven additional alternatives were evaluated in December 1969, and the mayor reversed himself (for the fifth time!) as these new options were put forward.

The final decision was not made until July 1970, eighteen months after D'Alesandro's initial decision to avoid Rosemont. The adopted bypass (Figure 28) impacted no homes; it still relocated hundreds of graves, but far fewer than earlier options. In December 1970 the original condemnation line was lifted by city council, finally ending the thirteen-year fight to save Rosemont. The decision to save Rosemont from the wrecking ball was celebrated locally and nationally, not just by highway opponents, but also in architectural and planning circles.

The city applied for and received $5 million in federal funds to rehabilitate the 483 acquired homes, giving first preference to previous homeowners that had relocated. The difficulties involved in relocating graves in Western Cemetery became one more impediment to building I-70. The segment died a very slow death, with the city formally dropping it in 1981. The Leakin Park chapter is more expansive on this subject.

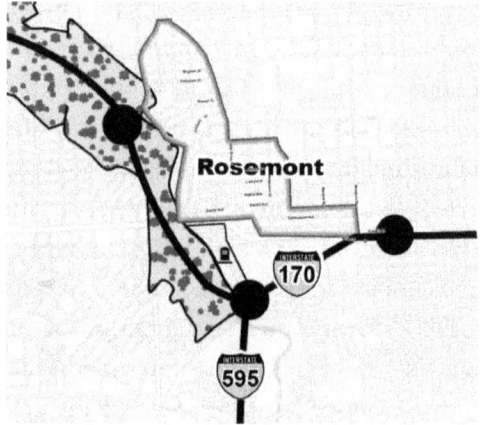

Figure 28. Rosemont Bypass adopted in July 1970 (the headstone symbol is Western Cemetery)

ROSEMONT, POST ROAD WARS

People won't burn down houses that they own.
Unnamed Republican senator on Congress' cynical reasoning for adopting the Section 235 mortgage subsidy program used to rebuild Rosemont homes

Rosemont's triumph was that the highway was first rerouted and later dropped. Most of the acquired houses were not torn down; they were later rehabilitated, so the physical fabric of the community was retained. However, the social fabric of this once close-knit community was torn asunder. So many of those hard-working families, sharing great pride in their neighborhood, had been forced to relocate by a city that did not recognize their value.

Two years after the condemnation line was lifted, Joe Wiles gave a sober-ing report to Baltimore City Council, bluntly stating that Rosemont "had been destroyed," partly by the forced exodus of middle-class homeowners and partly by the long period of time that Rosemont was under the cloud of condemnation, giving those left with no incentive "for maintaining and preserving their homes."[325]

Art Cohen visited Mary Rosemond around 1979 and observed that the neighborhood had deteriorated. "Just the whole weight of the expressway planning and the condemnation lines, the threat to the area, really the disre-gard of the area, had all taken a toll," he said.

However, it was not just that the social fabric had been interrupted. Author Emily Lieb was highly critical of the manner in which the city man-aged the rehabilitation and resale of the acquired homes. She said contractors cut corners and used below-standard materials. Complaints about the low quality of work attracted the attention of Congressman Parren Mitchell. His investigation concluded that new homeowners, lured by favorable financing under the Section 235 program, were in danger of buying "a home with a thirty-year mortgage only to have it fall apart in ten."[326]

With low down payments (only $200) and subsidized interest rates (set at 20 percent of income), the Section 235 program attracted "mostly first-time homebuyers hovering just above the poverty line," according to Lieb. Many of these newcomers were ill-equipped for homeownership. They fell behind on upkeep, which was more than they bargained for partly because of the contactors' poor workmanship, and this once beautifully maintained neighborhood began to deteriorate.[327] Subsidized housing may have been nec-essary to reoccupy all those mistaken acquisitions, but the end result seemed to hasten rather than stem neighborhood decline.

A 1988 news article gave voice to neighborhood fears about drugs and crime. Long-time residents complained that they had to be accompanied on walks to the corner store. Middle-class parents found their kids lured into the world of drugs and fast money. The homeownership rate had declined from 72 percent in the late '60s to 54 percent in 1980, still higher than the city-wide average of 47 percent.[328]

In general, the city has not done well in retaining the Black middle class. As discriminatory housing practices in the suburbs slowly receded, many Black families that could afford to pulled up stakes and moved out. Of course, there is always a push-pull axis in considering urban versus suburban locations. The city was not offering enough to "pull" them back in, but crime, drugs, schools, and policing problems provided plenty of "push."

Ironically, highway relocations (supplemented by the $5,000 bonus for "replacement value") provided a big part of the first push of Black populations into the County part of the Liberty Road corridor. At a 1969 US Conference of Mayors meeting in Cleveland, D'Alesandro proudly announced the puncturing of the "White noose" around the city, saying, "We are seeking and getting housing for inner city residents in the counties." D'Alesandro declared that "hundreds of homes are involved; the breakthrough has been made." He later clarified that about one hundred former Rosemont households had moved to the County.

His fellow mayors were astounded. Henry Maeir, mayor of Milwaukee, asked incredulously, "Do you mean to tell me you got [Black] people moved into affluent suburbs?" Cleveland Mayor Carl Stokes was quoted as saying, "I'm moving to Baltimore."[329] Of course, this was progress—African Americans were starting to have the same freedom of choice enjoyed by White people, but the downside was that Rosemont and other middle class and predominantly African American neighborhoods in the city were suddenly competing with the suburbs, and, more often than not, losing. Worse, Baltimore did not even know it was a contest.

While other neighborhood battlegrounds featured in this book are clearly in either the victory or defeat column, Rosemont was both—a spectacular win and a crushing defeat.

X. BLOWS AGAINST THE EMPIRE II

MIKULSKI AND SCAR

Barbara Mikulski is somewhat of a phenomenon in Baltimore. She emerged virtually unknown from East Baltimore's ethnic neighborhoods and conducted a grassroots door-to-door campaign which managed to unseat the incumbent councilman in her district. She is a forceful voice in the city council and an articulate representative for the ethnic community.
Phyllis K. Wilson, Greater Baltimore Committee, memo from November 15, 1972, to Urban Affairs panelists

MAD member Mary Logan volunteered to assist Barbara Mikulski in the 1971 councilmanic elections because of her opposition to the Road. Mikulski was not on the Democratic slate, so it was an uphill climb. Mary, in a 2019 interview, recalled handing out Mikulski's literature on election day and running into a gregarious local man who was handing out a straight Democratic ticket. "I told him why I liked Barbara," she said, and "he started handing his literature out, [but] telling people, 'Well, I want you to vote for these two people, but you can vote for her Polack rather than mine.'"

There were more than a few voters who pulled the lever for Mary Logan's Pole: Mikulski got the most votes in the First District. As election returns came in, the Movement Against Destruction (MAD) anxiously counted their gains. They conservatively assumed that they could only count on elected officials that were also members of MAD: Barbara Mikulski, Robert Douglas, Robert Fitzpatrick, Alexander Stark, and Wally Orlinsky. This was a coming-of-age moment for highway opponents. Newly elected Mayor Schaefer still held the cards, but expressway skeptics had earned a seat at the table. More importantly, they finally had a spokesperson in a position of authority: Barbara Ann Mikulski. I use the phrase "position of authority" loosely—after all, Mikulski was just one vote in an eighteen-member body. However,

Baltimore's future US senator was a larger-than-life personality who commanded attention and respect; she gave expressway opposition both legitimacy and an amped up megaphone.

SOUTHEAST COUNCIL AGAINST THE ROAD'S (SCAR'S) INCEPTION

When I interviewed Senator Mikulski in 2020, she described her initiation into the Road Fight through the University of Maryland School of Social Work. Her mentor, Sister Mary Vera, had asked her to meet with Sister Elaine Lowery and Captain Tom Fiorello, a fellow student and former military man interning with UDCT. Fiorello told Mikulski that highway-impacted communities had no say in the matter, and their homes were being acquired below appraised value with minimal relocation benefits. "They were afraid...to fight the political machine," Mikulski recalled.

They asked her to come to a meeting at St. Stanislaus Church.* The senator attributes this invitation to her family name. "My grandmother had one of the most prominent Polish bakeries in Baltimore. Dad had a grocery store. His father-in-law also had a grocery store.... Quite frankly, if people were hungry, our family extended credit. My grandmother was beloved. So, the name Mikulski meant something. It stood for integrity and compassion and being rooted in the community." She attended the meeting, listened to their fears, and was completely drawn into the issue, she says, "because it was not about losing your house. It was about losing your community."

Her response reveals her budding political thought process. "I felt we could fight City Hall because there was going to be a bond referendum on school construction, which we were for. We were absolutely for it. But if we threaten to withhold votes, then maybe we had some degree of power." Mikulski suggested that a smaller group convene to do two things:

---

* We previously dubbed UDCT the "planner insurgents" for their astonishing role in aiding and abetting the enemy. Here we add to that legacy: UDCT intern Captain Tom Fiorello was responsible for recruiting the number one Road Warrior, Barbara Ann Mikulski.

We had to give ourselves a militant name, and we had to create the illusion of power that we were more than the twenty people in that room. So, we went down the street to Glyphis' Tavern, which is the corner of Fell Street, Anne Street, and Thames Street. We met there over a glass or two of Ouzo. That is how we came up with the name SCAR, Southeast Council Against the Road. SCAR then proceeded to meet on a bi-weekly basis in the basement of Holy Rosary Church because the priest, Father Mike Miller, wanted to be active and help the community and so on. That was where we met and that is how it got started.

At this point Joe McNeely picks up the story thread, explaining how Mikulski and SCAR helped to form Southeast Community Organization (SECO). In the wake of the 1968 riots, Mikulski (already familiar with the issues) was hired for the summer of 1969 as a community organizer to create "multi-faceted neighborhood organizations" that could counter White flight and disinvestment. That organization later became SECO. Mikulski's job was to assess community issues, match them with potential leaders, and then "figure out how to move them." The most explosive of those community issues was the highway, and the leader Mikulski identified was Gloria Aull.

GLORIA AULL'S ARMY OF HOUSEWIVES

Robert Moses once dismissed his New York City critics as "just a bunch of housewives." Just as in the Big Apple, Moses' Baltimore highway plans succumbed to a determined group of road-fighting housewives. In separate interviews, Mikulski and McNeely each repeatedly returned to the emergence of women as leaders of SCAR and SECO. Mikulski recalled "the rise of women claiming their power [over] the political clubs [and their] cigar-smoking, smoke-filled rooms… Women had [influence] but it had been in ethnic heritage organizations and so on." She continues, "every area had their own leadership," but it was mostly women who challenged convention, be that for the expressway system or for libraries, schools, and housing.

When McNeely speaks of the women of SCAR, his tone is reverent. Though most have now departed this world, he wanted to give credit where credit is long overdue. Not one of them had a resume that would impress, but each rose to a leadership role that defied their humble beginnings. He ticks off the list: Gloria Aull, Jean Hepner, Delores Canoles, Sophia Maloney, Eleanor Lukowski, Elizabeth Hunt, Betty Hyatt, Matilda Koval...

> These were housewives, and they were smarter than shit—they were the ones that mobilized the people, studied the issue, did the analysis, came together and taught themselves...the regulations. Betty Hyatt ended up on the school board. Delores ended up on the liquor board.... Jean Hepner, another housewife, she and her husband bought Captain Fell's House on Fell Street... She was just sweet and loving...everybody liked her. She was the secretary of every committee she ever got on. [Many of these women] became the leadership of [SECO] for twenty years... SCAR was a practice run.

For the SCAR part of the SECO community organizing machine, Gloria Aull was the ringleader. Aull's family history is typical of Canton-Highlandtown. Her grandmother's family emigrated from Hamburg, Germany, at the turn of the century, lured by the promise of jobs: Canton, sometimes called the nation's first industrial park, offered plentiful jobs in packing houses, canneries, and the copperworks.[330] Gloria's Mother[†] bought their house on the border of Canton and Highlandtown with a five-dollar bill as down payment. McNeely said:

> Gloria was probably the smartest-person-in-the-class type of person at Patterson High. Girls weren't supposed to go to college, [so] she got married; her husband worked in the factory; she raised three kids on Kenwood Avenue... She was incredibly smart and articulate and active; she could

---

† McNeely said Gloria's mother "had the most amazing foul mouth of anybody I'd ever met... We'd be aghast."

attract people... She was...pretty sophisticated [considering that she was] mostly self-educated and had...spent her whole life in Canton. She was one of the first people that Barbara identified as a natural spark plug. She loved Canton; she'd get involved in every issue. She didn't like taking the forefront as a leader, she liked encouraging other people to become leaders.

Senator Mikulski, her emotions rising even though all this was fifty years past, spoke of the sacrifices made by Aull and the other leaders of SCAR:

They put their heart into it, and they put their pocketbook into it. Whatever we did, we had to raise money for ourselves, and we were fighting the State Highway Commission....And it was controversial. We were called a lot of names. We were called communists. We were slandered about our backgrounds. They would just want to continually undermine us... Some of them cast incredible disparagement. But they really stood fast.

Following the Road Fight, Gloria acted as Treasurer of Southeast Development, Inc., a SECO subsidiary. In 1977 she was elected to the Board of Directors of the National Center for Urban Ethnic Affairs.[331] When she passed away in 1993, there was an outpouring of accolades that went well beyond the Road Fight. Mikulski said, "She was one of the founding mothers of SECO...and she could really bring out East Baltimore. She was equally good at stopping roads and playing pinochle." Gloria's sister, Joan Hoffman, noted that Gloria had chaired a national committee that lobbied for the Family Leave Act. When Aull was debilitated by the cancer that later killed her, Joan took advantage of that very law to take care of her sister.

McNeely remembers another small but significant story about Gloria's funeral. Former IDBC Director (and later Secretary of Transportation) Dick Trainor was in attendance. McNeely interpreted this as a "Grant respects Lee" moment, but I can't help but wonder if Trainor was there to send out silent appreciation for someone who prevented him from making the biggest mistake of his professional career.

221

Senator Mikulski is fond of telling the story of how SCAR managed to give the appearance of a widespread movement, when in reality, it was the same people meeting under different organization names. "We got started with about eight of us meeting seven times a week in groups under different names to create the illusion of power. There are two sources of power: money and large numbers. We didn't have lots of money. All we had was each other. Our strength rested in activating [or creating the illusion of] those large numbers."[332]

Joe McNeely has a knack for helping you understand the big picture with engaging stories. He gave me a crash course in community organizing principles: You need short-term doable objectives so that everyone can see progress. While stopping the Road might be the real goal, your first step might be to "get a meeting with Dick Trainor." Trainor, he said, is a tall guy who wears cowboy boots. "He makes a useful icon."

Then, if requesting the meeting doesn't work, you take the meeting to Trainor, which leads Joe to imparting this anecdote: "[We] showed up to disrupt the ribbon cutting for BWI… the women in our group decided to find the tallest women we could to stand up to Trainor; they came up with four women that were five-eleven to six foot; then we helped them get three-inch heels so that when the four of them stood around Trainor he [wouldn't be] looking down—they could look him in the eye." Needless to say, the four chosen representatives did not include Barbara Mikulski.

Of course, SCAR could turn folks out for hearings, too. On June 29, 1971, they may have charted new territory among highway opposition groups—350 people showed up for a hearing that had actually been *canceled* two weeks before. No, this was not a mistake—highway officials had canceled the meeting, but SCAR decided to hold it anyway. The thinking was that the audience was not highway officials, who were not listening anyway; it was the media and the attendees themselves, bolstering their resolve. In other words, preaching to the choir is a useful community organizing vehicle.

SCAR IN ACTION

SCAR meeting minutes reveal an energized group of doers, the polar opposite of pontificators. A thumbnail impression emerges: octopus-like, with tentacles spreading out to suffocate the highway at every possible weak point. A few excerpts suffice:

> 500 posters prepared and distributed... 50 letters were directed to the mayor's home with the help of the 7th and 8th grades at Saint Stanislaus School... prepared "action list" for taxpayers, also distributed by middle schoolers... drafted press release to explain federal regulations... secured a blowup of a bulldozer in the demolition area for use at the display booth... letter published on the front page of the East Baltimore Guide... a "condemnation kit," prepared by MAD, to be distributed to people in the acquisition area... meetings set with Western Electric and other industrial businesses... Reverend Al Baumann will mimeo 3,000 action lists and distribute 200 buttons... 27 people representing 13 organizations were present at a Canton-Highlandtown meeting and voted to join Fell's Point in the fight against the road.

Those excerpts were taken from only one meeting: March 27, 1969.

SCAR and SECO worked tirelessly with other groups, often creating multi-racial coalitions to strengthen the hand of each participating organization. This included MAD, of course, but we also find vocal SCAR/SECO representatives Betty Deacon and Ms. M. L. Dashiell in news articles about the shortage of replacement housing in Sharp Leadenhall.[333] As cited previously, there was similar coalition building with the famous Baltimore humanitarian Bea Gaddy and with Lucille Gorham for her work in the

Middle East neighborhood. Senator Mikulski stressed that it was important for SCAR and SECO to counter "what the John Gardner Urban Coalition crowd was saying, that 'Oh, the White working class are the enemy against Black people.'"

By 1975, SCAR had receded in the highway fight. In a 1974 interview Mikulski said, "To me, it's amazing citizens persevere at all. Because we did this in our own time. People took off from work, people made tremendous personal sacrifices, and that's why I said we're worn out." SCAR's impact, much like MAD's, did not include any slam-dunk wins over the Road establishment. However, by uniting southeast Baltimore, by forging inter-racial coalitions, by adding to the steadily rising mountain of criticism, and by cultivating future leaders, they left a lasting and powerful legacy.

CITY COUNCIL

In organizing SCAR and SECO, Mikulski gained a reputation as someone who could forcefully articulate the needs of the community and generate enthusiasm for a new way of getting things done. When she ran for city council in 1971, Mikulski separated herself from SECO so the organization would not be seen as a political group. However, the parallels were plain to see. She and SECO both represented a challenge to the backroom councilmanic fiefdoms that had controlled southeast Baltimore politics for decades. And she knew all the issues because she attended all the meetings in establishing SECO: "I knew about the library, and I knew about the fact that Betty Deacon and other moms were also advocating for the dyslexia program at school G-15. I knew about the truck task force. So, you see…ours was kind of a federation of issues of which the Road was an anchor because it cut through so many neighborhoods."

The Mikulski name, as noted above, was both well-known and highly respected. She recalled that once, going door to door, a woman had asked her, "Now, tell me, kid, are you any relation to Mikulski's Bakery?" Hearing that, yes, it was Mikulski's grandmother, the woman said, "If you are half as good as your donuts you will be okay." Mikulski remembered telling her campaign team, "I feel like I am going to spend...the rest of my political career [trying to be] as good as my grandmother's jelly donuts."

In that same 1971 Council race, Mikulski became a national spokesperson for the all-but-forgotten working class White ethnics. In fundraising for SECO, Mikulski connected with Monsignor Geno Baroni, a Catholic priest who was organizing urban ethnic parishes. Mikulski and Baroni were on the same page in that, "We do not think of ourselves like Chicago and what Dr. King's experience [was] in Chicago."‡ They both felt that "White and Black people were pitted against each other, but we were fighting for crumbs...when both communities were being disinvested in."

Baroni asked Mikulski to speak at a conference at the Catholic University of America. It was a high-profile event with Senator Edmund Muskie as the keynote speaker. However, it was Maryland's *future* senator who commanded the most media attention. Capturing the essence of the issue in a single pithy phrase, she was widely quoted saying, "America is not a melting pot. It is a sizzling cauldron." Continuing, she attacked the conventional view of White ethnics:

ART COHEN ON WATCHING MIKULSKI IN ACTION

Art Cohen said in a 2019 interview: "I had known Barbara as a work associate and a colleague... I met her and the people from her Emergency Unit at DSS... We did a lot of work as a team...trying to...combat the effects of the poverty and racism in Baltimore."

Some time after she had decided to run for city council, Mikulski invited Cohen to one of her talks on the east side. He was shocked, as he put it, "To discover a completely new Barbara I hadn't even known was there. She has a great, powerful, bull horn voice, you know, socking it to the audience about what needed to be done and what was wrong... It was a pretty impressive, and it was an eye-opener for me."

‡ In 1966 Dr. King's Chicago march was attacked by White supremacists. Dr. King was hit on the head by a brick. After this incident, King said Chicago was the most racist city in the US. See: https://allthatsinteresting.com/racism-in-chicago.

The ethnic American is sick of being stereotyped as a racist and dullard by phony White liberals, pseudo Black militants and patronizing bureaucrats. He pays the bill for every major government program and gets nothing or little in the way of return... The ethnic American is overtaxed and underserved at every level of government... In many instances he is treated like the machine he operates or the pencil he pushes. He is tired of being treated like an object of production.[334]

This speech led to articles in the *Washington Post* and the *New York Times*. Mikulski remembered that the author of the *Times* article called her and said, "My editor would like you to write an op-ed about what you were saying because, coming out of Baltimore, you are a very different kind of voice." Mikulski's famous op-ed, "Who Speaks for Ethnic America?" appeared in the *Times* on September 29, 1970. The themes were similar to her speech, but she added one note right out of SECO's call for organizing southeast Baltimore: "The ethnics find that the only things being planned for their areas are housing projects, expressways, and fertilizer factories."[335] As Mikulski said, "That made me nationally famous. I did not seek it."

In June 1971, Mikulski wedded the plight of White ethnics to the highway issue at an expressway hearing at St. Brigid's Hall:

My great-grandparents, grandparents, and yours too, came to this country looking for an American Dream. Their dream was that, through hard work and honesty, they could own a home that no king, kaiser, or czar could take from them on some whim. Now in 1971 the dream has turned into a nightmare. The State Roads Commission and City Hall are taking from us the very homes we have struggled for all our lives. It's not right. It's not fair. And it's not going to happen."[336]

Seven months later, Mikulski was attempting to line up support for two proposals: one to repeal the condemnation lines for the entire 3-A expressway system and another to cut $30 million from the capital budget for highways. She was expecting a close vote, but instead got an education in the strong mayor form of government. After fourteen hours of testimony and with the vote approaching, she began looking at her colleagues for non-verbal cues. "Then I knew that the light at the end of the tunnel was the train coming toward me because nobody would look at me. They were looking at their shoes. They were looking at cornices in the ceiling." Her efforts landed only four votes, which was three votes more than Councilman Ward rounded up in a similar effort in 1967; at least you could say the trend was going in the right direction.

There were similar defeats in subsequent years, which draws us to an interesting question: Why is Mikulski regarded as the number one Road Warrior when her role in city council yielded so little gain? A good question that I will address in Chapter 17.

JOE McNEELY ON MIKULSKI'S FAMOUS BOX:

I was the one who invented the box for her to stand on, because when we were campaigning against Mathias, she was behind the podium somewhere, but nobody could see her…I grabbed some wood from my basement in Fell's Point and whipped it together.

XI. THE CANTON BLITZKRIEG

You have to hand it to DPW Chief Bernard Werner. He was right, and what happened to Canton might be Exhibit A. Werner was the city's top advocate for barging ahead with the 1962 10-D plan: no deviations responding to aggrieved parties, no dallying with more studies, no Design Concept Team— NO, NO, NO! Canton was Werner's road-building version of the blitzkrieg: acquire, relocate, demolish, pour concrete—get on with it before they knew what hit them.

The print was hardly dry on the May 1967 condemnation ordinance when the city started acquiring properties in Canton. Only a year and a half later SCAR gained inspiration for their acronym from the gash through Canton (Figure 29): 215 houses acquired, 500 people moved, buildings

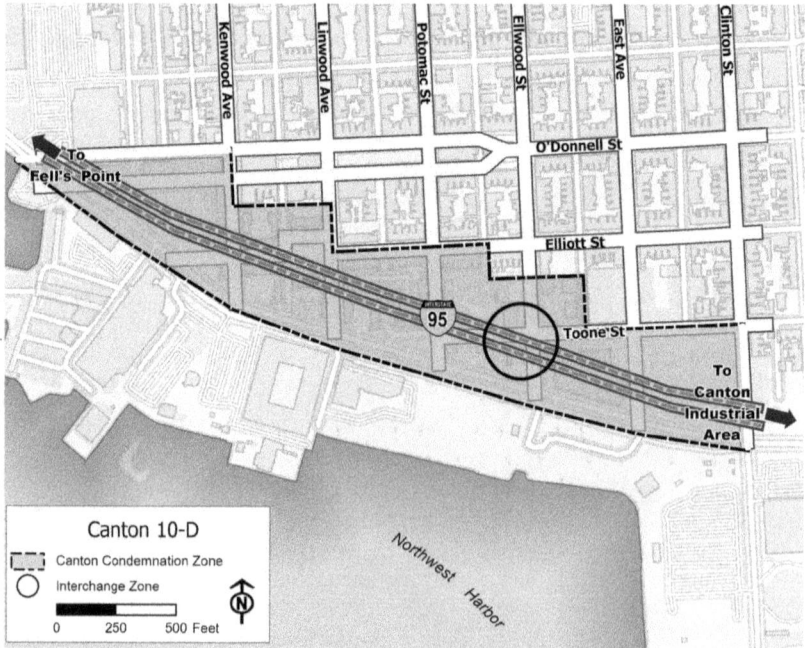

Figure 29. The Canton blitzkrieg path of 10-D (1961) and 10-D Modified (1967) (Scott Jeffrey, MS, GISP)

228

razed, all before the opposition really got organized. If Werner had held sway over the entire expressway system, the rest of the disastrous 10-D alignment would have followed the Canton example, and highway opponents all over the city would be looking at already demolished corridors and wondering what is the point of opposing the darn thing—there isn't much left to save.

Raymond Bahr is Canton's informal historian. When I interviewed him in November 2020, he asked me the same question that I was going to ask him: Was our impression correct, that Canton did not raise much of a ruckus to fight the original acquisitions? Part of the reason is that the city moved in quickly, before the opposition got organized, but the other reason is that most of the impacted residents were willing sellers.

Bahr characterized Canton in the 1960s as a "White ghetto." It was run-down but lacked the history and quirkiness that was so central to saving Fell's Point. For years Canton's wealthier residents had been moving across the city line to Dundalk, Essex, and Eastpoint. The same faction that embarrassed the Preservation Society at public meetings in 1967 was present in Canton—they wanted the relocation money to exit a declining neighborhood and move to the County. Bernard Werner was only too happy to oblige them.

However, one part of Werner's theory was later proven wrong—he postulated that neighborhoods like Canton would not organize an opposition force after expressway acquisitions were completed and houses were razed. That was not the case: In late 1968 Barbara Mikulski and Gloria Aull came together to form SCAR.

Canton, in the Road Fight, was primarily represented through SCAR (covered previously). Canton also played a strong role in the Southeast Truck Task Force, which knocked the pins out from under the rationale for the Road in southeast Baltimore.

"JUST NOT BETTY DEACON"

Southeast Baltimore had one issue that the mayor could claim the expressway would solve: Too much truck traffic was going through predominantly residential areas. Neighbors complained that trucks roared down their streets, creating intolerable noise and smog while rattling everything in their houses that was not nailed down. Schaefer often cited the removal of trucks from neighborhood streets as a key benefit of the expressway. This is where Betty Deacon entered the picture.

In later life Ms. Deacon obtained an advanced degree and served as state director for Senator Mikulski, as well as chief of staff for the president of Baltimore City Council. But, when she took up the truck issue, she was a housewife without a high school diploma. She organized the other neighborhood housewives, forming a group called Neighbors United, with the truck route issue as their primary concern. First, they met with the businesses that were generating the traffic and concluded that completion of I-83 would not address a significant part of the problem.

In early 1972 Deacon's group proposed that the city form a Southeast Truck Task Force to explore options, but Mayor Schaefer turned a deaf ear—the communities assumed his non-response was due to his need for the truck diversion issue as a rationale for the expressway. This stalemate led to a protest action and quite a memorable story. Deacon recounted the truck route protest in a 2018 interview, with Joe McNeely adding his recollection of the events:

> At 5 p.m. on a Friday evening, just north of Lombard Street on Kresson, we gathered our motley crew to stop traffic. My heart was beating. Like, I could not believe it. We had a lot of elderly people came—everybody came out to support us, but the older people were not going to get out in the middle of the street. We waited until there were two trucks coming along to begin and we walked out in the middle of the street. Some people with baby carriages started crossing back and forth. I had my son Brian in a stroller as did other women. But soon we had a parade of baby carriages and older people moving back and forth across the street, even some clergy in their white collars. We tied up traffic all the way down to the port.

The reaction of the truck drivers in the front two trucks was not pleasant.

The truck driver in the east lane came up and started edging forward towards us like he was going to run into us if we did not move. At this point, one of our local ministers got out in front and put his hand on the front of the truck! And the truck started, and he moved forward, and [our minister] just stood there and started going under the truck. This is when all the elderly people came out in the middle of the street because now, you were going to run over our minister!

It was the most unbelievable thing I ever saw. I was scared to death, but he stayed there. Finally, I went up and I banged on the trucker's door, and he opened his window and he said, "Get out of my way!" And I said, "Please, please. Please, will you work with us? We are trying to get the mayor to set up a truck task force, so you can get through our neighborhoods easier." He said, "Well, I have got to be in such a place at such a time," and I said, "Can you just give us thirty more minutes?" So, he shut his door, he sat there, he did not say anything and never moved the truck again.

Then the other trucker [got agitated]. He started to come out of his truck with a length of pipe he kept under his seat to protect the truck. Luckily one of the guys in the neighborhood was a truck driver himself; he pulls out his Teamsters card and says, "Hey, hey wait a minute!" The guy sees the Teamsters card and stops. [Our guy] explains to him what we're trying to do. And the trucker says, "Well, hell, I'm being paid by the hour, I'll sit here as long as you want." So, the two of them went to a bar to have a beer. When the cops finally showed up to make us clear out, we couldn't find the guy to move his truck.

Somebody calls the police, and the captain is there from the Southeast Police Station, and he said, "What are you people doing in the street? What do you want?" And I said, "We would like a meeting with the mayor. We want a truck task force for this community." And he said, "Well, let me get back to you." So, he went somewhere and made a phone call, and he came back, and he said, "Mayor Schaefer said he will meet with three or four people. Come down to City Hall now, but he said that one of them cannot be Betty Deacon."[337]

Schaefer, possibly trying to avoid blame for danger to the parish priest, did agree to form the Southeast Truck Task Force. In 1973, they did find and agree to non-highway solutions for routing the trucks. This was real progress for southeast Baltimore, but a loss for I-83 advocates. When the city pressed forward with the Fort McHenry Bypass, that created another truck bypass option and further weakened the case for I-83. Without the truck diversion issue, it became exceedingly difficult for highway planners to claim that I-83 would benefit southeast communities. It was one more issue where the mayor was losing in the court of public opinion.

KIDDIE CORPS FOR HISTORIC PRESERVATION

By the mid-1970s it was apparent that Fell's Point and Federal Hill had gained leverage, possibly even the winning hand by virtue of placing their neighborhoods on the National Register of Historic Places. While highway planners were bending over backward to avoid Fell's Point, the plan for Canton was still an elevated highway.*

Canton's leaders scoped out what it would take to achieve National Register status, but it was an uphill climb—they did not have their own Bob Eney or Jack Gleason to do the spade work. However, Eney did offer to train people and supervise the work. This led to an unconventional volunteer group: Canton enrolled grade schoolers from St. Brigid's to collect information.

McNeely recalled that Bob helped eighth graders do a historic survey of Canton. "So now the eighth graders were [saying]…'that's a 1940s cornice,' and 'look what they did with the brick.' And the factory worker father is

---

* David Chapin, former IDBC staff, said he thought there was a late 1970s plan to extend the Fell's Point tunnel through much of Canton. I have not found written confirmation of that plan.

going, 'What the eff you talking about, the *cornice*?' The kids are developing a pride for their buildings in Canton and the parents are getting influenced by this."

Historian Nancy Schamu remembered that a local church rector got his "fourth graders to interview their grandparents and do stories about their families living in Canton, and that was all part of an effort in that neighborhood to keep the interstate highway out... You know, you just see all these little kids with notebooks going to talk to their grandparents and...they don't realize they're fighting the highway."

This may be two versions of the same story, or perhaps the fourth and eighth graders were both involved but in different tasks. The main point—that Canton's historic status was gained through Bob Eney-supervised child labor—remains. The kids must have done a good job. Although the process took about three years, Canton was approved for the National Register in January 1980. And chalk up another point on Bob Eney's road-fighting resume—he must have been a natural at communicating history and architecture to these kids.

However, National Register status came in right at the end of the Road Wars—it was likely too late to impact the final decision to drop the Fell's Point-Canton segment. Also in 1980, the city council reevaluated the expressway plan and recommended dropping I-83 through southeast Baltimore—Canton's new status as a historic area is not mentioned in their report. Regardless of its impact on the Road Fight, the historic designation undoubtedly helped Canton turn the corner and come back as a desirable place to live and work.

CANTON, RACE, AND THE ROAD

There is one more issue we must address: Canton was not a bastion of racial tolerance. Charlie Duff, President of Jubilee Baltimore, claimed that this made Canton less prominent in the coalition-building critical to the success of highway opposition groups:

There just weren't enough people of any one kind or in any one neighborhood to have the political muscle to stop all of the Interstate Highway Division. The neighborhoods where people were able to cross the lines of class and race and form alliances tended to survive, and the places and people who couldn't do that tended not to survive.... Canton was very different than Fell's Point...The preservationists didn't care about [Canton] because the houses were too new and undistinguished.... Canton was very, very worried about race, and they saw almost everything in racial terms. They needed some allies, and they couldn't get the preservationists...and they didn't want to be a part of the citywide MAD because there were colored people at the meetings.

To clarify, SCAR (which represented Canton) was prominent in cross-racial coalition building. However, Duff is referring to Canton in its own right. Canton's record on race becomes important because SCAR faded from prominence in the Road Fight in the mid-seventies when Canton was still slated for an elevated highway.

In 1982, the Canton Improvement Association and its president, Tom Canoles, proposed a senior citizen's building as one anchor for redevelopment of vacant highway parcels. The community review of that project became a fight with heavy racial overtones. Tom said in a 2020 interview, "Many of the people that were opposed to [the project] didn't want an integrated senior complex in there." The opposition was strong enough to chase the facility out of Canton—it was built in Fell's Point instead.

The bottom line is, for various reasons including race, the fact that clearance happened before the opposition got organized, and the delay in getting National Register status, Canton was not a strong player in the highway opposition camp. Canton was saved largely on the coattails of Fell's Point. When the Fell's Pointers forced the adoption of the underwater tunnel option, the whole Lower Jones Falls/Fell's Point/Canton segment became too expensive, and Canton was spared.

It is in the post-Road-Wars comeback that the Canton star shines more brightly.

COMING BACK, STRONGER

Canton's decline was not just the residential acquisition area. The water-dependent businesses that occupied the Canton waterfront were subject to the same economic decline that impacted Fell's Point. Other businesses closed or moved due to direct highway acquisitions, but according to Tom Canoles, the impact was greater than just the highway corridor. "When those companies are planning their future, if they know that the government might come in and take their property, they don't plan to stay there. They plan to move." What this mass exodus left behind was not pretty (see sidebar).

Raymond Bahr had a local pharmacy in Canton that closed due to the highway acquisitions, not because the property had been acquired but because he lost his clientele. Canoles maintains that St. Brigid's School succumbed to the same phenomenon and was forced to close. The community also had to fight to keep the Canton Branch of Enoch Pratt open.

In the residential section north of Boston Street there was more damage spreading out from the highway acquisition corridor. Canoles recalled:

AN UNROMANTICIZED VIEW OF THE WATERFRONT

David Carroll, Department of Planning's coastal resources manager in the late 1970s and early '80s, had to correct some community representatives who were recalling the old waterfront through "rose-colored glasses":

"The shoreline was horrible. I mean derelict boats, rotting piers... I can remember going to a neighborhood meeting...they kept having sort of a retro memory of how wonderful it was to be able to get to the shoreline. So, I found these slides of before they did the demolition of the packing houses all along Boston Street.

"I showed it to them and said, 'Oh, this was the great old days?' ...I had a picture of this tomato packing company right next to Chester Street... It was all these rotting tomato peels and rinds. And so I said, 'The reality, folks, you have a lot of history and connections here, and we understand that, but you never had unfettered access to an [attractive or pristine] waterfront.'"

(Source: David Carroll interview by Evans Paull and Bob Hewitt, 2017)

O'Donnell Street went into decline, the blocks from St. Casimir's and Lakewood Avenue, all the way up through to Potomac Street, that whole area went into much more decline... They were setting fires in the empty houses... We had to fight to get [remaining vacants] all torn down...

We wanted to preserve what was left of the housing stock in the community so that we would not end up becoming a slum... What happens in a community like Canton, where you have generational changes, the parents pass away or the aunt or uncle passes away, and the younger people in the family inherit the property. They were just dividing it into two properties and renting it out. It doesn't really add to a healthy neighborhood because there's no connection, no buy-in to the community concept of the neighborhood.

Canoles does credit Mayor Schaefer for being receptive and supportive of the neighborhood's efforts to rebuild, saying Schaefer bought into most of what they were trying to achieve, including "straightening out the zoning, getting O'Donnell Square Park [established], getting the park pavilion roof from the old Canton market moved to the Canton playground; we had Canton parades..." and the list goes on.

In Canton, similar to Fell's Point and Federal Hill, the community eventually came back stronger than it was before the highway. "The road had a terrible impact, but it also coalesced the community to action. [The end result was] a community that now has real economic vitality," Canoles said. Some of that comeback was precisely a result of mistaken highway acquisitions. The redevelopment of vacant parcels in the right-of-way created positive momentum that eventually encompassed everything that had previously been underutilized or undervalued. It was a complete makeover.

Three sites sparked this transformation. The first was the Anchorage townhouses at 2300-2500 Boston Street, forty three-story townhouses completed in 1982. The Anchorage pioneered waterfront residential space for the Canton-Fell's Point shoreline, heretofore regarded as a future-less place where the highest and best use was an interstate highway. The behind-the-scenes story about the Anchorage and the Waterfront Promenade is detailed below.

Second is the Canton Waterfront Park on the vacant industrial land just west of Clinton Street. The *Sun* took note that the targeted area was once known as "baptizing shore, a place where Protestant preachers brought locals into Christianity through prayer and a swift dunk in Baltimore's harbor." Mayor Schaefer was quoted as saying, "Someday a beach with sand will go down to the water there. It's a very beautiful view. I want a beach there." City planner David Carroll deftly sidestepped contradicting his boss: "I think that, when the mayor called it a beach, he was trying to push people's imaginations…. We do not anticipate encouraging people to go into the water."[338] The park provided an exceptional amenity for newcomers while setting the stage for a different view and role for the waterfront.

Third was Canton Square townhouses, 124 units on the site of demolished rowhouses just north of Boston Street. By 1987 some of them commanded as much as $235,000, to the shock and dismay of former residents who had been forced out and came away with as little as $3,500.

A 1988 news article elicited pithy comments from former residents. Mercedes Stevens commented, "That Canton renaissance is putting salt into the wound. You go back there now and say this was mine and now other people are living here." Helen Wisniewski said, "It's like sticking a knife in your heart." Stevens captured the bottom line: "If the Expressway had been built, you'd say, 'Well, who wants to live there anyway?'"[339] The only way the city may have been able to bring back former residents was through subsidized housing, as Mildred Moon and Sharp Leadenhall eventually succeeded in developing for their neighborhood. However, Canton was dead set against subsidized housing because of racial fears. With subsidized housing off the table, there was no way to accommodate former residents in the new properties.

BALLOONS, DOGS, AND THE WATERFRONT PROMENADE

Other cities were coming to us and asking, "How did you do this?"
Al Barry, former Deputy Director, Baltimore City Department
of Planning, referring to the Waterfront Promenade

The Promenade at Harbor East Apartments† advertises that "You won't find a more desirable location anywhere else." These apartments at 1001 Aliceanna Street command rents from $1,500 for a studio to $2,800 for a two-bedroom apartment. That the word *promenade* is now a moniker for a desirable, walkable urban waterfront location is a coup for Baltimore's farsighted city planners. The concept of a continuous public walkway at the water's edge may seem like an obvious public good from a modern-day perspective. But at the time it was a radical departure and a singular innovation.

While that apartment building in Harbor East may be laying claim to identification with the Waterfront Promenade, it was down the road apiece in Canton that the principle was established back in 1981. The story of the Promenade starts at the end of the Road Wars. The I-83 connector was going to hug the waterfront all along the Canton/Fell's Point/Harbor East shoreline, with the waters' edge sometimes in the right-of-way and sometimes isolated from adjoining neighborhoods by the intruding expressway. Had the expressway been built, the whole concept of a Waterfront Promenade would have been far less appealing.

When the city abandoned that segment, suddenly numerous waterfront parcels were available. The Inner Harbor had established the precedent that the water's edge should be public, but most of the Inner Harbor waterfront was already publicly owned. The farsighted (and oft-cited) Wallace, Roberts, & Todd 1964 Inner Harbor masterplan emphasized public space not just at the waters' edge but for the majority of the redevelopment area. In contrast, the Harbor East/Fell's Point/Canton waterfront consisted of mostly privately

---

† The site that became the Promenade Apartments would have been buried under a massive nine-block concrete and steel interchange under the 1962 10-D plan. The 3-A plan, adopted in 1969, was less land-intensive, but the six-lane expressway still would have obliterated the site.

owned industrial properties. There was no unifying plan. For decades, highway plans had heavily impacted any vision of a new kind of waterfront. No plan, no money, no authority—it was a prescription for chaotic redevelopment with each project claiming the waterfront as an extraordinary amenity to be enjoyed only by the few who lived there or parked their yachts behind locked gates in the adjoining marinas.

Into the breach stepped two city planners, Larry Reich and David Carroll. Reich, you will recall, was the Director of Planning who spoke on behalf of the highway system at a key public hearing in 1972. Carroll worked for Larry as the Chief of Coastal Resources Planning.

I interviewed Carroll, along with Al Barry (former Deputy Director of Planning), to gain perspective on Reich's background‡ and vision for the waterfront. Reich had worked in Chicago and Philadelphia, with a history of implementing big ideas. "The Chicago waterfront...was something that certainly influenced his feelings toward waterfront redevelopment... He talked about Chicago all the time," Barry said.

Carroll added, "Chicago had the Burnham Plan way back in the early 1900s—they had made the decision to devote a lot of their lakefront to public access and parks."

"It was a model in a lot of ways," Barry said. Reich's experience in Philadelphia served more as an example of what NOT to do with the waterfront: "Philadelphia has screwed up its waterfront [with] their expressway [I-95]," Barry said. "It's not hard to make that leap between what [Reich] is doing now [1980s in Baltimore] and how he was influenced [by Chicago and Philadelphia]."

Barry described Reich's management style as "more based on ideas and finding out who might be the best person to deal with those ideas as opposed to

---

‡ Reich told one story that is worth memorializing even though it had nothing to do with the Road Wars. It appeared in the *Sun*, as follows: "On leave in Paris [Reich] found himself standing next to a woman he thought he recognized. 'You're Gertrude Stein, aren't you?' he said. 'Yes,' said Ms. Stein, the famous American writer. 'You know, I came here hoping to see some art and all the museums are closed,' Mr. Reich lamented. To which Ms. Stein replied, 'Well, why don't we go see Pablo?' Mr. Reich spent the afternoon in a storage warehouse with the famed artist Pablo Picasso, a large array of Picasso's paintings, and Gertrude Stein.

SENATOR MIKULSKI ON
LARRY REICH

"I did not realize what a
visionary he was until years
later. I am a great admirer
of Larry Reich, and not
only what he did from the
standpoint of a professional
planner…[but] the way he
organized his department,
and what he saw city planning was. Indeed, he [ini-
tiated] the whole concept
of neighborhood planners,
one of whom helped us
with SECO…That was so
important…"

some hierarchical notion of management…
It was one of the things that drove some people crazy." Reich set a tone and established
a vision, then delegated and empowered his
staff to take their own initiative.

Carroll was one of many staffers who
thrived in that environment, saying, "I was
given remarkably free rein… As a planner, it
was an incredible blessing." Carroll's lateral
connections to federal agencies (just the kind
of connections that a more controlling manager would have nixed) were the key to the
birth of the Waterfront Promenade.

Carroll said the precedent for the
Promenade was established at the Anchorage project at 2300-2500 Boston Street.
Lou Grasmick, an influential businessman,
owned a lumber yard that needed to relocate
from Pier 5 in the Inner Harbor. The Boston
Street parcel had been in the highway right-
of-way until the city moved the Fell's Point alignment to the underwater tunnel. Grasmick acquired it in 1981 with the intention of moving the lumber
business there.

Reich had his design staff prepare some drawings of what a redeveloped
Boston Street waterfront could look like. Then he arranged a meeting with
Grasmick. Grasmick showed Reich his plan for the relocated lumber business,
but Reich stopped him midstream and said, according to Barry, "that relocation would be the dumbest thing he could do." Grasmick responded, "What
are you talking about? Nobody talks to me that way." Reich showed him the
Planning Department sketches, and Grasmick quickly got over the rebuke
as he considered this alternative view of Boston Street. He was intrigued and
later confirmed with the mayor that the city was looking for waterfront residential in that area.

Grasmick, although a novice as a developer, took the next step—he hired his own architect to flush out what a redeveloped and upscale waterfront might look like. But Reich, with David Carroll overseeing the details, had his in-house design team do the same. There was one significant difference in these dueling design plans: the Planning Department version had a public walkway along the waterfront; Grasmick's plan was for a private waterfront.

Carroll described how the Planning version prevailed and a precedent was set for what would later become seven miles of Waterfront Promenade stretching from Key Highway all the way to Canton Waterfront Park.

Where the rubber met the road, we had a strong working relationship with the Corps of Engineers, and this was just when Lou was looking to do the Anchorage, which he called the "outpost."

Lou [Grasmick] comes in—he wanted to build just a bulkhead, everything private, and the marina. We had been working on [public access issues] and we said, "Lou, you really need to do public access." He said, "That's bullshit. I'm not interested. I'm going to be selling these houses for $150,000 to $175,000, and I don't want people walking in front of the houses."

The Corps of Engineers came to us and said, "We have an application from this guy, what do you want us to do with it?" We said, "No, he's filling in at that point and not for public use." We had developed this policy that the federal agencies agreed to, that fill could only be allowed for water-dependent or water-related uses or...for public access. So that became the operative [policy], and, I think, for the first time in the United States that that became [Corps policy].

Grasmick and his marina partner (Marinas International) attempted to pull strings to reverse this decision. Meetings with Grasmick reached an impasse when Carroll and Reich insisted that he would have to pay for the Promenade. "He was like...going nuts. He says, 'I'm going to see Schaefer. This is bank robbery,'" Carroll said. "The way we sold it was: We got the neighborhood on our side; we got the [industrial] maritime guys on our side;

and the federal agencies on our side. ...So he had nowhere to go. We said, 'Look, this is a core principle of the Inner Harbor. The water belongs to the public...and we have a right to access it."

There ensues a meeting with the mayor where Reich, Carroll, and Sheldon Lynn (Deputy Director of Planning) show Schaefer the concept plan with the public promenade. Lynn was nervous about going up against the influential business owner. He told Carroll, "Don't say a word about public access, don't say anything about it." Carroll responded, "Yes, well then, what's the plan of the meeting then?" Planning's schematic representation sold the concept despite Lynn's avoidance of the elephant in the room.

Carroll continued:

I mean, how could you go against it? ...It was kids holding balloons and dogs running around. Yeah, [Carroll laughs] balloons and dogs, [but it also showed the public promenade].

The mayor was saying, "What's this?" and, "What's that?" and, "Lou has been talking to me about the promenade." So, I went through the whole spiel about the Corps of Engineers and federal agencies. And he said, "Oh yeah, the Corps of Engineers—they are in favor of it?" And I said, "They want to know... what we're in favor of, and for us to tell them everything about [our] harbor [policies]."

Carroll comments that the mayor was predisposed to liking the concept because of the military connection vis-à-vis the Corps of Engineers.[§] Carroll continues:

[Larry Reich added] "We think we should do the same thing we did in the Inner Harbor... just not as big." Mayor, "Okay, Okay." And eventually he says, "Good idea." Schaefer, again, "Yes, good idea." Then the

---

§ Schaefer served in World War II, directing hospitals in England and western Europe. After the war he continued in the Army Reserves, retiring as a colonel in 1979.

mayor said, "Do it," so we did it... And that was it.

He [Grasmick] got squashed, because then Lou realized that, if he wants this project to move forward in his lifetime, it [balking at the Promenade] wasn't a winning strategy. So, we went to Lou and said, "We're ready to get you permits for this promenade." And he did it.

Carroll gives the mayor credit for sanctioning these kinds of policy innovations. "I would go to these big conferences mostly with coastal planners, and I would start telling them, 'Well, we had this meeting with the mayor about a public promenade and he said, do it.' They'd sit there... slack-jawed, because it would take them ten years to convince their commissioners or mayor or development authority to do anything like that."

For the next several years the promenade was enforced as land-use policy, not through familiar mechanisms like zoning and urban renewal plans, but really by jawboning bolstered by the Anchorage precedent and the support of the Corps of Engineers. The first place the policy was formalized was the Canton Waterfront Plan adopted in 1984. It included an appendix that made the public promenade a required easement, to be paid for and maintained by the property owner. The plan set out specifications for size, materials, locations, etc.

The policy was later enshrined in the Planning Department's 1986 *The Harbor Book*, the 1989 *Marina Masterplan*, and then in several urban renewal plans, gradually producing what we see today—an almost continuous public walkway stretching for seven miles, a jewel of urbanism, and a victory for everyday Baltimoreans.

I asked Carroll if Baltimore's successful implementation of this policy was unique, since many cities showcase their redeveloped waterfronts. He stressed that Baltimore was the first and probably most successful city to establish a continuous public walkway without using extensive public acquisition or eminent domain. The Planning Department also played a significant role in spreading best practices by "explaining how to do it, and why it was important, and the economic impacts and advantages to jurisdictions. We hosted several conferences here."

IN APPRECIATION...

On several occasions I have attended First Thursday concerts at Canton Waterfront Park. Here I am a fish out of water, one of the few silver-hairs in a sea of young people, many of whom live in the waterfront communities of Federal Hill, Harbor East, Fell's Point, and Canton, all of which owe their revival to the Road Warriors featured in this book.

It would be a good guess that many of the attendees arrived at the park by walking at least a mile or two on the Waterfront Promenade. Do they ever stop and wonder how all this came about? Absent the dedicated public service of Larry Reich and David Carroll, Baltimore would likely be saddled with private enclaves from Key Highway to Canton. Instead, we have an urban gem for all to enjoy.

XII. SHARP LEADENHALL SURVIVES THE TRIFECTA OF SLUM CLEARANCE

Sharp Leadenhall's roots as a proud community of African American Freedmen were ripped apart in the late 1960s, another community destroyed by acquisitions for highway plans that were later changed. Two highway plans and one urban renewal plan left a decimated community—more than eighty percent of the residents had been relocated.[340] The last plan would have saved a substantial part of the neighborhood, but by then there were only a few blocks left to save. A lesser person might have cited a line from the serenity prayer, "God grant me the wisdom to accept the things I cannot change," and moved on, but Mildred Moon was neither serene nor accepting, and the words "I cannot change" were never uttered from her lips.

Moon fought long and hard before finally acknowledging that I-395 was, in fact, one thing that she could not change. In a 1975 look back at her community's fight against the highways, Moon admitted her frustration, saying, "I [originally] thought we could save our community, but I woke up one day to realize we weren't getting anywhere. There were more tenants here than elsewhere, and the landlords were selling the houses out from under them. In areas like ours it was a losing battle… We never wanted the Road, but there was nothing we could do about it."[341] Still, the tenacious Ms. Moon was a Road Wars heroine not for holding back the highway plan but for her valiant, persistent, and at least partially successful attempt to rebuild Sharp Leadenhall from the ashes of slum clearance schemes.

The origins of Sharp Leadenhall lie in a late eighteenth century neighborhood on the southwest side of downtown near Pratt, Charles, Eutaw, and Lee Street—a diverse mix of African American Freedmen, Germans, and Quakers, all attracted by jobs in nearby industries. The Quakers were fierce abolitionists, and many were active in the Underground Railroad. It is not coincidental that African American Freedmen settled in a corridor where their presence was accepted by Whites who rejected slavery.

Much of the link between Quakers and African American Freedmen revolves around one man: Elisha Tyson (whom Tyson Street is named for—see Chapter 3). Tyson was not just an abolitionist and participant in the Underground Railroad, he also challenged and thwarted dozens, perhaps hundreds, of attempted kidnappings intended to return slaves and former slaves to the South. He even employed a vigilante group to hunt down kidnappers. He further aided more than a thousand African Americans to gain Freedman status by filing lawsuits on their behalf.[342] Sharp Leadenhall housed the largest enclave of Freedmen in Baltimore, with many, perhaps most, of those Freedmen gaining legal status as a result of Tyson's lawsuits.

It was Tyson and other Quakers, working in concert with African Americans, who founded the Baltimore Abolitionist Society (at Sharp and Pratt Streets) in 1789, the first such society below the Mason-Dixon line. Together with African American Methodists and German Baptists, the Quakers also helped establish the first school for African Americans (the African Academy of Baltimore) at that same location in 1797. The school site later became the Sharp Street United Methodist Church, the first Baltimore City church with a predominantly Black congregation. The church proudly retains its Sharp Street name even though it has relocated to the Madison Park neighborhood. When Tyson died in 1824, his funeral was attended by ten thousand African Americans, more than two-thirds of the city's African American population.[343]

The seeds planted by Tyson and the Quakers became a multi-racial and multi-denominational anti-slavery support system with a lasting impact. At least three of these historic churches are still in existence today: the German-affiliated Old Otterbein Church on Conway Street, the Ebenezer AME Church on Montgomery Street, and the Leadenhall Baptist Church* on Leadenhall Street. There is also evidence that at least two (Sharp Street Methodist and Ebenezer AME) were active in the

---

* Leadenhall Baptist Church is the second oldest continuously occupied Black church in the city. Its first service was held in a local blacksmith shop in 1873. The church is also on the National Register of Historic Places.

Underground Railroad. Attracted by these churches and institutions, the Black population grew and spread southward to the area we now call Sharp Leadenhall.[344]

The population rose to a high of seven thousand in the 1930s and 1940s,[345] but, at the same time, the city rezoned much of the area to allow a range of commercial and industrial uses.† The resulting mix of building types is still evident today.

The area remained poor and consisted mostly of rental properties, many lacking indoor plumbing. Resident William Good, interviewed by the Sharp Leadenhall Planning Committee for a 2004 video, acknowledged that in the 1950s "the outhouse [was] in the back; it was wooden outhouses, although they had running water; they had toilets inside." There was also a public bath house. Hilda Singleton, another resident, recalled, "It was something to get a bath; [mostly] you had to go dirty." Leanna Clifton added, "My mom rented a room. It was like a rooming house, and we had three beds in there: [one for] my mother and my father; I had a bed by myself 'cause I was the only girl; and [one for] my three brothers."[346]

As a small Black neighborhood in mostly White South Baltimore, it was easy for elected officials and the city to ignore the area—so the city infrastructure remained substandard. Good said "there were mostly dirt roads." City planners, myself included, might examine these conditions—lack of indoor plumbing, check; overcrowding, check; substandard infrastructure, check; predominantly rental with absentee landlords, check —and conclude that Sharp Leadenhall was a slum.

Still, the area elicited loyalty, held together by neighborliness. Singleton said, "Everybody knew everybody. This is how it was." June Spratley, another resident, added, "I mean, you could walk from one house to another and smell food, [the neighbors would say] 'come on in, y'all, and have something to eat.' We could go to any house in the neighborhood…"

From the Sharp Leadenhall Oral History Project, long-time residents (interviewed in 2011) looked back at the neighborhood that used to be,

---

† Likely the first attempt at "Negro removal" in Sharp Leadenhall.

saying, "It was all like one big family... Your children couldn't do anything wrong without their parents knowing it, and, if a neighbor saw you doing something, he'd take care of it right there, and let your parents know."[347]

Fifth-generation resident Bernice Daniels said, "I was born in the 1930s on Plum Street in a house that is torn down... At one time about a hundred of my relatives lived here. Now, [because of the highway and urban renewal acquisitions] it's only me and four of my children." For the Sharp Leadenhall Oral History Project, longtime residents remembered the highway acquisitions. One recalled, "It was sad, because people had been livin' in the same house fifty, sixty years, and never owned the house. They raised families... oodles and oodles of children in one household."[348]

If we take these interviews at face value (even though some undoubtedly romanticized the past), available indicators draw us to conclude that Sharp Leadenhall was not a healthy place and the city might have done residents a favor by relocating them; yet longtime residents maintained that it was a neighborly place where folks watched out for each other and guided successive generations toward positive outcomes. There is also the question of what the city would relocate them *to*. Relocation assistance to renters was modest, and there were long waiting lists for public housing, which, even if available, may not have improved living conditions. Years later all the public housing high rises were either changed to senior housing or torn down because the environment was dangerous and unhealthy. Poor but stable Sharp Leadenhall would have to compare favorably to that. It was yesteryear's "affordable housing," albeit with a ton of code violations.

It was neighborhoods like Sharp Leadenhall that led to a general reevaluation of urban renewal and slum clearance policies in the 1980s and '90s. As one commentator put it, "These neighborhoods weren't really slums. They were areas where African Americans had been contained through private covenants, government zoning, and [other mechanisms]. While the housing was run-down due to overcrowding and poverty, the neighborhoods at large were still functional, full of churches, groceries, restaurants, and shops."[349] Critics of urban renewal, like Jane Jacobs, Herbert Gans, and Chester Hartman, have even advocated to eliminate the word "slum" as a term loaded with bias that encourages misguided decision-making. Gans wrote back in 1965:[350]

Entire neighborhoods have frequently been destroyed, uprooting people who had lived there for decades, closing down their institutions, ruining small businesses by the hundreds, and scattering families and friends all over the city. By removing the structure of social and emotional support provided by the neighborhood, and by forcing people to rebuild their lives separately and amid strangers elsewhere, slum clearance has often come at a serious psychological as well as financial cost to its supposed beneficiaries.

Conventional wisdom in city planning in the mid '60s still favored slum clearance via both urban renewal and highway construction. Sharp Leadenhall was in the crosshairs for both the 1962 10-D plan and the 1967 "10-D Modified" plan. The 1962 plan swiped through the neighborhood east to west, wiping out four blocks and bisecting the community into northern and southern sections. (See Figure 30.)

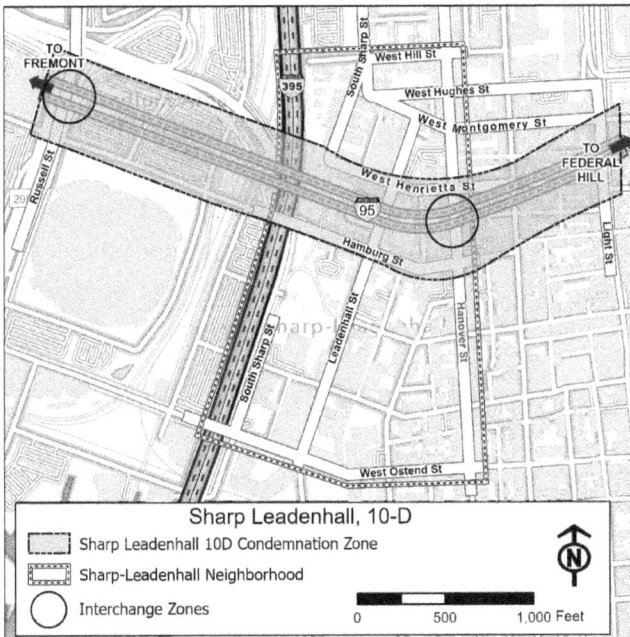

Figure 30. the 10-D path through Sharp Leadenhall, bisecting the neighborhood (Scott Jeffrey, MS GISP)

In 1967 Sharp Leadenhall became a pawn in the condemnation ordinance battle. From 1962 to 1967 the most controversial highway segment was the southwest section near Carroll Park. Although displacement numbers were comparatively low, the southwest/Carroll Park neighborhoods were organized and turned out hundreds of opponents at public hearings. Sixth District city councilmen represented both Sharp Leadenhall and Carroll Park; while they advocated for the Carroll Park neighborhoods in a "fall on the sword" fashion, the record is silent on their advocacy of Sharp Leadenhall.

When UDCT arrived in Baltimore in 1967 their first task was to revisit the Carroll Park problem. UDCT examined three alternative routes. All three moved the highway to the industrial corridor southeast of Carroll Park (where I-95 was later built), but there was not an easy solution to the problem of how to get from Carroll Park to Federal Hill and the bridge over the Inner Harbor.[‡] Two options lessened or removed the impact on Sharp Leadenhall; one, dubbed the "Sharp Leadenhall alignment," exacerbated the impact. UDCT recommended the Sharp Leadenhall route. Their reasoning: "It was felt that there was a greater need for clearance and redevelopment in the Sharp Leadenhall Corridor."[§][351]

The new "10-D Modified" (see Figure 31 and Appendix 1-C) route buried Sharp Leadenhall at the intersection of two superhighways: I-95 (running north to south and laying waste to eight mixed residential and commercial blocks) and the I-70 southwest connector (running east to west and displacing mostly commercial properties at the north end of Sharp Leadenhall.[352] 10-D Modified was adopted by condemnation ordinance in November 1967.

[‡] This reevaluation of the southwest segment was a year and half before UDCT's recommendation that the Federal Hill/Inner Harbor crossing be abandoned in favor of the Fort McHenry crossing.

[§] It is doubtful that UDCT came to this conclusion (that Sharp Leadenhall should be targeted for clearance) of their own volition. City development officials were almost certainly calling the shots. Once again, Robert Moses-like thinking was still alive and well in 1967.

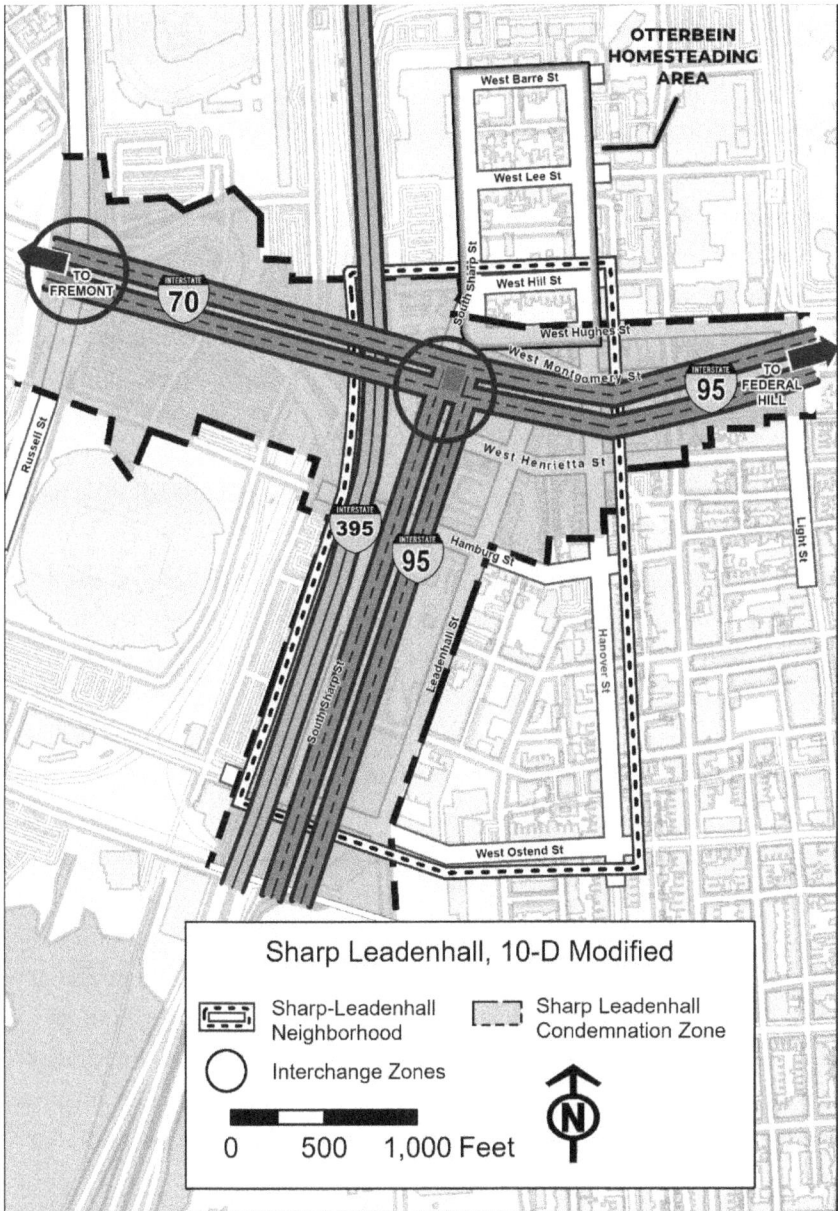

Figure 31. 1967 10-D Modified put Sharp Leadenhall at the intersection of two superhighways, I-95 and I-70. The Otterbein Urban Renewal Area additionally displaced more residents at the north end of the neighborhood. Note that I-395, as built, frees up the four blocks between Sharp Street and Leadenhall Street. (Scott Jeffrey, MS, GISP)

Then, one year later in December 1968, Mayor D'Alesandro ditched 10-D modified for 3-A, with the I-95 Harbor crossing at Fort McHenry instead of Federal Hill. The new alignment was linked to downtown via the I-395 spur. I-395 used the same north-south corridor through Sharp Leadenhall as the 10-D modified alignment, but at six lanes instead of eight, the right-of-way narrowed by one block, staying west of Sharp Street rather than Leadenhall Street.[353] That narrowing would have freed up four blocks from the Sharp Leadenhall condemnation area; however, because Locust Point put up a huge fight against the Fort McHenry route, Sharp Leadenhall stayed in limbo from 1968 to 1973, except that it was worse than limbo because acquisitions continued even though the city's plan had changed. Once again, Sharp Leadenhall was a pawn relative to the more influential White neighborhoods, this time Locust Point. In 1973 the city finally adopted the revised plan and officially sanctioned the narrower condemnation area for Sharp Leadenhall.[354]

In the meantime, the neighborhood had gone downhill. As the 1976 environmental impact statement for I-395 dryly phrased it, "Forces which contributed to the decline of this area included general obsolescence of the structures, considerably worsened by the 1967 Highway Condemnation Ordinance and the resulting lack of investment."[355] The tragedy of Sharp Leadenhall was that, if that last highway alignment had been the original route, much of Sharp Leadenhall would have been saved, at least from highway acquisitions.

However, in addition to the highway acquisitions, the city also adopted the Inner Harbor West Renewal Plan in 1970, and parts of the neighborhood were once again targeted for clearance, this time to support a vision of upgraded neighborhoods adjacent to the Inner Harbor. The renewal area included three blocks and about a hundred houses at the northern end of Sharp Leadenhall, now reclassified as Otterbein.[356] The city then decided against razing the houses—instead, they offered them to homesteaders under the Dollar House Program.¶ With renovations typically requiring $35,000

¶ Under this program, city-owned houses were made available to new owners who paid only $1 for the property but were required to bring it up to code and live there within a set period. After 18 months in residency, homesteaders received the deeds to the houses. The city also passed bond issues to offer low interest loans (up to $37,000) to enrollees.

($191,000 today), the few African Americans that were left were mostly unable to participate, so Otterbein transitioned to a mostly White enclave.

Sharp Leadenhall was thus victimized by two highway plans and one urban renewal plan. A total of 360 houses were razed, displacing 620 families and 3,000 residents.[357] The Sharp Leadenhall Planning Committee said "only 500 holdouts remained in the wreckage of Baltimore's oldest African American neighborhood."

The final highway plan was at once a happy and sad development. Sad that much of the neighborhood had been relocated for highways that were not built, but happy that there was an opportunity to remake Sharp Leadenhall with some semblance of its former role as a strong and historic neighborhood for lower income African American families. This is where Mildred Moon made her mark, using her leadership abilities and quiet forcefulness to rebuild Sharp Leadenhall in a manner that those original African American Freedmen might approve.

MILDRED MOON, "THE MAYOR OF THESE PARTS"

Five years after Mildred Moon passed away in 1992, people still knocked on the door of her former home on Ostend Street. According to Greg Simon, the subsequent owner of the property, "They stop by and want to see her. Then they want to come in and see what the place looks like. One guy told me, 'You're living in the house of the mayor of these parts.'" Charles Yim, owner of a neighborhood convenience store, was dealing with nearby drug dealers. He said, "We've called the police, but it doesn't work. You know the person I'd like to call at a time like this, the person who always got the job done. Mildred."[358] In 1993 the former Hamburg Street Bridge was rechristened in her name.

Senator Mikulski had vivid recollections of Mildred and characterized her as a "beloved and unique and tireless advocate for that community." Jay Brodie (former Housing Commissioner) regarded Moon as one of the most effective community leaders he had encountered in his long career in city government. He said, "She was forceful and determined, but always diplomatic and personable. The way she commanded attention for her small African

American community in an overwhelmingly White district was an exceptional example of community leadership."

Melvina Moss, Mildred's daughter, reflected on how Mildred got things done. "She used to call Mayor Schaefer—she only talked to people at the top—and she let her feelings be known. But she would always hug Schaefer. And she liked to tell angry people, 'Anger destroys. Take a deep breath and carry on.'"

In the anti-highway sphere, the earliest issue where Moon made important progress was not Sharp Leadenhall but rather the system-wide issue of relocation, particularly for renters. In 1970 she got the attention of US Transportation Secretary Volpe. The news reported that "Mr. Volpe was visibly moved by Mrs. Mildred Moon, who spoke off the cuff of the tribulations of displaced friends. 'Tell them to please not displace any more people until they find some place for them,' she said. Moon continued, 'I'll meet you any place at any time of day to show it to you like it is.'" Volpe followed the meeting with a blunt warning to cities: "We will not approve any construction until any city, not just Baltimore, can show us that people have been relocated...to a decent place to live."[359]

While some credit Moon for getting the highway reduced in size, it was the later redevelopment of abandoned right-of-way where Moon left her indelible mark.

THE CITY'S IOU – AFFORDABLE HOUSING

Moon's main objective was to renovate, rebuild, and re-establish affordable housing consistent with Sharp Leadenhall's history as a well rooted African American neighborhood. It was a daunting task; more than half the former neighborhood stood vacant: some owned by the city, some cleared by the city, some vacated under the cloud of condemnation lines later lifted—all run down.

The first win came in the early 1970s before the final highway plan was adopted. Moon first convinced the city to stop acquiring properties for the (abandoned but still-on-the-books) 10-D modified right-of-way and to stop knocking down acquired houses; thirty were saved from the wrecking ball and later rehabilitated.[360] When the condemnation line was officially narrowed in 1973, Moon persuaded Schaefer to commit $2 million in renewal funds for parcels freed up from condemnation. Highway dollars were also committed to replace lost facilities—Solo Gibbs Park and Sharp Leadenhall Elementary were both built on land acquired for earlier highway plans.

Moon and the community continued to press Housing Commissioner Brodie (who replaced Embry in 1976) for redevelopment that would produce new affordable housing. A 1977 *Baltimore Sun* article cited the community's growing impatience with the city. "After years of acquiescence residents of this once thriving Black community have begun to organize and demand that the city fulfill its pledge to rehabilitate houses condemned in the late 1960s for an expressway that has since been realigned.... Standing near a string of boarded-up and buckling rowhouses on Leadenhall Street... Bernice Daniels said, 'But the only thing we've gotten is more bulldozers and more promises.'"[361]

Eventually Brodie and the city delivered. Vacant city-owned rowhomes on Bevan and Henrietta Streets were the first part of the city's commitment to the neighborhood. In a 2018 interview Michael Seipp (a Housing Department staffer from that time) said, "That was the big issue when I was in [the Housing Department]... Otterbein [had been] a Black community and all the Blacks got relocated, and the vast majority of the people coming in with the dollar houses were White. So how do we take...a piece of what was left over from Otterbein and make sure it went to Sharp Leadenhall folks?" Some units were sold directly to Sharp Leadenhall residents, and twenty-three others were enrolled in the Scattered Site Public Housing Program. Many of these were the same homes Moon had saved from the wrecking ball in the early '70s.

Then in 1979 the city came to an agreement with a private developer to build Sharp Leadenhall Courts, an affordable development including an eighty-unit elderly mid-rise, eighty rental townhomes, and thirty-seven Section 8 apartments.[362] The redevelopment occupied much of the remaining vacant land taken for the mistaken highway acquisitions. The city gave former Sharp Leadenhall residents priority for the new units.

If an academician were designing a study to test the hypothesis that the pre-highway Sharp Leadenhall really had been a well-functioning community (not a "slum"), he/she would have jumped at the chance to analyze whether and why former residents took advantage of this chance to come back. There is no quantitative data, but two articles in the Sun provide anecdotal evidence, by virtue of the recorded comments of people who did exactly that: they moved back.[363]

Their stories capture in human terms what the old neighborhood meant and what the new neighborhood represented. One returnee was Mary Lee Moore, an elderly woman who was relocated twice but moved back to a "bric-a-brac filled Ostend Street house." She said, "We fixed this place up all right, but I miss my old neighborhood. We were there thirty-eight years. My husband had to close up his store when the people started moving away. Now everything is different." Moore had been relocated once for a highway that never materialized and a second time due to urban renewal condemnation later redeveloped as an Otterbein dollar house. "One day I passed by and stood for a long time looking at [my old house]. Finally, a White lady came out and asked me if I'd like to take a look inside. It was so lovely; it was like a palace. I could hardly recognize anything. When we had it, it was just an old house."

Another returnee was Ms. Jannie White. White felt fortunate to be residing in a city-owned house on Hamburg Street but also worried about former neighbors that were not so lucky. She said, "I praise the Lord for bringing us to this beautiful house… So many people had to move into projects in Westport and East Baltimore, or they just went away. I wish more of them could have homes like this."

Patricia Thompson lived in the 700 block of Hanover Street; her house was condemned then sold in the Otterbein Dollar House Program and renovated into a fashionable townhouse of "nothing but glass," she said. After living on Division Street near North Avenue, Miss Thompson would have preferred to return to Hanover Street, but she was "not disturbed that those homes are mostly inhabited by middle- and upper-class renovators. 'It's real nice over there, but it's too expensive,' she said. 'It's much nicer than it used to be around here. The houses were so shabby and cold before.'"

Ida Pinckney and her husband Harvey were glad to be back in Sharp

Leadenhall, reunited with old friends. They had also rented on South Hanover Street but were forced to move. Ida commented, "I liked the changes—I just wish I had it up on Hanover Street." Mercedes Johnson and her brother Wade Dunn had been evicted from their parents' home on Hill Street. Mr. Dunn was glad to be back, saying, "We lived on the east side, but it was a rough place. I always wanted to come back to South Baltimore."

Surprisingly, of all the people interviewed by the *Sun*, only one voiced lingering resentment over being forced to move or being replaced by wealthier White people residing in their former homes. Derrick Corbin said, "I feel we were railroaded out because we were offered money to leave and there was never any intention of having us back. I don't have any resentment of the people who moved into the dollar houses, but the government knew we were poor people and couldn't afford to rehabilitate. Where are we going to get $50,000 to rehabilitate to government standards?"[364]

This is hardly a rigorous analysis, but it appears that former residents were anxious to come back and re-create that sense of neighborliness they remembered from the time before highways and urban renewal. While Sharp Leadenhall may have ticked all the boxes to be defined as a "slum," it was better than available alternatives, and highway alignments designed to wipe out the neighborhood were, as Tom Ward characterized Bolton Hill's venture into "Negro removal," simply immoral.

If it is true diversity you seek, look no further than Sharp Leadenhall. When you take a walk through Sharp Leadenhall today, the contrasts are jarring. There is the new Hanover Cross apartment building, where one-bedroom units start at $1,500 per month, but just up the street there is the Sharp Leadenhall Courts subsidized apartment complex, part of Mildred Moon's legacy and now a little rundown. North of those apartments you find the upscale renovated townhomes of Otterbein, but Leadenhall Street, which should connect the two areas, is closed at this juncture, giving the illusion (or perhaps portraying the reality) that the two neighborhoods are separate and distinct.

There are Scattered Site Public Housing units almost cheek-by-jowl with smartly renovated townhomes, as fine as any in Federal Hill. A gleaming new mid-rise office building on Ostend Street stands in stark contrast with older industrial buildings mostly in decline. The Baltimore Station building at 130 West Street captures the divergent picture of Sharp Leadenhall in a single building: the beautifully renovated fire station houses a complex of services and a shelter for the homeless.

Clearly the forces of gentrification have been at work for quite some time. The average sale price for houses in Sharp Leadenhall is currently $250,000, well above the means of the original inhabitants.[365] The demographics are changing too: in 1990, 84 percent of 881 residents were Black, but by 2010 the percentage had fallen to 68 percent.[366] One private demographic service estimates that the neighborhood population is now over 60 percent White.[367]

These opposing views of Sharp Leadenhall came into focus in 2009 when community leaders proposed a local historic designation to solidify Sharp Leadenhall's historic roots as a haven for African American Freedmen. The Planning Department study included several blocks that are now considered "Otterbein" even though their history is more aligned with Sharp Leadenhall.

Within that study area there is a small National Register historic area dubbed "Little Montgomery Street." When those residents made their case for National Register status back in 1982, they contended that the district was the "only coherent remnant of the Sharp Leadenhall neighborhood in South Baltimore."[368] However, when the current residents considered whether they should be in Sharp Leadenhall's local historic district in 2009, they said no, that such a designation would impede property values. Those opposed succeeded in changing the boundary, in effect denying the basis of the earlier National Register designation that had undoubtedly contributed to the district's inflated property values, which start over $300,000 and go as high as $650,000.[369]

You might think Mildred Moon would have rested on her laurels after all her accomplishments, but the opposite was true. A 1996 news article said, "After her husband died [in 1986]…Moon seemed to lose her balance. She spent all her time in community work and didn't sleep or eat properly. Her friends and her daughter believe overwork contributed to her failing health and sudden death in July 1992 from pancreatic cancer."[370] She was sixty-eight.

The 2004 City Planning Neighborhood Survey, cited above, opened with two sentences that I now employ to close the Sharp Leadenhall chapter:

Underneath the current nomenclature and neighborhood boundaries is a rich history that illustrates the Baltimore African American experience, a history that rises to national significance. The Quaker and African American histories along the Sharp Street corridor present a story of extraordinary importance.

A story (I add) that was nearly obliterated, but remains at least partially intact because of one determined woman: Mildred Mae Moon.

XIII. BLOWS AGAINST THE EMPIRE III

CORRUPTION

Engineers lost whatever sheen remained on their war-torn image when the entrenched system of political bribery came to light in 1972-1974. These were the scandals that brought down Vice President Spiro Agnew and Baltimore County Executive Dale Anderson. A mountain of evidence against Agnew led to his resignation in October 1973 and prevented a court trial at the time, but a later civil suit found Agnew guilty and assessed damages of $147,500 ($979,000 today) for kickbacks he received from engineering and public building contracts. Anderson, Agnew's successor as Baltimore County Executive, apparently continued past practices, leading to his conviction and a prison term in 1974.

Those implicated included quite a few of the defenders of the old 10-D plan: J. E. Greiner Co. and two SRC chairmen—John B. Funk and Jerome Wolff.* Baltimore's highway plans were now suspect; the engineers and public officials who supported them had claimed their recommendations were driven by analytical tools, but the growing scandals revealed not just financial self-interest but corruption.[371]

The lengthy and thorough investigation never implicated IDBC or any of Baltimore's elected officials or government employees, but they did ensnare engineering firms that were getting some of the largest city contracts. A March 1974 *Sun* column reported that "seven of the sixteen engineering firms that are designing the expressway system and two former heads of the State Roads Commission who helped plan it are being investigated...indicating an interest in the project that may have little to do with providing efficient transportation to the public."[372]

---

* Bernard Werner's name was never associated with the kickback scandals; however, because he worked for Greiner both before and after his stint as DPW director, his role in fighting new highway alignments had a degree of guilt by association.

Wolff was *the* central figure in the Agnew case. In the early 1960s Wolff was a deputy in the Baltimore County Department of Public Works. When Agnew was elected as governor in 1967, he made Wolff head of the SRC. When Agnew was elected vice president in 1968, Wolff moved again to work for Agnew in Washington. In 1970 he became President of Greiner Environmental Systems. Throughout this period, playing four different roles, Wolff maintained one point of continuity—he was Agnew's bagman. In the Agnew civil trial Wolff stated that his attic was filled with documentation that detailed "every corrupt payment he participated in with Agnew."

At least three of Agnew's documented bribes came from Greiner;[373] three more Greiner pay-offs were part of the Dale Anderson case. Greiner was also under suspicion for cost overrun approvals and a bribery scandal in New Orleans. In a 1974 interview, Carolyn Tyson of MAD connected Baltimore's highway plan, the insider engineering firms, and the political figures under scrutiny:[†]

We made a study recently of the contractors who have gotten either the design or the preliminary engineering contracts on the whole 3-A system, and we found that two thirds of the mileage was covered by contracts that are involved with either Mr. Agnew or Mr. Mandel and a small part with Mr. Schaefer. Matz-Childs [implicated in the Agnew scandals] all down for I-95; the Greiner Company has most of I-83... Zollman Associates is associated with Mr. Mandel and that's part of their Tidewater outfit; they had the Fort McHenry contract.[374]

Over in Leakin Park...that's covered by a firm named Volkert [David Volkert Co.]... They've been indicted for bribery on a job down in Louisiana.[375] ...They also have done other work on the road that we consider a conflict of interest. They will design a segment and then they will also get the contract to write the environmental impact statement.[376] Now you can't expect them to be neutral... You know they're going to justify what their company has already designed.[377]

[†] To verify Tyson's contentions, I added footnotes to Tyson's text.

Ms. Tyson went on to raise the ultimate irony of MAD's ongoing fight against highway backers and the engineers that provide their technical support. "An engineer, who's not in any of these companies and hasn't been in the Road Fight, laughed one time, and he said, 'Well, the longer you folks put off their building the highway the happier you're making the consultants and the designers and all… They're raking it in… Every time the opponents force a change in the alignment, that requires a whole new set of plans, designs, and impact statements.'"

This is quite a humorous twist on the Road Wars: Imagine Greiner and Matz-Childs disparaging highway opponents in meetings with the mayor while anonymously bankrolling MAD and SCAR in hopes that their actions would lead to yet another round of highway alternatives with the attendant contracts. It might be an even better investment than bribing unscrupulous politicians. A bribe might get your firm a leg up on your competition, but you were all competing for the same slice of pie; plus, your competition was likely doing the same thing, so the cost of winning those contracts was going up. The alternative? Make a bigger pie.

While we are in a humorous vein, we also note that Baltimore's engineers were not an entirely unamusing lot. In one 1973 newsletter they ran a column that skewered EPA's environmental regulations, entitled "God and EPA." The article imagines that God, in promoting his plan to create heaven and earth, had to go before the Heavenly Environmental Protection Agency (HEPA) council. After a lengthy back and forth with HEPA over the required permits, "God announces 'that I want to complete the project in six days.'" At this time, He was advised by the Council that his timing was completely out of the question. HEPA would require a minimum of 180 days to review the application and the environmental impact statement; then, there would be public hearings. It would take at least 10 to 12 months before a permit could be granted. God said, "Oh to hell with it."

XIV. LEAKIN PARK,
A 1,200 ACRE "HIDDEN GEM"

I've shown dozens of people the spectacular 100-foot overlook above the confluence of the Dead Run and Gwynns Falls streams and they are invariably amazed. One autumn day a companion said he had been traveling to Vermont to see the vistas no more beautiful than this one in Baltimore City, and this is just where they planned to put a 90-foot-high bridge across the Valley.

George L. Scheper[378]

I-70 traverses 2,115 miles beginning with an interchange at I-15 near Fort Cove, Utah; it then passes through Glenwood Canyon in Colorado (generally regarded as a stunning engineering feat), crosses five states comprising the Great Plains and the Midwest, intersects briefly with Wheeling, West Virginia (the author's hometown and the original destination for B&O Railroad), spans the Alleghenies in Pennsylvania, then descends gently toward megalopolis, only to meet an unceremonious end at the I-70 Park-N-Ride just outside the Baltimore City line. Here there is a convenient turn-around for the many incredulous motorists that expected I-70 to meet up with... well, something more than a Park-N-Ride.

It is at this point that, rather than a roadway, one finds a plaque. It reads as follows:

The abrupt end of Interstate 70 symbolizes a controversy that engaged Baltimoreans from the 1940s to the 1980s. Plans envisioning an East-West Expressway and the linking of three Interstate Highways stirred up fierce opposition. Citizens formed protest groups, such as... VOLPE, spoke out at hearings, and joined together in a biracial coalition to protect their neighborhoods and preserve Leakin and Gwynns

Falls Parks. The city, nonetheless, started to buy and demolish properties along the proposed routes. Eventually officials made substantial changes and withdrew the plan to extend I-70 through the two parks.

The sign credits two city council members, Barbara Mikulski and Norman Reeves, for leading the fight to save the parks. More about their actions below.

THE HIGHWAY FIGHTERS' MOST CREATIVE ACRONYM

In Baltimore, our anti-road activists seemingly stayed up late to come up with acronyms that would get their point across and be easily remembered. RAM, SCAR, and MAD are simple, direct, and effective.

But the prize for the most creative acronym goes to VOLPE, Volunteers Opposing the Leakin Park Expressway: The Secretary of Transportation at that time was John Volpe.

George Nilson, the attorney that filed *VOLPE v. Volpe*, recounted, "That was my contribution… So, I thought it would be sort of amusing if the lawsuit…would be captioned "VOLPE versus Volpe" because people would think it was a domestic relations case about a couple whose marriage was coming asunder, and it was sort of exactly that."

WHAT WAS AT STAKE?

"Shhhh." Leakin Park's neighbors may hope this book does not encourage the general public to explore this astonishingly beautiful but lightly used oasis of nature in the city. They don't want their little secret to get out—that because of Leakin Park's grisly reputation (sometimes referred to as "Leakin Memorial Gardens"), they have a relatively uncrowded little slice of heaven at their doorstep. The inside joke in the neighborhood is that residents secretly fan the flames, perhaps ghostwriting social media posts to protect their own almost private wilderness from the masses.

Contrary to popular opinion Leakin Park was not saved so Baltimore's criminals would have a convenient place to stash dead bodies. I accept this reputation of the park as fact, although this does not mean that park goers are in danger—those bodies originated somewhere else.

A walk on Leakin Park's uncrowded trails is a "twofer"—nature inter-mixed with history. Using the moniker of "the Ghosts of Leakin Park," blog-ger Cham lures curious readers (expecting, perhaps, a lurid guide to where and how the dead bodies were dumped) and pivots to the park's forty-some notable artifacts, ruins, and relics. How many parks can boast a description like this? "Leakin Park, rife with its mysterious dark history and haunting intrigue, is filled with artifacts, and the flotsam and jetsam of yesteryear. The park played host to a wealthy Winans family's Crimea estate, several mills, the Mt. Holly Inn, an old trolley line, two cemeteries, a Bollman Truss bridge, and the home of Dr. Jesse William Lazear, who cured yellow fever. [Take a hike and] have fun searching for yesterday's debris."[379]

Cham's list of curiosities continues: Orianda House (built in 1854 and an outstanding example of Italianate architecture); Winans Chapel; the Bergner Mansion; a wonderfully picturesque waterwheel; two springs; a water tank; a three-mile mill race (now covered over); and the remnants of a stone outhouse, the caretakers' quarters, the Hudnut farmhouse, a root cellar, an icehouse, and a "mock fort." The mock fort—a stone barrier with fake wooden cannons (no longer present)—is a bit of a mystery, as there are two theories on its purpose. One is that it was meant to deter the Union army, because Winans was staunchly pro-Confederate. If true, the battlement failed—Union soldiers used Winans' orchard for firewood. The other theory is in keeping with the Winans' Russian-themed Crimea Estate: that the fort was modeled after the Russian defense in the Battle of Balaklava, immortal-ized in Alfred Lord Tennyson's poem "The Charge of the Light Brigade."[380]

If your walk through Leakin Park stimulates research on Ross Winans, there is a wealth of historical intrigue there, too. Although from a family of horse breeders in New Jersey, Winans made his first mark on society in the 1820s helping Peter Cooper build the Tom Thumb engine that would eventually make horse travel an anachronism.* He worked as a train-building engineer for B&O in the 1830s, later splitting off and running his own engine assembly operation in the Mount Clare area of Baltimore City. His business produced about three hundred engines total. He pioneered the use of coal instead of wood to power the engines, gaining a number of patents while also generating some controversy. One account maintained that he gained a reputation as someone who would steal other people's ideas, patent them, and charge licensing fees or sue others who employed similar devices. Winans' two sons, Thomas and William, followed in his footsteps and added significantly to the family fortune by building engines for the Russian Czar Nicholas I in the 1850s.[381]

In the early 1860s Winans led a pro-Confederacy contingent in the Maryland General Assembly. He burned a bridge in the Monkton area of northern Baltimore County and became a target of Union generals. His arrest by Union forces in 1861 was tied to the story of General Butler's occupation of Federal Hill (See Federal Hill chapter).

Controversy also swirled around the city's acquisition of Leakin Park. The park was first envisioned in 1922 when J. Wilson Leakin bequeathed his downtown mansion to provide funds for a park that would bear the Leakin name. But it took twenty years for Baltimore to make up its mind.

In 1904 and again in 1926, Frederick Olmstead Jr. advocated for park expansion in the river valleys of Gwynns Falls and Dead Run (including the Crimea/Winans estate). His 1926 report read: "This valley [Dead Run], of all those discussed, has been freer from defacement by man's activities. It is considered by all who view it as one of the very best bits of scenery near Baltimore."[382] However, the city and the Park Board disregarded these reports and adopted a "sprinkle the money around" plan for citywide park and playground improvements funded by the Leakin bequest. Mr. Leakin's sister contested the plan in court as inconsistent with the intent of the bequest, and the city was forced to reconsider. Olm-

---

* I wonder, was Ross Winans viewed as the black sheep of the family for helping to invent the device that undermined the family horse business?

stead was again consulted in 1939, and he again recommended the Crimea estate. Finally, in 1941 the city purchased 241 acres of the Crimea; then added more acreage in 1948, eventually meeting up with Gwynns Falls Park.[383]

The two parks together now comprise over 1,200 acres, the largest park in the city and the second largest woodland park in an Eastern US city. Most of the acreage is regarded as wilderness, featuring extensive old-growth (never logged) forest, a true rarity for a city park.

Hikers, bikers, and naturalists often express surprise at the serenity and beauty they encounter in the parks. If the highway had been built, you can bet no All-Trails reviewer would have commented: "For a nice quiet hike in the woods, check this one out"; or "Gwynns Falls River makes this ride truly serene at times."[†] But commenters also note indications of neglect as trail signage is often confusing or completely absent. And all those artifacts and ruins on Cham's blog—you are mostly on your own to find those, as well.

The centerpiece of the trail system is the fifteen-mile Gwynns Falls hike-bike trail that runs all the way from that I-70 Park-N-Ride to the Inner Harbor. Had the expressway been built, it is doubtful that anyone would have thought a hike-bike trail was a good idea.

I overlaid the highway plan on a map of park trails, facilities, and events. There were nine points where hiking trails would have intersected or run directly adjacent to the highway. Because the park is long and narrow, there is very little acreage that would have been more than a half mile from the highway. The Carrie Murray Nature Center, one playground, four tennis courts, the annual Herb Festival, and the Chesapeake & Allegheny Live Steamers were right in the expressway path. Within a quarter mile (certainly close enough to be bothered by the expressway) were Outward Bound, Orianda House, Winans Chapel, the Mushroom City Arts Festival, and the Leon Day ballfield.

---

† More comments from www.alltrails.com: "This is an absolutely wonderful trail. So woodsy and pure nature at its best." "So many beautiful trails to choose from at this park." "Love. Love this forest! I used to go off trail and found many, many beautiful adventures. Forever in my heart." "Love it. Great hike." "I've ridden this trail for a little over 8 years and have never had a problem with not feeling safe." "Wonderful amount of migratory birds to see." "A great hike!... The views were great." "Pretty streamside path and lots of woods." From Trip Advisor: "Leakin Park will not disappoint in beauty or history. For walkers, runners, hikers, and bikers, there is so much beauty to explore."

It would be exceedingly odd to call a 1,200-acre park a "hidden treasure," but, in many ways, it is exactly that. The unique natural beauty of the park, in addition to its noteworthy history, should mean that it functions more like a regional or state park. There should be a visitor center where park users can get trail guides, information about upcoming events, a guide to the old-growth forest and abundant flora and fauna, and a leaflet on the fascinating history of the park. Wayfinding signs, both in the park and getting to the park, would make the park more user friendly. Trails should be well-marked and supplemented by branches that take the visitor to artifacts and ruins. With those kinds of improvements park utilization would increase, which would undoubtedly make more people comfortable enough to venture out and give it a try.

Returning to the central issue of highway impact, the park is a good example of what Congress had in mind when it added the landmark 4(f) provision to protect public parks. However, from my personal vantage point, there is a more pointed question not envisioned in the 4(f) legislation: Since Gwynns Falls Leakin Park is a rare example of an urban wilderness park, and since its neighboring communities are now majority Black, what is being done to enhance the environmental education of city kids? Are these parks that activists worked overtime to protect now helping city kids gain an appreciation for the natural world? In my opinion, these questions are the final reckoning for the highway vs. park balance sheet. To answer them, I interviewed several program administrators.

City kids in nature

They're not just playing in nature, they are: learning, creating, sensing, believing, relaxing, exploring, observing, wondering, connecting, discovering, appreciating, understanding, experimenting...
Penny Whitehouse, MotherNatured.com

Mary Hardcastle has the enthusiasm of a cheerleader and the altruism of a woman devoted to a just cause. As the director of the Carrie Murray Nature Center, Hardcastle is used to encountering skeptics. She notes that even some teachers say, "Where am I going? I do not really want to take the kids out there." But she says, "Once they arrive and see how magical it is here, people change their tune. Honestly, a lot of people that have come here are thrill-seekers, [but they] change [too]... They come out here trying to find these places they have read about, and then they see what is really here. They are like, 'Wow. I am going to hike up trails... just enjoy the park.' It is so beautiful in all seasons."

She thinks the dead body issue has been sensationalized and misrepresented by the media, a vestige of past problems that are not representative of conditions today. "I have been working in this park for years with other organizations," she said. "I have never been involved in anything that felt unsafe." The center's kids have been out on Leakin Park's secluded trails every day with halfway decent weather for more than four decades, and they have never run into anything that remotely suggested foul play.

Carrie Murray Nature Center was established by the city in 1986, only a few years after finally folding its cards on the expressway. Orioles Hall-of-Famer Eddie Murray made the initial gift to start the center in memory of his mother, whose "gentle spirit and strength of character greatly influenced her twelve children."[384] When plans for the center were first announced in 1985, Murray said, "I would not be the ballplayer I am today if it wasn't for my father and mother."[385]

Hardcastle describes the center as a forest immersion experience. It offers after-school, summer, and full-time day care programs, all geared to experiential learning about the natural world. Adding in school field trips, several outreach programs (bringing nature to "your front door"), and special events, Carrie Murray reaches ten thousand students a year, almost all city residents. Parents and teachers frequently comment "that when they are out with the kids, they are shocked that the student who is the restless or maybe a problematic child in the classroom is the one on the trail that is really engaged, calm, interested, focused, behaving really well, and following directions. They are like, 'Wow. This is a completely different child.'" And parents often report more healthy activity levels back on the home front—kids are less tethered to devices, and "just being more active and running around changes their endurance and their weight." Those restless, possibly hyperactive kids "just seem to be a little… calmer, but also just more healthy."

Research on the positive impacts of nature back Mary's observations and go several steps further. One article found that "hundreds of studies now bear on this question, and converging evidence strongly suggests that experiences of nature boost academic learning, personal development, and environmental stewardship."[386] That Gwynns Falls Leakin Park is so close to so many city kids is a huge bonus, because exposure to the natural world can be ongoing and evolve—it is not a one-and-done experience at a national park or rural hideaway.

I asked Mary if the center could have located elsewhere in the park (remember the highway alignment went right through the Carrie Murray site). She responded, "This location is in the heart of the old-growth forest that is unique and so special. I would say that this was the right place for the Nature Center to be…. When children arrive here who have not necessarily been in a woodland area or under the tall and old-growth tree canopy, it just opens up a world of wonder for them, to know that that is right in their backyard."

The Carrie Murray Center is not the only organization attempting to connect city kids to the natural wonderland they live next door to but know nothing about. The Outdoor Recreation Division of the Department of Recreation and Parks offers similar programs that take city kids on hiking, biking, and camping expeditions, with Gwynns Falls Leakin Park as a primary destination. Program director Molly Gallant sees Gwynns Falls Leakin Park—with its old-growth forest, pristine stream valleys, and twenty miles of trails—as the key resource that puts Baltimore in a leadership position over other cities trying to do the same thing.

Outward Bound, located on another site that would have been impacted by the expressway, is a third organization linking city kids to the park's natural resources. Their "Police Youth Challenge" program is described by Director Ginger Mihalik as follows: "If you come out here any Thursday, you will see the Baltimore City Police Department and kids out here playing together on the ropes course, building relationships that would never have happened

Figure 32. City kids experiencing nature in Leakin Park, photo credits from top left: Mary Gallant, Carrie Murray Nature Center (twice), and Baltimore City Department of Recreation and Parks

Figure 33. Outward Bound's Insight: Team Building for Youth Program (Source: Chesapeake Bay Outward Bound)

271

without this structure… Kids need to trust the cops and the cops need to trust the kids."

Leakin Park is thus being used in ways not necessarily envisioned by either the Congressional authors of the 4(f) provision or the environmental activists that filed suit and stopped the Road. The dead bodies issue has led to significant underutilization of the park by those who would ordinarily be attracted to a unique urban wilderness. However, the park is admirably performing an even more important function: giving city kids an experience in nature that is improving lives and will undoubtedly pay dividends over time.

HIGHWAY THROUGH THE PARK

On June 7, 1971, Walter Sondheim, probably the most revered figure in Baltimore's urban renaissance, wrote a revealing letter to the editor of the *Baltimore Sun*. There had been a hearing on the Leakin Park segment, and highway supporters had invoked Sondheim's good name in making the case for the segment. Sondheim was clearly irked. In 1964 Mayor McKeldin had asked Sondheim to chair a committee to recommend an alignment for the route through Leakin Park. Sondheim's 1971 letter clarified the record. He said the highway through the park was presented to the committee as a fait accompli; he then quotes from his committee's report:

The committee wishes to make clear at the outset that it feels it is most unfortunate to have expressways slashing through public parklands. Parks are a precious public amenity, difficult to obtain and seemingly more difficult to retain. Thus, it behooves us to protect and maintain present parklands in every way that we can…

Some parks are more nearly unique, more nearly irreplaceable than others, and it is these the city should be most diligent in preserving. Nature has endowed Baltimore with some truly magnificent stream valleys which offer to a widespread segment of the population nearby stands of century old trees, inspiring topography, and watershed streams. These are settings that the urban man finds essential to well rounded, healthy city life, and, to date, he has not learned how to create such areas on his own. Thus, to destroy such areas is to remove them forever from the city's natural resources.

The Sondheim Committee's persuasive disclaimer came close to a rebuke of McKeldin, almost an out-and-out rejection of the charge to the committee; however, that disclaimer had been ignored in 1964 when the protest over the Leakin Park segment was *where* it should go, not *if* it should go. When Sondheim brought the issue back up in 1971, it fit into an onslaught of criticism. In those seven years, everything had changed.

The plan to route the expressway through Leakin Park was first proposed in the 1957 Interstate System Concept Plan. While Baltimore fretted about the impacts of that plan on Tyson Street and Mount Vernon, the ruination of Gwynns Falls Leakin Park was seemingly classified as acceptable collateral damage for the greater good. The 1962 10-D plan recommended a southerly route through the park, generally following the Dead Run/Franklintown Road stream valley (see Figure 34). The engineering mentality was again holding sway—that was the most direct and level route from point A (I-70 approaching from the west) to point B (the southeastern corner of Gwynns Falls Park).

Nine neighborhood associations, supported by the influential CPHA, banded together and forced the city to examine alternatives.[387] This led to the creation of the Sondheim Committee, which reluctantly recommended a more northerly route through the parks as the least damaging to both the environment and adjoining communities.

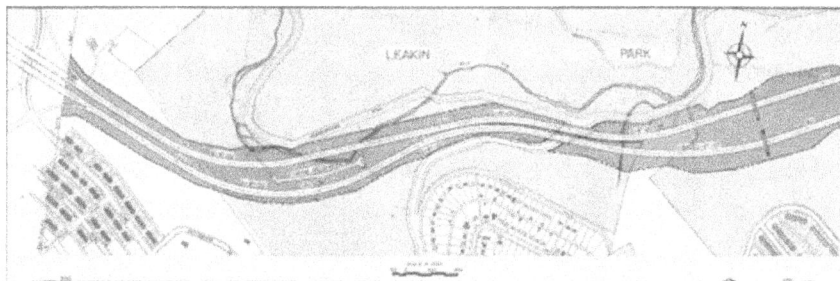

Figure 34. 1962 10-D Plan, the southern route through the parks (Source: Expressway Consultants, Interstate Highways 70-N and 95, East-West Expressway, 1961)

In 1967-1968, UDCT re-reviewed the options and endorsed the northern route with some modifications, including a six-hundred-foot tunnel under the Crimea section.‡ 388 (See Figure 35.)

There is evidence that Nathaniel Owings had been an early advocate for an alternate route avoiding Leakin Park. He had asked UDCT engineers to examine the possibility of accessing Franklin-Mulberry coming up from I-95 rather than down through Leakin Park. They refused, citing "the givens."389 This option (later named I-595) was incorporated into the overall 3-A plan, but it was in addition to the Leakin Park segment rather than instead of it.

UDCT was also responsible for a sub-contractor study, ostensibly aimed toward advancing the highway plan, except it actually aided the opposition. In 1969 UDCT hired Robert H. Giles Jr. to prepare an ecological assessment.

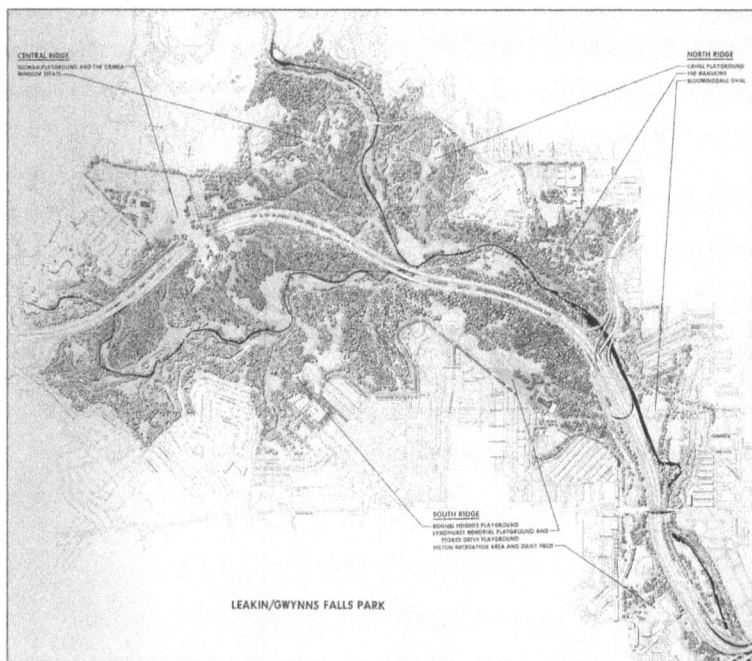

Figure 35. UDCT's 3-A plan—I-170 through Leakin/Gwynns Falls Park using the "northern alignment" (source: Urban Design Concept Associates, Leakin-Gwynns Falls Corridor Development Plan, Segment 9)

‡ Stew Bryant makes another appearance in VOLPE's archives. In June 1972, the meeting notes say, "Stew Bryant visited Sierra Club [headquarters] in San Francisco. They will go along if we need more money [for the Leakin Park lawsuit]."

Giles report

The Giles Report was prepared at the request of community representatives, but IDBC presumably funded it with an eye toward complying with 4(f) requirements. There is an intriguing document attached to the Enoch Pratt Library's copy of Robert Giles' 1969 report. The attachment was written by George Scheper, representing VOLPE, and Carolyn Tyson, representing MAD. Scheper says that the report was so unfavorable to the highway-through-the-park plan that IDBC attempted to bury the findings. Scheper said:

> The community representatives never heard another official word about this study. The reason it was suppressed is that, to the road planners' chagrin, the Giles Report is a devastating documentation of the destructiveness of the proposed road. Professor Giles formally delivered his report to the State Roads Commission (SRC) on January 30, 1970. No community representatives were invited, but some individuals privately received word of the meeting and attended uninvited.
>
> [The incognito activists reported that] after his summary of his report, Professor Giles was closely questioned by hostile highwaymen. He reiterated even more forcefully that the road plan could have nothing but a destructive impact on the park, that Leakin Park was a unique natural area, that further study would document even greater damage than his report showed, and that he had no specific recommendation for salvaging the park with the road. After the [uninvited] citizens asked further questions of him, a [highway] official present loudly asked, "How the hell did you get into this meeting?" and suggested that they be put out. (They were not.) The policy of the SRC from that point on was to keep the report unavailable and to misrepresent it in their subsequent [documents].

Carolyn Tyson's note adds that the report was made available only by making an arrangement to read it at IDBC's offices. Tyson continues, "Fortunately, since then, an individual who obtained a copy *in an unknown manner* has lent it to us for duplication" (emphasis added). The "unknown manner" was most likely through a UDCT staffer; suspect number one is Stew Bryant, who seemingly had little concern for his job security while repeatedly sharing with the community information his bosses and clients wanted held close to the vest.

Giles' primary task was to provide a technical ecological assessment of the impact of the highway on the park: defining, for example, the presence of wildlife and the degree to which certain species might be reduced or threatened. Giles, however, did not want to make the same mistake that Walter Sondheim made in 1964, burying a disclaimer in the preface; rather he placed his opinion—that the highway through the park was a monumentally bad idea—directly in his report. He spends the first eight pages expounding on the sanctity of such parks and admonishing highway officials for even considering destructive highway plans. Giles extolls the benefits of parks, as if he needs to instruct the ill-informed about the places where Man:

(1) can find conditions scaled to be compatible with his human potential; (2) avoid density stress; (3) feel safe from…air pollution, radiation, noise pollution, and water shortage; (4) experience diversity that is freeing of mind and spirit; and (5) gain the physical necessities for life…. [If] we are not to throw out any effort at achieving a properly designed, integrated city environment, we must maintain the open ground, the parks, and walkways and natural areas, along with the built-up land… Open space [should be regarded as] a fixed element… of an equal order of consideration with any kind of development.

He references Yellowstone National Park, calling it "irreplaceable…and immovable… It must be preserved in site or not at all. You can't build a city there and find another place for the national park." Giles stopped short of describing Leakin Park as "irreplaceable," but he was quite clearly implying that it was. Much like Walter Sondheim, he did not want his good name associated with the destruction of this unique wilderness in the city.

While Giles' opinion was as clear as a bell, the technical ecological assessment was more nuanced. He cited damage to groves of 100-to-200-year-old trees, loss of open space, and destruction of habitat for a variety of birds and animals; however, those impacts were relative, not absolute. Giles concluded that, "The initial decision to build a highway through the park thwarts many of the opportunities and alternatives for Baltimore to provide for its citizens' basic human needs." He then offers up the key conclusion that road builders would repeatedly cite: "There appeared to be no single catastrophic natural losses due to the highway."[390]

After the Giles report leaked out to the community, highway opponents used it as a key part of their anti-highway literature and public statements. IDBC was again put on defense and forced to include a number of references to the Giles report in the environmental impact statement (EIS). Approval of the EIS was withheld for several years mostly because of air quality issues, but the Giles report did not help the cause.[§]

Mitigation: Negotiate improvements or oppose?

MAD meeting minutes from November 30, 1970, noted: "Suit by conservationists on the Leakin Park segment not certain at this time pending extravagant offers of joint development proposed by Design Concept Team."[391] This was the other side of UDCT's modus operandi—remember, our previous intersections with joint development included the unrealistic Harlem Park platform and the scorned Fell's Point proposal for retail and tourist shopping under the elevated highway. For Leakin Park the joint development plan was for $5 million ($33 million today) in improvements, essentially creating more active recreation facilities in areas of the park that had been mostly passive. The plan called for three swimming pools; four playgrounds; twenty-seven miles of new foot, bicycle, and bridal paths;

---

§ I have not uncovered a paper trail leading to a smoking gun, but I have to suspect that Owings and UDCT knew precisely the kind of report Mr. Giles would write when they hired him. This appears to be UDCT's insurgent planners striking again. In my 45-year career as a city planner I have never encountered anything remotely like the consultant-client relationship in the Baltimore Design Concept Team.

thirty tennis courts; five ball fields; picnic areas; stream valley protection; and an improved park lighting system.[392]

There was one key difference between Leakin Park and other joint development plans: Harlem Park and Fell's Point plans were mostly unfunded "blue sky" wish lists, but Leakin Park improvements were potentially eligible for 90/10 federal funds because they compensated for the loss of park acreage. This created the classic dilemma of public policy decision-making: negotiate or oppose? Outright opposition is risky because you lose a seat at the table. Michael Seipp (later serving multiple roles as a respected community development professional) was a young community organizer when he volunteered with VOLPE in 1971. In a 2018 interview he explained the dilemma. "What if we lose? We'd lose the park; we'd lose everything. Shouldn't we be fighting for concessions? Shouldn't we be fighting to have buffers or things in that vein?" There were meetings between the compromisers and "the hardline folks" saying, "No road, no road, no road," Seipp said. "The 'No road' group won out completely, that there was not going to be any negotiations."

My interviews and research led to a question about the "no road" group vs. those inclined to negotiate improvements: Was there a racial split in that White environmentalists comprised the "no road" camp, compared to African Americans that wanted to see more active recreation facilities for their children and were therefore more inclined to negotiate?

I asked longtime VOLPE member Barry Blumberg about this underlying race issue in a 2020 interview. He remembers VOLPE as remarkably diverse and inclusive. He said, "We met with the neighborhood associations all around the park and got them involved… And, in the meetings and fundraising I attended, there was [always] a large group of African Americans."

The public record of hearings in May 1971 and December 1972 does not reveal any substantial split in the community. Of 250 community speakers, only four spoke in favor of the highway as the best way to gain the recreation facilities Leakin Park needed.[393] Anna J. Clinkscales,¶ President of the

---

¶ Ms. Clinkscales had a few interesting notches in her activism belt. On December 21, 1973, she delivered a 10,000-signature petition to the White House in support of a beleaguered President Nixon, saying Nixon "was the greatest president that ever lived." In October 1972

Leakin Park Improvement Association, was the only supporter representing an organization.

However, when I interviewed Iris Reeves (the wife of African American Councilman Norman Reeves and a three-term city councilmember in her own right), she confirmed that many African American families were more favorable to the joint development package, while White folks were more inclined to outright opposition. So, the evidence is mixed and the issue unresolved; however, on one point all are in agreement: Ms. Reeves' husband, Norman, played a critical role in backing VOLPE's no-compromise stance.

The revered Mr. Reeves

"He had a presence about him," said fellow VOLPE activist Barry Blumberg, expressing the universal characterization of Norman Reeves as a person of strength and stature despite his slight build and physical handicaps due to muscular dystrophy. Reeves' name is commemorated on the plaque that marks the end of I-70 just before Leakin Park. In the park there is also a Norman Reeves nature trail, a serene 1.4-mile hike symbolically located where the noisy pollution-generating highway would have gone. Had he lived (he passed away in 1983), Reeves probably would have declined to be singled out in this fashion. Indeed, there is a long list of VOLPE activists who merit more than a mention.

Reeves, however, does deserve the accolades. He was one of the two individual plaintiffs in the VOLPE lawsuit that stopped the highway. He was so respected and admired that his presence gave the highway fight legitimacy. Further, his deep roots in the civil rights movement helped neutralize any feelings that VOLPE did not represent African American communities adjacent to the park. Lastly, Reeves' election to city council in 1979 sounded the death knell for the highway through the park, partly because Schaefer did not want to go up against the highly regarded Mr. Reeves.

---

her support for Nixon led to a spat with Councilman Emerson Julian. She complained that her "Democrats for Nixon" sign posted at the Leakin Park Association office had been taken down, implying that Julian was responsible. Julian said, "I'm sorry someone else beat me to the sign."

In the early days of their relationship Norman's wife, Iris, said she was shocked that Norman's mother made no allowances for his disability. At the time Iris thought, "What is it that she does not get about his limitations? …What is wrong with this lady?" However, as time went on, she realized that Norman's fortitude came from his mother's insistence that "there wasn't anything that [he could not] accomplish." As a result, Norman "never let [his disability] get him down… He was tough."

In Maryland's civil rights struggle, Norman was a leader of the University of Maryland Black Coalition and a supporter and friend of noted civil rights leader Walter P. Carter. They carpooled together, but Iris remembers that Carter was an unreliable participant because "we never knew whether Walter was going to be in jail following a civil rights protest." Ms. Reeves also recalled that Carter once enrolled she and Norman in a public accommodations protest at a Mount Vernon hotel, and the protesters were met by a group of "young men in Nazi-type uniforms and German Shepherd dogs… That was something…kind of frightening."

Reeves ran for city council three times, losing narrowly in both 1971 and 1975, the latter election marred by a name-is-the-same dirty trick run by rivals. When he finally won in 1979, the long hill he had climbed was celebrated as a victory for determination in the face of monumental obstacles. The *Sun* reported that the "[inauguration] day was dominated by Mr. Reeves… The 44-year-old muscular dystrophy victim repeatedly received the biggest applause at the Civic Center and also got so many kisses that his face became smeared with lipstick."[394]

He died four short years later, having won the respect and admiration of all he encountered. He had been a civil rights activist, social worker, teacher, and politician, but mostly he was known as a doer who would not let his disability slow him down. The *Sun* editorial page lamented the loss of "quite simply the best city councilman… If there was any group whose legitimate interests he might have overlooked, it might have been the handicapped. He didn't know he was one."[395]

THE VOLPE PUTSCH

If Canton was the premier example of pro-highway forces in blitzkrieg mode, VOLPE was the highway opponents' rapid-fire counter offensive. The speed with which VOLPE achieved a favorable decision must have stirred both awe and jealousy from highway warriors who had labored for years and invested thousands of man-hours with little to show for it.

The VOLPE putsch took less than one year from inception in August 1971 to filing the lawsuit in October 1971 to the court-ordered injunction issued on June 8, 1972. Leakin Park opponents had accomplished in nine months what it took Fell's Pointers a decade to achieve.

How, precisely, was this quick result achieved? The chain of events goes back a little further to August 1970 when the Southeast Chapter of the Sierra Club put out a strongly worded position paper opposing the expressway through Leakin Park.[396] However, 1970 closed with a huge setback: in December the Interior Department backed the Federal Highway Administration and approved the city/state 4(f) statement. The approval recognized that alternatives were not feasible, that it was impossible to replace the 150 acres of park lost to the highway, and agreed that the $5 million improvement package was sufficient mitigation for the loss.[397]

In early 1971 the Sierra Club reached out to George Nilson, a young attorney who later served as Deputy Attorney General of Maryland and Baltimore City Solicitor. Mr. Nilson came to Baltimore in 1970 as a recent graduate from Yale Law School, his second post-graduate degree after city planning. These two specialties led Nilson to Piper Marbury, which was handling the legal work for the Rouse Company's ambitious plans for building the Columbia New Town; those areas of expertise also made Nilson an ideal candidate to take the helm in the battle against the Leakin Park expressway. Nilson recounted:

I personally was a strong environmentalist—I guess I picked that up during my education. I was a member of the Sierra Club, and [connected to the Sierra Club and the Natural Resources Defense Council…

[His contact at the Sierra Club said,] "Would you be interested in taking a look at the situation in Baltimore and in Leakin Park?" And I said, "Sure." I think the first person that I talked to locally…was a guy named Lyle Horn, he actually lived in Roland Park…and he was also a member of the Sierra Club and an environmentally concerned citizen.

Lyle Horn is a key part of the story—Horn was Chairman of the Conservation Committee of the Greater Baltimore Chapter of the Sierra Club and authored the August 1970 letter opposing the expressway through the park. It was Horn who put Nilson in touch with the neighborhoods of Dickeyville, Windsor Mills, Hunting Ridge, and Ten Hills; it was Horn who lined up Sierra Club funding for a good part of the legal expenses; and Horn served as the first President of VOLPE.

LYLE HORN, UNIFIER AND MOTIVATOR

Lyle Horn was "the right guy, at the right place, at the right time," according to fellow Leakin Park activist Barry Blumberg. "He motivated and inspired people. Lyle got you to think optimistically that you were going to win. He got us moving and staying on target."

We have spoken before about the importance of "bridge people" who can work productively and amicably with people they may not have a lot in common with. For Leakin Park, it was vital that leadership pull together those with a strong environmental ethic (who were mostly White) and the neighbors and park users (who were majority Black). Horn, who was married to a Black woman,* was that rare guy who "talked the talk and walked the walk."

* If Lyle and his wife were married more than four years prior to the events described, they would have been in violation of Maryland's anti-miscegenation laws, which were repealed in 1967.

Nilson organized a neighborhood coalition, knowing that "it would be really important to have a local advocacy group involved in any litigation." The May 26, 1971, hearing brought out both neighborhoods and environmental protesters. Ironically, it solidified the opposition—all now convinced that the highway could only be stopped through legal action.**

Federal rules required two hearings: one on the location of the highway corridor and one on the design of the highway after the corridor was set. The May hearing was labeled a "design hearing." The city and state contended that the "location hearing" requirement had been met in system-wide hearings in 1962 and 1967. Opponents claimed no information was imparted about the location of the Leakin Park segment at those hearings. The May 1971 hearing only added to opponents' frustration: they were there to state that no ameliorative improvements would change the basic issue, that the park would be substantially destroyed by the highway; however, they were told those comments were not germane to this "design hearing."

Sun columnist James Dilts beautifully articulated the growing frustration on both sides of this dispute:

> In the files of the Interstate Division office are some 1,500 pages of testimony taken at hearings before the 1969 DOT rulings went into effect [the two hearings rule]. Since then, beginning in August 1969 with Rosemont, there have been seven hearings held resulting so far in over 800 pages of testimony. Along with the letters and the statements that are added later (313 letters on the original Rosemont hearings alone), [the record] is almost uniformly against the proposed expressway...
>
> But the eloquence stirs briefly in the air and is shortly forgotten in the files of the Interstate Division. The highway engineers long for the end of these exercises in community catharsis and for the day they can at last get to their drawing boards. They are perhaps beginning to feel they never will.[398]

** It is no wonder highway planners resisted setting up these hearings. They usually accomplished little except to unify the opposition.

VOLPE was created in August 1971 as a coalition of the Sierra Club and the local communities. The *Baltimore Sun* marked the event with a change in their editorial stance, saying for the first time, "Leakin Park would be destroyed by the proposed highway. There is no doubt of that." The column pointed out that Secretary Volpe had said that "some expressway segments can't be built at all."

To assure their standing in the lawsuit, VOLPE acquired twelve acres of land contiguous to Leakin Park. To reserve all funds raised for the lawsuit, VOLPE performed a minor miracle to acquire the property without spending a single dollar: Private property owners donated land to VOLPE (a non-profit) and gained tax deductions spread over ten years.[††399]

On October 12, 1971, VOLPE filed the lawsuit.[400] The Sierra Club and the National Resources Defense Council (NRDC) joined VOLPE and two individuals (including Norman Reeves) on the plaintiff side; the defendants included the city, state, and federal governments. The basis of the complaint was the insufficiency of public hearings for the Leakin Park segment, the government's failure to demonstrate that "no feasible and prudent alternative" existed, and their failure to carry out "all possible planning to minimize harm to such park," therefore violating the 4(f) clause in the Highway Act of 1966.[401]

The courts separated the 4(f) issue from the public hearings issue because the *Ward v. Ackroyd* lawsuit filed by Tom Ward similarly attacked the sufficiency of public hearings. Much to the surprise of highway opponents, the 4(f) issue was never needed—the public hearings decision was the obstacle road builders never overcame.

In his June 8, 1972, decision, Judge James R. Miller first dismissed the defendants' claims for rejecting the lawsuit—that the plaintiffs lacked standing to sue and that the state was protected under the doctrine of sovereign immunity. The judge agreed that road builders had not met the requirement

---

†† VOLPE held those twelve acres for fifty years as an insurance policy against future threats to the park, finally transferring the land to the Friends of Gwynns Falls Leakin Park on the occasion of VOLPE's fiftieth anniversary on November 12, 2021.

for a "location hearing," i.e., they had bypassed required public discussion of the highway's location when they held the May 1971 "design hearing." The judge rejected the defendants' assertions that the 1962 and 1967 hearings were sufficient, partly because the alignment had changed after 1962 and partly because earlier hearings were system wide and had little focus on Leakin Park.

The injunction ordered defendants to cease all highway implementation activities until "a new corridor public hearing has been held…to obtain information concerning the economic and social effects of such a location, its impact on the environment, and its consistency with the goals and objectives of such urban planning as has been promulgated by the community." At the time, it was viewed as a temporary setback by friend and foe, the first inning of a nine-inning game.

Mayor Schaefer said, "The ruling will not stop me from proceeding with the essential parts of a total transportation system. One of the worst things that could happen to our city would be more study and looking for more alternative routes."[402] This dogged determination to continue building the expressway wherever he was not blocked led to the disastrous decision to build the I-170 Highway to Nowhere even though it might never link up with any other expressway segment.

George Nilson forced off the case

Greiner Company wears the blackest hat in the Road Wars saga. Greiner authored the disastrous 10-D plan, then continued promoting that plan even though the city had adopted 3-A; they spied on their fellow consultants at UDCT; they allegedly bribed both Agnew (as governor and later as vice president) and County Executive Anderson, recouping their bribery investments many times over in cost overruns. Further, Greiner Vice President Edward Donnelly testified before Congress, opposing a modest proposal to use Highway Trust funds for joint development, which would have been enormously helpful to Baltimore. But the clincher for black-hat status was the manner in which they forced George Nilson off the *VOLPE v. Volpe* case.

When Nilson resigned, he declined to comment to the media, and Donnelly denied that Greiner had anything to do with it.[403]

Stu Wechsler described Greiner as "a bunch of thugs." I thought this was a little extreme, but after interviewing Nilson, I cannot really argue with this characterization. Fifty years later, Nilson described exactly how Greiner used underhanded methods to have him removed.

[Defense attorney] Larry Rodowsky...in a move which was clever and arguably sinister...decided that he would have...one of [Greiner's] senior vice presidents, [Bruce A. Herman‡‡], be a witness at the preliminary hearing. The fact of the matter is that the Greiner Engineering had virtually nothing to do with the issues in the lawsuit...but they were, at the time, represented by Piper and Marbury, the firm that I was with.

So, we hadn't sued them and didn't consider them a relevant player...But Mr. Rodowsky, who I've known for many years and who I like and respect, put [Herman] on the witness stand. ...He was Irish and he had a temper and a short fuse. ...During the break, I went over to Henry Conway [attorney for Tom Ward, whose lawsuit had been joined to *VOLPE v. Volpe*] and I said, "I'm not going to cross-examine this guy." I said, "It's a cross-examination that's worth having; it's up to you. He has no business being here, but he is here, and the judge is probably going to let him testify, but I don't think it serves our purposes for me to be the one to cross-examine him."

So, Henry Conway cross-examined him. [One news article reported that Conway "raked Herman over the coals."] [Herman] sort of scowled at us the whole time that he was on the witness stand.... He clearly didn't like us because we were trying to stop an expressway. ...[So Herman] calls one of the senior partners of Piper...I'm sure he

---

‡‡ James Dilts interviewed Bruce Herman and asked him how a highway engineer lays out an expressway route. Herman said, "Well, you sit down with a map and see what looks like a good line, and then you go out in your car, and see if there's too many churches in the way." *Baltimore Sun*, "How not to run a roadway...," Feb. 25, 1968.

used a few expletives and gets very upset. Our senior lawyer went to Mr. Marbury…and they said they needed to talk to me. I said I was actually about to get on a plane the next day and go down to visit my family…

So, we met at eight o'clock [at the airport] and they basically said, "You cannot continue to be involved in the case because the Greiner Company has raised a conflict." …I said, "There is no real conflict; they're not a party; I haven't sued them; they don't really have a stake. If they were a party I would totally understand, but just because they were put on a stand as a witness—and I strongly suspect that that was done to get rid of me—that doesn't mean we should abandon my clients in West Baltimore and my clients, the Sierra Club and the Natural Resources Defense Council. They are firm clients, and they do have a stake in this matter that the Greiner company doesn't."

But it was Mr. Marbury and a senior partner on one side of the conversation and me on the other.

When Nilson returned from vacation, he had been removed from the case.

George Nilson went on to have quite a distinguished legal career including a five-year stint as Baltimore City Solicitor,[§§] but many years later people still thanked him for his role in stopping the highway through the park. Once while door-knocking for a political campaign, several neighbors recognized him and thanked him. Another time he and his wife were biking through Dickeyville and an older lady stopped her gardening to thank him. Nilson remembers that she said, "I've lived here for thirty-five years and I was one of your clients, and I just want to thank you ten years or twenty years later for all your good work."

"So, you know," Nilson said, "the expressway followed me a little."

[§§] Had time travel been possible Nilson might have filed another cleverly named lawsuit against his own future role in defending the City: *Nilson v. Nilson*.

The Leakin Park segment slowly ebbs away, but why?

If it was hard to tell precisely when and how the Fell's Point segment was finally defeated, it was even more nebulous for Leakin Park.

Following the injunction in June 1972, the city issued a new draft Environmental Impact Statement (EIS) on November 10, 1972; then held the required location hearing December 14-16. Six hundred people attended and eighty-six spoke, almost all opposed. Speaking for VOLPE, Barbara Holdridge quoted renowned Baltimore author Gerald W. Johnson, who had staked out the moral high ground by characterizing the city as "swapping... the last scrap of primeval nature left anywhere near Baltimore...for a continuous stream of metallic monsters, hideous to the eyes, hellish to the ears, pestilential to the lungs, murderous to flesh and bone, and destructive of property values in a mile-wide strip."[404]

The hearings were not just polemics. By this time, the Movement Against Destruction (MAD) and other opposition groups were far more educated on the technical and analytical data used to justify the expressway. At the same time, MAD also loved to use a bit of levity to keep up morale while garnering attention to the cause. Two articles captured both sides of MAD's approach. The first, "l-70N foes sing Leakin Park lullaby," highlights MAD's mini songfest; Art Cohen sang his "Road Building Blues," then he joined Mary Logan (MAD and South Baltimore activist) in singing a satirical version of "America."

The second article highlighted MAD's now impressive record of taking on the experts. Allan H. Marcus, a Johns Hopkins University mathematics professor and MAD member presented a 21-page critique of the new EIS, attacking the analytical underpinnings of I-70 and criticizing highway planners for their "failure to establish the need for the expressway; failure to consider meaningful alternatives and regional context; and failure to describe land use and travel demand assumptions on which traffic projections are made." He also maintained that the air and noise pollution impacts were underestimated and the case for the "no road" alternative was weighted incorrectly.[405] In June 1973, EPA issued a critical review of the EIS, citing some of the same issues raised by Marcus. MAD's strategy of diving into the technical sphere seemed to have paid off.

The revised EIS and the location hearing were an attempt to meet the requirements of the injunction so the city could proceed with the highway. However, that logical next step never happened. Two IDBC staffers told me that in 1973-1974 priority for I-70 was downgraded relative to the top priority, which was I-95. From 1973 to mid-1975 the Leakin Park plan was stalled. In June 1975 the city announced that a new EIS had been prepared, and they were going back to court to have the injunction lifted.[406] VOLPE again ramped up their opposition, including a walking tour of the park punctuated by a visual that must have been inspired by MAD's stunt, when Art Cohen cut sheets the width of the expressway and marched them through City Fair. VOLPE's Jastro Levin wound orange tape through the park to represent the wide swath of the eight-lane highway.[407] ¶¶

Here the paper trail is thin, but there was no real progress for two more years.

In 1976 Leakin Park was back in the news but not for progress, rather it was the reverse: support was eroding in city council. In September 1976 Council President Walter Orlinsky changed sides and introduced a bill to rescind authority for the I-70 Leakin Park segment. This was the second time Orlinsky had switched his allegiance. Originally one of the most vocal opponents to the expressway plan, Orlinsky became a highway backer in 1972, much to the chagrin of opponents.*** The 1976 about-turn resulted from fiscal issues: Orlinsky became incensed that the city was shifting the $1.7 million ($8.7 million today) cost of school crossing guards from motor vehicle revenue (MVR) funds to local funds because MVR funds were needed for the expressway. Councilwoman Mikulski had grown tired of Orlinsky's

---

¶¶ Jastro Levin's role in VOLPE is commemorated by naming two facilities, a trail and a picnic grove, in his honor.

*** In late 1971 Schaefer held a fundraiser for Orlinsky that paid off much of Orlinsky's campaign debts, estimated to be $30,000 ($214,000 today). It was widely assumed that there was a quid pro quo connected to this fundraiser: that Orlinsky would switch sides on the highway issue and back the mayor.

head-spinning flip-flops and made a few choice comments.[408] This and other issues led to a rift between them.[409] Orlinsky's bill failed as Schaefer again rallied support for the expressway even though his administration seemed to be making only half-hearted efforts to move it forward.

In March 1977 IDBC announced that new hearings would be held on the Leakin Park segment.[410] However, once again, the plan went to the back-burner. As the calendar turned to 1978, the Leakin Park segment was still on the books, but no one was writing the final chapter. This leads to the 1979-1980 reconsideration of both I-70 and I-83, addressed in Chapter 16.

What happened to the city's resolve to move forward with the Leakin Park segment? There were multiple factors. First, I-95 was "priority one" from 1973 on. Second, community opposition may have taken a toll. The mayor's coalition to continue the expressway plan may have been jeopardized if he had pushed forward with the Leakin Park segment. That coalition weakened in 1976 when Orlinsky abandoned the I-70 cause. Third, remember that the Leakin Park segment was dependent on the Rosemont Bypass, which meant acquiring plots in Western Cemetery—a slow, tedious, and time-consuming process. Fourth, although the court had not adjudicated the 4(f) issue, that potential legal obstacle undoubtedly reinforced the shift in priorities away from the park.[411] Fifth, EIS issues created a significant obstacle. But note also that the city took two full years to redraft the EIS after EPA's negative comments in June 1973. If I-70 had been the priority, surely the city would have moved more rapidly.

All of the above were formidable obstacles, but there were similar obstacles for I-83 on the east side. The mayor and the city left no stone unturned in prosecuting I-83, but that zeal seemed distinctly lacking when it came to Leakin Park. While much of the Road Wars story portrays Mayor Schaefer charging forward with ill-conceived highway plans, the languid pace of the Leakin Park segment calls that view into account. The do-it-now mayor seemed magically transformed into the do-it-later guy when it came to Leakin Park. I can't help but wonder, did the mayor have a soft spot for the park?

Recall that, from 1960 to 1967, Schaefer was a Fifth District councilman, which included most of the Leakin Park neighborhoods. Schaefer also warned highway planners all the way back in 1961 that they were underestimating the potential for opposition in this part of the city. He knew these people and these neighborhoods. There must have been many personal exchanges with constituents that he respected—was there a cumulative effect that sowed the seeds of doubt? Is it possible that the 1972 injunction, which seemed like a small bump in the road at the time, became an excuse for inaction?

When Norman Reeves was elected to city council in 1979, it may have been the last nail in the coffin for the Leakin Park segment. Iris Reeves confirmed that, "Schaefer did have a lot of respect…for Norman, and they butted heads, but he knew that Norman was going to…stand his ground… They were just both being really… bullheaded about things, but he did have a lot of respect for the positions that Norman took." When city council forced a reconsideration of highway plans in December 1979, Schaefer said he was "not wild about" the expressway through the park, and that he had asked highway planners to prepare alternatives that would emphasize mass transit instead.[412]

My theory is that the 1979 reversal was not the abrupt change it seemed to be at the time. This was not Schaefer folding his cards and admitting defeat. Rather, this decision had been building a long time—it appears that the mayor's heart was just not in it.

XV. BLOWS AGAINST THE EMPIRE IV

FALLON'S FALL AND BUSTING THE TRUST

It was a stunning victory for environmentalists. After the first Earth Day in April 1970, really at the dawn of the modern environmental movement, the League of Conservation Voters named twelve congressmen and senators as "the Dirty Dozen" and worked to defeat them. The number one prize: Baltimore's George H. ("H" is for highways) Fallon. The *New York Times* described his defeat by Paul S. Sarbanes in the Democratic primary: "George Fallon, veteran of thirteen terms in the House of Representatives and chairman of the Public Works Committee, was eliminated almost solely because of his fanatic devotion to highways and the highway lobby."[413] It was symptomatic of the changing times—expressways were no longer the simple benevolent carriers of workers to jobs and families to vacationland.

Fallon, you will recall, was the Baltimore congressman who drafted significant portions of the 1956 Federal-Aid Highway Act, including the centerpiece: the self-funding Highway Trust. Thereafter, Fallon played a pivotal role as guardian of the sacrosanct Trust.[414] The self-funding mechanism for expressway financing (fueled by highways that enabled people to live further from their jobs and abandon public transit) had grown from $1.0 billion in 1957 to $5.4 billion in 1969; meanwhile public transportation, which had to compete for funds with all other federal priorities, was pegged at a paltry $175 million.[415]

While the imbalance was plain as day, the Road Gang was quite the well-oiled lobbying machine. Senators and congressmen in key positions were practically on their payroll. In October 1968, business-friendly *Forbes Magazine* ran an article entitled, "The US's lopsided Transportation Budget," estimating that the highway lobby was spending $500 million annually, including campaign contributions to members of Fallon's House Committee on Public Works. The highway lobby was not just the engineering companies, carmakers, and road builders—it included a host of affiliated industries and businesses. According to the *New York Times*: "oil, rubber, construction, asphalt and limestone industries; the car dealers and renters, bus lines and trucking concerns that depend on the highways; the banks and advertising agencies with clients in the companies involved; and the American Automobile Association."[416]

J. N. Robinson, retired Director of the DC Department of Highways, said, "If the highway people ever had a friend in Congress, that would be George H. Fallon."[417] In 1968, facing a challenging primary, Fallon got a huge boost from the American Road Building Association (ARBA) in the form of a testimonial event that raised $13,000 ($113,000 today), most of it from road-building interests.[418] The ARBA president went on to organize and chair the "National Committee to Re-elect George Fallon," again, dominated by highway contractors and engineers, including Edward J. Donnelly, a Greiner engineer who was later implicated in the Agnew bribery schemes.

In 1968, Fallon's unshakable belief in freeways led an action that climbs the scales of reprehensible and indefensible public policy. In 1967, the new Washington, DC, city council voted to expunge the controversial Three Sisters Bridge from the city's transportation plan and to designate more than twenty miles of unpopular freeways for further study. In February 1968 the district court ruled in favor of the local anti-highway coalition, finding that there had not been adequate public hearings for the bridge and four planned highways.[419]

As author Ben Kelley phrased it, "The court's opinion may have been written in vanishing ink, so far as [Fallon's] House Committee on Public Works was concerned."[420] The committee amended the 1968 Transportation Reauthorization Act to include a provision that ordered the District to build the Three Sisters Bridge and the four challenged highways. Further, by working with the House Appropriations Subcommittee, Fallon was able to withhold funds for building Washington's Metro system until the council approved the bridge and highway plans. The ensuing crisis over who was in charge of the District's transportation program took seven years to resolve.

Luckily, Baltimore was not a congressional fiefdom, and Fallon's pro-highway committee was almost powerless over the anti-highway sentiment taking hold here.

From 1965 to 1970, the highway lobby turned back all manner of proposals to cut the Trust Fund budget, merge federal transportation programs, or allow cities to trade in highway funds for transit. President Johnson tried to trim the budget in 1966, but backed off after, as one observer noted, he was "filleted and fried by all the good old boys who didn't want their country deprived of a mile of paving it deserved."[421] Maryland's Governor Mandel attempted to get the Governor's Association to support a program merger, but the highway lobby turned that back as well. Maryland's Senator Joseph Tydings (D) co-sponsored several bills to allow cities to switch highway funds to mass transit, but those proposals were dead on arrival. In 1969 the Nixon Administration tried a variation on the program merger concept, a transportation program block grant, but that was a non-starter too.

However, the cumulative effect of all these proposals, each advertised as a more sensible way to fund transportation, had turned a microscope on the Highway Trust Fund and the lobbying machine that had consistently twisted public policy to serve their own purposes. The highway interests knew they were in trouble when mainstream magazines aimed broadsides at the Highway Trust Fund and its self-interested lobbyists. A March 1969 *Readers Digest* article titled "Let's Put the Brakes on the Highway Lobby" bluntly accused the lobby of "riding rough-shod over development of a sane transportation system in the United States."[422]

In October 1969 the most mainstream magazine in America, *Life*, published a satirical article about the Highway Trust Fund. "Kill the Hill! Pave that Grass!" was a take-no-prisoners rebuke of the highways-beget-more-highways mentality:

As for parks, clean air, trout streams, grass, and secluded neighborhoods, we'll all be better off…when we face up to the fact that they are rapidly being outmoded…the rights, needs and importance of automobiles have superseded the rights, needs, and importance of humans in many areas

294

of our culture… Nor will those fruitless protests become more effective. There's a reason: the Highway Trust Fund—a pork barrel of such magnitude that no congressman, senator, governor or state highway official can possibly ignore it. [423]

The author concluded, quoting Baltimore's own George Fallon: "Any cutback in the highway program would [amount] to breaking faith with… motorists."

In 1969 Boston made headlines as a city that said "no" to the highway trough, as Mayor White ditched two planned highways. That officials were willing to part with hundreds of millions of dollars is telling, but they weren't happy about it; so they brought Senator Edward Kennedy into the issue and he became a legislative leader for busting the trust.[424]

In February 1970, Mandel tried to accomplish at a state level what he had failed to do nationally—he proposed creating a State Department of Transportation with all transportation funds in a single pot. Although federal trust fund dollars would still have to be used for highways, the clear intent was for Maryland to bend the rules as far as they could in making their own transportation decisions. The highway lobby went on high alert, with Maryland AAA leading the charge. AAA put out a four-page flier entitled "Maryland's Phony Funnel," portraying this completely overt move as a shady "behind the scenes" effort to take Highway Trust Fund dollars and divert them to "other purposes than those for which it was collected from the motoring public."[425] The flier went out to 200,000 Maryland AAA members.

By 1970 the battle to bust the trust had become a test of America's moral fiber—democracy, it seemed, was being subverted by lobbyists over the interests of the public. The implication of this convoluted policymaking was that America was succumbing to needless pollution. Public opinion had clearly shifted.

Newspaper editorials were turning in favor of busting the trust. The *Baltimore Sun*, for example, worried that "an estimated 60 percent of the pollution we breathe comes from automobiles. Cities will figuratively and literally strangle if urban mass transit on a big scale doesn't supplement private, individual travel. The easiest and most logical way to pay for it would be—at least in part—with Highway Trust funds."

Still, in 1970 the highway lobby turned back legislative proposals, both broader bills that would have unified transportation funding (Senator Kennedy's approach), and narrower bills that would have allowed states and localities to trade in Highway Trust dollars for transit (Tydings-Bingham bill). Fallon remained rigid, saying: "This committee cannot, I can say in

THE HIGHWAY LOBBY STRIKES BACK

In the midst of all this bad news, the US Bureau of Public Roads was feeling a little defensive. Bureau Director Ralph Bartelsmeyer decided to go on a PR campaign because "some people are trying to make us into black-hatted villains."

The first news release backfired. It proudly declared: "The budding basketball star of tomorrow could be a kid that learned how to dribble, pass, and shoot because an interstate highway came through his neighborhood. This same youth, who wiled away hours of his life wondering what to do next, can now cavort on a basketball court under a structurally modern viaduct." It only took a little digging to discover that this referred to a Wilmington, Delaware, highway that had slashed through Wilmington's Black ghetto, displacing hundreds of families but leaving behind one sun-robbed playground.

After another embarrasing release ("thousands of ducks and birds found a quiet resting place in the middle of a highway"), the campaign was halted. (Source: *The Pavers and the Paved*)

Later, the highway lobby tried another PR makeover. The Wall Street Journal covered the campaign with the tongue-in-cheek headline, "The Highway Lobby Aims to Prove there is no Highway Lobby, Road Builders Mount Campaign to Convince America That It Yearns for More Asphalt."

good conscience, devote any money other than for highway purposes because the people using them are being charged for them."[426]

FALLON'S DAY OF RECKONING

The 1970 congressional elections took place amidst this upheaval. The growing environmental movement was now laser focused on the Highway Trust Fund. The League of Conservation Voters and Environmental Action amassed a $42,000 war chest for their Dirty Dozen campaign to unseat the most environmentally unfriendly politicians, with the largest single contribution, $8,000 ($59,000 today), going to Fallon's opponent, Paul S. Sarbanes.[427]

When Sarbanes, a state delegate, announced his candidacy to unseat Fallon, he said, "The problems facing us as a nation call out for a dramatic reordering of priorities. We must redirect our resources and attention back to urban centers and to the quality of life for those who live there. More roads… are not what is so desperately needed."[428]

Baltimore never had the opportunity to vote on the Baltimore highway plan;* this primary election was the closest thing they got to a referendum, with Fallon's unwavering support of the Highway Trust Fund and Sarbanes' opposition representing the pro- and anti-expressway sides of the local debate. Fallon maintained his opposition to Governor Mandel's bust-the-trust initiative, saying, "the taxpayers have already paid for highways they have not gotten yet… If you don't have highways, I don't know how the city is to be served." Sarbanes supported Mandel and accused Fallon of an "appalling lack of sensitivity." Sarbanes said flatly, "Funds that are being spent on the Interstate Highways should be diverted to create a rapid transit system."[429]

Sarbanes ran a grassroots, door-knocking campaign attacking Fallon's aloofness, lack of communication with voters, and his ties to Washington lobbyists, pointing out that "more than two-thirds of Rep. Fallon's campaign chest in the 1968 election came from members of this highway lobby."[430]

---

* In the early 1970s, the city began borrowing against future motor vehicle revenues to finance the growing local share, but they avoided local bond issues, fearing likely defeat at the polls. Instead, they sought and were eventually approved to use a state bond program.

Sarbanes also held a fundraiser spoofing lobbyist-backed political events. Charging only $10 per person, he claimed to have "screened guests for lobbyists, and there aren't any here." His campaign manager pilloried the whole concept of event sponsors, saying our "honorary sponsors…are all dead." However, each had impacted the candidate's life. A *Sun* article explained, "They ranged from Pericles, the Athenian statesman who reflected Sarbanes ethnic background, to John Naismith, the inventor of basketball, reflecting Sarbanes' captaincy of the Oxford University basketball team."[431]

Sarbanes defeated Fallon in the primary and then won the general election, launching a distinguished thirty-six-year congressional career. It was the longest congressional stint in the state's history until it was surpassed, by exactly one day, by Barbara Mikulski. It might seem coincidental at first glance that Maryland's two longest tenured congressional figures both launched their careers fighting against highways. However, it also makes sense—there was no other issue that stayed on the front pages for forty years. No other issue even comes close.

The perplexed former-congressman Fallon commented, "I used to be complimented on the great job I was doing for the highway program. Now that is the thing that is used against me." He added, "I thought I was helping people."[432]

TRUST-BUSTERS FINALLY PREVAIL

With George Fallon vanquished, the bust-the-trust movement held out new hope for a change in the 1972 Transportation Reauthorization bill. But the irrepressible highway lobby, now under the umbrella of the Highway Users Federation for Safety and Mobility (HUFSAM), was in fine form for another battle. A determined but underfunded group of mainly environmental activists, dubbed the Highway Action Coalition, coordinated an energetic bust-the-trust effort.

The *Sun's* James Dilts visited both offices and described the David vs. Goliath battle being waged in the halls of Congress.[433] HUFSAM occupied "plush offices" that housed a staff of fifty, bankrolled by a budget that was north of $3 million. Veteran activists of the late '60s and early '70s will likely slip into a nostalgic mood when they read Dilts description of the Highway Action Coalition: a ramshackle space, "which seems to be sort of a commercial Chelsea Hotel† and in a similar state of physical decay." He added that, "A lot of people run around the halls with guitars." Dilts asked John D. Kramer, the guy directing a staff of four in a valiant effort to take on the well-heeled protectors of the Trust, about their funding sources. "That's the problem. We don't have one," Kramer said. "Neither I nor anyone else on the staff has been paid in a month."[434]

The mismatch was quite apparent, as one commentator further described: "One anti-highway man counted nearly 30 highway lobbyists working the corridors of Capitol Hill as the House proposal headed toward a vote recently." Lobbyists were writing checks in the hallways outside of the committee room.

On September 19, 1972, the Senate voted 48-26 in favor of the Cooper-Muskie amendment, which allowed cities to shift highway funds to transit. The amendment had gained additional traction partly because President Nixon parted ways with Republican leadership to endorse the amendment, and partly because two high profile businesses, Ford Motor Company and Mobile Oil Company, published full-page ads supporting a more balanced approach to transportation.

However, the House, still in the grips of the highway lobby, steadfastly resisted any change. The conference committee deliberated for two months with neither side giving ground. The resulting stalemate killed the Transportation Reauthorization bill, which was revisited in early 1973. This stalemate actually benefitted the trust-busters—highway funds were dwindling, threatening to create a significant gap in the federal highway gravy train. Nothing like a pinch in the pocketbook to bring a reluctant negotiator to the table.

In 1973 the same stalemate occurred, and these seemingly irreconcilable bills again went to the conference committee. After three months of wrangling, several "last best offers," and many newscasts pronouncing negotiations "deadlocked," the conference committee adopted a compromise that would

---

† The Chelsea Hotel in New York City was known as a center of bohemian culture, attracting many iconic figures from the Beat generation and the counterculture, including Jack Kerouac, William S. Burroughs, and Allen Ginsberg.

transition to more flexible use of trust funds over time. The Highway Trust Fund was finally busted, and cities could use the "Interstate substitution" provision to shift highway funds to transit, dollar for dollar. The legislation also almost doubled the capital grant program of the Urban Mass Transportation Administration from $3.1 billion in 1973 to $6.1 billion in 1975.

The conference committee's bill passed both houses and was signed into law by President Nixon on August 13, 1973. Nixon said: "The legislation I sign today represents an important forward step for our country, not only in providing for better and more balanced transportation but also in related fields such as environmental protection, highway safety, energy conservation, and community development." Secretary of Transportation Brinegar was more emphatic, calling it "the single most important piece of legislation that the Department of Transportation has been called upon to administer."

The *St. Louis Globe-Democrat* announced gleefully, "The powerful highway lobby finally got a well-deserved kick in the teeth." The *Baltimore Sun*: "On balance, it clearly establishes that the highway lobby is no longer the unassailable power it once was. The nation desperately needs new priorities in urban transportation and the…[new law] is a major step in the right direction."

As Agnew stood behind Nixon when he signed the bill, the *New York Times* was breaking the story that Agnew and Jerome Wolff were now targets of the Maryland corruption investigation. The article said Assistant Prosecutor George Beall "appeared to be concentrating on highway construction and engineering contracts" in their probe. These two seemingly disparate events—the enactment of bust-the-trust legislation and the emergence of the Agnew bribery scandals—were linked. In both cases, the public had said "No more" to the manner in which transportation decisions were being made—the cozy relationships between engineers, road builders, lobbyists, and politicians would no longer rule the roost.

A much later look back found that states and localities used the substitution provision to redirect $9.8 billion in highway funds, dropping 343 miles in planned interstate highways.[435]

Back in Baltimore, highway opponents all across the city had a brand-new battering ram to continue hounding Mayor Schaefer about the city's

300

ill-advised pursuit of expressways over transit. Further, these new options for Highway Trust dollars became a divisive issue between the mayor and the state: Transportation Secretary Hughes was now additionally taking into account the energy crisis spawned by OPEC and trouble in the Middle East. He said his department's "first priority" in Baltimore was construction of the rapid transit system. A *Baltimore Sun* reporter asked Schaefer if the change in the federal landscape would affect Baltimore City priorities. Schaefer replied tersely, "We believe expressways are not in conflict with clean air."[436]

A *Baltimore Sun* reporter captured a befuddled Fallon after his election defeat in 1970. "It was as if the veteran, 13-term, 68-year-old Democratic lawmaker could not really believe his defeat in Tuesday's primary election... He did not know what he would do after leaving office and wasn't even sure what his pension would be. He was 'surprised' by the upset, but conceded that, 'Mr. Sarbanes put on a very vigorous campaign, the most vigorous I've ever seen in my district...'"

Fallon then largely disappeared from public life. He enjoyed one last honor: AASHO invited him to their annual meeting and bestowed a certificate of appreciation, memorializing his appearance by designating the day as "George Fallon Day." Fallon said, "Over the years I have been involved in Congress with many people, but nowhere have I felt so much at home as being with the American Association of State Highway Officials; you represent America in the finest sense." Although he had many opportunities to continue work in the political realm, Fallon said, "I had thirty-two years in public office and that's enough."

When he died in 1980 after a long battle with emphysema, the *New York Times'* obituary called him the "Father of the Interstate System," but the general public recalled little of his thirteen terms in Congress. His name is enshrined on the Federal Building in Baltimore's Charles Center. In that grand opening ceremony back in 1965, Fallon's speech was short. He said, "It's nice to be remembered."[437]

IMPORTANT NOTE

At this point we have completed the deep dive into the geographic battles and cross-cutting city-wide issues that dominated civic discourse from 1967 to 1975 and completely upended the balance of power in the expressway fight. Here we return to a chronological accounting for the period 1976 to 1982.

XVI. 1976 – 1982

There is no benefit that can come from expressways that even remotely balances the cost of removing people…I cannot approve or encourage any expressway that will lead to further dislocation. But if you take I-95 as a tunnel under Fort McHenry, you are talking about something that does not dislocate and honestly serves transportation. In contemporary life, roads are the transportation link that makes the city work.[438]

Walter Orlinsky, President of Baltimore City Council, just before switching his allegiance to backing Schaefer's expressway plan

By 1976-77 the balance of power had shifted. In Fell's Point, the Preservation Society's no-compromise stance had the implicit or explicit backing of the courts and the President's Advisory Council on Historic Preservation. The city was forced to accept that only the Cadillac version of the I-83 connector (the underwater tunnel south of Fell's Point) was acceptable. As Fell's Point went, so went Harbor East and Canton. On the west side, Franklin-Mulberry was under construction, but resolution of the Leakin Park injunction was going in slow motion, at about the same speed that Western Cemetery plots were being relocated.

This will shortly lead us to the city-wide issues that sunk the expressway ship, but first there are two more geographic battlegrounds to consider.

INNOVATIONS—MLK AND FEDERAL HILL, I-395 AND OTTERBEIN

David Chapin of IDBC was essentially self-taught in the field of highway engineering, not a field one usually associates with self-instruction, but Chapin's colleagues were not surprised—they regarded him as brilliant. IDBC staffer

303

Gene Bober remembers Chapin as "just amazing…hard-working, creative, thoughtful, articulate." Chapin graduated from Princeton, then "spent some time building a stone wall around his parent's property in Ruxton. And then, somehow he got on the Interstate Planning Department payroll through this federal jobs program. He taught himself to speak 'highway,' then he taught himself the basics of highway engineering." Renovators and homeowners in Otterbein should be especially grateful that Chapin's self-education led to a community-saving innovation.

Much of the Road Wars saga portrays the city, in general, and IDBC, in particular, as on the wrong side of history. However, in planning Martin Luther King Jr Boulevard and I-395, a different view emerges: that dedicated and resourceful employees came up with creative solutions that lowered the impact of highways on neighborhoods.

We have looked at MLK and I-395 three times. First, the so-called "westside connector" (connecting I-70 to the Jones Falls expressway near Mount Royal) was defeated in 1968 when the Planning Commission recommended a boulevard instead. Later that same year UDCT's 3-A plan, adopted by Mayor D'Alesandro, called for a crescent-shaped boulevard ringing downtown's westside, distributing traffic from the I-170 (Franklin-Mulberry) and the I-395 spur. Third, I-395 was the segment that narrowed from eight lanes to six, freeing some of the land that Mildred Moon and Sharp Leadenhall used to rebuild the neighborhood as an African American enclave with affordable housing.

In 1970 the city released a plan for the thirty-three-block-long "City Boulevard" (later referred to as "Harbor City Boulevard" and later yet as "Martin Luther King Boulevard") extending from the Mount Royal area to the intersection of Light Street and Key Highway in Federal Hill. (See Appendix 1-F—City Boulevard) There were controversies and accommodations along the whole stretch, including a depressed section under Pratt and Lombard Streets that was changed to at-grade intersections at the behest of the Little Lithuania community.[439]

There were significant public controversies in two areas: the Federal Hill Historic District and Otterbein. The city spared Federal Hill from an I-95 harbor crossing by adopting the Fort McHenry Bypass, which, after a pro-tracted controversy from 1968 to 1975, became the Fort McHenry Tunnel. But that was not the end of the story—MLK Boulevard (Figure 36) was still going to take 150 properties (70 in the historic district) to tie into Light Street (for traffic going downtown) and to Key Highway (for traffic bound for Locust Point). Although the plan was primarily for an at-grade boulevard, it would be elevated (and look very much like an expressway) at the point where it crossed over I-395.

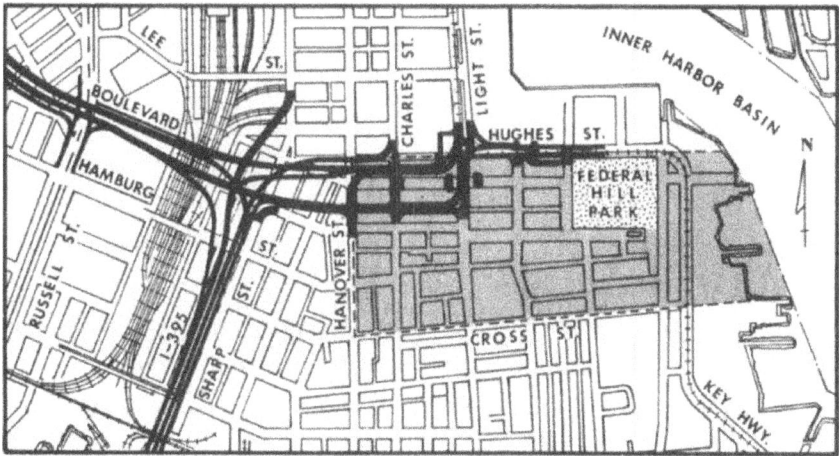

Figure 36. (Later named) MLK Boulevard, extended into the Federal Hill Historic District and tied into Light Street and Key Highway (source: Federal Hill Historic District, Federal Section 106 Informational Report, February 1974).

Federal Hill community groups faced the same dilemma as Fell's Pointers and Leakin Park protectors: negotiate a deal or maintain outright opposition. In contrast to the other two groups, Federal Hill decided to nego-tiate. In February 1975 the Federal Hill Neighborhood Association and the Preservation Society backed (at least in concept) the option they regarded as the least damaging. Attorney Geoff Mitchell's position paper for the Preservation Society said they "would not oppose Alternate No. 5."[440] * This

---

* I have not been able to reconstruct the why's and wherefore's of Federal Hill's decision to negotiate and endorse, in concept, the destructive boulevard plan. This may have boiled down to personalities. But I suspect the following: it was only shortly before this time that the main

frankly comes as quite a shock: Those 150 properties to be razed included 87 that had been categorized as either "must be preserved" or "should be preserved" vis-à-vis the same federal historic preservation regulations (Section 106) that were key to saving Fell's Point.[441]

A lengthy negotiation dragged into January 1976, centering largely on appropriate mitigation measures, such as several pocket parks. The city became frustrated with the lack of resolution and decided to play hardball, but the resulting showdown backfired. On January 27, 1976, mayor's representatives held a confidential meeting with Federal Hill leaders and gave them an ultimatum: absent community endorsement, they would build the boulevard without any of the negotiated improvements. They further threatened to dispose of unneeded city-owned property "by selling...for the highest possible prices in order to minimize their financial losses, regardless of any impact that this would have on the neighborhood." Further, "homesteading proposals for the unit block of E. Montgomery would be stymied."[442]

Community leaders were prepared to accept the ultimatum and may have done so except for the actions of young Charlie Duff, at the time a just-out-of-college volunteer for the Preservation Society. Duff recounted what happened in a 2018 interview:

> The Interstate Division got the leaders of the Federal Hill neighborhood association to agree to endorse...[MLK] as an elevated highway across Montgomery Street as far as [Light Street]... I don't know how...but they did. And there was some boring neighborhood association meeting on a Sunday in February; there were about five of us at the meeting. The president at the moment, Jim Craig, said that they had decided to agree on this and that it was wonderful because city was going to build

route of I-95 was officially shifted to Fort McHenry; compared to I-95 cutting a wide swath through Federal Hill, the boulevard plan looked like a scalpel instead of a sledgehammer. I'm sure IDBC's renderings made the boulevard look like an asset. An additional factor is that there were many properties in the vicinity of Hughes, Montgomery, and Charles Streets that were so rundown that they were causing a lot of concern—those involved may have thought these properties were not salvageable.

a bunch of vest pocket parks throughout Federal Hill. I went back and informed the Road Warriors that Federal Hill was about to capitulate. Between then and the next meeting Jane Spreinger and several others and I knocked on every door we could and had a hundred people at the next meeting and overthrew the leadership. They resigned in disgust and Federal Hill stayed in the Road Fight.

Duff's recollection matches up with historical records; it was at precisely this time that the community position hardened. Further, internal Preservation Society documents reveal an in-house controversy revolving around Jim Craig's leadership of the neighborhood association, including concerns that he had a conflict of interest due to properties he owned.[443] When the Federal Hill Committee on the Road made their report, they were unequivocal "that our present policy of opposition to any proposed interstate road through the Federal Hill Historic District be maintained without any qualifications."[444] Jim Craig's name was not listed as a committee member,† consistent with Duff's description of an overthrow of leadership.[445]

Throughout this book I've taken great pains to document all the times that destruction of waterfront and historic areas was narrowly averted. We can now add to this list the northwest quadrant of Federal Hill, almost destroyed with the shocking acquiescence of Federal Hill and the Preservation Society, right up until the last possible moment when twenty-two-year-old Charlie Duff sounded the alarm.‡

The impasse spurred the creative juices of Robert Embry, Commissioner of Housing, who had his own reasons for opposing the boulevard extension into Federal Hill: It would bisect and constrict the redevelopment he had championed in Inner Harbor West/Otterbein and Federal Hill.[446] It was Embry, my interviewees agree, who came up with the creative scheme that was later built:

---

† However, Rosemary Craig (presumably Jim's wife) was listed as a committee member, which leads me to further speculate that there were some interesting discussions of the boulevard issue in the Craig household.

‡ I sent this section of the book to Charlie for fact checking. He emailed me back a few corrections, but also this comment: "I feel as if I might actually have justified my existence."

The boulevard would end at I-395, and access to Light Street, the Inner Harbor, and downtown would be via I-395 (extended north by a half mile) and a widened and pleasantly landscaped Conway Street. (See Figure 37, below.)

Embry's Conway Street solution freed up those 150 properties. Much like Fell's Point and Canton, interest in rehabilitating city-owned properties got the ball rolling; then it kept rolling and rolling... Soon the problems associated with derelict properties were replaced by a whole new set of issues related to gentrification. In the larger scheme of a downtrodden city, many people, myself included, feel those are good problems to have.

Which brings us to Embry's adjoining redevelopment area: Inner Harbor West, specifically Otterbein. Embry's Conway Street solution had one major downside: The extension of I-395 to Conway Street was a very unwelcome neighbor for Otterbein homesteaders. Once slated for clearance and new development as part of the Inner Harbor West Renewal Area,§ several blocks of Otterbein had been saved from the wrecking ball in January 1977. The city was now expanding on the success of the Dollar House Program to salvage and renovate 105 deteriorated homes. The new I-395 alignment put the highway right next door to Otterbein, both the homesteading part and the new development known as Harborwalk. Homesteaders balked at shelling out $35,000 to fix houses next door to an expressway.

One homesteader,¶ environmental planner Henry Fostel, raised the rhetorical decibel level as he cited air quality impacts: "To accept such a health risk as part of the decision to construct the proposed highway would be more than the usual callous, reckless, and irresponsible bureaucratic action.

§ Some records refer to at least part of Otterbein being acquired for the highway.

¶ Homesteaders can be a cantankerous lot. The Otterbein Association's newsletter is titled "The Mullion" as "a reminder of the night when, after four hours of discussion, the homesteaders were deadlocked over the standard regarding window mullions." (source: https://www.theotterbein.org/wp/history/).

It would be within the bounds of criminal law to consider this action part of a conspiracy to commit murder." Housing Commissioner Embry responded, "Everybody wants the road someplace else. I would prefer no roads at all, but since it looks as though we have to have them, we have to place them where we can save as many houses as possible."[447]

However, Embry was able to move I-395 west by one critical block because of a technical solution attributed to (the self-taught non-engineer) David Chapin. Gene Bober was there when Chapin came up with the plan. "David came to see me one day and he said, 'You know, I've been thinking about this. We could pick up the highway and literally move it west, towards the warehouse, and put it over top of the B&O trench like a lid, making the trench into a tunnel. And we could put roads across the trench.'" Chapin had already calculated all the grades and clearances—it worked. It was a creative solution that no one else, including a bevy of well-paid engineers, had thought of. (See Figure 37 on the following page.)

Bober said it took two years and added $10 million to the costs, but the result was well worth it. The Federal Reserve Bank was built on the resulting development parcel, a perfect buffer between the highway and Otterbein. The 1997 expansion of the Baltimore Convention Center was also facilitated by the new alignment; the proposed six-lane section of I-395 would have provided a much larger separation of the new part from the old part and may have killed the project.

The Otterbein homesteading program became a renowned urban comeback success story, but it might not have gotten off the ground except for "the David Chapin innovation." MLK went under construction in 1978 and was completed in 1982 at a cost of $77 million.

Figure 37. The 1976 alignment of I-395, only a few feet away from Sharp Street and Otterbein; the "as-built" alignment moved away from Otterbein and creating space for the Federal Reserve and the Convention Center expansion of 1997, all due to Chapin's innovative solution. (Scott Jeffrey, MS GISP)

Critics frame the boulevard as yet another example of the White establishment's weaponization of transportation against the interests of the African American community. Lawrence Brown, a professor at Morgan State University, explained that "[the MLK name] belies the way in which the actual street itself is a primary marker of racial segregation in the city. MLK Boulevard in Baltimore basically creates a boundary between the midtown/downtown area and then Black West Baltimore." [448] Articles in the *Baltimore Brew* have suggested MLK's footprint is far too wide, partly because of "capacious" landscaping and partly because the boulevard was designed to take traffic from the non-existent I-170. [449]

On the positive side, first and foremost, MLK is NOT an expressway. And it is, most agree, physically attractive, an asset to the neighborhoods and downtown districts that adjoin it (for this we can also credit IDBC staff who successfully sold the feds on funding many of these beautification elements). It also diverts downtown traffic away from Mount Vernon thoroughfares such as Maryland Avenue/Cathedral Street, Charles Street, and St. Paul Street. Maryland Avenue/Cathedral Street was recently reduced to one lane for cars and one lane for bikes, an innovation that would have been impossible without MLK Boulevard. This appears to be the best-used bike path in the city, clearly an asset for urban living.

The University of Maryland Bio-Park is the largest and most significant new investment on the west side of MLK, an exceptionally unlikely development had the boulevard been built as an expressway. Comparing MLK to a no-build option is just speculation, but my personal speculation is that the attractive boulevard, as well as the improved access, was a significant positive factor for establishing the bio-park. Other redevelopment areas just west of the boulevard (the Barre Circle homesteading area, the mixed income Heritage Crossing project, and the future redevelopment plans for Poppleton and State Center) are all likely in that same category, i.e., all benefiting to some degree from the attractive boulevard.

BLOWS AGAINST THE EMPIRE V—EPA AND AIR QUALITY

In 1976 Baltimore's expressway and air quality plans were caught up in what can only be described as a pissing match between the US EPA and the US Department of Transportation (DOT). EPA found Baltimore's expressway plans "inconsistent" with the Clean Air Act and "strongly recommended" that no more money be spent until the program was changed to reduce driving and encourage public transportation. The recommendation carried a threat that Baltimore's highways might become ineligible for federal funds.[450]

Only one month later two federal transportation agencies flatly rejected EPA's recommendation. DOT held the trump card—EPA's opinion was advisory, and DOT was rejecting EPA's advice. DOT did acknowledge that "there are problems with respect to air quality, but we cannot conclude that there is a basis for withdrawing certification."[451] The announcement settled a long-running dispute between the State Department of Health and EPA on one side and the state and federal transportation agencies on the other, with local advocates lining up behind whichever side meshed with their preconceived notions.

To those inclined to believe that, at least in the world of public policy, there is no such thing as "unbiased" numbers or "objective" analysis, this long-running war over air quality impacts is the perfect illustration of that point of view. In all, between 1973 and 1976 there were no less than six studies to project the air quality impacts of Baltimore's highway segments. EPA's model pegged the Carroll Park Golf Course receptor at 35 parts per million (ppm) of CO (a violation), but the Maryland State Highway Administration's number for the same location was 9.6 ppm (well within the standard). [452] I suspect that both sides were guilty of skewing the numbers, but I found archival evidence that at least some EPA officials were leaning into advocacy rather than even-handedly implementing federal law.

The Preservation Society's minutes in July 1972 reported, "[EPA officials] were very familiar with the activities of the anti-highway groups in Baltimore, and they encouraged us to think of new areas in which to file suits, since legal action plus community pressure have proven to be the most effective tactics."[453] The Movement Against Destruction (MAD) archives also reported a series of friendly communications with EPA: "Our contacts will line up appt. with their lawyers. Willing to appear in court, even come down for condemnation…hearings before city council if helpful. I am seriously concerned that you discuss our actions with John Collins, at Philadelphia… He is their authority who has reviewed and criticized all of Interstate's environmental impact statements. He ought to be fully informed about what we are doing, even though he cannot officially promote, etc."[454]

I'm sure the Preservation Society and MAD were only too pleased to welcome EPA as comrades in arms. It certainly solved a lot of problems like insufficient funding and reliance on volunteers.

MAD had a long history raising air quality issues as a potential legal matter to halt the highways. MAD's 1972 lawsuit asked the courts to require a regional EIS to assess areawide air quality impacts of the full 3-A system. MAD lost, but then filed a second lawsuit in 1974 specifically alleging that the 3-A system would violate the Clean Air Act. The second lawsuit lost, as well, but EPA and the State Department of Health adopted both issues from a regulatory point of view.

EPA – BUREAUCRATIC OVERREACH

In this same time period, an Appeals Court decision (*Sierra Club v. EPA*) required EPA to create local and state air quality plans if state and local governments failed to do so on their own. EPA's resulting plans went to war with the automobile, causing quite an uproar, while also providing EPA's critics with fodder for ridicule.

One plan banned on-street parking in downtown Boston; another closed Main Street in Springfield, Massachusetts; in frigid Fairbanks, Alaska, EPA proposed to make it illegal for drivers to run their cars on idle for more than five minutes. William F. Chouinard of the Boston Chamber of Commerce called EPA's plan "laughable."

EPA's plan for Baltimore was to reduce auto traffic within the metropolitan area by an astonishing 65 percent of anticipated levels in 1977.

Responding to regulators' concerns, IDBC hired a consultant to carry out a regional analysis of system-wide impacts, both economic and environmental. (This was not an EIS per se—the courts had determined that was not required.) The resulting 1973 study found that "building the 3-A system versus doing nothing appears to have little effect on air pollution levels."[455] Both EPA and the State Health Department disputed that conclusion, causing yet more delay but producing quite a windfall for businesses with air quality modeling expertise. The result was the above-referenced war over numbers, assumptions, and methodologies, only settled in 1976 because DOT held the trump card.

The significance of all this is "not much" and "quite a lot" at the same time. No highway segments were stopped because of air quality regulations, but there were delays. Plus, this was one more issue piled onto the ever-growing mountain of roadblocks and just-plain-headaches that IDBC had to contend with, which is a convenient segue to the end of the Road.

"TIME ON THEIR SIDE":
THE QUIET TRIUMPH OF THE OPPOSITION

> *That's what we all thought: if we keep dragging it out, it'll die of its own weight.*
>
> Joe McNeely, first director of SECO

In October 1975, Councilmember Mikulski was preparing for an expressway hearing and wrote a two-page memorandum to Council President Orlinsky with a series of concerns. At the same time, James Dilts issued one of his typical barrages of expressway skepticism in the *Sun*. On November 6, IDBC Deputy Chief Bill Hellmann responded with a fourteen-page memorandum.[456] More than the details of this debate, I call your attention to the ratio: it took fourteen pages to defend against three pages of criticism, a ratio of more than four to one.

This, in a nutshell, is what happened to Baltimore's expressway plan. Generically, you could say that every roadblock thrown out there by opponents was "X," but each roadblock required some multiple of "X" to overcome it, which is why Interstate Division was often taking one step forward while going two, three, or four steps back. And this explains the phrase that multiple interviewees used: "We lost every battle, but we won the war."

Highway opponents deserve substantial credit for all the obstructionist tactics that produced delay after delay and forced expensive modifications that eventually broke the budget. However, it was not just highway opponents who were responsible for all the delays—in some ways highway builders were their own worst enemies. Many delays in the 1960s were internal. At times highway planning was almost a comedy of errors, featuring bureaucratic in-fighting, useless power struggles, and a whole lot of foot-dragging—the polar opposite of the proverbial "well-oiled machine."

As you recall from the Federal Hill chapter, State Roads Chairman John Funk unwittingly aided and abetted the enemy when he held up the decision on 10-D (for 18 months!) because he wanted to wait for the altogether useless Wilbur Smith Associates study to be completed.

City decision-making was also subject to fundamental and costly errors: Recall that Councilman Tom Ward was able to delay the condemnation ordinances for (Ward says) two years, simply because the McKeldin Administration had not followed the correct administrative process.

A 1967 news account, "East-West Plan Stymie," captured four sources of significant delay around April 1967; none had anything to do with community opposition, lawsuits, environmental impacts, or tearing up historic communities. "For more than a year the city and the State Roads Commission battled over the engineering firms to be hired to design the project until they finally reached a compromise... Then progress stopped again last spring when the Federal Bureau of Public Roads ruled that henceforth it would have official dealings only with the state." The article then shifts to a chicken-and-egg controversy—the city was holding up their condemnation ordinance, awaiting federal approval of the 10-D alignment, but the feds were withholding approval until the city's condemnation ordinance was adopted. This stalemate was only broken when Councilman Schaefer trekked down to Washington and flatly told federal officials "there would be no condemnation ordinance" without federal approval of the alignment. On top of all that, the power struggle over the creation of UDCT cost another six months.[457]

Recall also that the government delayed examining real alternatives for Fell's Point for three years *after* the historic designation. In the meantime both the opposition and the obstacles were building to the point that the government ended up in a poor bargaining position.

To this considerable record of self-flagellation, add back in the delays and obstacles attributable to the opposition: a barrage of mostly on-target criticism, including challenged procedures, critiques of EIS reports, six lawsuits, and federal regulators' muscular backing of community positions (the Advisory Council on Historic Preservation, Department of the Interior, and EPA).

Highway opponents should also be credited for the clear shift in public opinion. The disappearing consensus meant greater scrutiny of everything from a modified highway ramp to a flawed 4(f) statement. Every *i* needed to be dotted, every *t* crossed. There were no shortcuts, but there were plenty of detours.

On May 20, 1970, Transportation Secretary Volpe received a communication that must have struck him as odd. The Reverend A. Otto Baumann II of St. Paul's Lutheran Church in southeast Baltimore sent a memo with the subject "The Feasibility of Baltimore City, Maryland, Financing its Share of the East-West Expressway." It was a scholarly work citing findings from divergent and credible sources and concluding that there was no way for the city to finance its share of the 3-A system. The Reverend Baumann, obviously an amateur in capital accounting and budgeting, had pinpointed the Achilles' heel of the expressway plan ten years before William Donald Schaefer admitted that the city could not afford the plan he had championed for most of his political life.

Baltimore's somewhat daffy comptroller, Hyman Pressmann, was the first high-ranking city official to question the city's ability to finance the expressway system. He registered his skepticism in February 1969, predicting that MVR funds would be insufficient to pay the local match, and "some of the services now financed by the Fund…would have to be borne by the property owner."[458] (Unfortunately, local news records do not reveal any evidence of Pressmann applying his signature poetic skills to this topic.)

As you recall, MAD's Carolyn Tyson produced an annual exposé on this issue, carefully documenting how the city was moving activities formerly funded by MVR (such as local street resurfacing and school crossing guards) to local fund sources, which meant that either cutting other parts of the budget or raising taxes. Of course MAD had an agenda, so the influential and even-handed CPHA conducted their own analysis in 1973, which showed that these "silent transfers" amounted to fourteen cents on the property tax rate just for fiscal year 1973, and the cumulative impact over several years was twenty-nine cents on the property tax rate.[459]

The *Baltimore Sun*, after reviewing a number of reports on this issue, concluded, "In a few years as much as $15 million will be needed yearly in local taxes to finance operations which were funded by motor vehicle revenue before expressway bonds got first claim."[460]

By 1976 the *Sun* had pronounced the expressway plan a "graveyard for city dollars."[461] Cost increases relative to 1972 (the last time the system was re-evaluated) amounted to a whopping $700 million, a 61 percent increase.[462]

In 1977, with the Advisory Council on Historic Preservation ready to weigh in on the Fell's Point segment, the city dropped a less expensive landside tunnel, leaving only the Cadillac tunnel under the harbor south of Fell's Point; then the ACHP said the Lower Jones Falls segment should be a boulevard or a tunnel, and that segment turned into a Cadillac, too.

But it wasn't just the expensive alterations—in the late 1970s inflation and interest rates rocketed up, putting an exclamation point on the old adage that "time is money." On the other side of the ledger, motor vehicle revenues were going down. Gas taxes were a constant cents per gallon rather than a percentage of gasoline sales, so rising gas prices did not lead to any increase in MVR funds. In the category of "good news, bad news," MVR funds were further hit by a combination of less driving (responding to the OPEC oil embargo and the high price of gas) and more fuel efficient vehicles.

The I-70 and I-83 segments were whipsawed by a lethal combination of delay, cost increases, and revenue declines such that, by 1976 to 1977, most knowledgable people thought the highway plan was simply infeasible—most people, that is, except one William Donald Schaefer.

But then, in 1978 and 1979 a different view of the waterfront began to emerge: "The Gold Coast." In Fell's Point there was heavy and immediate interest in the former city-owned properties even though many were little more than a shell. Developers were eyeing Fell's Point waterfront properties like the old National Can plant and the former B&O warehouse for upscale apartments. The *Sun* editorialized that, "The acreage to be buried under concrete is no longer the waste land of a decade ago, when the expressway route was selected; it is prime development land. [If built] the expressway…will become an immovable obstacle to realization of the Gold Coast potential."[463] My theory is that it was these development trends, as much or more than all the delays and cost increases, that finally sowed the seeds of doubt in our economic-development-oriented mayor.

In the 1979 city council elections the expressways were not the most hotly contested issue; in fact it is hard to find candidates weighing in one way or another. It was as if the words employed to make or break the case for the expressways were all used up—the English language afforded no more opportunities to say something insightful or even meaningful on the topic. But the other reason expressways were not a hot-button issue was that even highway backers saw the handwriting on the wall. Everyone seemed to be just waiting for Schaefer to come around to that point of view, too.

Only three days after the inauguration of the new city council, Orlinsky introduced City Council Resolution No. 23, which charged the Policy and Planning Committee with "reviewing the current plans to complete Interstate-70 and Interstate-83 in light of present conditions." The resolution passed on December 10, 1979, the same day it was put in the hopper. The mayor said that he welcomed the chance to review the expressway plan. He defended I-83 but commented that he was "not wild about" the Leakin Park segment and that Franklin-Mulberry could be linked up to I-95 from the southwest rather than I-70 through Leakin Park.[464]

This set in motion the expressway gut check that was many years over-due. It appears that the mayor let this unfold without trying to control the outcome, almost entirely new territory for the man who clearly wanted to be the father of Baltimore's expressway system, much like Ike was to the other 43,000 miles of interstate highway.

The mayor was essentially ceding control of the issue to city council, but he almost certainly knew what their decision would be. I presume that all of the issues described above had an impact, but my interview with Bill Hellmann, chief of IDBC at the time, steered toward delay as the number one factor. He said Schaefer was less motivated by opposition or even the pocketbook issue; rather it was a looming federal deadline and the possible loss of funds. "I think that's what drove his decision more than people arguing 'we don't need that' or 'that's the wrong thing to do'… I think he realized, 'if I can't get these approvals, we can't afford to lose the money'… Interstate transfer was driven by that date. I think he came to the conclusion that I can't roll this dice. These are big bucks that we don't want to lose."

Hellmann is referring to the September 30, 1983 deadline for requesting withdrawal of Interstate segments and substitution of transit and other road proj-ects. That date was four years hence, so I am inclined to conclude that it was one more reason to reevaluate rather than "THE REASON." The city council's anal-ysis focused on the fiscal issues and never mentioned a pending federal deadline.

In January 1980, the City Council Policy and Planning Committee held a new round of hearings for I-83 and I-170.

Bill Hellmann delivered new cost estimates: I-70 was now a $620 mil-lion dollar project; I-83 was tipping the scales at more than $1 billion. Total: $1.62 billion, requiring a local match of at least $162 million, both figures representing just the cost for the two unbuilt segments. This was roughly triple the costs of only a few years before.

In city council hearings on the issue Leakin Park advocates were shocked to discover a new comrade in their midst: Bill Boucher of the Greater Baltimore

Committee. Boucher testified that "present conditions and lack of funding… necessitated a re-examination of the city's prior commitment for I-70." As to the Fell's Point segment, "in view of the financial circumstances and present conditions of high inflation and reduced motor vehicle revenue tax, the Greater Baltimore Committee was not prepared to make a recommendation one way or the other on the withdrawal of its prior commitment for I-83 at this time."[465]

All eyes turned to Schaefer, but he kept a low profile while the committee deliberated, which meant that all eyes shifted instead to the mayor's trusted Finance Director, Charles Benton. Never much of a public speaker, Benton dead-panned his way through the numbers. Much of it was bad news, but Benton had always found a way to justify the city's astronomical highway financing commitments, for example, saying, "We can't afford NOT to build these highways." But this time Benton's conclusion was different: "We have to stop when we complete projects now under construction unless there is some more money forthcoming. We have no money to do any more than what we have currently committed."[466]

Perhaps there was a gasp from the audience. Did he just say what we thought he said? With the room buzzing at what they had just witnessed, Benton left behind his written testimony, which was even more decisive: "The city could not realistically raise the $160 million needed to complete I-83 and I-70; there appears to be no realistic alternative sources of funding for either I-83 or I-70; current financial circumstances, therefore, preclude either alternative." Benton recommended that both segments be dropped.

Taking escalating costs into account, the committee estimated that the local match may climb to $200 million. They examined steps the state had taken to supplement declining MVR funds, but determined those measures were not even counterbalancing the decline. The committee concluded that neither I-70 nor I-83 was "financially realistic for the city," and that while I-70 was the "least desirable" segment, the $100 million local share for I-83 made that segment prohibitive given the decline in MVR funds.[467] The only segment that survived the committee's scrutiny was the Lower Gwynns Falls connector (I-595), which the group said should be considered to connect Franklin-Mulberry (Highway to Nowhere) to I-95.

The Mayor stayed in the background even as the committee's recommendations came to light. Perhaps he did not want to be the executioner for the expressways he had championed, or (more likely) he was holding his cards close to his vest to have a little more leverage in the new high stakes game of redeploying funds. Still, the mayor's point of view was implicit in the testimony of Bill Hellmann and Charles Benton, and in concert with Bill Boucher. It had taken overwhelming and indisputable evidence, but the mayor had finally and irreversibly changed his mind.

POLITICS AND TRADE-INS

When Baltimore City lost six percent of its population from 2010 to 2020, Dr. Seema Iyer (Associate Director, Jacob France Institute) analyzed the differences between Baltimore and other large northeastern cities that saw population increases in that decade. "The biggest difference between Baltimore and these other East Coast cities is, believe it or not, the fact that we do not have an excellent transit and transportation system…" Iyer continued, "If you look at Philadelphia, Boston, [Washington], all of them have been investing in their transit system for many decades, and they're now reaping those benefits."[468]

Iyer particularly contrasts Baltimore and Washington, DC, which had similar demographics in the 1960s through the 1980s, but Washington is now in its third decade of reversal and growth. Part of the reason that the District has been on a steady upward trend is that, all the way back in 1976, more than $1 billion in highway funds was reallocated to building the Metro. (Remember Sammie Abbot and Reginald Booker from Chapter 5—this was their legacy.) In Baltimore this trade-in happened a critical five to eight years later in 1981-1983, and the resulting switch to transit was far less robust.

The gas crisis of the mid '70s was over, and transit was no longer viewed as the silver bullet, the universal answer to our oil dependency, our polluted air, and our increasingly troublesome urban-suburban dichotomy. Baltimore's streets had suffered years of neglect while expressways monopolized available funding, and neighborhoods were clamoring for local street resurfacing and reconstruction more than transit. Additionally, the Reagan Administration was cutting all manner of domestic spending, so switching highway dollars to transit was far less likely to leverage other federal transit dollars. Years of high inflation and high interest rates had eroded the purchasing power of the trade-in dollars. In short, the window of opportunity where Baltimore might have established a fully functioning mass transit system had passed, perhaps never to return.

How did these trade-ins work? Although these abandoned highway plans were 100 percent in Baltimore City, the purse strings were held by federal and state governments, and decisions were subject to their priorities. The Regional Planning Council (where Baltimore had one vote out of six) also had to pass on the plan. Most importantly, the Highway Act of 1976 expanded the bust-the-trust Interstate Withdrawal and Substitution Program to allow transfers to highway and street projects, as well as transit projects. Bottom line: There were a lot of hands in the till. The city was a major player, but the city did not control the process. With all that as background, the following is a close approximation** as to what happened.[469]

I-70 was submitted for Interstate Transfer in July 1981 and approved in September 1981. $216 million went to: the Metro extension to Johns Hopkins ($160 million/74 percent); Baltimore City highways ($42 million/19 percent); and suburban highways ($14 million/6 percent). The suburban highway wish list that passed Regional Planning Council was pared way down from $48 million;[470] so superficial evidence suggests that Schaefer, assisted by Bill Hellmann and IDBC, had cut a good deal for the city. This transfer is a good representation of the pro-city, pro-transit principles that underlie this book. If these percentages had set a precedent for later trade-ins, there would be little room for complaint from either city boosters or transit advocates. Unfortunately, the later trade-ins did not follow suit.

In early 1983 the city canceled I-595, the proposed connector between I-95 and Franklin-Mulberry (thereby leaving the "Highway to Nowhere" embarrassingly unconnected to anything). I-595 and I-83 were submitted

---

** Researching the use of these funds was exceptionally difficult. Decisions announced at one point were often later changed. The city trade-ins were lumped together with other non-city projects, so it became quite problematic to isolate exactly what happened to the city dollars. David Chapin, IDBC acting director for much of this period, was a great help in sorting all of this out.

for interstate transfers in July 1983 and approved in September. A whopping $864 million was generated ($241 million for I-595 and $623 million for I-83). The larger numbers likely attracted more suitors, as it appears that suburban and highway interests muscled their way into larger shares of the proceeds. Initially the funds were distributed as follows:

- $217 million for the Charles Center (downtown) to Johns Hopkins subway line
- $99 million for a busway that would parallel I-83 through north central Baltimore City and Baltimore County
- $25 million for a suburban bus program
- $323 million for city highways, including President Street Boulevard and other improvements in southeast Baltimore designed to improve traffic flow in lieu of I-83
- $200 million for suburban highways, including several that might be classified as "sprawl generators," like Route 100 and Route 10 in Anne Arundel County

The percentages for this distribution are 39 percent for regional transit, 37 percent for city highways, and 23 percent for suburban highways—certainly not the rush to embrace transit envisioned when the Highway Trust Fund was first broken in 1973.

But then the deal was restructured. On March 18, 1983, the *Baltimore Sun* lamented that the city was losing the services of William K. Hellmann, "the city's highly efficient chief road-builder," calling him "one of those civil servants who gets things done… A talent of his magnitude…will be missed."[471] Hellmann moved to the private sector but was then recruited to serve as Governor Hughes' Secretary of Transportation in 1984. His top two priority projects were finishing the National Freeway (later I-68) in Western Maryland and building the Nanticoke Bridge on the Eastern Shore, both ranked as the state's worst traffic bottlenecks and both impeding economic development.

Hellmann, of course, had intimate knowledge of the Interstate Transfer Program. As the guy "who gets things done," Hellmann masterminded a complicated deal that involved dropping the north central busway project, retooling financing of the Canton Seagirt Marine Terminal, and funding the National Freeway and Nanticoke Bridge.[††] By that time (summer of 1984) there were few supporters of the busway—community opposition had taken hold, and Secretary of Transportation Bridwell (the chief proponent) was no longer in a position to defend his pet project.

Funds from the canceled busway went to the National Freeway ($47 million), the downtown-to-Johns-Hopkins Metro line ($21 million) and several smaller transit station and bus projects ($32 million). Hellmann told me Mayor Schaefer, who was setting the stage for a gubernatorial run, had nothing to do with structuring the deal. "[Schaefer] made it clear he would only support my proposal regarding National Freeway and the Nanticoke River Bridge if the Governor, Senate President, and Speaker of the House agreed to make [the Metro extension to Johns Hopkins] Maryland's number one transit priority."[472] Hellmann accepted 100 percent credit or blame, depending on how you looked at it, for the deal, saying it was "the right thing to do," and that it solidified his role as State Secretary: "This is a good move to let them know that I'm going to be Secretary for the whole state, [not just] for the Baltimore region."

The mayor's aides, perhaps looking forward to a change of scenery, were "ecstatic after the perfect deal."[473] Schaefer, who announced his run for governor nine months later in June 1985, was only too happy to tout his part in approving Hellmann's deal. "He played it to his advantage in Western Maryland and the Eastern Shore," Hellman said. Pro-business interests from both ends of the state flocked into the Schaefer camp—he won both the primary and the general election by landslide proportions. A later I-68 MDOT "success story" handed out accolades to Schaefer, "who as mayor agreed to a financial plan that involved Baltimore City federal funding entitlements."[474]

Transit advocates, undoubtedly lost in the shuffling and reshuffling of the deck, did not weigh in, but they should have taken note: the transit share of this second round of trade-ins dropped to 34 percent.

[††] Available records do not indicate that city expressway funds were used for the Nanticoke Bridge.

When you total up both trade-ins, only 42 percent was used for transit, a deflating number for the many anti-highway activists hoping that their efforts would lead to (or at least point toward) a city with a fully functioning transit system, a viable alternative to car dependence and sprawling growth patterns.

Highways outside Baltimore City (and outside the region in the case of the National Freeway) made off with $261 million in former city highway funds. There are two ways of looking at this. One is moral outrage: Baltimore has so many disadvantages in competing with suburbs for new investment; when we finally came to our senses and discarded the highway plan intended to mitigate those disadvantages, those same suburbs got to pick our pockets and further subsidize sprawl. The other point of view is that this was the price that Schaefer and city advocates had to pay to gain funding for city priorities, especially the Metro extension to Johns Hopkins. Both points of view are correct; unfortunately, this was how interstate transfers worked—it was the only game in town.

SHORTCHANGED???

Before we let Schaefer off the hook for this debacle, I have to ask: Would the old Don Schaefer—the guy who made a career out of defending the city and chasing after every last dollar to improve it—would THAT GUY have approved of a deal that sprinkled $261 million of city-designated funds all around the state? Would the old Mayor Schaefer have raised a ruckus over this unfair deal that the new gubernatorial candidate Schaefer took to the electoral bank? Might he have shouted from the rafters that the new Schaefer had given up without a fight, that new Schaefer was more concerned about getting elected than standing up for the city? This was the yin and yang of William Donald Schaefer, a truly complicated figure whose legacy was laid bare by the Road Wars.

XVII. LEGACY REVISITED

SCHAEFER'S ALBATROSS? MIKULSKI'S CALLING CARD?

MAYOR SCHAEFER: "MY WAY AND THE HIGHWAY"

The former two mayors ignored the Planning Commission. He [Schaefer] wants to BE the Planning Commission.
> David W. Barton, resigning as Chairman of the Baltimore City Planning Commission in 1972, following a dispute with Mayor Schaefer over highway plans[475]

The Road Wars featured two towering figures: Mayor William Donald Schaefer, the number one road prosecutor, and Senator Barbara Mikulski in the role of chief antagonist. This characterization places Schaefer on the wrong side of history, with Mikulski basking in the limelight of a virtuous cause. However, it is not that simple.

The annals of the decades-long expressway battle are rife with examples of rogue city councilmen just not getting the big picture, much to the consternation of the mayor. In one council meeting, a councilman publicly accused the mayor of dodging his responsibility, saying, "I've written you letters about this, I've called you, I've come to see you, but we don't seem to be getting anywhere... Until you sit down with us and work out a route acceptable to the districts, I can tell you the expressway is in real jeopardy." Accused of insensitivity to the human costs of the highway, the mayor bristled. "Do you think I have some desire to go around the city and put people out of their homes?" According to the *Sun*, after an hour and half of wrangling, "the mayor rose abruptly, and, with thinly veiled sarcasm, thanked the councilmen for 'a very interesting afternoon.'"[476] Then he left the meeting.

Readers familiar with Schaefer's impetuous and combative demeanor, not to mention his reputation as the highways' last bastion of political support, can be excused for misinterpreting this account: this was *Councilman* Schaefer getting under the skin of *Mayor* J. Harold Grady in a 1962 committee hearing. This little anecdote illustrates the almost universal principle of public debate, that "where you stand depends on where you sit." Although Schaefer was seen as a staunch ally of the road builders, this encounter with Grady was not the only instance that Schaefer, as councilman, sat in the position of a highway critic.

In 1961, he warned highway planners "to pay more attention to neighborhood protests...over the expressway slice through Leakin...and Gwynns Falls parks." The account continues, "Schaefer believes that, if the opposition continues to be brushed off in 'routine answer' fashion, the present muttering may grow to a roar."[477] In 1966 he became the chief critic of the southwest expressway (later I-95), forcing a study to determine whether the city really needed both the southwest expressway and I-70 through West Baltimore. (If only he had reversed that thinking: if the southwest expressway is built, I-70 might not be needed.) In 1967 he held up condemnation ordinances because DPW was threatening to severely limit UDCT's role.[478] In 1968, Schaefer (as city council president) was a key figure in saving Federal Hill and scrapping the 10-D and 3-C(2) plans. Schaefer's support of 3-A was, in a word, huge—he was likely the tiebreaker between the engineers and DPW on one side (favoring 10-D) and the development agencies and GBC on the other (favoring 3-A).

C. Frazer Smith captured the essence of Schaefer in his political biography:

He was maniacal, unpredictable, and politically incorrect—aggressively so. He knew that his rough edges were assets. He was, like every modern politician, an actor, ever on stage, projecting his own image as he promoted his city... Schaefer was a 24-hour man, a 100 percenter, an overachiever who was maddeningly unsatisfied with the grandest accomplishment. To keep pushing, to remain optimistic, to assault his

friends with new demands required a lack of balance. His genius was
to see this; his strength was to endure it.[479]

Sun writer Richard Ben Cramer put it this way: "The mayor is not slick
but, after twenty years of campaigning, Mr. Schaefer and his closest aides have
turned his lack of club stylishness into an asset. They consciously portray him
as a simple dogged laborer for Baltimore's betterment.... Regardless of where
he is, he is ready to pull out a dog-eared 39-cent notebook to record the complaints of the citizenry."[480] As a city councilman, city council president, and
then mayor from 1972 to 1985, Schaefer held to a pro-business, pro-econom-
ic-development mantra. But he also cultivated a pro-neighborhood image,
bolstered by his famous trips through neighborhoods where department heads
were ordered to fix everything from a broken streetlight to rats in the alleys.

He earned the loyalty of many who worked for him. Bill Hellmann, in
a 2018 interview, said of Schaefer, "He was clearly the best boss that I ever
had, and I worked for (a whole range of) politicians later at DOT.... I always
found him as an outstanding elected official who did what he believed in his
heart was the right thing to do.... I never saw him make a decision politically,
for political gain."

Schaefer was also Baltimore's chief cheerleader at a time when the city
desperately needed just that. And he succeeded to a large degree—under his
watch, this downtrodden city was successfully sold as a tourist destination,
something no one thought possible right through the late '70s. This role led
to some amusing promotions, such as "think pink positive," which involved
repainting curbs and benches pink, surely one of the most ridiculed attempts
at re-branding ever undertaken by a city.

Another humorous instance of boosterism emerged when Schaefer
seemed quite annoyed that Baltimore was left off a list of cities that might be
targets of terrorism. He said, "I know you [the reporter] don't think Baltimore
is any good, but Baltimore is a right good place. Baltimore is a well-known
place, and there is no reason to think we're exempt from terrorist attacks."[481]

David Chapin (Interstate Division staff from 1974 to 1984, interviewed
in 2017), recounted a story told by others that illustrated Schaefer's famous

impatience, as well as his tendency to become obsessed by certain odd details. Chapin explains that Schaefer sometimes attended the meetings of the City's Coordinating Committee, leading to this exchange:

One day Schaefer comes to the meeting and lets everyone know how frustrated he is: "*Every time* I drive to work from West Baltimore down Mulberry Street I see this abutment being built (at the end of the Franklin Mulberry corridor, where the roadway was coming up out of the ground.) And there's just one person working on it!" He goes on, with some fairly choice words. "Every time... EVERY TIME...I see only one guy, just one guy. I told you about this the last meeting. And before. Did you do anything? No!" The others attending the meeting were trying to find a place to hide under the table or an excuse to go to the bathroom... And at the end of it... Schaefer says, "Why only ONE g-d fella to do it?" [No one answers the question] "Why do you never pay attention to anything the mayor asks for? Just one g-d worker on the job." There's absolute silence—nobody knows what to say.... And then Dick Trainor, who was sitting at the other end of the table, facing Schaefer, puffing on a cigar, calmly says: "You got to admit, Mr. Mayor, he's one hell of a worker."

Another Road Wars example of Schaefer's famous myopia comes from J. Randall Evans, who served Schaefer as Baltimore Deputy Housing Commissioner and Maryland Secretary of Economic and Community Development. Evans recounted how Schaefer became fixated on one dilap- idated house, a city acquisition in Fell's Point. "One night about 4:30, he calls me into his office and says, 'Young man, I'm sick and tired of hear- ing your excuses. I want that fixed up by morning." Evans bought a set of curtains and put them up at the house (by climbing on the shoulders of an aid because there was no floor) along with a sign that read "Brought to you by Mayor William Donald Schaefer and the Citizens of Baltimore." Schaefer called Evans at 9:00 a.m. "You could hear him smiling through the phone."[482]

Schaefer has gotten an enormous amount of credit for the Inner Harbor, even though the credit should go to Planning Director Arthur D. McVoy, (for the initial concept), the Greater Baltimore Committee (for promoting it), Mayor McKeldin (for adopting it), and Mayor D'Alesandro (for the initial implementation). Bob Embry (interviewed in 2018) said Schaefer had actually opposed the original Inner Harbor Renewal Plan. "He was wedded to Connolly's Restaurant on the pier down there," Embry said. "He was the Chairman of the Judiciary Committee that handled the urban renewal plans, and, according to Tommy [D'Alesandro], he was the one councilman that caused all of the trouble.... Schaefer had nothing to do with it, in concept. He's like a Nixon and the landing on the moon—he just happened to be there."

Embry then offers up another issue where Schaefer's image and persona were not in sync with his internal biases: he said Schaefer was "not overly sympathetic with Black aspirations," which he illustrated as follows:

> I remember one time, he and I were at something where Parren Mitchell was speaking. Parren was very articulate and very forceful on civil rights issues, discrimination, racism, and so forth... Schaefer and I walked out on the platform together, and he said something to the effect of, you know, what an outrageous thing that Mitchell was saying. And then one time in his office he said to me... "I know you're soft on the Blacks..." He came from a White working-class, non-college educated background and I think, in his heart, he was a Republican... I think he deserves credit for overcoming his background through his public actions.

Embry's recollections represent candid moments that run counter to Schaefer's considerable record of working productively and amicably with African American leaders. We have portrayed Schaefer as afflicted by near-fatal pro-highway bias, but Embry's recollections open up the issue of racial bias, which could have entered into the mayor's decisions related to Franklin-Mulberry and Sharp Leadenhall. These are such sensitive and difficult issues that I hesitate to draw a conclusion other than to say that Schaefer was the product of a time when city leaders all across the country had little hesitation in using highways and urban renewal as vehicles for slum clearance, almost exclusively targeting lower income minority neighborhoods.

When Schaefer was elected mayor in the fall of 1971, the man and the job became closely intertwined. The powerful road building apparatus was at his disposal, and he would use it to overcome all obstacles and get the job done. If you were against the highways, you were against HIM. Carolyn Tyson (MAD) said, "I think it's unfortunate...[that the highway] has become identified with him—he has identified it in some way with himself, so that an attack on that particular policy has become an attack on him. That's not the point."

Schaefer and highway wars are a textbook case study of confirmation bias—Schaefer had made up his mind, and the only information he allowed to penetrate his thinking reinforced what he already believed. As his administration progressed into the mid-'70s, mounting legal and fiscal obstacles, not to mention the erosion of public support, would have led a level-headed person to re-evaluate. Schaefer turned a deaf ear to all of it. Bob Embry agreed that Schaefer was obsessed with implementing the expressway system and blinded to the obstacles in front of him. "He was a stubborn person, and he didn't want to be pushed around.... He didn't want to hear all this criticism and controversy. And, I don't think he cared particularly where it went, but when there was a plan to go someplace, he saw it as his job to get it done."

The road wars tended to bring out the worst side of Schaefer's personality—his pettiness, his tendency to fixate on points of disagreement, as well as his inclination to turn policy matters into issues of personal antagonism. He tended to be dismissive, even disrespectful, of highway opponents. In a 1974 interview Schaefer dismissively described highway opponents, saying, "There is one lady [presumably Lu Fisher] who writes letters to the editor all the time. I tried to talk to her, but she's very emotional. She's opposed to it, and, if she wasn't opposed to this, she'd be opposed to something else."[483]

This hearkens back to Robert Moses' characterization of New York highway opponents as "just a bunch of mothers."

Schaefer was not above using threats to try to force opponents to back down. Minutes from the Preservation Society in 1971 refer to Schaefer's threat to overwhelm Fell's Point with traffic if they did not agree to a highway plan: "He said, if we win the lawsuit, he would build the road to Wolfe St. and then disperse the traffic into Fell's Point!"[484] The City (MLK) Boulevard section of Chapter 17 chronicles a series of threats, which temporarily succeeded in neutralizing opposition to an incursion into the Federal Hill Historic District. Chapter 5 speculates that it was Schaefer who caused Art Cohen to lose his job as Director of CPHA.

In January 1975, Schaefer threatened Locust Point with elimination of city services if they continued opposing the Fort McHenry route for I-95. Councilman Dominick Leone had inquired about $7,500 budgeted for Latrobe Park play equipment. Leone said, "[Schaefer] jumped up and said, 'I killed it. I'm sick and tired of those people harassing me and attacking me after what I've done for them. I'll take away anything they ask for.'"[485]

At one Board of Estimates meeting Schaefer harassed Jennifer Multhopp, a Baltimore City librarian opposing the highway through Fell's Point. The news account said, "She was visibly shaken after completing only half of her prepared testimony… Schaefer asked repeated questions about where she lived, whether she rented or owned her residence, if she was married, where she worked, how much she made, how much her husband made, and how much rent it was." Multhopp had responded, "Why is that relevant?" but Schaefer did not answer.[486]

To no one's surprise, Schaefer confronted the *Sun's* James Dilts a few times. "If Mayor Schaefer didn't like something," according to Dilts, "he came right up to the fifth floor [newsroom] and complained about it. Sometimes he would call out reporters by name."[487]

In 1979, wanting to put the Road Wars behind him, Schaefer participated in a choreographed ceremony at Fell's Point Square to "bury the hatchet" with

Preservation Society President Charlie Duff. Charlie Duff, the elder's son, recounted the story in a 2018 interview: "They took my old boy scout hand axe, Lou Gerber from Budeke Paints got some gold paint, painted the damn thing. Oh, they had a box of dirt. My dad and Mayor Schaefer got out in the middle of market square and buried my gold-painted Boy Scout hand axe in a box full of dirt, formally burying the hatchet."

In a 2004 interview Schaefer expressed regret he held onto the Road plan long after he should have reevaluated, but also laid the blame on the engineers. "At that time, I really believed in engineers. I thought that when an engineer proposed [something], it was right. I learned later on that we had to make our own decisions, but I listened to engineers... I learned that they [don't always] want to do the right thing, but they're out to make money. This would have been a major moneymaker for them. They would have made millions and millions of dollars."[488]

As much as this book portrays Schaefer in his worst moments, the times when he allowed himself to be blinded by self-interested engineers and the lure of federal highway dollars, I feel compelled to end this section on a positive note. I find it hard to paint Schaefer into the "black hat" corner when everything he did, including his wrong-headed support for the expressways, was born of his almost religious zeal for improving the city.

Schaefer surrounded himself with really good people, people who shared his dedication to bettering the city, professionals that were the polar opposite of political hacks. This book, I hope, has illuminated the good works of at least some of these well-regarded professionals: folks like Bill Hellmann, Bob Embry, Larry Reich, Jay Brodie, and David Carroll. David Chapin, another well-regarded staff person who got his start at IDBC, offered up a fitting conclusion to this section:

> Schaefer, he was remarkable in so many ways. He was very quick to latch onto ideas and push them. He went on a trip to San Antonio—saw the River Walk. Having decided to not build the I-83 expressway, We were planning President Street along the Jones Falls. He...we all... wanted to keep the Fish Market; but he also wanted to keep a building

that was at the corner of the Fallsway and Baltimore Street, a four-story concrete industrial building. Even if it had been redone it would have been an ugly building. It was right smack in the middle of where this boulevard would have to go in order to miss the Fish Market. He wanted to keep it all. He was inspired by what he had seen [in San Antonio] and wanted to get people thinking outside the box about the pedestrian environment along the Jones Falls. He was genius, sometimes a crazy genius. I think it was remarkable. He was Schaefer.

BARBARA MIKULSKI—NO. 1 ROAD WARRIOR?

The only people served by this expressway are people living in the county, and they aren't paying for it. We're paying for it with our homes, our neigh-borhoods, and our taxes.[489]

Barbara Mikulski

The anti-expressway movement is so identified with Senator Barbara Ann Mikulski that an Elkridge resident wrote a 2017 letter to the editor of the *Sun* and forcefully argued that the Highway to Nowhere should now go somewhere: "Now that she is out of office, why not take the opportunity to finish what we started and complete the East-West Expressway to downtown?"[490] It was a shocking thought, that some people were under the impression that a single woman—at the time one member of an eighteen-member city council—had exerted such control over events that the entire federal-state-local government highway-building apparatus was thwarted, bent to her will.

Incredulously, the Mikulski-stopped-the-road hype even extended to the Oval Office. President Barack Obama awarded Mikulski the Medal of Freedom at a White House ceremony on November 24, 2015, repeating an often-told claim that the senator played THE lead role in the stop-the-road movement. "Let's just say you don't want to get on the wrong side of Barbara Mikulski. *She stopped 'that' highway* [emphasis added]." Mr. President! Really? Are you taking literary license in the interests of a PR event? Or did a Mikulski staffer get a little carried away in feeding information to your office?

In a 2004 campaign flier Mikulski claimed, "I led the fight to defeat a highway development that threatened historic Fell's Point." When Tom Ward saw the flier he blew a gasket, not an uncommon occurrence for the pugnacious Irishman. He fired off an angry letter to Mikulski (with copies to the news media), accusing her of going well beyond the exaggeration typical of political campaigns. "Your lies and outrageous statements that you had any part in stopping this road beggars anything I have ever heard a politician say." Ward, never one to mince his words, wrote another letter accusing Mikulski of "lying through her teeth."

As my 2016 interview with Ward was coming to a close, he brought the conversation back to Mikulski, saying, "[She] talks about Helen's Bar… That's bullshit, she was never down there at Helen's Bar. Lots of misinformation floating around about the expressway, and it always surrounds Barbara Mikulski. Outstanding ten women, and she's in the book, and it's all about how she saved the highway. Bunch of shit. It's not true. She did a lot of work after the highway was killed."

This issue was a bit of an obsession for Ward—he wrote no less than thirteen letters to various organizations and individuals who had authored articles, made plaques, or delivered speeches that credited Mikulski with stopping the expressways,[491] arguing that "at no time during this entire time when I was present at every hearing and every meeting, did Barbara Mikulski do or say anything to stop this road. She never wrote a letter, never made a public statement, nor appeared at a public meeting."[492]

Ward maintains that Fell's Point was already saved by the time Mikulski was elected to city council in 1971, that it was the Preservation Society's actions that saved Fell's Point and Mikulski was not involved in the Preservation Society; therefore, she was a Johnny-come-lately and a political opportunist. Historian Nancy Schamu agreed, noting that "[Mikulski] was involved in the whole I-70 thing; I'm not arguing about that, but she wasn't there [for Fell's Point]."

Additionally, the *Baltimore Brew* published two articles that questioned the senator's road-fighting credentials. One cited Ward's version of events and concluded "Mikulski has… gone too far in bragging about her putative accomplishments. She played no significant role of record in saving Federal Hill, Fell's Point, and Canton from the original East-West Expressway. It is long past the time for her to come clean about that salient fact."[493] The other article cited a number of misstatements by Mikulski and concluded that she "did not stop the expressway through Fell's Point. Rather, the plan dragged on until it became too impractical and expensive."[494]

I asked Senator Mikulski about these issues when I interviewed her in 2020. In the middle of the pandemic her files were inaccessible; so, even if she had wanted to respond point by point, she did not have the evidence at her fingertips. Her responses were appropriately general, even deferential to her detractors. First, she credited the Preservation Society, calling their plan to file a lawsuit based on Federal Register status a "brilliant strategy." She also credited Tom Ward. "Judge Ward… and his wife were very important figures, and [they created] a lot of positive change." Tom and Jack Lapides, she added, "were really very good…on the issues of race and change… These men had their own great record. I do not know why Tom was so sour about that."

Additionally, she distinguished the role of the two organizations, that "They [the Preservation Society] initially were into saving houses. We [SCAR and SECO] were into saving communities. It was a different mentality." Mikulski said. "We, eventually, were all working together…and out of that, I think was a very potent force… The [only] ones who have it in their mind that we were not working together is Tom [Ward] and Jack [Lapides] sitting up there in Bolton Hill… We never saw each other as at odds with the Preservation Society." She maintains that "this chip on their shoulders…does not come from Fell's Point," because Bob Eney, Jack Gleason, Jean Hepner, and others believed "we were all in it together."

The Fell's Point Fun Festival is where their differing approaches came together: "The preservationists wanted to show how historic we were, and we wanted to show the vitality." Mikulski thought the Fun Festival brought the preservationists down to earth, because they initially had "the attitude that… the whole corridor was the other side of the tracks."

If the only question was "Who put up the critical roadblocks that stopped the Road from tearing up Fell's Point?" then the Preservation Society deserves the most credit. Mikulski was not part of the Preservation Society; ergo Lu Fisher, Bob Eney, Jack Gleason, and Tom Ward were the saviors, not Mikulski.

However, that view is deceptively simplistic. Just with respect to Fell's Point, Mikulski and SCAR were extraordinarily strong allies for the Preservation Society, and Mikulski's statement that they were all working together is absolutely true. Remember, the Preservation Society was met with considerable hostility until SCAR (and later SECO) was formed and unified southeast Baltimore against the highway. Absent SCAR and SECO, the Preservation Society could have been marginalized as unrepresentative and elitist.

There is also considerable evidence that Mikulski was influential in Schaefer's decision to consider the underwater tunnel south of Fell's Point (which later proved to be beyond the city's ability to finance). As noted in the Federal Hill Chapter, Mikulski initiated a deal to accept the Fort McHenry Bypass in exchange for putting the Fell's Point segment in the underwater tunnel. Although she does not remember this now, I found four supporting documents in addition to the GBC minutes.[495] Additionally, Mikulski's advocacy of Fell's Point brought key stakeholders into the fight. It was Mikulski who gained a key ally when the CPHA Transportation Committee opposed all four of the UDCT alignments through Fell's Point and Canton.

Preservation Society attorney Geoff Mitchell defended Mikulski, saying, "I view it as a team… [Mikulski] played a very important role, and she played it in the right places. She played it in City Hall. She played it in the newspapers. She got publicity, and believe me, nobody objected to that. I mean, all this was required to get the result that we got. Without this, we wouldn't have done it."*

More importantly, our current accounting needs to consider geography beyond Fell's Point. There is a nomenclature problem that clouds the

---

* Mitchell, clearly in the Mikulski camp for this controversy, also extolled Mikulski's role with these memorable words, "She never passed up a chance to rub William Donald Schaefer's nose in it."

geographic issue: Many people use Fell's Point as a shorthand for the Road Wars in general, because it is the most well-known part of the Road Wars. Mikulski's PR team may be guilty of oversimplification in using this familiar moniker, but no one should crucify a politician for using terms the average voter understands. The real test is: Did Mikulski play a strong role in defeating the highways in general?

City-wide, Mikulski had been hoisted into a leadership position even before her election to city council in 1971. In June 1970, Mikulski was noted as a community spokesperson in a meeting with Secretary Volpe regarding relocation assistance. Mikulski, along with Mildred Moon and others, left an impression—promises were made that no one's house would be torn down until those affected were relocated to decent, affordable dwellings.[496]

Mikulski was the master of what is now called, somewhat derisively, "soundbites." The media grew to rely on Barbara to articulate the opposition's position in a fifteen-second whir of biting analysis. She described the Fell's Point tunnel as "a tube of pollution." Her cryptic analysis of joint development: "They'll get the development, and we'll get stuck with the joint." Displaced residents were the "new refugees," and (my personal favorite) UDCT was the "Urban Design *Concrete* Team." These statements, multiplied by the hundreds of times she was quoted in the media, or delivered a speech at a hearing, or shouted through a megaphone at a festival, took a toll on support for the highway plan. Mikulski acknowledged, "I was always good with the media." I would add, if Twitter had been operating in 1970, Mikulski might have slayed the freeway dragon in months rather than years—the 140-character limit would have been no problem.

A continuing theme in this work is that this shift in public opinion was an essential part of why the Road plan failed. I take issue with the *Baltimore Brew* article that concluded, "Barbara Mikulski did not stop the expressway through Fell's Point. Rather, the plan dragged on until it became too impractical and expensive." The plan dragged on and became too expensive largely because of relentless community opposition. Mikulski was the voice of that movement.

Mikulski and SCAR were also important coalition builders, including with the African American communities of Rosemont and Sharp Leadenhall.

Mikulski said this was an extension of relationships built in the civil rights movement. She "had been a...foot soldier in the early days of civil rights," the senator said. "I do not mean to puff that up...I was a marcher like everybody else. I was not in leadership, but when the name Mikulski came up, they said, 'Oh, that is Barbara. Barbara worked in the poverty program.'" As one example, when Mikulski and SCAR testified at the Rosemont hearings in August 1969, it had to help Joe Wiles and Mary Rosemond press their case.

In a 1974 interview, Mikulski explained how these alliances were formed. "It was interesting...there are people who like to look at my neighborhood, which [is] blue collar European ethnic, and say they were racists. And yet it was our community—Canton, Highlandtown, Fell's Point—that formed the alliance with Rosemont; that then was, in many ways, the basis [for a unified anti-road coalition, MAD]."

Ward's broadsides at Mikulski imply that she is a political opportunist, using the expressway issue to pad her political resume. Here I agree with Stu Wechsler, who said, "She definitely capitalized on her efforts, but I don't think her efforts were designed to be capitalized on. She had legitimate concerns with the issues she espoused." Art Cohen agreed with this, saying, "I think she really cares about the community... The Road Fight is just one part

MIKULSKI'S POPULIST CHARACTERIZATION OF UDCT

"The Design Concept Team came down with their plans... Their idea of citizen participation was for us to tell them what kind of shrubs we wanted alongside the highway, not whether we wanted the god damn thing or not... [They] had $5,000 [now $30,000] worth of tape recorders, movie projectors, slide projectors, audio visual gizmos to sell us the road, to convince us [we need] the road. And we had two or three bake sales, 50-50 raffles and so on to get enough money so we could take a bus to Annapolis."

(Source: Mikulski's 1974 interview, part of the East-West Expressway Collection, Maryland Historical Society)

of the efforts that she made on behalf of her community." Many other interviewees made similar comments.

Additionally, I call your attention to the fact that Mikulski purchased a property on Ann Street that was right in the highway corridor. Tony Norris (who later owned the same property) said there were "three occasions where she was ready to come down, fold her arms, all 4'10" of her, and…lie down in front of the bulldozers." Your garden-variety political opportunist is not ordinarily willing to invest in condemned property or risk life and limb to make a stand in front of the bulldozers.

ATOP THE MARQUEE

This all reminds me of a movie where a well-known star is given top billing, even though there are lesser-known actors who contributed equally to the success of the film. Among those lesser-known stars, Tom Ward may have the most legitimate claim to the marquee, right up there with Barbara Mikulski. Unfortunately, Ward did not accept this oversight graciously and went to his grave harboring resentment for the senator. Perhaps this book can give Tom some peace, because we now acknowledge all those lesser-known actors, not just Ward, but also Bob Eney, Lu Fisher, Art Cohen, Norman Reeves, Stu Wechsler, Shirley Doda, John Wells, Nathaniel Owings, Stew Bryant, Mary Rosemond, Gloria Aull, James Dilts, Joseph Wiles, David Barton, Esther Redd, Mildred Moon, Jack Gleason, Carolyn Tyson, Geoff Mitchell, and George Nilson. Their victories were our victories.

XVIII. PERSPECTIVES

It took Baltimore almost forty years to settle on the highway plan it now lives with. Did the right plan get built? Or were highway planners forced to make compromises that actually did not make sense, leaving the city at a competitive disadvantage?

Let us circle back to John Bragdon's 1959 critique of the interstate system, prepared for (and then ignored by) President Eisenhower. Bragdon's thesis was that city highways, by and large, should not be through-routes; central business districts (CBD) should be served only by spurs, eliminating through traffic while saving near-CBD neighborhoods from needless destruction. Bragdon would have endorsed what eventually happened in Baltimore: The only through route (I-95) was moved away from downtown to a mostly industrial corridor, and three truncated spurs (B-W Parkway, I-395, and the JFX) serve the CBD.

Most of my interviewees agreed with this, but there was one whose opinion I valued above all others, Bill Hellmann. Hellmann started at IDBC in 1966, became director in the mid-'70s, then went on to be appointed Secretary of the Maryland DOT, serving from 1984 to 1987. Regarded as a consummate professional, respected by all who worked with him, Bill was the guy I wanted to reflect on the sufficiency of the highway Baltimore built. Hellmann said,

> I think we built the right roads... I think the I-95 route was the correct decision... The city is better today because of I-95. I think the concept we developed and built for the I-395 extension and Martin Luther King Jr. Boulevard was a good decision. I think the decision to not build 83 but to build the President Street Boulevard was a good decision... and it's better they did not build I-70 through Leakin Park. .... In retrospect I think all the build decisions were probably good decisions except for Franklin-Mulberry ... Hindsight is always 20/20.

David Chapin (IDBC) reflected on that same question, saying, "The roadways that were built have served a great purpose and served the city well; and thank goodness we didn't build the ones we didn't build. And then there's I-170, which we should not have built... If we were going to do all that damage to the Franklin-Mulberry corridor...it would have been nice for it to have...made some transportation sense.... But since it wasn't connected, it should never have been built." He also adds that, although he thinks building I-70 through Leakin and Gwynns Falls Parks would have been a mistake, the traffic analysis done back in the day was correct in predicting "a very significant amount of congestion on the beltway from I-70 down to I-95."

Chapin ranks I-95, with the Fort McHenry tunnel, as the road that had to be built, saying, "I can't imagine Baltimore functioning now without I-95 being there. I-95 now carries 130,000 vehicles a day."

On balance, here is one area of public affairs where Baltimore stands out relative to numerous cities who got it wrong and are now trying to undo the mistakes of the past.

But Chapin then goes to a future-looking perspective that had not occurred to me: Might another thirty years provide a whole new perspective on all of this? "It will be interesting to see if, in thirty years, people say, 'Why was I-95 built there? We have this fantastic Port Covington area that's all developed now, but it's separated from South Baltimore by this horrible highway. Tear that highway down!' The city changes."

THE WRONG FORK

[The city should avoid] being pushed into a box that soon could be filled with bad highways, bad debts, and an outraged public.[497]
David Barton, Chairman of the Planning Commission

My thoughts go back to John Wells, the former public housing resident and bus driver who led RAM and had an enormously significant win when the state and federal governments agreed to alter fair market value and give homeowners up to $5,000 in additional "replacement costs."

If Baltimore had dropped the Highway to Nowhere when it became apparent that it had a slim chance of linking up, Wells might have stayed in the neighborhood, might have applied those leadership skills to doing positive things in the city, might have been a great role model for the next generation. Instead, Baltimore ripped out his home and treated him so badly that he used that extra $5,000 to become one of the early African Americans to break the color barrier in Baltimore County. How many more John Wellses were there?

We cannot pin the later decline of West Baltimore and Harlem Park solely on the Highway to Nowhere. The highway was clearly an accelerant of decline, but the 1968 riots, the loss of manufacturing jobs in the 1980s and 1990s, and the devastating influence of crack cocaine were at least equally responsible for the precipitous decline.

But in the realm of transportation decisions and their impact on the community, the summer of 1973 was when Baltimore had a chance to set a new course away from destructive highways and toward a sustainable transit-geared future. This is when IDBC's dedicated staff conducted the courthouse vigil, awaiting Judge Thomsen's decision on the MAD lawsuit seeking an injunction to stop I-170 through the Franklin-Mulberry corridor. There was a June 30 federal deadline to get underway or risk losing federal funds. On June 20 the judge rejected the MAD lawsuit. The *Baltimore Sun* article that announced the judge's decision also said that city council was going to take up Mikulski's expressway-stopping amendments. The bills had been held up for months but were suddenly headed for a vote, apparently because the mayor knew they would be defeated.

At the same time, forty miles to the south, the House-Senate Conference Committee was finally making progress on the bust-the-trust transportation bill. The issue had been debated and rejected in each of the last five years, but suddenly there was hope. Nixon had thrown his weight behind it, the press had adopted the issue as a barometer for the nefarious influence of self-interested lobbyists, and the highway-friendly House conferees were feeling pressure because the highway spigot was running dry.

On June 24 Franklin-Mulberry went under construction. Less than one month later, the bust-the-trust bill passed Congress. It was signed by President

Nixon on August 14, 1973. News outlets and political pundits hailed a new day; cities could finally choose to spend federal transportation money on locally determined priorities. Harry Hughes, Maryland's Transportation Secretary, was completely on board with the switch.

Two months later the OPEC oil embargo brought US dependence on foreign oil into focus—the country's gas-guzzling cars, linked to distorted transportation funding, were the problem, and mass transit was the solution. This was the most opportune moment for Baltimore to make a course correction and supplement transit plans with an infusion of highway dollars. However, Schaefer still had pro-expressway blinders. When he cashed in his highway chips in 1981 to 1983, transit growth was incremental, not the wholesale switch that highway opponents were fighting for.

The "road not taken" in the mid-1970s was a road leading toward a stronger central city, with both downtown and the neighborhoods bolstered by the backbone of a complete transit system. It is well established in the literature that public transit has a centralizing effect on land use, both residential and commercial. This is what transportation economists call "the agglomeration effect."[498] Transit-accessible areas have a competitive advantage over non-accessible areas—transit both uses and encourages the density of highly urbanized areas. Highways, on the other hand, have a decentralizing effect, encouraging destructive sprawl.

The later plan for the Red Line followed roughly the same corridors as the failed highway plans for I-70/I-170 through West Baltimore and I-83 through southeast Baltimore. If Schaefer had not obstinately clung to detrimental highway plans, I-70/I-170 and I-83 could have been swapped for a much earlier version of the Red Line. It would have been a natural fit.

Just switching highway dollars to transit dollars, even in the mid-1970s, would not have singlehandedly created that complete transit system. It would have taken larger infusions of state and federal dollars; so, that alternate reality is dependent on larger commitments at all three levels of government. But, for West Baltimore, it takes less imagination to envision transit making a huge difference.

Transportation barriers –
Inner city residents cannot
access suburban jobs

The Baltimore Opportunity Collaborative and the Baltimore Metropolitan Council put out a 2014 "Study of Barriers to Employment Opportunities in the Baltimore Region." The following are a few excerpts:

"Most Baltimore Region residents living in low-income neighborhoods cannot effectively travel by public transportation to growing job centers in areas north and south of Baltimore City."

"Nearly a quarter of job seekers (23 percent) report that they lack a driver's license."

"A quarter (25 percent) of job seekers indicate they cannot get to jobs by accessing public transportation."

"Travel from [inner city neighborhoods] via public transit to nearby job centers like the BWI airport area requires travel times that exceed one hour and fifteen minutes."

"Less than one-fifth of the region's jobs (18.2 percent) are transit accessible, and even fewer jobs are transit accessible in the construction sector, in manufacturing, in transportation and logistics, in information technologies, and in business services."

"85 percent of all new jobs will be created outside of Baltimore City, but growing job centers… are not well served by public transportation."

By 1973, the Franklin-Mulberry strip had been acquired and demolished, so abandoning the highway plan would not have been easy; redevelopment would have been an overwhelming task. But what if a 1973 version of the Red Line had been prepared as an alternative use of the right-of-way, and what if Schaefer had been open-minded about the switch to transit? Baltimore could have carried out a transportation project that would have been an asset to West Baltimore instead of a liability.

Then, with a transit line instead of a super-highway running down Franklin-Mulberry, the community would look much better for redevelopment. The later historic designation for Old West Baltimore would have dovetailed with mass transit and community development activities to create positive momentum. Then too, as manufacturing jobs disappeared in the late 1970s and 1980s, the transit line would have connected lower income job seekers to alternative employment centers such as Woodlawn, Dundalk, and, after the North Central line was completed, to Timonium, Hunt Valley, and the airport area.

When I interviewed US Transportation Secretary Foxx in 2020, he gave an off-the-cuff treatise on these kinds of transit investments:

> [In these depressed areas] you can't just put the line in there. But...if you've got good planning associated with it, you can really catalyze a lot of economic opportunity. What's exciting about that for a city like Baltimore is that, someone who's now taking three buses to get to a job someplace, maybe the job pops up down street. It both provides a mechanism to connect jobs beyond the neighborhood, but it also starts to make it more attractive for jobs to come into the neighborhood. That's part of what is possible with these investments.
>
> Look, investments like the Red Line are very expensive... But you know, you had a lot of money you spend with [social] support programs, and a lot of lost economic opportunities because we don't provide great education everywhere...great health care everywhere, or frankly, quality food everywhere.

Baltimore had a chance to counter suburbanization with a transportation tool that would have helped the city grow while lowering the later impacts of manufacturing losses and the insidious effects of the drug trade. We failed.

THE ROAD WARS AND THE "BLACK BUTTERFLY"

Dr. Lawrence Brown coined the phrase "Black Butterfly" as a succinct way to describe the racial/socioeconomic division of Baltimore: White and relatively wealthy from the north central strip to South Baltimore and the southeast waterfront, but mostly Black and mostly poor for huge swaths of West Baltimore and East Baltimore. This characterization has struck a chord, and many view the on-going changes to Baltimore through the lens of the Black Butterfly.

The Road Wars exacerbated this duality.

Building the Highway to Nowhere sent Harlem Park on a downward spiral from which it never recovered. Rosemont and Sharp Leadenhall survived, but they too suffered from disinvestment and festering social ills after losing many stable families to relocation. This downward cycle might have been avoided or lessened if the city had cashed in its highway chips for a transit lines, but that was a non-starter for the city's leadership.

In contrast, the White waterfront neighborhoods of Federal Hill, Fell's Point, and Canton were able to capitalize when condemnation lines were lifted. You could argue that highway acquisitions, in the long run, actually accelerated redevelopment by making many contiguous houses and parcels available at the same time. The positive psychology of an area on the comeback trail became a self-fulfilling prophecy.

The unfortunate result of all of this was to intensify the racial divisions that come under the banner of the "Black Butterfly."

For more: www.theblackbutterflyproject.com

THE LONG VIEW

In July 1949 Mayor Thomas D'Alesandro, Jr., became frustrated that his crosstown expressway bills were going nowhere in city council. He organized a meeting that included not only all the Democratic councilmen but also the old-line Democratic bosses he assumed were pulling the strings: William Curran, Ambrose Kennedy, Patrick O'Malley, George Della, Joseph Wyatt, and James "Jack" Pollack. Word of the meeting leaked out to the press, and D'Alesandro was engulfed in a firestorm of criticism—Republicans accused him of pandering to unelected shadowy figures and termed it "a flagrant threat to representative government in Baltimore... If they have the power he credits to them, he should be fighting it not encouraging."[499] Three of the bosses, unaccustomed to public scrutiny, declined to attend. Pollack issued an "Emancipation Proclamation" so that certain councilmembers could vote their conscience. Some Democratic councilmen boycotted the meeting so as not to be seen as puppets. Needless to say, D'Alesandro's efforts to create a pro-expressway coalition (thankfully) landed in fallow ground.

In 1953 the Mount Royal Democratic Club was founded by Tom Ward and several other Bolton Hill residents as an alternative to the Jack-Pollack-dominated machine.* Jack Lapides joined the group in 1959. Ward and Lapides led Mount Royal for over a half century. Both also played critical roles in the Road Wars. In 1963 Ward was elected to city council from his Mount Royal Club base, one chink in the armor of the old guard in the city's Second District (north central Baltimore). In 1966 the Mount Royal Club was part of a broad coalition that wrested control of the state's Democratic Central Committee from Jack Pollack.

---

* A *Baltimore Sun* op-ed piece in 2017 referred to a theory I have also heard from other sources: The wide thoroughfares leading to and occupying the west side of Druid Hill Park (Auchentoroly Terrace, Reisterstown Road, McCulloh Street, and Druid Hill Avenue) amounted to Jack Pollack's own personal expressway to his home on Anoka Avenue. The op-ed piece supports recent efforts to restore the adjacent community's connection to Druid Hill Park by way of design changes consistent with "complete streets" principles. (Daniel Hindman, "Right a past wrong by opening access to Druid Hill Park," *Baltimore Sun*, Oct 19, 2017.)

Ward lost his re-election bid in 1967, but Mount-Royal-backed Robert Douglass won a Second District council seat. It was a racial breakthrough that Mount Royal put Douglass, an eastside African American, on their ticket. Five incumbents were defeated, and the *Sun* reported that "the returns apparently demolished the fragile one-vote majority by which the Pollack and Reed factions have maintained their control of councilmanic patronage."[500]

In 1970 SECO was organized, one of five umbrella community organizations that substantially replaced the previous role of political bosses. By involving thousands of people and seventy-five different organizations, SECO became the focal point for bottom-up community development activities through the 1970s and into subsequent decades. Joe McNeely (SECO's first director) described their role:

> [SECO] wasn't put together as an anti-road organization, it was put together as being multifaceted, multi-issue agenda, and building a strong organization of power that could displace the political machine. In September of 1970 the rezoning of the city was underway, and the First District council people refused to meet with the neighborhood organizations. The only people they would meet with were political clubs, and [SECO was able] was to create a new mode of mobilizing and organizing.

Multiply the SECO inroads to also represent the other umbrella groups.

In the 1971 councilmanic election, the feisty social worker and Road Warrior Barbara Mikulski whipped the machine, getting the most votes in the First District (southeast Baltimore) race. In my 2020 interview she expanded on this point: "What defined me was that I was…not part of the political machine… In the words of the late great Shirley Chisholm when she said she was 'unbought and unbossed.'… [I said] I am going to be an independent Democrat speaking to the community needs, not the needs of downtown… or the political organization." The Road, she continues, was the most prominent and current issue that exemplified how her constituents felt powerless and how she acted to fill that void. "We knocked literally on the doors of City Hall, [but] the big highway guys, etc., they just blew us off…. So, there was a lot of pent-up frustration, and I said, 'You can claim your power. It is your power. But at City Hall, I will try to give voice and effort,' and that is what I did. And that is why I beat the political machine."

In 1971 the New Democratic Club (NDC) split off from the Mt Royal Democratic Club and forged a coalition with the Black Eastside Democratic Organization. NDC swept the three Second District council seats, including the election of two highway opponents, Robert Fitzpatrick and Robert Douglass. Fitzpatrick co-sponsored Mikulski's highway stopping ordinances in 1972 and Douglass spoke at the founding meeting of MAD.

It is not coincidence that Mikulski, Ward, Fitzpatrick, and Douglass, all part of the anti-highway group, were also key in overthrowing the political machine. Nor is it an accident that the rise of anti-highway activism coincided with the time that the old-line bosses faded from power. It was all due to community activists stepping up and saying the neighborhoods' interests were not being represented. In this same 1971 election, Paul Sarbanes ran for Congress as an independent Democrat and defeated George Fallon, defender of the Highway Trust and candidate of the Democratic machine. Sarbanes, too, was in the anti-expressway camp.

The old guard was giving way—progressives were coming into power who drew their strength from communities rather than entrenched political organizations. As the expressway battle was gradually resolved and the city recovered from the riots, the energy brought by this new generation of community leaders produced a city on the vanguard of urban transformation. Neighborhoods organized, redevelopment plans were prepared, and every turn for the better was hoisted up as a success story at City Fair.

William Donald Schaefer, although he made unforgivable mistakes by building the Franklin-Mulberry Highway to Nowhere and squandering the mid-'70s transit opportunity, was an unabashed city booster and made this troubled city believe that it could come back. And it did.

But no fix is permanent, and the forces of pessimism and disinvestment are back.

We now face a moment in Baltimore's history not unlike the challenge of overcoming the riots and wrong-headed highway acquisitions. In the aftermath of Freddie Gray, the Gun Trace Task Force, and the crack cocaine epidemic, much of Baltimore appears to be spiraling downward. Baltimore suffered through a betrayal of leadership when two mayors behaved like modern-day versions of the old bosses: They were in it for themselves, and the downward spiral continued. There is now a critical need for selfless leadership, a new vision, and grassroots support for change. Not unlike the 1970s, a new generation needs to step up, craft new approaches, build new partnerships with private and public entities, restore trust and hope and pride, and work tirelessly to right the ship and get Baltimore back on a positive path.

But there is one key difference between then and now: It would be naive to expect that the federal government will be the kind of partner in urban reinvention that it was in the 1970s. Further, the city's fiscal ability to act on any new vision is severely constrained. The private sector needs to step up, but there is only one governmental unit with the resources to make that new vision a reality: the State of Maryland.

I asked my two highest ranking interviewees to step back and add some perspective. Secretary Anthony Foxx responded:

> The opportunity [is there] to start tearing away some of those factors that contribute to poverty and to a lack of economic mobility—that's exciting. That's what our country should be doing. That's what I think is one of the defining issues of the century, is can we still ensure economic prosperity for those who clamor for it and create the pathways for that?
>
> I know there will be another moment in time, where something like the Red Line comes up. And the same old questions will emerge: Is this city ready for this? Can it manage it? Is this going to do anything? Is it putting money to nothing? The answer is, we've got to get past all that, because an entire generation is coming along and they're either going to be net contributors to the overall economy or not. If we just write them off, that's not a good formulation for this country.

I know how hard this is. I mean, ultimately, as much as we want to imagine ourselves as a country that's fully integrated and fully together, we still have fissures and repairing those fissures is hard. It is extremely hard work...

It is really important for our society to have this conversation. Baltimore, it is a beautiful city. It is a city with an immensely proud history, but it's also a city that has a very troubled history when it comes to lifting up its people. And, as long as that's true, it will never live up to its potential. That is really the goal is to see a place like Baltimore and the people of Baltimore all live up to their potential.

Senator Mikulski said:

Well, I think there is a lot of community spirit. I think there are a lot of very spunky grassroots organizations today. Many belong to the umbrella organization of BUILD, which is a very viable and dynamic organization. [Some organize] around crime and violence, [like] the moms that have organized [to] end the violence.

We have had a big problem with mayors over the last decade, and it has taken its toll. We have had two indictments of mayors. We have had one mayor after the Freddie Gray trouble. The shock and awe of the Freddie Gray uprising took its toll on Mayor Rawlings-Blake.... Now I think [there is new hope] with Brandon Scott.... There is new technology.

One of my big fights if I were in City Hall would be the digital divide, and it is not only our young people having the tools of technology, but Comcast and their lackluster approach to ensuring connectivity to our homes and small businesses.... It is the Eastern Avenue for the Latino Community. It is the work that still goes on along Pennsylvania Avenue, really the whole work that could be done with small business, [for example] in Edmondson Village.

Senator Mikulski, still incredibly articulate and outspoken, still a mouthpiece for the dispossessed, and still just as feisty as when she got on the bullhorn for "Radio Free Fell's Point" at the 1969 Fell's Point Fun Festival, left me with one final anecdote that I now employ as a closing:

> What made me famous and then all of this got attached to me… The day of the Fell's Point Festival, when one of the TV stations came up and we had a little storefront on Thames Street, down where the Brassworks is now…. So, we had these maps that showed the expressways here. This is what is going to be taken… It was like a ground zero of a nuclear attack. So, when TV showed up, some of the people manning the booth said, "Barbara, you talk… You are pretty mouthy, and you get up there and talk." That is when I said, and it came to me, it was not planned or rehearsed, "The British could not take Fell's Point. The termites could not take Fell's Point, and god damned, the State Roads Commission cannot take Fell's Point, either." Well, I was all over the media.
>
> Interviewer (incredulously): "That was just like a spur-of-the-moment thing that just came to you?"
>
> Sen. Mikulski: "That is exactly right. So, it was spur-of-the-moment."
>
> Interviewer (myself), thinking: *How do you do that?*

I could have taken a month of Sundays and still would not have been able to come up with a single memorable phrase that so well encapsulates the forty-year struggle to Stop the Road.

APPENDIX 1. MAJOR HIGHWAY ALIGNMENTS AND BATTLEGROUND NEIGHBORHOODS

APPENDIX 1-A. BATTLEGROUND NEIGHBORHOODS
A BRIEF GUIDE

Please use this description with the maps on the following pages.

FROM WEST TO EAST:

LEAKIN PARK – The 1,200-acre park is surrounded by mostly middle-income neighborhoods. At the time of the Road Wars, some of the area was in transition from White to Black. The area is now predominantly African American; however, some sections (Windsor Hills in particular) have been stably integrated for many decades.

ROSEMONT – At the time of the Road Wars the neighborhood was solid middle class and African American. Rosemont was under the cloud of highway acquisition for fifteen years; 483 dwellings were acquired before the alignment was changed in 1971 (and dropped in 1980). After these acquisitions, the area went into decline, but it is still above average in measures such as the percent of dwellings in homeownership.

HARLEM PARK AND FRANKLIN-MULBERRY – A lower income African American neighborhood with rental properties predominating, twenty blocks of Harlem Park were acquired in the late 1960s. The infamous "Highway to Nowhere" was built starting in 1973 and completed in 1979. The area is now plagued by crime and drug-related social pathologies; housing abandonment is outpacing renewal efforts.

Appendix 1

SHARP LEADENHALL – At the time of the Road Wars, Sharp Leadenhall was a lower income African American neighborhood with rental properties predominating. It was nearly wiped out by two highway rights-of-way and an urban renewal plan; the area is now exceptionally diverse, with subsidized housing geared to lower income African American residents in an uneasy co-existence with predominantly White rehabbed properties.

FEDERAL HILL – At the time of the Road Wars, Federal Hill was a mixed-income and mixed-race community with industrial uses mixed in, especially along the waterfront. After the area was freed up from the highway right-of-way, renovation of historic property, along with new infill and industrial conversions, completely remade the community. Gentrification spread southward and inland, encompassing much of the South Baltimore peninsula.

HARBOR EAST (AKA INNER HARBOR EAST) – A mostly industrial area at the time of the Road Wars, the area was freed up when I-83 through southeast Baltimore was abandoned in 1980. The area was completely transformed, starting in about 1995, to Baltimore's highest value waterfront redevelopment area. New development includes high rise apartments and offices with a lively mix of retail uses on the ground floors.

FELL'S POINT – Historically a seaport community with port-related commercial and industrial uses at the waterfront and rowhomes slightly inland, Fell's Point was in decline at the time of the highway acquisitions. After condemnation lines were lifted, vacant homes were renovated by young adventurous urban dwellers. New investment snowballed as industrial lofts became upscale apartments, and trendy bars and restaurants replaced the seedy establishments of the past.

CANTON – A lower-middle-class White ethnic area before the highway acquisitions, Canton followed Fell's Point's lead: the highway acquisition area became new infill; waterfront industrial lofts were redeveloped as apartments, condos, and marinas; and young people renovated rowhomes, resulting in a gradual shift from older White ethnics to young city dwellers.

Appendix 1-B—10-D plan
1961 Expressway Consultants

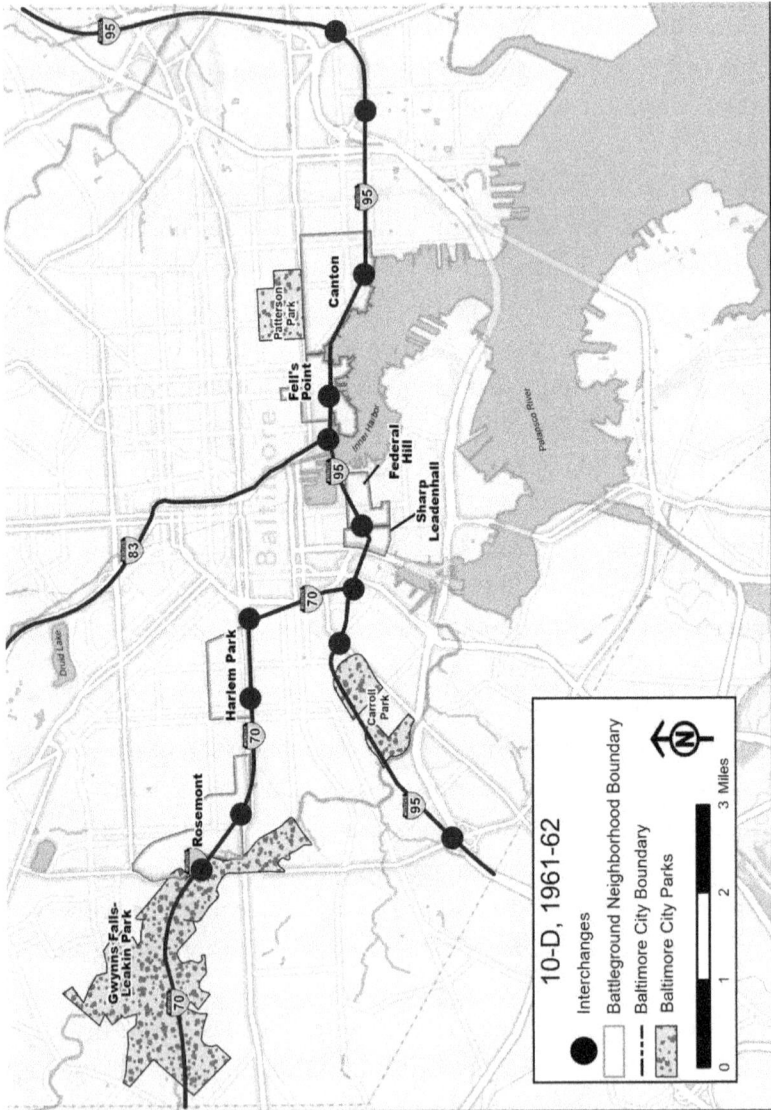

Appendix 1-B. The 1961-62 10-D alignment. Multiple sources, but primarily: Expressway Consultants, "Interstate Highways 70-N and 95, East-West Expressway," 1961 (Map by Scott Jeffrey, MS, GISP).

Appendix 1

Appendix 1-C—10-D modified
1967

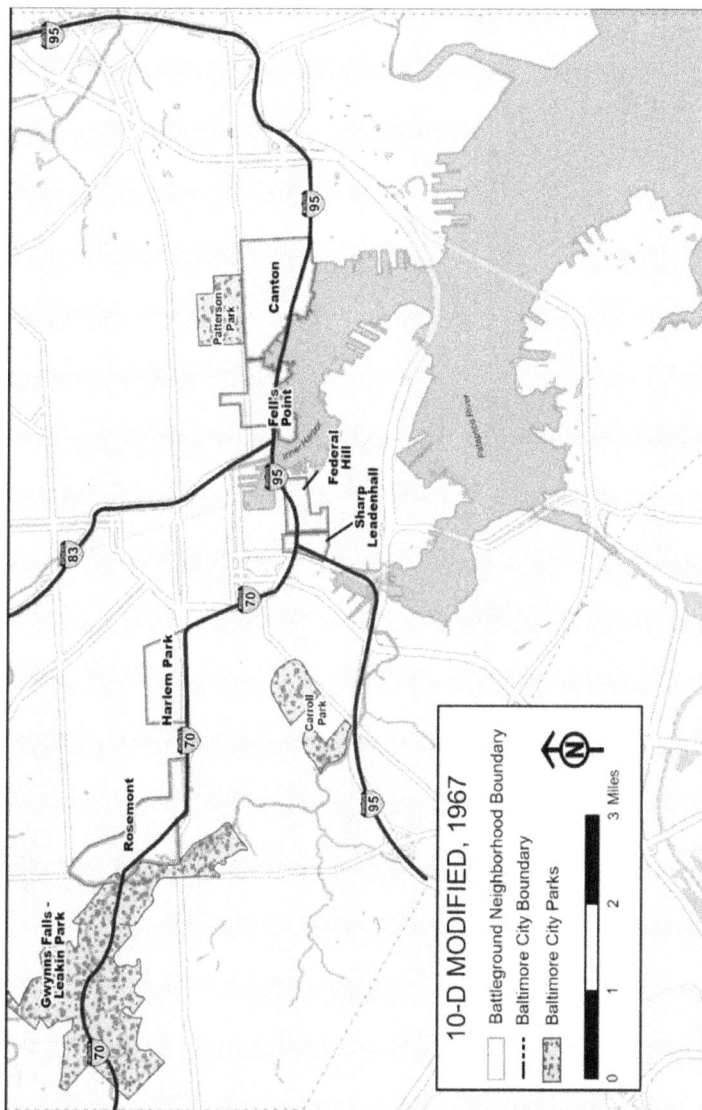

Appendix 1-C. 10-D Modified, adopted 1967, repealed 1973. Source: "Case Report, Section 106, I-83, Historic Preservation Act of 1966, Gay Street to I-95, January, 1977," (Map by Scott Jeffrey, MS, GISP).

357

Appendix 1-D—3-A Plan
Urban Design Concept Team (UDCT) 1968

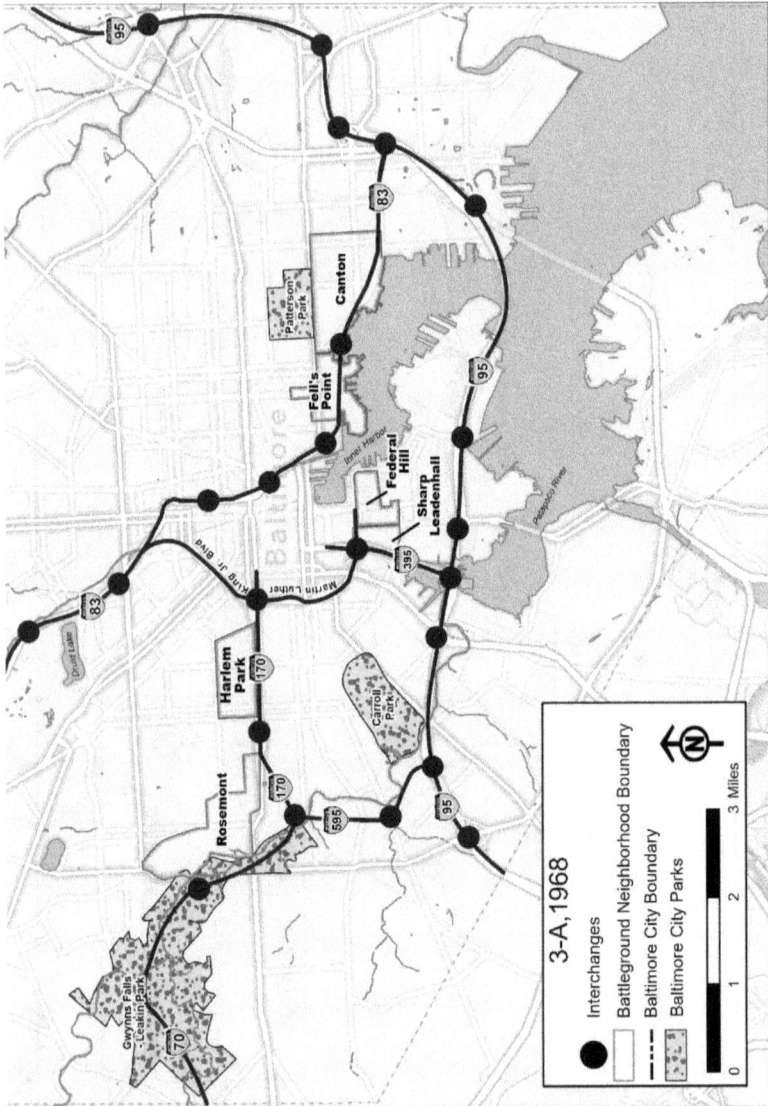

Appendix 1-D. 3-A system, adopted 1968, but not fully implemented until 1975. Multiple sources, but primarily: "Case Report, Section 106, I-83, Historic Preservation Act of 1966, Gay Street to I-95, January 1977." (Map by Scott Jeffrey, MS, GISP)

Appendix 1-F—City Boulevard
UDCT, 1970. Later named Martin Luther King, Jr. Boulevard

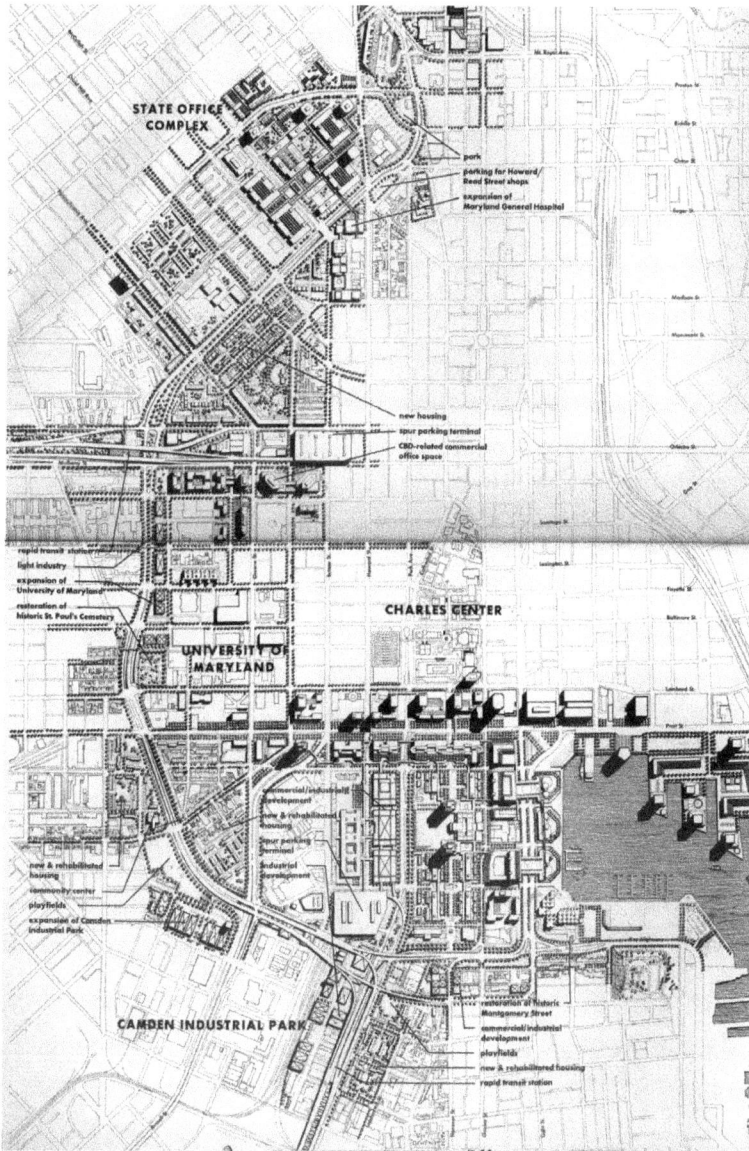

Appendix 1-F, City Boulevard (later Martin Luther King, Jr. Boulevard) from Urban Design Concept Associates, 1970, Corridor Development, Segment 11

APPENDIX 2.
ROAD WARS PROTAGONISTS

Left: Joe Axelrod, Interstate Division; John Wells, RAM; and Esther Redd, RAM. (Source: David Allison, Innovation Magazine, "the Battle Lines of Baltimore," spring, 1969. University of Baltimore Langsdale Library, Digital collections, Rosemont Community Association, 1950-1968.)

Lu Fisher presenting an award to Tom Ward at the Preservation Society's Founders Day event in 1992 (Source: The Society for the Preservation of Federal Hill and Fell's Point).

Shirley and Victor Doda marker located at Fort Avenue and Latrobe Park Terrace, acknowledging the Doda's role in changing the Fort McHenry bridge to a tunnel

Art Cohen, MAD, with his self-penned "Baltimore Highway Blues."

Appendix 2. Road Wars Protagonists

*Left:
Rosemont
activist: Joe
Wiles (Source:
Baltimore Sun)*

Rosemont activist: Mary Rosemond (Source: University of Baltimore RLB Library, SCAR collection)

Norman Reeves, Councilman and VOLPE activist (Source: Iris Reeves)

Bob Eney, Preservation Society, (source: 2004 Oral History Interview, Jacqueline Greff, Tonal Vision, Fells Point Out of Time)

James Dilts, Baltimore Sun, Courtesy Penny Williamson

Bob Embry, Housing Commissioner. Source: "Fell's Point, 1975," historical video from Department of Learning Resources at Montgomery College.

Jack Gleason, Preservation Society, leading a meeting while smoking cigarettes that later killed him. From Jacqueline Greff, Tonal Vision documentary video, "Fell's Point 1975," courtesy Montgomery College.

Barbara Mikulski in 1975 as a councilmember. (Source: University of Baltimore, RLB Library, SCAR collection)

Joe McNeely, SECO/SCAR

Mildred Mae Moon, Sharp Leadenhall, (Source: Solo Gibbs historical marker for the Gwynns Falls Trail)

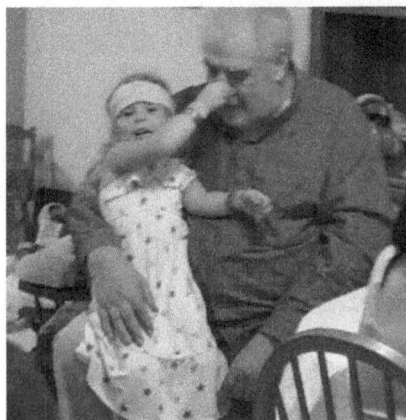

Stu Wechsler, MAD, CORE (Source: Facebook)

APPENDIX 3. EASY REFERENCE

CAST OF CHARACTERS

Positions listed are those held at key points in the Road Wars; other positions are noted if relevant.

Joseph Axelrod, Chief, Interstate Division of Baltimore City from 1968-1973

Raymond Bahr, Canton historian (Interviewed)

Al Barry, (later) Deputy Director, Baltimore City Department of Planning (Interviewed)

Bernard Berkowitz, Mayor's Physical Development Coordinator under Schaefer (Interviewed)

Gene Bober, Chief of Joint Development, Interstate Division of Baltimore City, 1971-1977 (Interviewed)

Bill Boucher, President, Greater Baltimore Committee (interview transcribed)

Alan S. Boyd, US Secretary of Transportation, 1967-1969

Lowell K. Bridwell, Director, Federal Highway Administration, 1967-1969; Secretary of Transportation for the State of Maryland

Claude S. Brinegar, Secretary, US Department of Transportation, 1973-1975

M. J. "Jay" Brodie, Deputy Commissioner of Housing and Community Development for Baltimore City, 1968-1976; Commissioner, 1976-1984 (Interviewed)

Irwin Brown, Chief of Staff to Baltimore City Council President Orlinsky (Interviewed)

Stewart Bryant, Skidmore, Owings & Merrill; Urban Design Concept Team

Steve Bunker, Fell's Point historian (Interviewed for Fell's Point Out of Time living history project)

Lynn Butler, Movement Against Destruction; Relocation Action Movement (1974 interview transcribed)

Tom Canoles, President, Canton Improvement Association, 1980s (Interviewed)

David Carroll, Coastal Resources Planner and Chief, Coastal Resources, Baltimore City Department of Planning, 1974-85; Secretary, Maryland Department of Environment, 1993-1994 (Interviewed)

David Chapin, Chief of Joint Development Planning, Interstate Division of Baltimore City; Assistant Transportation Coordinator for Baltimore City (1981-1984); Assistant Secretary for Policy and Government Affairs, Maryland Department of Transportation (Interviewed)

Art Cohen, President, Movement Against Destruction, January-July 1969 (Interviewed)

Thomas D'Alesandro III (AKA "Young Tommy"), President, Baltimore City Council, 1963-1967; Mayor of Baltimore 1967-1971

Steve Bunker, long-time Fell's Pointer, (interviewed for Fell's Point Out of Time)

Betty Deacon, SECO; SCAR; Southeast Truck Task Force (Interviewed)

Hugh G. Downs, Chief, Interstate Division for Baltimore City 1965-1968

James Dilts, columnist, the *Baltimore Sun*

Charlie Duff, Preservation Society, early 1970s; President, Jubilee Baltimore (Interviewed)

Robert Embry, City Housing Commissioner, 1968-1976; Mayor's Transportation Coordinator, 1973-1976 (Interviewed)

Bob Eney, Preservation Society (2003 interview transcribed)

Lucretia "Lu" Fisher, founding member, Preservation Society (2003 interview for Fell's Point Out of Time)

John Fowler, President's Advisory Council on Historic Preservation (Interviewed)

Anthony Foxx, Secretary of Transportation for Obama Administration, 2009-2017 (Interviewed)

John B. Funk, Chairman and Director, State Roads Commission, 1959-1966

Sheila Gaskins, playwright, *The Last House Standing, a play about the Highway to Nowhere* (Interviewed)

David Gleason, Preservation Society (Interviewed)

Jack Gleason, Preservation Society (2003 interview transcribed)

Bill Hellmann, Deputy Chief and Chief, Interstate Division for Baltimore City, 1970-1983; Mayor's Transportation Coordinator (late 1970s); Secretary, Maryland Department of Transportation, 1984-1987 (Interviewed)

Dave Hollander, VOLPE; Friends of Gwynns Falls Leakin Park (Interviewed)

Peter Hopkinson, Skidmore, Owings & Merrill, Urban Design Concept Team

Denise Johnson, Director of CultureWorks. (Interviewed)

Mark Joseph, Mayor's Physical Development Coordinator (late 1970s), (Interviewed)

Ed Kane, Baltimore Water Taxi (Interviewed for Fell's Point Out of Time living history project)

Norman Klein, Skidmore, Owings & Merrill, Urban Design Concept Team

Julian "Jack" Lapides, Senator, Maryland General Assembly; member and General Counsel, Preservation Society

Pierce Linaweaver, Director, Baltimore Department of Public Works, 1968-1973 (Interviewed)

Mary Logan, Movement Against Destruction and South Baltimore/Federal Hill activist (Interviewed)

Theodore R. McKeldin, Mayor of Baltimore, 1943-1947 and 1963-1967

Joe McNeely, first Director, Southeast Community Organization (Interviewed)

The Honorable Barbara Ann Mikulski, SCAR, councilperson, later Congresswoman, U.S. House of Representatives; Senator, U.S. Senate; (1974 interview transcribed, also interviewed in 2021)

Ashley Milburn, arts activist, Culture Works

Geoff Mitchell, Attorney, Semmes, Bowen & Semmes (representing the Preservation Society) (Interviewed)

Robert Moses, New York kingpin of highways and public works, brought in as a consultant to Baltimore in 1944

George Nilson, Attorney, Piper Marbury (representing VOLPE in the *VOLPE v. Volpe* lawsuit) (Interviewed)

Tony and Laura Norris, long-time Fell's Point residents; owners, Bertha's Restaurant (Interviewed)

David Nutter, Urban Design Concept Team; Baltimore City Department of Planning (Interviewed)

John Pearce, Maryland State Historic Preservation Officer

Norman Ramsey, Senior Partner, Semmes, Bowen & Semmes (represented the Preservation Society)

Esther Redd, neighborhood leader and activist, Relocation Action Movement; Movement Against Destruction

Larry Reich, Director of Planning, Baltimore City Department of Planning, 1966-1990

Jimmy Rouse, Movement Against Destruction (Interviewed)

William Donald Schaefer, President, Baltimore City Council, 1967-1971;

Appendix 3. Easy Reference

Mayor of Baltimore, 1971-1986; Governor of the State of Maryland; Comptroller of the State of Maryland

Nancy Schamu, historian and long-time staff, Maryland Historic Trust (Interviewed)

Michael Seipp, VOLPE; Baltimore City Department of Housing and Community Development (Interviewed)

Glenn Smith, Rosemont resident; Transit Equity Coalition (Interviewed)

Romaine Somerville, Director, Baltimore City Commission on Historic Preservation; Executive Director, Preservation Society (Interviewed for Fell's Point Out of Time living history project)

William Struever, urbanist; consultant; developer (Interviewed for Fell's Point Out of Time)

Betty Bland Thomas, Sharp Leadenhall Planning Committee (Interviewed)

Richard H. Trainor, Chief, Interstate Division of Baltimore City, 1974-1978; Secretary, Maryland Department of Transportation, 1987-1991)

PJ Trautwein, long time Fell's Pointer, (Interviewed for Fell's Point Out of Time)

Carolyn Tyson, President, Movement Against Destruction, 1972-1973 (1974 interview transcribed

George Tyson, President, Movement Against Destruction, 1975 (interviewed)

David Wagner, Interstate Division of Baltimore City; Administrator, Mass Transit Administration; Deputy Secretary, Maryland Department of Transportation; Administrator, Maryland Port Administration (1974 interview transcribed)

Mark Wasserman, Mayor's Physical Development Coordinator, 1981-1986 (Interviewed)

John Wells, President, Relocation Action Movement

Tom Ward, Councilman, Baltimore City Council 1963-1967; founding member, Preservation Society; plaintiff in two highway opposition lawsuits (Interviewed Ward and his son, Patrick Ward)

Stuart Wechsler, Congress for Racial Equality; activist member, Relocation Action Movement; President, Movement Against Destruction, August-December 1968 and July-December 1969 (Interviewed)

John Weese, Skidmore, Owings & Merrill; Project Manager, Urban Design Concept Team

John A. Volpe, Secretary of Transportation, 1969-1973

John Wells, President, Relocation Action Movement, 1967-1968

Bernard Werner, Director, Baltimore City Department of Public Works, 1958-1968

Penny Williamson, James Dilts' wife (Interviewed)

Jerome Wolff, Chairman and Director, Maryland State Roads Commission, 1967-1968; Greiner Engineering, (early 1970s); chief witness in the Agnew bribery scandal

Norman Zassek, Canton Improvement Association (1974 interview transcribed)

Steve Zecher, Urban Design Concept Team (Interviewed)

ACRONYMS

ACHP – US Advisory Council on Historic Preservation
BPR – US Bureau of Public Roads (absorbed into the FHWA in 1967)
CORE – Congress for Racial Equality
DOT - US Department of Transportation (created in April 1967)
FHWA – Federal Highway Administration (under DOT in 1967)
IDBC – Interstate Division for Baltimore City
MAD – Movement Against Destruction
MDOT – Maryland Department of Transportation
RAM – Relocation Action Movement
SCAR – Southeast Council Against the Road
SECO – Southeast Community Organization
SRC – Maryland State Roads Commission
SOM – Skidmore Owings & Merrill
UDCT – Urban Design Concept Team
VOLPE – Volunteers Opposing Leakin Park Expressway

ENDNOTES

Note that interviews conducted by the author are only footnoted if clarification as to the source is needed. The author's interviews are noted in Appendix 3, "Cast of Characters."

1. Barbara Mikulski, 1974 interview, Maryland Historical Society, East-West Expressway Collection.

2. Anthony Foxx, "Reconnecting America in the 21st Century," *Aspen Journal of Ideas,* September/October 2015. http://aspen.us/journal/editions/septemberoctober-2015/reconnecting-america-21st-century, accessed 1/23/2017.

3. Rafael Alvarez, "New Canton rises on painful memories: Residents from two decades ago still pine for the homes..." *Baltimore Sun,* Jun 19, 1988, pg. 1A; ProQuest Historical Newspapers.

4. Tony Norris, Interview with Evans Paull, 2019.

5. *Baltimore Sun,* "Building a papier-mâché bridge from the refuse of citizen crossfire on the East-West Expressway," Apr 26, 1972; ProQuest Historical Newspapers, pg. C6

6. Robert A. Caro, *The Power Broker, Robert Moses and the Fall of New York,* Vintage Publishing, 1975, pp. 318-319.

7. *Baltimore Sun,* "Moses Group Favors Franklin Expressway," October 11, 1944.

8. *Baltimore Sun,* "Expressway Would Raze 200 Blocks: All Existing Buildings Would Be Destroyed," Oct 16, 1944, pg. 20; ProQuest Historical Newspapers.

9. Emily Lieb, "White man's lane, Hollowing Out the Highway Ghetto in Baltimore," in Elizabeth Nix, *Baltimore '68 : Riots and Rebirth in an American City,* edited by Jessica Elfenbein, and Thomas Hollowak, Temple University Press, 2011.

10. Louis J, O'Donnell, "House Group Votes Against Expressway: Reports Heard, However, State ..." *Baltimore Sun,* Mar 27, 1945, pg. 20; ProQuest Historical Newspapers.

11. *Baltimore Sun,* "Down Goes Another Plan," Dec 11, 1946; pg. 12, ProQuest Historical Newspapers.

12. "Baltimore's Future," *Baltimore Sun,* Nov 30, 1947; pg. 12.

13. A modern-day survey of 17 European cities with over one million in population found that only 34 percent of all trips were undertaken in a car. Similar to Baltimore in the 1940s, European city dwellers made two out of three trips via walking (22%), biking (5%), and transit (39%). Fergus O'Sullivan, "Breaking Down the Many Ways Europe's City-Dwellers Get to Work," *CityLab,* Oct. 18, 2017. https://www.citylab.com/transportation/2017/10/riding-bikes-buses-trains-in-european-cities/543141/. And "Modal share," Wikipedia, https://en.wikipedia.org/wiki/Modal_share.

14. Gary Helton, *Baltimore's Streetcars and Buses, Images of America,* Baltimore Streetcar Museum, Apr. 2008.

15. Gary Helton, *"Baltimore's Streetcars...*

16. The account of the truck brigade draws on the following: Earl Swift, *The Big Roads,* pg. 58-85; Dwight D. Eisenhower, *At Ease: Stories I Tell to Friends,* Eastern Acorn Press, 1967, pg. 155-168; and "Daily Log of the First Transcontinental Motor Convoy," Eisenhower Library Archives, Washington, DC to San Francisco, Cal, July 7th to Sept. 6, 1919.

17. Swift, p. 67.

18. Swift, p. 68

19. Eisenhower Library Archives, "Daily..."

20. Eisenhower Library Archives, "Daily…"p. 167

21. Swift, p. 157-158

22. Swift, p. 158-159

23. Swift p. 247

24. Lee Mertz, "The Bragdon Committee," https://www.fhwa.dot.gov/infrastructure/bragdon.cfm.

25. Tallamy was a disciple of Robert Moses. The Sun's James Dilts described Tallamy as follows, "a former superintendent of the New York State Department of Public Works… who in 1926 had come down from Niagara to sit at Moses' feet for private lectures on the art of Getting Things Done -- and who told the author that the Interstate Highway System was built by principles he had learned at those lectures. Moses was not merely the friend of the federal road builders, he was their idol." James Dilts, "A Brief History of Baltimore's Transportation Planning," 1977, from University of Baltimore, MAD Collection.

26. (author unclear) Memorandum for the Record, April 6, 1960, Eisenhower Archives, https://www.eisenhower.archives.gov/research/online_documents/interstate_highway_system/1960_04_08_Meeting.pdf.

27. Lee Mertz, The Bragdon Committee, https://www.fhwa.dot.gov/infrastructure/bragdon.cfm

28. Lee Mertz, the Bragdon Committee…

29. *Baltimore Sun*, "Fallon Ends His Campaign: Takes Final Fling At GOP Rival For Congress," Nov 5, 1944; pg. 15.

30. *Baltimore Sun*, "Fallon Makes Reply To Ellison Defense," Oct 30, 1944, pg. 13; ProQuest Historical Newspapers.

31. Nathaniel A. Owings, *The American Aesthetic*, Published by Harper & Row, 1969. University of Baltimore Special Collections, MAD Collection.

32. Emily Lieb, "Slum Clearance A La Mode: The Battle For Baltimore's Tyson Street," *The metropole blog*, Baltimore, Metropolis Of The Month, Nov. 26, 2018. https://themetropole.blog/2018/11/26/slum-clearance-a-la-mode1-the-battle-for-baltimores-tyson-street/ (accessed 7.17.21).

33. *Baltimore Sun*, 800 Protest Path of Road: Want Expressway Rerouted," Mar 8, 1957; pg. 8; ProQuest Historical Newspapers.

34. *Baltimore Sun*, "Tyson Street Seen Doomed: Faces Destruction," Jul 19, 1957; pg. 8, ProQuest Historical Newspapers.

35. *Baltimore Sun*, "Tyson Streeters Tell Mayor They Plan Fight to Finish," Aug 21, 1957, pg. 23; ProQuest Historical Newspapers.

36. *Baltimore Sun*, "2,700 Visitors Give $4,000 To Save Tyson Street Fund," Oct 21, 1957, pg. 8, ProQuest Historical Newspapers.

37. *Baltimore Sun*, "House Backs Plan to Save Tyson Street," Mar 1, 1958; pg. 7, ProQuest Historical Newspapers.

38. *Baltimore Sun*, "Liss Backs Tyson Cause: Councilman Sees 'Beacon' For City's Future," Sep 11, 1957, pg. 12, ProQuest Historical Newspapers.

39. Dimento, Joseph F.C., and Cliff Ellis, *Changing Lanes, New Visions of Urban Freeways*, MIT Press, 2013.

40. Draft Environmental Impact Statement, Interstate Route I-70N, Vicinity of Existing I-70n At Ingleside Avenue in Baltimore County, Maryland to vicinity of Baltimore Street

and Ellicott Driveway In Baltimore City, Maryland, November 10, 1972. From MAD collection, University of Baltimore, RLB Library.

41. Baltimore Department of Planning, *Study for the East-West Expressway*, January, 1960, pp 20 and 59.

42. *Baltimore Sun*, "Vision and Action, Jul 17, 1956, pg. 12; ProQuest Historical Newspapers.

43. Baltimore Department of Planning, *Study for the East-West Expressway*, January, 1960, p. 49

44. Michael P. McCarthy, "Baltimore's Highway Wars Revisited," *Maryland Historical Magazine*, Volume 93,2 (Summer 1998), pp 142-143.

45. McCarthy, p 148.

46. Frank P L Sommerville, "Consultants' Route Favored: Businessmen's Committee Takes Expressway Stand," *Baltimore Sun*, Jan 9, 1962, pg. 36; ProQuest Historical Newspapers.

47. McCarthy, p. 149 – 153.

48. J Anthony Lukas, "At City Hearing Irate Crowd Hits Planned Expressway," *Baltimore Sun* Jan 31, 1962, pg. 34; ProQuest Historical Newspapers.

49. Charles V Flowers, "Expressway Choice Asked: City Seeks Decision to Aid Traffic, Renewal Plans," *Baltimore Sun*, Jul 26, 1962.

50. *Baltimore Sun*, "Protest Meeting Set Tonight on New Expressway Plans," Feb 20, 1962, p. 25, ProQuest Historical Newspapers.

51. *Baltimore Sun*, "Mckeldin Challenged: Engineers Unit Asks Mayor To Name Road Eyesores," Nov 20, 1963; ProQuest Historical Newspapers.

52. John E. Woodruff, "City Told it Acts Alone on Bridge: Roads Unit Bars Comment On New Harbor Plan," *Baltimore Sun*, Oct 15, 1966, pg. B20; ProQuest Historical Newspapers.

53. Earl Swift, *The Big Roads, The Untold Story of the Engineers, Visionaries, and Trailblazers Who Created the American Superhighways*, Houghton Mifflin Harcourt, 2011, p. 65.

54. Jacques Kelly, "Thomas H. Ward, longtime city judge and former council member, dies," *Baltimore Sun*, Mar 06, 2016.

55. Charles V. Flowers, "Ward Would Ban New Expressway: To Ask Other Councilmen to Help Defeat It," Dec 19, 1964, pg. 32; ProQuest Historical Newspapers.

56. *Baltimore Sun*, "$50 Expressway Plan," Apr 10, 1965, pg. 12; ProQuest Historical Newspapers.

57. *Baltimore Sun*, "Expressway Bill Voted Suit Is Vowed: Ward Threatens Action As Council Approves The Sun," Nov 21, 1967, pg. C24; ProQuest Historical Newspapers.

58. Mayor Theodore R. McKeldin letter to Joe Axelrod, Acting Director of Planning, December 21, 1965, Tom Ward personal papers, now available at the University of Baltimore library.

59. Nick Madigan, "Dose of law, order on the street," *Baltimore Sun*, November 07, 2007.

60. Tom Ward personal papers, now available at the University of Baltimore library.

61. *Baltimore Sun*, "Findings," Jan 5, 1968, pg. C22; ProQuest Historical Newspapers.

62. Raymond A. Mohl, "Stop the Road, Freeway Revolts in American Cities," *Journal of Urban History*, Vol. 30 No. 5, July 2004 674-706.

63. U.S. Department of General Services, Section 106: National Historic Preservation Act of 1966, https://www.gsa.gov/real-estate/historic-preservation/historic-preservation-policy-tools/legislation-policy-and-reports/

section-106-national-historic-preservation-act-of-1966 (accessed 7.19.22)

64. Bob Levey, Jane Freundel Levey, "End of Roads," *Washington Post*, Sunday, November 26, 2000.

65. Douglas B. Feaver, "No New Freeways Slated for District," *Washington Post*, October 30, 1978. https://www.washingtonpost.com/archive/politics/1978/10/30/no-new-freeways-slated-for-district/73617023-5f32-4617-99ae-edf7eab5192a/ (accessed 7.19.22).

66. *Baltimore Sun*, "Expressway Opponents Vilify Officials," Aug 7, 1969, pg. A10. ProQuest Historical Newspapers.

67. Helen Szablya, "Betty Deacon," transcribed interview available, https://archive.org/details/deacon_betty_01. (accessed 7.19.22)

68. Kermit C. Parsons, *The Baltimore Wars,* Cornell University, unpublished draft, p. 279-280

69. *Baltimore Sun*, "Foes Of Highway Rev Up Strategy In Angry Parley," *Baltimore Sun*, Aug 4, 1968; ProQuest Historical papers.

70. Parsons, p. 280

71. "In Baltimore new options are opened and alliances formed," University of Baltimore, RLB Library, Greater Rosemont Collection, 1950-68.

72. Lin Butler, Church of the Brethren and secretary to MAD, 1974 interview, East-West Expressway Collection, Maryland Center for History and Culture, transcribed by the author.

73. Earl Swift, P. 275.

74. Greg Freidman, "The Freeway Revolts: A Brief History of an Important Baltimore Grassroots Movement," July 24, 2013. http://envisionbaltimore.blogspot.com/2013/07/the-freeway-revolts-brief-history-of.html, accessed 1/28/2017.

75. Carolyn Tyson, 1974 Interview, East-West Expressway Collection, Maryland Center for History and Culture, transcribed by Evans Paull.

76. James Dilts, "Analysis: Highways obsess a poor, gas-short city," *Baltimore Sun*, Feb 24, 1974; ProQuest Historical Newspapers.

77. Carolyn Tyson, "Why the City is Broke," Movement Against Destruction, Feb. 22, 1974.

78. E-mail, David Hollander to Evans Paull, 10.26.20.

79. Norm Klein (UDCT staff) died in 1975 at 53 years old. John Weese (Project Manager of the Baltimore UDCT) died in 1985 at age 65. Joe Axelrod (Chief, Interstate Division), died in 1981 at age 75.

80. James D. Dilts, "The Changing City: Concept Team: Off Into The Sunset," *Baltimore Sun*, Jan 24, 1971, pg. D3, ProQuest Historical Newspapers.

81. James D. Dilts, "The Changing City: Concept Team: Off Into The Sunset," *Baltimore Sun*, Jan 24, 1971, pg. D3, ProQuest Historical Newspapers.

82. Library of Congress, "Waters of Destiny," https://www.wdl.org/en/item/14208/. And https://www.youtube.com/watch?v=rSwJaPlPvG0, (accessed 7.19.22)

83. Swift, p. 271.

84. Dimento and Ellis, p. 40-43.

85. Parsons, p. 19-20

86. James Macnees, "Federal-City Plan Aims at Road Design: New Concept Expected To Set Pattern For Nation," *Baltimore Sun*, 24 Sep 1967, Pro Quest Historical Newspapers.

87. Hopkinson, email to Evans Paull, noted in Jan 28, 2021 email, Evans Paull to Peter

Hopkinson, Dave Nutter, and Steve Zecher.

88. Parsons, p. 41.

89. Nathaniel Owings, "Urban Transportation Planning Concepts," *Traffic quarterly*. v.21, April, 1967. https://babel.hathitrust.org/cgi/pt?id=mdp.39015021323186&view=1up&seq=196.

90. Raymond A. Mohl, "Stop the Road..." 674-706.

91. John E Woodruff, "Schaefer's Road Advice: Give Up Plan," *Baltimore Sun* Aug 21, 1966, pg. 26, ProQuest Historical Newspapers.

92. *Baltimore Sun*, "Agreement Reached on Expressway: City Officials, Roads Agency in Accord," Feb 17 1967, pg. C24, ProQuest Historical Newspapers.

93. *Baltimore Sun*, "Expressways' Design Team Would Transcend Prettying," Apr 20, 1967, pg. C20. ProQuest Historical Newspapers.

94. *Baltimore Sun*, "Expressways' Design Team Would Transcend Prettying," April 20, 1967, University of Baltimore, Digital Archives, Regional collection.

95. *Baltimore Sun*, "Wolff, Werner Criticize Owings: Expressway Feud Develops Over Degree Of Control," Apr 20, 1967, pg. C20, ProQuest Historical Newspapers.

96. Horace Ayres, "Foes of Federal Hill Expressway Route Unite," *Baltimore Sun*, February 2, 1967, University of Baltimore, RLB Library, Digital Archives, Regional Collection.

97. Baltimore City Department of Planning, *Report on Lee-Hill Street Route*, January 4, 1963.

98. John E. Woodruff, Park Board Threatens Expressway - Seeks Guarantee From City For Federal Hill Extension, May 17, 1967, University of Baltimore Digital Archives, Regional Collection.

99. Woodruff, John E, "Park Board Threatens Expressway: Seeks Guarantee from City for Federal Hill Extension," *Baltimore Sun*, May 17, 1967

100. Janalee Keidel, Planning Board 'Capitulates' on Freeways," *Baltimore Sun*, May 27, 1967, Preservation Society archives.

101. Parsons, p. 106

102. Parsons, p. 101

103. Parsons, p. 116

104. Parsons, p. 181-182

105. The Fort McHenry Bypass was not a UDCT invention. It first appeared in Baltimore's highway plans in the 1949 "Tentative Transportation Plan."

106. Parsons, 193-196.

107. Wagner to Downs, IDBC memorandum, 12 July 1968, SOM/UDCA, cited in Parsons, p. 277

108. Parsons, P. 209

109. Parsons also indicates Axelrod knew about a secret meeting Owings had with Stewart Udall, Secretary of the Interior. Parsons comment is, "It seems Axelrod had established a "spy" in SOM's Washington Office." (Parsons, p. 353)

110. Parsons, p. 213.

111. Parsons, p. 301.

112. Parsons, p. 309.

113. Parsons, p. 313.

114. Parsons, p. 281

115. Parsons, p. 318

116. Memo, Wagner to Axelrod, 23 August 1968, cited in Parsons, p. 315.

117. Parsons, p. 322

118. *Baltimore Sun*, 26 August, 1968, cited in Parsons, p. 343.

119. Parsons, p 347-348.

120. Parsons, p. 353.

121. Parsons, p. 353.

122. Parsons p. 354.

123. The account of the speech is based on: Nathaniel A. Owings, "Baltimore and the Fifth Dimension," speech delivered at the Citizens Planning and Housing Association Fall Meeting held September 24, 1968, Lord Baltimore Hotel, Baltimore, Maryland, as cited in Parsons, p. 355-358; and Jane Keidel, "City Freeway Woes Likened To Viet War: Owings Says Growth Of Problem Leads To East-West Dilemma," *Baltimore Sun*, Sep 25, 1968, pg. C26, ProQuest Historical Newspapers. NOTE: There are some confusing uses of punctuation and verb tenses in the Parsons account. It is often difficult to discern quotes from Owings vs. paraphrasing from Parsons. Keep in mind that Parson's manuscript was a draft.

124. Parsons explains the "'Fifth Dimension in Planning' as referring to the new stress on public participation in decision making. Owings used the example of the audience at the Czech pavilion of EXPO 67 being able to decide (at the final crisis in a romantic film) on two opposite plot options by pressing a button... Owings believed that his speech to the CPHA was a distinct step in the process of planning in the fifth dimension, because the audience represented a broad spectrum of citywide interests.

125. Jane Keidel, "City Freeway Woes Likened To Viet War: Owings Says Growth Of Problem Leads To East-West Dilemma," Sep 25, 1968, pg. C26, ProQuest Historical Newspapers.

126. Parsons, p. 360

127. Parsons, p. 361

128. *Baltimore Sun*, 5 October 1968, cited in Parsons, p. 363.

129. *Baltimore Sun*, "Soft on People," Oct 6, 1968, pg. K4, ProQuest Historical Newspapers.

130. Axelrod to file, Subject: Meeting Held on September 30 with Concept Team Representatives for Discussion of Expressway Route Modifications, 1 October 1968, cited in Parsons, p.

131. Parsons, p. 363

132. Parsons, p. 364

133. Parsons, p. 372

134. *Baltimore Sun*, "Expressway Dove," Oct 1, 1968, pg. A12; ProQuest Historical Newspapers.

135. Parsons, p. 370

136. Parsons, p. 365.

137. *Baltimore Sun*, Oct 31, 1968, cited in Parsons, p. 371.

138. *Baltimore Sun*, "Two-for-One Plan." Oct 31, 1968, *Baltimore Sun*, ProQuest Historical Newspapers.

139. John B. O'Donnell, "Mayor's Route Choice Averts Harbor Span, Bypasses Rosemont: ...," *Baltimore Sun*, Dec 24, 1968; pg. C16; ProQuest Historical Newspapers.

140. Louise Campbell, "Architects of hwys treading forbidden turf divert threat to significant parts of city," *City Chronicle*, Jan, 1969

141. John B. O'Donnell, Jr. "Werner Says 3-A Will Clog City Streets: Ex-Works Chief Asks Mayor to Change Roads Plan," *Baltimore Sun*, Jan 2, 1969, pg. 40; ProQuest Historical Newspapers.

142. John B O'Donnell, "City's 3-A Route Wins Approval of U.S. Agency," *Baltimore Sun*, 18 Jan 1969, B20; ProQuest Historical Newspapers.

143. Janelee Keidel, "2 Planners Are Removed From Urban Design Team," *Baltimore Sun*, May 17, 1969, pg. B22; ProQuest Historical Newspapers.

144. Janelee Keidel, "Orlinsky Blasts City Design Unit: Planners Accused Of 'Breach Of Faith' On Highways," *Baltimore Sun*, Jul 19, 1969, pg. A12; ProQuest Historical Newspapers.

145. Janelee Keidel, "New Road Accord Reached," *Baltimore Sun* Sep 21, 1969 pg. SP13 ProQuest Historical Newspapers.

146. John O'Donnell, "Expressway Priorities Are Revised: Planning Commission's Proposals Are Put Last in Program," *Baltimore Sun*, 12 Sep 1969, C26. ProQuest Historical Newspapers

147. Greater Baltimore Committee, "Report of the Transportation Subcommittee to Greater Baltimore Committee Regarding the Status of the East- West Expressway," June, 1970, University of Baltimore digital archives, Regional Collection; and Kathy Kraus, "SRC Charged With Fighting Expressway: Toll Losses Feared If Expansion Proceeds," *Baltimore Sun*, Jun 14, 1970, p. 20, ProQuest Historical Newspapers.

148. Greater Baltimore Committee and Maryland Chamber of Commerce, "A Report to the Governor and the Mayor on the Crisis Developing Out of Baltimore's Failure to Move Forward with Its Freeway Program, October, 1970, University of Baltimore digital archives, Regional Collection.

149. James D. Dilts, "The Changing City: Concept Team - Off Into The Sunset," *Baltimore Sun*, Jan 24, 1971, pg. D3, ProQuest Historical Newspapers

150. James D. Dilts, "The Changing City: Concept Team - Off Into The Sunset," *Baltimore Sun*, Jan 24, 1971, pg. D3, ProQuest Historical Newspapers

151. *Baltimore Evening Sun*, "Mayor urged to send aides to explain highway policies," (undated) from the Preservation Society's archives.

152. James Dilts, "Locust Point bridge spurs angry debate: crowd of 500 at roads panel hearing," *Baltimore Sun*, Mar 31, 1971, pg. C22, ProQuest Historical Newspapers.

153. James D. Dilts, "New Harbor Bridge Study Set: Outside Consultant To Seek Alternative To Fort McHenry Span..." *Baltimore Sun*, Jun 24, 1971, pg. C20; ProQuest Historical Newspapers; and *Baltimore Sun*, "Actions Taken By Maryland General Assembly," Apr 9, 1971, pg. A8, ProQuest Historical Newspapers

154. Barry Rascovar, "Mayor Asks Roads Agency To Reconsider Tunnel Plan," *Baltimore Sun*, Jun 18, 1971, pg. C15, ProQuest Historical Newspapers

155. Edgar L. Jones, "A Conspiracy against the Expressway, not of Silence, but of Talk," *Baltimore Evening Sun*, Sept., 1971, Baltimore City Archives, Mayor William Donald Schaefer, BRG 9-42, Box 48.

156. Karen E. Warmkessel, "Tunnel ceremonies special for activist who fought City Hall to standstill," The *Baltimore Sun*, Jun 19, 1980, pg. D7, Baltimore City Archives, Mayor William Donald Schaefer, BRG 9-42, Box 48.

157. Reutter, Mark, "Santa Claus may bring Mayor Schaefer an enormous 'Bravo' scroll,"

Endnotes

The *Baltimore Sun*, Sep 4, 1978

158. Email Mary Logan to Evans Paull, "Transcripts and road fight in S Balt," Feb 21, 2021.

159. Greater Baltimore Committee, Sub-Committee on Transportation, Report on The Proposed 10-D-TL Interstate System," November , 1971, University of Baltimore digital archives, Regional Collection, Greater Baltimore Committee

160. Note that the Preservation Society's endorsement of the Fort McHenry Bypass happened the year before in March 1971. James D. Dilts, "Fort McHenry Bypass: Expressway opponents …," *Baltimore Sun*, Feb 28, 1972, pg. C16; ProQuest Historical Newspapers.

161. James Dilts, "Fort McHenry Bypass…"

162. James d. Dilts, "The road battle at Fort McHenry," *Baltimore Sun* Dec 8, 1974, pg. K1, ProQuest Historical Newspapers.

163. Roads to the Future, http://www.roadstothefuture.com/Fort_McHenry_Tunnel.html.

164. However, there was significant residential displacement for the downtown connector, I-395 through Sharp Leadenhall. See chapter 12.

165. Ports of America, Chesapeake, https://www.pachesapeake.com/ (accessed 7.19.22)

166. Maryland Port Administration, South Locust Point, https://mpa.maryland.gov/Pages/south-locust-point.aspx (accessed 7.19.22)

167. *Baltimore African American*, "X-way protestors term it: 'white man's road in the black man's neighborhood,'" September 18, 1971.

168. Ashley Halsey III, "A crusade to defeat the legacy of highways rammed through poor neighborhoods," *Washington Post*, March 29, 2016.

169. *New York Times*, "Baltimore tries drastic plan of race segregation," December 25, 1910, https://www.nytimes.com/1910/12/25/archives/baltimore-tries-drastic-plan-of-race-segregation-strange-situation.html.

170. Antero Pietila, *Not in My Neighborhood: How Bigotry Shaped a Great American City,* Ivan R. Dee, publisher, Chicago, p. 36

171. Pietila, p. 58.

172. Pietila, p. 50. Note the Baltimore Heritage account of Preston Garden's history acknowledges that there was thriving African American neighborhood that was knocked out by the park plan, but the account stresses the city beautification objective and does not mention "Negro removal." https://explore.baltimoreheritage.org/items/show/71 (accessed 7/12/2020)

173. J Anthony Lukas, "Mount Royal Fight Looms on Renewal: Neighborhood Split on Clearance of Linden," The *Baltimore Sun*, Mar 14, 1960; pg. 28. ProQuest Historical Newspapers.

174. *Baltimore Sun*, "Race and Renews," letter to the editor, Dec 1963, p. 22.

175. The author suspects that the 30 percent homeownership rate counted land installment contracts as rentals, and the "close to 50 percent" estimate counted land installment arrangements as homeownership. Sources, respectively: Mohl, R.A, "Stop the road: Freeway revolts in American cities," *Journal of Urban History* 30 (5): 674-706; and Amanda K. Phillips De Lucas, "Producing the 'Highway to Nowhere': Social Understandings of Space in Baltimore, 1944-1974," Cary Institute of Ecosystem Studies, Engaging Science, Technology, and Society 6 (2020), 351-369.

176. Baltimore Heritage, "Harlem Park," https://baltimoreheritage.org/programs/harlem-park/, accessed 7.17.22.

177. Donald S. Frank, "An assessment of the stewardship program," July 1957, University of Baltimore, RLB Library, Greater Baltimore Committee collection, series III, box 1, folder "Harlem Park --- Urban Renewal."

178. Andrew M. Giguere, " '...And never the twain shall meet': Baltimore's east-west expressway and the construction of the 'Highway to Nowhere.' " June 2009, College of Arts and Sciences of Ohio University.

179. Blair and Stein Associates, *The Impact of the East-West and Southwest Expressways in Baltimore, a Socio-economic Assessment*, 1962. University of Baltimore, Digital Archives, MAD Collection.

180. James D Dilts, "City hopes to start corridor road soon," *Baltimore Sun*, Oct 10, 1972, pg. C22, ProQuest Historical Newspapers.

181. Blair and Stein   Associates, *Impacts of the East - West and Southwest Expressways on the City of Baltimore*, Maryland State Roads Commission, June, 1962.

182. Laurie Willis, "Road to remembrance; Reunion: Former childhood pals whose neighborhoods were broken up by the I-170 project plan to recall old times in a gathering today," *Baltimore Sun*, 25 Oct 2003, 1A, and *Baltimore Sun*, "Residents divided by I-170 plans meet again; Reunion, memories sweet for former city neighbors," 26 Oct 2003, 3B.

183. B*altimore Evening Sun*, "Road building and racial unrest are linked," February 13, 1968, Baltimore City Archives, William Donald Schaefer collection.

184. Richard Basoco, "West Baltimore is an ugly no-man's land," *Baltimore Sun*, April 9, 1968, Pro Quest Historical Newspapers.

185. James D Dilts, "The Changing City: "Expressway 'Victims' Fight Back," *Baltimore Sun*, Mar 17, 1968, pg. D3; ProQuest Historical Newspapers.

186. Archives of Maryland, (Biographical Series), Theodore R. McKeldin (1900-1974), MSA SC 3520-1484. https://msa.maryland.gov/megafile/msa/speccol/sc3500/sc3520/001400/001484/html/1484extbio.html, (accessed 7.19.22).

187. James Dilts, "Franklin-Mulberry highway's cost is double 1972 estimate," The *Baltimore Sun*, Oct 1, 1975, pg. C1; ProQuest Historical Newspapers.

188. James D Dilts, "The Changing City: Haunted Village, Living under the threat of an impending expressway takes a human toll that the highway engineers and other planners have not yet begun to count," *Baltimore Sun*, Oct 13, 1968, pg. D1. Pro Quest Historical Newspapers

189. Relocation Action Movement, "A History of the Relocation Action Movement," undated, University of Baltimore, Digital Archives, MAD Collection.

190. Relocation Action Movement, "A history…"

191. Gene Oishi, "Agnew Asks Acquisition Policy Study: Families Displaced by Expressway Prompt Governor's Move," The *Baltimore Sun*, Oct 14, 1967, pg. B20, ProQuest Historical Newspapers

192. James D. Dilts, The Changing City: "Haunted Village…"

193. James D Dilts, "The Changing City: "Haunted Village…"

194. Norman M. Klein, "Baltimore Joint Development Project," Skidmore, Owings & Merrill, paper presented at the Conference on Joint Development, 1968, Highway Research Board.

195. Dilts, James D, "3-block platform project postponed," *Baltimore Sun*, Jun 13, 1972; p. C15, ProQuest Historical Newspapers.

196. Dilts, James D, "3-block…"

197. Klein, "Baltimore Joint…"

198. Klein, "Baltimore Joint…"

199. Highway Research Board, "Joint Development and Multiple Use of Transportation Rights-of-Way, Proceedings of a Conference Held November 14-15, 1968 Washington, DC, National Academy of Sciences -National Academy of Engineering, Publication 1459, 1969, Washington, DC.

200. James D Dilts, "Franklin-Mulberry highway's cost is double 1972 estimate," The *Baltimore Sun*, Oct 1, 1975, C1, ProQuest Historical Newspapers

201. Maryland Department of Transportation, letter Richard Trainor to Mayor William Donald Schaefer, March 22, 1974, Mayor William Donald Schaefer, BRG 9-42.

202. William Donald Schaefer, letter to Susan Anderson, The New Democratic Club, Inc., March 27, 1974, University of Baltimore, RLB Library, MAD archives.

203. Carolyn Tyson, Letter to William Donald Schaefer, undated, but likely 1972, University of Baltimore RLB Library Digital Archives, MAD Collection, Carolyn Tyson correspondence.

204. *Baltimore Sun*, "One More Loop," Jan 26, 1983, pg. A10, ProQuest Historical Newspapers.

205. Aileen Canzian, "None spoke for blacks uprooted by highway," The Sun, Jun 2, 1980.

206. Andrew M. Giguere, " '…And never the twain shall meet': Baltimore's east-west expressway and the construction of the 'Highway to Nowhere,'" June 2009, College of Arts and Sciences of Ohio University.

207. Baltimore City Health Department, Baltimore City 2017 Neighborhood Health Profile, Sandtown-Winchester/Harlem Park, 2017.

208. JoAnna Daemmrich and Robert G. Matthews, "Highway idea aims to go somewhere: Schmoke wants homes back that road ended, The *Baltimore Sun*, March 16, 1997. https://www.baltimoresun.com/news/bs-xpm-1997-03-16-1997075027-story.html (accessed 7.19.22)

209. Carver Bain, "Arena Players draws on Baltimore history, November 17, 2016, Johns Hopkins University Newsletter, https://www.jhunewsletter.com/article/2016/11/arena-players-draws-on-baltimore-history/ (accessed 7.19.22)

210. Michael Dresser, "Hogan says no to Red Line, yes to Purple," *Baltimore Sun*, Jun 25, 2015.

211. Glenn Smith email to Evans Paull, June 3, 2020

212. Angie Schmitt, "Anthony Foxx Wants to Repair the Damage Done by Urban Highways, Mar 30, 2016, https://usa.streetsblog.org/2016/03/30/anthony-foxx-wants-to-repair-the-damage-done-by-urban-highways/ (accessed 7.19.22)

213. Sumathi Reddy, "Revival Hope Rides on Marc Rail Stop; West Baltimore Station Seen As Key To New Life In A Section Scarred By An Aborted 1970s Road Project," The *Baltimore Sun*, 23 Apr 2007, p. 1A.

214. Reddy, "Revival…"

215. JoAnna Daemmrich and Robert G. Matthews, "Highway idea aims to go somewhere: Schmoke wants homes back that road ended," The *Baltimore Sun*, March 16, 1997. https://www.baltimoresun.com/news/bs-xpm-1997-03-16-1997075027-story.html (accessed 7.19.22).

216. Society for Preservation of Fell's Point, Federal Hill, and Montgomery Street, Bob Eney, in memoriam, comment originally posted at Nextdoor Historic Fell's Point.

217. E. C Pelio, "Recreating Lost Neighborhoods: The House on Ann Street, Fell's Point, Baltimore City, Maryland," Remembering Baltimore Blog, Nov. 29, 2016. http://www.rememberingbaltimore.net/2016/11/recreating-lost-neighborhoods-house-on.html, (accessed 7.17.22).

218. Jacqueline Greff, "Bob Eney Interview," Tonal Vision LLC, Fell's Point Out of Time living history interview, January 21, 2004.

219. Greff, Fell's Point Out of Time, Bob Eney Interview…

220. Norman Rukert, The Fell's Point Story, Bodine & Associates, January 1, 1976

221. Post on the Preservation Society website, but now removed.

222. Scott Shane, The Baltimore Sun, "The Baltimore Slave Trade," June 1999, copied to the website: https://usslave.blogspot.com/2011/08/baltimore-city-slave-trade.html. (accessed 7.19.22)

223. Rukert, The Fell's Point… p. 69.

224. Soul of America, the Fun, Comprehensive and Trusted Black Travel Guide, Fell's Point. https://www.soulofamerica.com/us-cities/baltimore/Fell's-point/ (accessed 7.19.22)

225. Maryland Historical Society, Library Department, "A Safe Harbor: The Port Mission in Fell's Point, November 14, 2013. https://www.mdhistory.org/a-safe-harbor-the-port-mission-in-Fell's-point/, (accessed 7.19.22)

226. Hamilton Owens, Baltimore on the Chesapeake (Garden City, N. Y.:Doubleday, Doran & Company, Inc., 1941), 45-46, cited in Maryland Historical Society, Library Department, "A Safe Harbor: The Port Mission in Fell's Point, November 14, 2013.

227. Blair and Stein Associates, Impacts of the East – West and Southwest Expressways on the City of Baltimore, for the Maryland State Roads Commission, June 1962.

228. Mrs. Murray A. Fisher, letter to Urban Design Concept Team, Feb. 20, 1969. University of Baltimore RLB Library, SCAR digital collections, Preservation Society Position Papers, Design Concept Team.

229. Interview of Tom Ward by Evans Paull, John Kern, and Nate Pretl, December 15, 2015.

230. Jacques Kelly, "Waterfront neighborhoods slowly eroded." Baltimore Evening Sun, Feb 19, 1992.

231. Horace Ayres, Foes of Federal Hill Expressway Route Unite," Baltimore Evening Sun, February 27, 1967, University of Baltimore, RLB Library, Digital Archives, Regional Collection.

232. Tracie Rozhon, "Lucretia B. Fisher fought City Hall--and won," Baltimore Sun, Feb 15, 1976, pg. A24. ProQuest Historical Newspapers.

233. Jacqueline Greff, Tonal Vision, Interview of Romaine Somerville & Diana Hyde, Fell's Point Out of Time living history series, January 26, 2004.

234. Lucretia B Fisher, "Druid Hill Riots," Baltimore Sun, Apr 20, 1963, pg. 12; ProQuest Historical Newspapers.

235. Tracie Rozhon, "Lucretia B. Fisher fought City Hall--and won," Baltimore Sun, Feb 15, 1976, pg. A24. ProQuest Historical Newspapers.

236. Jacquie & Kraig Greff, Interview of Lu Fisher, Fell's Point Out of Time living history series, Tonal Vision, April 28, 2003. https://www.tonalvision.com/images/fpoot_transcripts/Lu_Fisher_042803.pdf (accessed 7.19.22).

237. Fisher, Lucretia B, "Heritage to Preserve," The Baltimore Sun, Mar 21, 1966; ProQuest Historical Newspapers, pg. A10.

238. Keidel, Jane L, "Renovations At Fell's Point Aid In Rediscovering Area," Baltimore Sun,

Dec 10, 1967; ProQuest Historical Newspapers, P. 36.

239. Tracie Rozhon, "Lucretia B. Fisher fought City Hall--and won," *Baltimore Sun*, Feb 15, 1976, pg. A24. ProQuest Historical Newspapers.

240. Jacquie & Kraig Greff, Interview of Romaine Somerville & Diana Hyde, Tonal Vision, Fell's Point Out of Time living history series, January 26, 2004.

241. *Baltimore Sun*, "Expressway Bill Voted Suit Is Vowed: Ward Threatens Action As Council Approves...," The Sun, Nov 21, 1967, pg. C24, ProQuest Historical Newspapers.

242. Frederick B. Hill, "Houses vs. the Highway," *Baltimore Sun*, Mar 9, 1967; Preservation Society archives.

243. Jane L Keidel, "300 Fell's Point Folk Hoot Down 'Silk Stockings,'" *Baltimore Sun*, May 24, 1967, pg. C28, ProQuest Historical Newspapers.

244. Jacques Kelly, "The Fell's Point Fun Festival Was City's Coming-Out Party," *Baltimore Sun*, Oct. 6, 2006.

245. Stephen A Bennett, "Fell's Point Throws Splash Party: Thousands Sample Art, Music, Food In Area Now Under Shadow Of Expressway," *Baltimore Sun*, 09 Oct 1967, C22.

246. Fell's Point Doom Turns to Boom," *Baltimore Sun*, April 12, 1967, University of Baltimore RLB Library Digital Archives, Regional Collection.

247. James D Dilts, "The Changing City: Fell's Point-Good-by To All That?" *Baltimore Sun* Feb 16, 1969, pg. D3. ProQuest Historical Newspapers

248. Norman G. Rukert, *The Fell's Point...* p. 97.

249. Baltimore Chapter of the American Institute of Architects, "Resolution on Fell's Point," May 26, 1969, University of Baltimore RLB Library, digital collections, Preservation Society Position Papers.

250. Letter William D. Elder to Mrs. Murray Fisher, Dec. 20 1968, University of Baltimore RLB Library, digital collections, Preservation Society records 1966 to 1969.

251. (Unknown author), "Notes on Presentation by Joseph Axelrod at the Engineers Club," October 29, 1969. University of Baltimore RLB Library, digital collections, MAD Collection.

252. *Baltimore Sun*, "Expressway Path Decried: Irate Citizens Get DiPietro To Sponsor Bypass Bill," May 23, 1969, pg. 3, ProQuest Historical Newspapers.

253. Janelee Keidel, "Thousands Throng To Fell's Point Fun Fest: Day Features Carnival, ..." *Baltimore Sun*

254. MAD Newsletter, December, 1969, Volume 1, number 6. pg. C22, Oct 6, 1969; ProQuest Historical Newspapers.

255. Tony Norris, Interview with Evans Paull, 2020.

256. Jacqueline Greff, Bob Eney Interview...

257. United States Department of The Interior, National Park Service, National Register of Historic Places Inventory - Nomination Form, Fell's Point Historic District, case number, 69-03-19-0001, March 28, 1969.

258. Undated letter to the Editor, from the papers of Tom Ward, later donated to the University of Baltimore RLB library.

259. The term "Mr. History" refers to a column in the Fell's Point Gazette that was attributed to Bob Eney, but Eney, who was dyslexic and had great difficulty writing, maintained that he never wrote the column.

260. Jacques Kelly, "Robert L. Eney, regarded as champion of Fell's Point, dies," the *Baltimore*

Sun,

261. Jacqueline Greff, Steve Bunker Interview, Fell's Point Out of Time Living History Project, Tonal Vision LLC, Dec. 7, 2003.

262. Letter Geoff Mitchell to Margaret Dougherty, Preservation Society archives.

263. Society for the Preservation of Federal Hill Montgomery Street and Fell's Point, "Position Statement," November 15 1968, University of Baltimore RLB library, Digital collections, SCAR collection.

264. Lu Fisher letter from Preservation Society to Urban Design Concept Team, February 20, 1969 University of Baltimore RLB Library, digital collections.

265. Baltimore Sun, "Corridor May Claim 100 Fells Point Houses: Proposed East-West Path ...," December 18, 1970, pg. C22; ProQuest Historical Newspapers.

266. Urban Design Concept Associates, Corridor Development, Segments 4 and 5, 1971.

267. James D. Dilts, "The Changing City: Concept Team: Off Into The Sunset," *Baltimore Sun,* Jan 24, 1971, pg. D3; ProQuest Historical Newspapers.

268. Preservation Society Meeting Minutes, June 24, 1970 and June 16, 1971, University of Baltimore RLB Library, digital collections, Preservation Society minutes, 1970, 1971.

269. Preservation Society, Minutes, June 20, 1973, University of Baltimore RLB Library, digital collections, Preservation Society, minutes, 1973.

270. Preservation Society Board Meeting, April 18, 1975, University of Baltimore RLB Library, digital collections, Preservation Society, minutes, 1973.

271. Preservation Society, Minutes, October 20, 1973, University of Baltimore RLB Library, digital collections, Preservation Society, minutes, 1973.

272. Preservation Society, Minutes, November 10, 1976, University of Baltimore RLB Library, digital collections, Preservation Society, minutes, 1974-86.

273. Preservation Society membership letter, January, 1977, Preservation Society archives.

274. Andrew M. Giguere, " '...And never the twain shall meet': Baltimore's east-west expressway and the construction of the 'Highway to Nowhere.' " June 2009, College of Arts and Sciences of Ohio University.

275. James Dilts, "100 Fell's Point Houses May Go," *Baltimore Sun,* Dec 18, 1970; ProQuest Historical Newspapers.

276. Kraig Greff, interview of PJ Trautwein, January 23, 2004, Fell's Point Out of Time living history project, Tonal Vision.

277. James D Dilts, "The Changing City: NECO And SECO Say-You Can Fight City Hall, The Sun, 09 May 1971. D3.

278. Email, Joe McNeely to Evans Paull, subject: "Mikulski, SECO/Gleason," 9.3.2020.

279. *Baltimore Sun,* "John C. Gleason Sr.," obituary, August 5, 1992. https://www.baltimoresun.com/news/bs-xpm-1992-08-06-1992219002-story.html (accessed 8/29/20).

280. Jack Gleason, interview, 1974, Maryland Center for History and Culture, East-West Expressway collection, transcribed by Evans Paull

281. The Urban Design Group, "Fell's Point historic district, Baltimore, Maryland, a survey, evaluation and interpretation of architectural and environmental values associated with structures and areas within the district," for Interstate Division of Baltimore City, August, 1970.

282. The *Baltimore Sun,* "Fell's Point Route Is Upheld," May 21, 1971, pg. A10. ProQuest Historical Newspapers.

283. Norman Rukert, *The Fell's Point...* p. 92.

284. Preservation Society, Minutes, August 16, 1972, University of Baltimore RLB Library, digital collections, Preservation Society, minutes, 1972.

285. Carolyn Tyson, 1974 Interview, East-West Expressway Collection, Maryland Center for History and Culture, transcribed by Evans Paull.

286. James D Dilts, "Expressways to spare harbor area," *Baltimore Sun*, Mar 30, 1974, pg. B20; ProQuest Historical Newspapers.

287. Nancy J Schwerzler, "Fell's Point residents fear I-83 will blight area," *Baltimore Sun*, Jan 29, 1975, pg. C1. ProQuest Historical Newspapers.

288. Department of Transportation, "Combined Location Design Public Hearing and Public Information Meeting, National Historic Preservation Act, I-83 Gay Street to I-95, Informational Summary," January 28th, 1975.

289. Preservation Society, resolution by the Historic Fell's Point and Federal Hill Fund, Inc. January 22, 1975, University of Baltimore RLB Library, digital collections, Preservation Society, Correspondence, 1970 – 1975. Note that a draft position paper in the Preservation Society acknowledges that the two underwater tunnel options had the least adverse impact. It is not clear whether this position paper was finalized and entered into the public record.

290. Richard Ben Cramer, "Mikulski anti-road rhetoric recalls her 3-A opposition," *Baltimore Sun*, Oct 15, 1975; pg. C2. ProQuest Historical Newspapers.

291. Richard Ben Cramer, "Mikulski anti-road rhetoric recalls her 3-A opposition," *Baltimore Sun*, Oct 15, 1975; pg. C2. ProQuest Historical Newspapers.

292. Lucretia B. Fisher, undated testimony (likely delivered at the hearings held by the Advisory Council for Historic Preservation, Feb 2-3, 1977), Society for the Preservation of Federal Hill and Fell's Point, University of Baltimore, RLB Library, Special Collections Department, "Correspondence re section 106 and Presidents advisory council."

293. Maryland State Historic Preservation Officer, "Section 106 case report, Maryland State historic Preservation Officer, Interstate 83 from Gay Street to I-95," January 17, 1977.

294. The Advisory Council on Historic Preservation, "On an undertaking by the Department of Transportation having an effect upon properties in Baltimore MD that are included in the National Register of Historic Places, that are National Historic Landmarks and that meet the criteria for inclusion in the National Register of Historic Places." Undated, reflects actions considered in Council meetings on May 4 and 5, 1977.

295. Tracie Rozhon, "Planning commission supports I-83, I-395 expressway moves," *Baltimore Sun*, Jun 10, 1977, pg. D4. ProQuest Historical Newspapers.

296. Donald Kimelman, "Expressway repeal accepted, releasing Fell's Point houses," The *Baltimore Sun*, May 26, 1977, pg. C24, ProQuest Historical Newspapers.

297. Ed Orser, "Race and Place in Greater Rosemont," Baltimore Heritage; https://baltimoreheritage.org/programs/race-and-place-in-greater-rosemont/, (accessed 7.19.22)

298. Blair and Stein Associates, "Impacts of the East - West and Southwest Expressways on the City of Baltimore, Maryland State Roads Commission, June, 1962.

299. Parsons, p. 206.

300. Parsons, p. 208.

301. Barbara Mikulski, 1974 Interview, East-West Expressway Collection, Maryland Center for History and Culture, transcribed by Evans Paull.

302. James D. Dilts, "Expressway, Now it's Money," *Baltimore Sun*, May 24, 1971; andParsons, p. 206.

303. James D Dilts, "Changing City--'We Must Destroy You To...'," *Baltimore Sun*, Aug 4, 1968, pg. FD3; ProQuest Historical Newspapers.

304. Earl Swift, *The Big Roads: The Untold Story of the Engineers, Visionaries, and Trailblazers Who Created the American Superhighways,* September 18, 2012.

305. Maryland State Roads Commission, "Chronology of Rosemont Bypass Studies, Location Study Report, I-170," Aug. 12, 1970, University of Baltimore, RLB Library, MAD collection.

306. Kermit C. Parsons, The Baltimore Wars, Cornell University, unpublished draft, p. 212.

307. Earl Swift, *The Big Roads*, p. 277.

308. *Baltimore Sun*, December 11, 1967 cited Parsons, The Baltimore Wars, p. 230.

309. This section uses the following sources: Earl Swift, *The Big Roads: The Untold Story of the Engineers, Visionaries, and Trailblazers Who Created the American Superhighways,* September 18, 2012; *Baltimore Sun*, "Joseph Sinclair Wiles, 84, vaccination gun inventor," (obituary) 11.25.98; *Baltimore Evening Sun*, "Post pharmacologist works to improve neighborhood," undated, University of Baltimore, RLB Library, Rosemont Collection; Kelly, Jacques, "An Activist's Gift of a History: A Longtime Collector of Neighborhood News Provides the Rosemont Community with a Detailed Archive, a Personal Diary, The *Baltimore Sun*, 21 Feb 2009, pg. A.5; Jacques Kelly, "Mary Rosemond, community activist, dies, Former elementary school teacher was a Rosemont leader who assembled a noteworthy archive of community life," *Baltimore Sun*, January 28, 2011.

310. Swift, pp. 231-235

311. Swift, p. 231.

312. Swift p. 234

313. Swift p. 234

314. Jacques Kelly, "An activist's 'gift of a history,' a long-time collector...," *Baltimore Sun*, Feb. 21, 2009.

315. *Baltimore Sun*, "Expressway Route," 14 Aug 1968, A10, Pro-Quest Historical Papers.

316. Christian Science Monitor, "Roads: In Baltimore, new options are opened and new alliances formed." Undated article, University of Baltimore, Digital Archives, Regional Collection, Rosemont, 1952 – 1968; and Memo Embry to D'Alesandro, August 7, 1968 cited in Parsons, 283.

317. James D Dilts, Changing City--'We Must Destroy You To...,' The *Baltimore Sun*, Aug 4, 1968, pg. FD3; ProQuest Historical Newspapers.

318. The *Baltimore Sun*, "Two-for-One Plan," editorial, Oct 31, 1968, pg. A18; ProQuest Historical Newspapers.

319. *Baltimore Sun*, "Owings Vows to Bar Road: Design Team Head Backs Foes of Rosemont Route," Jul 30, 1969, pg. A10; ProQuest Historical Newspapers.

320. Janelee Keidel, "An expressway bridges a gulf between people: Rosemont hearings draw ...," *Baltimore Sun*, Aug 17, 1969 pg. K2.

321. *Baltimore Sun*, "Expressway Opponents Vilify Officials," Aug 7, 1969, pg. A10, ProQuest Historical Newspapers.

322. *Baltimore Sun*, "Ulterior Designs Hinted In Urban Design Offices," Aug 27, 1969; pg. C6; ProQuest Historical Newspapers.

323. (Unknown author), "Notes on Presentation by Joseph Axelrod at the Engineers Club," October 29, 1969. University of Baltimore RLB Library, digital collections, MAD

Endnotes

Collection.

324. Movement Against Destruction, "MAD Statement, December 10, 1969." University of Baltimore, RLB Library, MAD archives.

325. Joseph Wiles, letter to Baltimore City Council, January 24, 1972, Rosemont Community Association, January 24, 1972. Baltimore City Archives, Mayor William Donald Schaefer, BRG 9-42, Box 77.

326. Lieb, "White man's lane…"

327. Lieb, "White man's lane…"

328. Jerry Bembry, "Drug trade, fear challenge a neighborhood's stability," *Baltimore Sun*, Sep 25, 1988, p. 1A; ProQuest Historical Newspapers.

329. *Baltimore Sun*, "Mayor Claims Big Housing Shift: Tells Cleveland Group Of Massive Move To County," Apr 11, 1969; pg. A7; ProQuest Historical Newspapers.

330. Dill McBride Stewart, "'The Road' That Turned Anger Into Unity," The *Baltimore Sun*, Nov 13, 1977; ProQuest Historical Newspapers.

331. *Baltimore Sun*, "Urban development group elects new board member," Jun 5, 1977; ProQuest Historical Newspapers.

332. Norman Rukert, "*Historic Canton,*" Bodine and Assoc, 1978, p. 91.

333. Kathy Kraus, "Home Crisis Is Aired At Road Debate: Need For Low-Income Housing Held Critical," *Baltimore Sun*, Aug 26, 1970, pg. C22; ProQuest Historical Newspapers.

334. Wikipedia, Barbara Mikulski, https://en.wikipedia.org/wiki/Barbara_Mikulski, (Accessed 7.19.22)

335. Barbara Mikulski, "Who Speaks for Ethnic America: He Came in Search of Freedom and a Job But What Did He Find?" pg. 43, Sep 29, 1970. ProQuest Historical Newspapers.

336. Barbara Mikulski, "Anti-Expressway Speech," Delivered at a Public Meeting at St. Brigid's Hall June 29, 1971, University of Baltimore, RLB Library, SCAR digital archives.

337. Originally from separate 2018 interviews of Betty Deacon and Joe McNeely; the stories were combined (using Deacon's version as the starting point) as a word document entitled "The Great Truck Blockade" and transmitted via email, Joe McNeely to Evans Paull, dated Dec. 3, 2020.

338. Rafael Alvarez, "Park planned for waterfront in Canton area," *Baltimore Sun* May 6, 1985, pg. 1D; ProQuest Historical Newspapers.

339. Rafael Alvarez, "New Canton rises on painful memories: Residents from two decades ago still pine for the homes…" *Baltimore Sun*, Jun 19, 1988, pg. 1A; ProQuest Historical Newspapers.

340. Baltimore City Department of Planning, Sharp Leadenhall Neighborhood Profile, 2004.

341. James D Dilts, "Sharp Leadenhall foes at the end of their road," *Baltimore Sun*, Oct 20, 1975, pg. C16; ProQuest Historical Newspapers.

342. Baltimore City Department of Planning and Commission for Historical and Architectural Preservation, "Sharp Leadenhall Historic Resources Survey," 2004.

343. Baltimore City Department of Planning and Commission for Historical and Architectural Preservation, p.7.

344. Baltimore City Department of Planning and Commission for Historical and Architectural Preservation, "Sharp Leadenhall Historic Resources Survey," 2004.

345. Mark Reuter, "Sharp Leadenhall is given rebuilding priority pledge," The *Baltimore Sun*, Aug 2, 1977, pg. C16. ProQuest Historical Newspapers.

346. Sharp Leadenhall Planning Committee, "Sharp Leadenhall, a Promise to Keep," Megaphone Project, https://www.youtube.com/watch?v=OLFHq94GikE (accessed 7.19.22).

347. Anthropology by the Wire Project, "Sharp Leadenhall Oral History Project," https://www.youtube.com/watch?v=0avcddvtZbk, (accessed 7.19.22)

348. Anthropology by the Wire Project, "Sharp…"

349. Scott Beyer, "How the U.S. Government Destroyed Black Neighborhoods, Post-World War II Urban Renewal Replaced Thriving Black Hubs with Highways and Public Housing. https://catalyst.independent.org/2020/04/02/how-the-u-s-government-destroyed-black-neighborhoods/

350. Herbert J. Gans, "The Failure of Urban Renewal," Commentary Magazine, APRIL 1965, https://www.commentarymagazine.com/articles/herbert-gans/the-failure-of-urban-renewal/, (accessed 7.19.22).

351. U.S. Department of Transportation and the Maryland Department, "Draft Environmental Impact Statement, Supplement, City Boulevard Ring… and I-395…," December, 1976. Google Books.

352. Properties impacted: I-95—blocks bounded by Henrietta, Leadenhall, Ostend, and Plum; Southwest connector—blocks bounded by Montgomery, Hanover, Henrietta, and Plum. Note it is not clear how many properties were acquired in the 10-D Modified condemnation line before 3-A was adopted and rendered much of the former condemnation line obsolete.

353. Jane L. Reidel, "Changes Backed for Expressway: an Amended Condemnation Law…," *Baltimore Sun*, Nov 4, 1967, pg. B18; ProQuest Historical Newspapers.

354. Tracie Rozhon, "Condemnation line narrowed in two expressway areas," *Baltimore Sun*, Jun 12, 1973, pg. C24, ProQuest Historical Newspapers.

355. U.S. Department of Transportation and the Maryland Department, "Draft Environmental Impact Statement, Supplement, City Boulevard Ring… and I-395…," December, 1976. Google Books.

356. The three blocks affected include all three of the blocks designated for Otterbein homesteading, bounded by Barre, Hanover, Hughes, and Sharp streets. Note that the northern boundary of Sharp Leadenhall is not well established and changed at various points in history. Several reference documents put the northern boundary at Hill Street. We are counting all three blocks because, historically, the neighborhood certainly extended that far north (to Barre Street), and because the demographic characteristics of the people that were relocated aligns with Sharp Leadenhall. Additionally, to the southwest of the homesteading area, much of the 800 block of Sharp Street was acquired under the Sharp Leadenhall Urban Renewal Plan but was later redeveloped as part of Otterbein.

357. Baltimore City Department of Planning, "Sharp Leadenhall" Community Profile, January, 2004.

358. Joe Mathews, "They still miss Mildred Dead 4 years, leader of Sharp Leadenhall is hard to replace," *Baltimore Sun*, Feb. 5, 1997.

359. Fred Barbash, "Volpe Might Delay City's Expressway: Displaced Residents Must Be Relocated," The *Baltimore Sun*, Jun 26, 1970, pg. C24, ProQuest Historical Newspapers.

360. James D Dilts, "Sharp Leadenhall foes at the end of their road," *Baltimore Sun*, Oct 20, 1975, pg. C16; ProQuest Historical Newspapers.

Endnotes

361. Mark Reutter, "Group seeks housing for Sharp Leadenhall," Aug 1, 1977, pg. C14; ProQuest Historical Newspapers.

362. Baltimore City Department of Planning, "Sharp Leadenhall" Community Profile, January, 2004.

363. Pamela Constable, "A community after the whirlwind," *Baltimore Sun*, Jun 28, 1981, pg. T1, ProQuest Historical Newspapers; and Jack Dawson, "Sharp Leadenhall folk return to neighborhood," *Baltimore Sun*, 28 June 1981, pg. T10.

364. McCarthy, pp 142-143.

365. Zillow. https://www.zillow.com/otterbein-baltimore-md/home-values/, (accessed 7.19.22)

366. Natalie Sherman, "Renewal plan brings hope, worry to Sharp Leadenhall," *Baltimore Sun*, 25 June 2014, pg. A.1.

367. http://www.city-data.com/neighborhood/Sharp Leadenhall-Baltimore-MD.html.

368. Baltimore City Commission for Architectural and Historic Preservation, listing for Little Montgomery Street, https://chap.baltimorecity.gov/little-montgomery-street (accessed May 16, 2022)

369. Telephone and in office conversations with Brent Flickinger, former District Planner, Baltimore City Department of Planning, Eric Holcomb, Division Chief, Commission for Historical and Architectural Preservation, and Evans Paull, 2021, and 2022.

370. Joe Matthews, "They still miss Mildred Dead 4 years, leader of Sharp Leadenhall is hard to replace, *Baltimore Sun*, Feb. 5, 1997.

371. Author Sidney Wong's analysis of UDCT contains a speculative footnote: "it was rumored that Agnew owned property in the 10-D corridor, and that might explain the resistance to 3-A." (Journal of Planning History, "Architects and Planners in the Middle of a Road War: The Urban Design Concept Team in Baltimore, 1966-71). One of my interviewees, Steve Zecher (UDCT staff) repeated this rumor; however, the only record I could find was a news article that linked Agnew to a property that was required for a Bay Bridge project, not the Baltimore highway projects.

372. James D Dilts, "Plenty of tracks, but no trains," The *Baltimore Sun*, Mar 3, 1974, pg. K3. ProQuest Historical Newspapers.

373. Robert A Erlandson, "Wolf admits taking $72,000 for self," *Baltimore Sun*, Jan 24, 1974, pg. A1. ProQuest Historical Newspapers.

374. Fred Barbash, "Ban placed on 2 firms tied to probe," *Baltimore Sun*, 11 Aug 1973.

375. James D. Dilts, "La. indicts city road contractor," The *Baltimore Sun* 26 Oct 1973: C24.

376. James D. Dilts, Designing firm also linked to 3-A impact study," 12 Oct 1973: C24.

377. Carolyn Tyson, 1974 Interview, East-West Expressway Collection, Maryland Center for History and Culture, transcribed by Evans Paull.

378. George L Scheper, "Debate and Discussion: Leakin Park, a Disputed Highway Route," *Baltimore Sun* (date needed)

379. Chams blogspot, http://chamspage.blogspot.com/2010/08/ghosts-of-leakin-park.html (accessed 7.10.22)

380. Johns Hopkins, "Crimea Estate at Leakin Park," Baltimore Heritage, https://explore.baltimoreheritage.org/items/show/30, (accessed 7.19.22)

381. Elkridge Heritage, "A thing or two to Know about Ross Winans," https://www.elkridgeheritage.org/knitn-picn/a-thing-or-2-abt-ross-winans/; https://en.wikipedia.org/wiki/Ross_Winans; and The Hopkins-Thomas Project, http://www.

thehopkinthomasproject.com/TheHopkinThomasProject/TimeLine/GenealogyPortraits/
RossWinans.htm, (all accessed 7.19.22).

382. Olmsted Brothers, "Report and Recommendations on Park Extension for Baltimore,"
1926

383. Friends of Olmstead Parks and Landscapes, "Leakin Park, Frederick Olmsted Jr.'s
Critical Advice," The Olmstedian, Volume 16, Issue 1, fall, 2006.

384. Carrie Murray Nature Center, https://www.carriemurraynaturecenter.org/about,
(accessed 7.19.22).

385. Katie Gunther, "Outward Bound comes to Baltimore," The Baltimore Sun, Aug 16,
1985, pg. C1, ProQuest Historical Newspapers.

386. Christopher Bergland, "8 Eye-Opening Ways Kids Benefit from Experiences with
Nature," Psychology Today, Mar 18, 2019. https://www.psychologytoday.com/us/blog/
the-athletes-way/201903/8-eye-opening-ways-kids-benefit-experiences-nature, (accessed
7.19.22).

387. Frank P L Somerville, "9 West Baltimore Sections Oppose Expressway Route,"
Baltimore Sun Jan 30, 1962; ProQuest Historical Newspapers.

388. Parsons, p. 219-220.

389. James D. Dilts, "Touted Road-Design Team Expiring In A Quiet Byway," Baltimore
Sun, 31 Dec 1970, B16, ProQuest Historical Newspapers.

390. Robert H. Giles, Jr. Ph.D., "An Ecological Study of the Influence of a Highway on
Leakin Park and Vicinity, A Report on Interstate Highway 70 North, segment 9, Leakin
Park, Gwynn Falls Park, and Vicinity; for Urban Design Concept Associates under a
contract with the Interstate Division of Baltimore City, September 27, 1969.

391. Movement Against Destruction, Minutes, November 30, 1970, University of Baltimore,
RLB Library, Digital Collection, SCAR, Movement against Destruction, "Miscellaneous
Papers."

392. James P Dilts, "Expressway Design Hearing Is Tonight," The Baltimore Sun, May 25,
1971, pg. A9; ProQuest Historical Newspapers; and "Design Hearing Information,
Interstate Route 70N, West City line to Hilton Parkway," May 25, 1971, Edmondson
High School.

393. James Dilts, "l-70N foes si11g Leakin Park lullaby," Dec 14, 1972, (Tom Ward papers);
and James Dilts, "Hearing Held On Park Section Of Highway," Baltimore Sun, May 26,
1971, pg. C8; ProQuest Historical Newspapers.

394. Antero Pietila, "Orlinsky, at inaugural, bids Schaefer rethink 1-70, JFX, look to old
railways," Baltimore Sun, Dec 7, pg. D1, 1979; ProQuest Historical Newspapers.

395. Baltimore Sun, "Norman V. A. Reeves," Feb 15, 1983, pg. A6, ProQuest Historical
Newspapers

396. Lyle Horn Letter to John Volpe et al, August 17, 1970 (Tom Ward personal files, later
archived at the University of Baltimore RLB Library).

397. Letter G. W. Hofe, Jr. (Director, Federal Programs Coordination, US Department
of the Interior) to Michael J. Gafferty (Acting Assistant Secretary, US Department
of Transportation) December 23, 1970, VOLPE personal archives, Barry Blumberg.
See also: Federal Highway administration, and State of Maryland Department of
Transportation, State Highway Administration, Draft Environmental Impact Statement,
Interstate route I-70, Ingleside Ave to Baltimore St and Ellicotts Driveway, original EIS
circulated April 28th, 1971. (Google Docs).

398. James D. Dilts, "The Changing City: Who Wants Expressway?" Baltimore Sun, Jun 6,

1971, pg. SD3; ProQuest Historical Newspapers.

399. Interview with Barry Blumberg conducted by Evans Paull, January, 2021.

400. There is considerable potential for confusion between several lawsuits related to Leakin Park. In May 1971 Tom Ward filed a suit against the Mayor and City Council based on the contention that the City was in violation of the original agreement under which the property was granted to the City by the trust of J. William Leakin. The courts ruled against Ward in that case, but Ward filed a second lawsuit (Ward v. Ackroyd) based on the insufficiency of the public hearings. That case was merged with the VOLPE case. Following the legal paper trail to another twist, the lead plaintiff was changed in the VOLPE case to "Sierra Club, Inc." Bottom line: VOLPE v. Volpe, Sierra Club v. Volpe, and Ward v. Ackroyd all raised the hearings issue, and all were decided by the same ruling.

401. Note that archival research (including VOLPE archives, PACER legal records, and a call the Clerk's Office for the U.S. District Court for the District of Maryland) has not resulted in recovery of the original Sierra Club/VOLPE complaint. The 4(f) side of the complaint is evidenced in newspaper records: Tom Huth, "Plan to run 70N through Baltimore parks opposed," *Washington Post*, November 2, 1971, Barry Blumberg, personal archives of VOLPE records; and James Dilts, "Leakin Route Suit Planned," *Baltimore Sun*, Sep 22, 1971, pg. C14, ProQuest Historical Newspapers. The public hearings side of the complaint is covered in the Court's June 1972 decision: Thomas WARD v. Richard ACKROYD, SIERRA CLUB, INC. v. John A. VOLPE, Civ. A. Nos. 71-930-M, 71-1118-M, United States District Court, Maryland, June 8, 1972. The author's assumption is that the courts separated the 4(f) case from the public hearings issue because the public hearings issue was common to both the Ward and the Sierra Club/VOLPE cases. The lack of a definitive paper trail on the 4(f) side of the issue leaves open the possibility that Sierra Club/VOLPE held back the 4(f) issue, wanting to see how the public hearings issue was adjudicated.

402. James D. Dilts, "Judge blocks park route for road, orders hearing," *Baltimore Sun*, Jun 9, 1972, pg. C24; ProQuest Historical Newspapers.

403. James Dilts, "Greiner accused of forcing lawyer out of highway suit," *The Sun*, Sep 14, 1972; p. A-17, ProQuest Historical Newspapers.

404. Barbara Holdridge, Statement for the Board of Trustees of Volunteers Opposing Leakin Park Expressway, Inc. (VOLPE), January 27, 1972, University of Baltimore, Digital Collection, Movement against Destruction.

405. James D. Dilts, "On the road and the parks," *Baltimore Sun*, Dec 24, 1972, pg. K1, ProQuest Historical Newspapers.

406. James D Dilts, "Highway men may try again for Leakin route," *Baltimore Sun*, Jun 30, 1975, pg. C14; ProQuest Historical Newspapers.

407. Jacques Kelly, "M. Jastrow Levin, 95, city teacher, advocate of Gwynns Falls Valley," *Baltimore Sun*, Sept 23, 2004.

408. *Baltimore Sun*, "Highway issue reopened as Orlinsky shifts sides," Sep 28, 1976, pg. C1; ProQuest Historical Newspapers.

409. Donald Kimelman, "Marriage' of Orlinsky, Mikulski ending," *Baltimore Sun*, Oct 4, 1976, pg. C1; ProQuest Historical Newspapers.

410. One of my interviewees remembered a hearing in this time frame, but I have not found written documentation. *Baltimore Sun*, "Leakin Park expressway plans to be revived," Mar 5, 1977, pg. B18, ProQuest Historical Newspapers.

411. In a 2017 interview, Bill Hellmann added to this point that Interstate Division had

been unable to gain the support of the Department of the Interior on the 4(f) issue. However, VOLPE archives retained by Barry Blumberg contained three letters from the Department of the Interior that simply clarified the conditions that must be met before full approval would be granted. These letters all referred to Transportation Secretary Volpe's conditioned approval of the full 3-A expressway system granted via a letter dated December 16, 1970. Volpe's conditions all related to implementation of UDCT's recommended park improvements/mitigation measures. The later Interior Department letters all reiterated that their agency would insist on implementation of the full UDCT-recommended package, but they also agreed with Volpe that there was no prudent or feasible alternative to going through the Park. These letters were: G Douglas Hofe, Director, Department of the Interior to Herbert F. DeSimone, Assistant Secretary, Department of Transportation, July 12, 1971; John Larsen, Assistant Secretary, Department of the Interior to Dan Ackroyd, Department of Transportation, August 23, 1971; and W. W. Lyons, Deputy Secretary, Department of the Interior to Joe Axelrod, Interstate Division, July 18, 1972. We have not uncovered Interior Department communications later than 1972, and it is possible that Hellmann's recollection corresponds to later positions, i.e. that Interior kept moving the goalposts.

412. Antero Pietila, "Mayor backs road plans, but voices doubts on I-70," *Baltimore Sun*, Dec 8, 1979, pg. B16; ProQuest Historical Newspapers.

413. By Ben A. Franklin, Rep. Fallon Loses in Maryland Race, *New York Times*, Sept. 17, 1970.

414. Weingroff, (multiple references)

415. Helen Leavitt, *Super Highway, Super Hoax*, Ballantine Books, 1971, p. 278

416. David E. Rosenbaum, "For the Highway Lobby, a Rocky Road Ahead," April 2, 1972. https://www.nytimes.com/1972/04/02/archives/for-the-highway-lobby-a-rocky-road-ahead.html, (accessed 7.19.22).

417. *Baltimore Sun*, "Fallon Honored by Road Groups," Oct 13, 1959, pg. 9; ProQuest Historical Newspapers.

418. Weingroff, p. 215.

419. Ben Kelley, *The Pavers and the Paved, the Real Cost of America's Highway Program*, Donald W. Brown, Inc, New York, 1971," p. 100-114

420. Kelley, p. 114.

421. O'Neil, Paul, "Kill the Hill! Pave that Grass!" *Life*, October 10, 1969, p. 126-134, as cited in Weingroff, p. 93-94.

422. Kelley, p.39-40.

423. O'Neil,"Kill the…"

424. Weingroff, 175-179

425. Ben Kelly, p. 59-61

426. Weingroff, p. 116

427. Weingroff, p. 116.

428. *Baltimore Sun*, "Sarbanes To Run For Congress: Delegate Will Seek To Unseat Fallon In 4th District," Apr 19, 1970, pg. 26; ProQuest Historical Newspapers.

429. G Jefferson Price, "Contrasts Mark Fallon-Sarbanes Contest," *Baltimore Sun*, Sep 7, 1970; pg. B16, and *Baltimore Sun*, "Fallon And Foes Discuss Issues: 3 Candidates In Primary Appear On Telecast," Aug 31, 1970, pg. C10; ProQuest Historical Newspapers.

430. Louis P. Peddicord, "Fallon Road Stand Scored: Sarbanes Criticizes Position on Trust Funds," *Baltimore Sun*, Aug 15, 1970; pg. B5; ProQuest Historical Newspapers.

Endnotes

431. Naomi S. Rayner, "Sarbanes Fund-Raiser Spoofs Real Thing," *Baltimore Sun*, Aug 27, 1970, pg. C8; ProQuest Historical Newspapers.

432. *New York Times*, "The Environmental Issue," November 6, 1970; https://www.nytimes.com/1970/11/06/archives/the-environmental-issue.html. (accessed 7.19.22).

433. Weingroff, "Busting… and Dilts, James D., "Trying to Crack the Highway Fund," The *Baltimore Sun*, October 1, 1972

434. Weingroff, p. 353

435. Richard Weingroff, Bust the Trust, abridged version, US Federal Highway Administration.

436. *Baltimore Sun*, "Hughes, Schaefer differ on roads vs. mass transit," Jan 15, 1974, pg. C6; ProQuest Historical Newspapers.

437. Weingroff, pp. 1254-1257.

438. *Baltimore Sun*, "Committed to action, city will compromise," April 26, 1972.

439. Donald Kimelman, "Schaefer considering road shift: Move would permit more homesteading in Inner Harbor,"Nov 20, 1976, pg. A1; ProQuest Historical Newspapers.

440. Letter, Geoff Mitchell, (Semmes, Bowen, and Semmes) to Richard H. Trainor, (Interstate Division for Baltimore City), February 10, 1975. Preservation Society Archives. The Interior Department's March 1975 review was consistent with the community's position, opposing all options except Alternative five (Letter Secretary of the Interior (signature illegible) to Richard Trainor (Interstate Division), March 18, 1975 (Barry Blumberg, personal VOLPE archives).

441. Informational Report for compliance with Section 106 of the National Historic Preservation Act of 1966, Boulevard Ring, Federal Hill Historic District. February 1974.

442. "Federal Hill and the Highway Problem," memorandum summarizing a January 27, 1976 meeting, George Klein, President of the Federal Hill Neighborhood Association and James Craig, Chairman of the FHNA with city representatives. University of Baltimore, Digital Collections.

443. Correspondence between Geoff Mitchell and Margaret Dougherty, February 1976, Preservation Society archives.

444. "The Road in Federal Hill," meeting of the Federal Hill Road Committee, July 6, 1976. University of Baltimore, Digital Collections.

445. The Society's Special Road Committee for Federal Hill, "Recommendations," undated; and "The Road in Federal Hill," meeting of the Federal Hill Road Committee, July 6, 1976. Both from Preservation Society archives.

446. Donald Kimelman, "Schaefer considering…"

447. Peter Ruehl, "Highway angers Otterbein residents," *Baltimore Sun*, Jan 23, 1977, pg. F1; ProQuest Historical Newspapers.

448. Tanvi Misra, "The Other Side of MLK Boulevard…" City Lab, April 11, 2018. https://www.bloomberg.com/news/articles/2018-04-11/the-broken-dreams-of-baltimore-s-mlk-boulevard. (accessed 7.17.22)

449. Gerald Neily, "Reviving the West Side can start by reducing the footprint of MLK Blvd," Baltimore Brew, October 16, 2014; https://baltimorebrew.com/2014/10/16/reviving-the-west-side-can-start-by-reducing-the-footprint-of-mlk-blvd/. (accessed 5.1.22)

450. James D Dilts, "Md. air, road plans held 'inconsistent,'" *Baltimore Sun*, Mar 18, 1976, pg. C1; ProQuest Historical Newspapers.

451. Dilts, James, "City highway plans certified for funds," The Sun, Apr 27, 1976, pg. C2; ProQuest Historical Newspapers.

452. Alan M. Voorhees and Associates, "Traffic Management Study for the 3-A Interstate System, Final Report, for the Interstate Division of Baltimore City, June 1977.

453. Preservation Society meeting minutes, July 19, 1972, university of Baltimore, SCAR archives, Preservation Society meetings, 1972.

454. "List of Volunteer Professionals," Movement Against Destruction, August 28, 1972.

455. Alan M. Voorhees and Associates, "Baltimore Regional Environmental Impact Study, a Summary of Findings," for the Interstate Division of Baltimore City, June 1974

456. Councilmember Mikulski memorandum to Council President Orlinsky RE: Informational Hearing on Transportation, October 20 1975; and Bill Hellmann, Deputy Chief, Interstate Division, memorandum to Frank Mucha, Finance Department RE: Expressway Program, November 6, 1975. Baltimore City Archives, Mayor William Donald Schaefer, BRG 9-42, Box 48.

457. Baltimore Sun, "East - West Plan Stymie: Many Expressway Route: Urged Over 28-Year Span," Apr 17, 1967, pg. C7; ProQuest Historical Newspapers.

458. Baltimore Sun, "Expressway Study Urged: Pressman Questions City's Ability to Pay Its Share," Feb 13, 1969, pg. A16; ProQuest Historical Newspapers.

459. Baltimore Sun, "The Hidden Costs of Expressways," editorial, April 16, 1973.

460. Baltimore Sun, "An Added City Expense that 'Snuck' In," May 2, 1972, pg. A16; ProQuest Historical Newspapers.

461. Baltimore Sun, "Graveyard for City Dollars," Oct 11, 1976, pg. A12. ProQuest Historical Newspapers.

462. James D. Dilts, "City highway system cost up 61% since '72," Baltimore Sun, Mar 10, 1976, pg. A1; ProQuest Historical Newspapers.

463. Baltimore Sun, "Eyes on City's Gold Coast," Feb 12, 1979, pg. A12; ProQuest Historical Newspapers.

464. Antero Pietila, "Mayor backs road plans, but voices doubts on I-70," Baltimore Sun, Dec 8, 1979, pg. B16; ProQuest Historical Newspapers.

465. Thomas J. S. Waxter, Chairman Policy and Planning Committee of the Baltimore City Council, "Report on Bill No. 23 - Concerning the Interstate Highway System for Baltimore City," June 23, 1980.

466. Antero Pietila, "Funds short for Leakin, 1-83 routes: City finance chief cites inflation, drop in gas tax revenue," The Baltimore Sun, May 6, 1980, pg. C1, ProQuest Historical Newspapers.

467. Waxter, "Report on Bill No. 23…"

468. WYPR, On the Record, "Baltimore City Shrinks, Maryland Redistricts. The 2020 Census Numbers in Play," interview with Seema Iyer, September 13, 2021.

469. The capital cost data in this section (the next four pages) comes from primarily: David Simon, "$825 million set for area transit plans," Baltimore Sun pg. A1, Jul 22, 1983; ProQuest Historical Newspapers; material provided by David Chapin, email to Evans Paull RE: Interstate Transfer, 2.9.22 (David Chapin, "General comments Interstate Substitution" with associated spreadsheets 02.09.22); and Memo, Virginia Kearney to Mayor William Donald Schaefer, RE: Interstate Transfer Funds – allocation, August 27, 1985. Baltimore City Archives, Schaefer collection, BRG 9-42, Box 48.

470. Regional Planning Council resolution, July 17, 1981, attached to letter James J. O'Donnell, Secretary, Maryland Department of Transportation to Ray Barnhart,

Administrator, Federal Highway Administration, July 28, 1981, Baltimore City Archives, Schaefer collection, BRG 9-42.

471. *Baltimore Sun*, "The End of 1-83," pg. A20, Mar 18, 1983; ProQuest Historical Newspapers.

472. William K. Hellmann email to Evans Paull, February 21, 2022 subject, "Your book."

473. John Frece, "Aides ecstatic after the 'perfect' deal: Everyone a winner, especially mayor," *Baltimore Sun*, Oct 3, 1984, pg. 17A; ProQuest Historical Newspapers.

474. Maryland Roads, Special Edition "Building the National Freeway," August 2, 1991.

475. The *Baltimore Sun*, "Barton Quits Planning Commission," February 22, 1972. University of Baltimore, RLB Library, Special Collections, MAD Collection.

476. The *Baltimore Sun*, "Councilmen," Feb 22, 1962;

477. *Baltimore Sun*, "From Mutter To Roar," Nov 27, 1961, pg. 14; ProQuest Historical Newspapers.

478. *Baltimore Sun*, "Wolff, Werner Criticize Owings: Expressway Feud Develops over Degree of Control," April 20, 1967, University of Baltimore, digital archives, regional collection.

479. C. Frazer Smith, *William Donald Schaefer: A Political Biography*, Johns Hopkins University Press, 1999.

480. Richard Ben Cramer, "Instead of vying for voters favor, Schaefer has them thanking him for running again," *Baltimore Sun* Aug 27, 1975. C1.

481. *Baltimore Sun*, "Schaefer couldn't have bombed with this audience," Feb 9, 1986.

482. Sandy Banisky, "Schaefer selects City Hall veteran for Cabinet post," The *Baltimore Sun*, Dec 31, 1986, pg. 1E, ProQuest Historical Newspapers.

483. William Donald Schaefer, interview in the City Dweller, March 10, 1974.

484. Andrew M. Giguere"…And never the twain shall meet": Baltimore's east-west expressway and the construction of the "Highway to Nowhere." A thesis presented to the faculty of the College of Arts and Sciences of Ohio University, June 2009.

485. *Baltimore Evening Sun*, "District angered by Mayor's Remark in Wake of Road Feud," Feb. 6, 1975 (Preservation Society archives).

486. Drew Marks, "Librarian Blasts Mayor," undated, unsourced news clipping, Preservation Society Archives.

487. Daniel j Gross, "Former *Baltimore Sun* columnist shares experience covering interstate, urban development boom," Posted by on May 18, 2011. https://danieljgross.wordpress.com/2011/05/18/former-baltimore-sun-columnist-shares-experience-covering-interstate-urban-development-boom/ (accessed 7.19.20)

488. Karen Francis, Road Wars Video, draft script, Jan. 2, 2006.

489. Barbara Mikulski, as a candidate for City Council, Public Meeting at St. Brigid's Hall, June 29, 1971; and in a 1974 Interview, East-West Expressway Collection, Maryland Center for History and Culture, transcribed by Evans Paull.

490. Jim Piel, "Revive Baltimore's highway to nowhere," *Baltimore Sun*, Letter to the editor, February 3, 2017

491. Tom Ward, personal files, now part of the Tom Ward Collection, University of Baltimore, RLB Library.

492. Tom Ward, letter to Ms. Kimberly A. G. Wilson, Sun National Staff, undated. (Tom Ward, personal papers, later archived at University of Baltimore.

493. Bill Hughes, "Did Senator Mikulski pull a Brian Williams and play loose with the

facts?" Baltimore Brew, Feb. 24, 2016

494. Gerald Neily, "The Senator and the Expressway," Baltimore Brew, April 29, 2011.

495. The author has found four other references to the deal described in this section. In two earlier interviews, Mikulski made references to the consideration of the underwater tunnel as an outcome of City Council's deliberations over her expressway condemnation repeal bills (1974 interview of Barbara Mikulski, Maryland Historical Society, East-West Expressway Collection; and Jerelyn Eddings, "Mikulski: Stepping up to the Senate," Feb 22, 1987, pg. R6 Baltimore Sun; ProQuest Historical Newspapers). Additionally, Tom Ward made a reference to the deal in March 1972, although his point of view was critical of the deal because, "No commitments had been obtained from the Mayor to stop the road through East Baltimore" (Tom Ward, "X-Way opponents quibble," Guide [May refer to East Baltimore Guide], 3.30.72. Tom Ward papers, now available at University of Baltimore Library.) In 1975 Council President Orlinsky also referred to this understanding, saying that, "He had voted for the road condemnation ordinances [i.e., against the repeal proposals] on assurances that the route would take an underwater route, rather than through the Fell's Point and Federal Hill historic districts," (Richard Ben Cramer, "Mikulski anti-road rhetoric recalls her 3-A opposition," Baltimore Sun, Oct 15, 1975, pg. C2; ProQuest Historical Newspapers).

496. Fred Barbash, "Volpe Might Delay City's Expressway: Displaced Residents Must Be Relocated," Baltimore Sun, Jun 26, 1970, pg. C24; ProQuest Historical Newspapers.

497. James D. Dilts, "Barton Quits Planning Commission," Baltimore Sun, Feb 18, 1972, pg. C15; ProQuest Historical Newspapers.

498. For example, see: Eric Jaffe, "Public Transit Is Worth Way More to a City Than You Might Think," City Lab, August 14, 2013, https://www.bloomberg.com/news/articles/2013-08-14/public-transit-is-worth-way-more-to-a-city-than-you-might-think (accessed 7.19.22).

499. Baltimore Sun, "Mayor Censured Over Conference: GOP Youth Head Sees Threat In Expressway Talks," Baltimore Sun, Jul 24, 1949, pg. 28; ProQuest Historical Newspapers.

500. John E. Woodruff, "5 Councilmen Lose In Democratic Vote," Baltimore Sun, Sept. 8, 1967; ProQuest Historical Newspapers.

ACKNOWLEDGMENTS

If I am lucky enough to get a few speaking engagements from publishing this book, my opening line will probably be, "I wrote this book because I'm a really bad golfer." If my lovely and very understanding wife, Rosemarie, could have cast a vote with future knowledge of how all-consuming this book would be, I'm quite sure she would have voted to be a golf widow instead of a book widow. However, since I had no desire to spend my retirement years demonstrating how not to hit a sand wedge, the book won out, and my gratitude and appreciation of Rosemarie's patience and tolerance gets top billing for my acknowledgments.

I also have a fabulous support group of family and friends who encouraged me, while offering critiques of long-winded early drafts. Prominent in this list are fellow city planner Al Barry, long-time friends Joe Mihalovich, Jan Serwint, Jean Engelke, Rick White, and Bob Hewitt, as well as the rest of my immediate family (Daniel, Mackenzie, and Ali [who also transcribed quite a few of my interviews]).

Of course, I am enormously indebted to my interviewees, all 55 of them. Many had only vague recollections of the facts, 50 years hence. And many were apologetic for not being able to shed much light as I peppered them with questions. But it was through these interviews that the book began to take a different form. What started out as an exercise in social science research and analysis evolved into something that I think (and hope you agree) is way more satisfying: a story about people.

Among those interviewees, there are three that I want to call out for particular recognition. Art Cohen (the second president of the Movement Against Destruction) met with me innumerable times and pointed me in many new and fruitful directions. Also, on my speed dial for help in communications, Denise Johnson (Arch Social Club) facilitated some of my best connections for people to interview and involve. David Chapin (former staff to Interstate Division) was my go-to guy to get the facts straight. Among the many facts he helped clarify, the section that addresses what happened when the city cashed in their highway chips (Chapter XVI, "Politics and trade-ins") is based mostly on his analysis.

There were several information sources that allowed me to probe deeper and give particular issues a more meaningful thrust. Patrick Ward (ex-councilman Tom Ward's son) gave me access to his father's personal files, which

4

are now available at the University of Baltimore Library. Another father-son hand-off resulted in my getting an inside view of the Urban Design Concept Team (UDCT, the consulting group that steadfastly ignored their overseers in the cause of saving the Inner Harbor and Federal Hill). Kermit Parsons, a Cornell University professor, had drafted a manuscript entitled, *The Baltimore Wars*, which gives a highly detailed account of UDCT's activities. Parsons passed away before he was able to publish the work, but his son Steve sent me the manuscript and granted permission to use the material.

I found more fresh material in the archives of the Society for the Preservation of Federal Hill and Fell's Point (courtesy Jeff Dewberry and David Gleason), VOLPE archives (courtesy Barry Blumberg), and the bookshelves of the Baltimore City Department of Planning (courtesy Eric Holcombe).

Since much of my research occurred during Covid restrictions, I also need to acknowledge that the staff at both the Enoch Pratt Library's Maryland Room and the Baltimore City Archives were especially helpful in gaining access to material.

Heather Shaw, my editor, also did a yeoman's job, especially in cutting down my voluminous narrative. Also contributing to team Stop the Road: my details-oriented GIS/computer-mapping specialist, Scott Jeffrey, MA GISP; my super-responsive web manager, Bev Bafford at Quad Computing; photographer, Larry Canner; and publicist Caryn Sagal—they each did a bang-up job.

Last but certainly not least, my publisher (Boyle and Dalton and CEO Emily Hitchcock, ably assisted by Clair Fink) was fabulous to work with. We had a difficult self-imposed deadline that caused B&D to jump through more than a few hoops at breakneck speed. Emily, prospective writers should note, has an interesting clause in her contract: "Both parties agree to *cheerful* cooperation and communication for the best possible project results," [emphasis added]. She certainly held up her side of that bargain. As a small publisher operating in the "hybrid" space (midway between traditional publishing and self-publishing), Boyle and Dalton was fast, responsive, and flexible, which was exactly what I needed. They cut at least a year and a half off the timeline relative to traditional publishing. The afore-mentioned spouse might have been reclassified as ex-spouse if I had gone the traditional publishing route. Either that or the afore-mentioned author might have been reclassified as the late author, E. Evans Paull.

ABOUT THE AUTHOR

Evans Paull spent 45 years as a city planner, working both in Baltimore and nationally on urban redevelopment issues.

He began his career in the Baltimore City Department of Planning as a generalist planner before specializing in the redevelopment of brownfields (vacant former industrial or commercial properties, the reuse of which is complicated by contamination).

After starting and managing Baltimore's Brownfields Initiative, he tackled these same issues at a national level, working first for Northeast-Midwest Institute before becoming director of the National Brownfields Coalition and finally running his consulting business, Redevelopment Economics. Many of his published articles, papers, and presentations still appear on the Redevelopment Economics website.

Paull has won several awards, including: *Brownfields Leadership Award, Phoenix Award* (for brownfields redevelopment), *Governor's Smart Growth Award* and *Professional Achievement in Economic Development Award* from the Maryland Chapter American Planning Association.

Paull is now retired. He resides in northwest Baltimore with his wife, Rosemarie. The couple has three children and one grandchild.

www.ingramcontent.com/pod-product-compliance
Lightning Source LLC
Chambersburg PA
CBHW031422270326
41930CB00007B/539